THE
PENNSYLVANIA MILITIA:

DEFENDING THE
COMMONWEALTH
AND THE NATION

1669-1870

SAMUEL J. NEWLAND, Ph.D.
Professor of Military Education
U.S. Army War College

Commonwealth of Pennsylvania
Department of Military and Veterans Affairs
Annville, Pennsylvania

The historical prints of soldiers used on this cover – from the First Troop, Philadelphia City
Cavalry; the First Regiment, Pennsylvania Volunteer Infantry; and the 48th Infantry Regiment,
Pennsylvania Volunteers – by Don Troiani, are reproduced courtesy of Historical Arts Prints,
P.O. Box 660, Southbury, CT 06488. The cover design is by Mr. James E. Kistler, Carlisle, Pa.

Dedication

Dedicated, respectfully, to Colonel (Retired) Walter M. Newland, USMC – fellow educator, fellow scribe, bona fide hero in the 1945 action on the *USS Franklin*, and perhaps most importantly my uncle, whose encouragement caused me to continue my military service and complete a very rich and satisfying military career. And to my wife Rhonda, who never complains about the time I spend with my other love: history.

Table of Contents

Preface

This book is the first of two volumes that will provide readers with a basic overview of the history of Pennsylvania's state defense forces, initially the militia and most recently the National Guard. It follows and expands an earlier publication called *The Pennsylvania Militia: The Early Years* that provided an overview of the militia's history through the end of the Revolutionary War. Although countless volumes have been written about Pennsylvania's history, there are many aspects that deserve additional attention.

The Commonwealth's history is rich and varied, making it one of the more fascinating of the 13 original colonies. Consider, for example, the personalities. William Penn, father of the American Quaker community, founded the colony. Benjamin Franklin, a man of varied and significant contributions, achieved his fame, politically and scientifically, in the Commonwealth of Pennsylvania. Generals Anthony Wayne and George G. Meade were Pennsylvanians, as too General of the Army George C. Marshall. The list of "who's who" politically and militarily is impressive. Significant events and locations also abound in Pennsylvania. Independence Hall and the Liberty Bell, two well-known symbols of American liberty, sit in close proximity to each other in Philadelphia. Valley Forge is only a short distance away. The best-known Civil War site, Gettysburg, is situated in the mid-state. In the western regions of Pennsylvania, George Washington's military career began, during the French and Indian War, at a place known as a Fort of Necessity. The list seems endless for the state whose history began with the chartering of the Commonwealth in 1681 and still has a significant impact on the nation today.

Even though many aspects of the Commonwealth's history are well-understood and well-documented in numerous books and articles, the role of the militia, known today as the National Guard, has not received proper attention. If an interested reader reviews available literature on the history of the Pennsylvania militia and National Guard, he will find only Major William Clarke's *Official History of the Militia and National Guard in Pennsylvania* and Frederic Godcharles' five-volume work on Pennsylvania, which includes a military volume. These two works have for several generations attempted to provide readers with the history of the Commonwealth's defense force. Clarke's work has merit, but it relies heavily on the legal history of the military and includes seemingly endless lists of units and officers that greatly distract today's readers.   Other than these two works, general histories on the Pennsylvania Guard and militia are virtually nonexistent.   Granted, any number of articles exist on significant personages in the history of the militia, on key battles in which they participated and on any number of Pennsylvania units and the campaigns, both state and federal, in which they participated.   Solid general histories on specific periods of the history of the militia and the National Guard in Pennsylvania are lacking.

The need for more research in this area was recognized by then Colonel Eugene Klynoot, then Chief of Staff of the Pennsylvania National Guard, who has been a friend and colleague since I was an analyst at the Army's Strategic Studies Institute in the late 1980s.   During a luncheon in 1993 I was asked if it would be possible to research and write a general history on the development of the militia in Pennsylvania.   Klynoot sought a history for Pennsylvanians that was both scholarly and readable and above all would accurately and objectively tell the story of the development of Pennsylvania's military forces.   Since that time, innumerable distracters have interfered with this project, but consistently Gene Klynoot has supplied resources and encouragement, which have made the first small book and now a full volume possible.   While I remain the sole author of this volume, he is without question the father of the project.   I will always owe now Major General Klynoot my thanks for his support and encouragement.

One comment needs to be included on style.   I have elected to use footnotes rather than endnotes for citations, because it is my hope that this volume will cause readers to examine other sources cited and future writers to do additional research on the early years of the militia.   For the reader who reads and uses citations, footnotes are far more convenient.   Furthermore, as an additional convenience for the reader, in each chapter the first citation of any work includes a complete bibliographical entry even if it has been cited in the previous chapter.   Subsequent entries are in a shortened form.   The method selected for citations was chosen in the hope that others will use my research as a base and work even more on the development of the militia in Pennsylvania.   Much more needs to be done on this worthy subject.

As with any project of this nature, I am indebted to any number of people and organizations for their assistance in researching and improving this book.   Mr. J. Martin West of the Fort Ligonier Association was from the outset of this project extremely helpful, furnishing research materials and providing many helpful suggestions on the early drafts.   The staff of the Military History Institute (MHI) has also been particularly helpful in supplying a significant number of relevant documents. From the beginning, Mr. John Slonaker, chief of the reference branch, and staff members Nancy Baylor, Dennis Vetock and Rich Baker were consistent resources for this project. Also from MHI I must thank Mike Winey and Randy Hackenburg, both solid Pennsylvania military historians, for their assistance and advice. I could not have asked for better support than I received from MHI. At my place of employment, the U.S. Army War College, thanks go to Jim Kistler, a fine artist and friend, for his excellent work on cover design. Both Mr. Kistler and Narin Sum have also been excellent resources for creating quality maps from my crude drawings. My colleagues at the War College, Lieutenant Colonel Robert Mellot and David Birdwell, have also been extremely helpful with the reproduction of numerous images.

From the Commonwealth's historical services I would like to thank Mr. Bruce Bazelon, Bureau of Historic Sites and Museums, Pennsylvania Historical and Museum Commission (and currently on loan to the Army), for the use of his rare books, his advice and assistance. Early in my research, Mr. Frank Suran, state archivist, was extremely helpful in making a significant number of bound volumes of Pennsylvania archives available to the Military History Institute for my research and that of future Army officers. In addition, I owe thanks to Mr. Charles Oellig, recently retired from the Pennsylvania Historical and Museum Commission, for his multiple edits of the draft, his excellent advice, and the use of some of his documents on the history of the Commonwealth.

Above all, I must thank a number of people from the Pennsylvania Army National Guard. I owe a particular debt of gratitude to Lieutenant Colonel Paul Ragard, the last commander of my old unit, the 128th Military History Detachment. His consistent support and encouragement was simply outstanding. Major James Casarella was also helpful with his editing and support. Early in this project, Captain Gary Schrecengost, an enthusiastic and well-trained Pennsylvania historian, provided a substantial amount of research materials to the author. His assistance was extremely helpful. A very special debt of gratitude is owed to Lieutenant Colonel John Maietta, Public Affairs Officer for the State Area Command. He has been a friend and ally whose assistance, edits and technical advice have been invaluable and without whose assistance this manuscript might not have been published. I am also greatly indebted to Lieutenant Jason Wynnycky, whose skill in layout and publishing techniques has taken my typed manuscript and made it a book. Sincere thanks to my old friend and longtime associate J. Craig Nannos, whose advice and encouragement throughout the writing of this book was of great assistance. And last, but cer-

tainly not least, Major General Eugene Klynoot who originated this project and
has consistently supported it and many of my other historical ventures.

Finally and most importantly I thank my wife Rhonda and son Daniel
for their tolerance. No book is ever completely written on office hours, and
their patience for at least my mental absence and often physical absence on
many evenings and weekends, while I was completing this book, is greatly
appreciated. While all of the above mentioned have contributed and assisted,
the author alone must accept responsibility for any and all omissions and all
errors of fact.

Carlisle, Pennsylvania
Samuel J. Newland, Ph.D.
Professor, Military Education
U.S. Army War College

Illustrations and Maps

Color illustrations following page 70

CHAPTER 1

Prelude: The Quaker Factor

Not fighting but suffering . . . so faith and patience suc-
ceed fighting in the doctrine and practice of this people.

– William Penn, 1694

fter years of neglect in many historical accounts, military historians and journalists are beginning to devote serious attention to the role of the militia, citizen-soldiers or the National Guard in the nation's defense. This recognition, though somewhat belated, is appropriate because the nation's earliest military history and its oldest military units still in the force structure are in the National Guard, the direct lineal descendant of the militia. Thus, it is not surprising to find that Captain John Smith, a founder of the Colony of Virginia, is also a founding member of that state's earliest military organization. The same is true in the Massachusetts Bay Colony, where Captain Miles Standish helped to establish that state's military tradition in 1620. Both men are prime examples of the citizen-soldier, the militiaman, who embodies the notion that citizens share a responsibility to defend their country. The military organiza-tions in the Bay Colony in 1636 are recognized by the Center of Military History as the oldest military units in continuous existence in the United States.[1]

That the earliest history of the nation's military resides in the militia – today's National Guard – is logical because the original thirteen colonies were founded by British settlers who brought with them the language, customs and military traditions of their home country. These early settlers, faced with a harsh and hostile environment, found that they had to rely on the military tra-ditions of the mother country because in the early colonial period the Crown did not send significant bodies of regular troops to North America. With the

---

[1] In Massachusetts lineages there were originally four military units which were linked back to the year 1636: the 101st Engineer Battalion, the 181st Infantry, the 182nd Infantry and the 101st Field Artillery. Regrettably, force structure reductions are taking their toll, and some of these lineages are in danger of being lost or consolidated.

exception of Queen Anne's War, 1704-1713, the colonies were largely responsible for their own defense.

The militia system, though traditional to the British Isles, had received
additional impetus in the decades immediately preceding colonization. During
the reign of Queen Elizabeth, the threat of an invasion by Spain had resulted
in a Muster Law of 1572 that required male citizens to muster and train in militia units. The early settlers in New England, faced by contingencies such as the
Pequot War of 1636-1637 and King Phillip's War, 1675-1676, found it necessary to use this Elizabethan law as a model. The law required militia commanders to arm, muster and train their commands, in order to be prepared on
short notice for any type of military contingency.

In most of the original thirteen colonies, the militia, based on the
Anglo-Saxon tradition,[2] was a sensible method of defense. It gave the citizen
the responsibility to actively participate in the colony's defense – a responsibility that was included in the charters of the original colonies and, because the
militia was a locally based system of defense, was responsive to the demands of
the citizenry who comprised its ranks. Furthermore, militia service was solidly
grounded in centuries of British tradition and was an accepted part of the citizenry's duties. In general, it was assumed that all healthy, free, male citizens
between the ages of 16 and 60 owed an obligation of military service to their
community and to the Crown. Thus, every citizen, as described, was legally
obligated to procure a suitable firearm, meet regularly for training and be prepared at all times to defend his community.

Among the original thirteen colonies, the Commonwealth of Pennsylvania has a unique history regarding defense in general and the militia in particular. Pennsylvania's unique history in defense matters originated in its earliest period. Its first official experiences with the militia system were rather indi-
rect, for they actually began prior to the organization of the Commonwealth
and were under the authority of the laws of a contiguous colony. In the early
17th century, portions of present-day eastern Pennsylvania were settled by the
Swedes and Dutch. Both countries exhibited interest in the extreme eastern
parts of the present-day Commonwealth as early as the 1620s. The English,
however, regarded both the Swedish and Dutch presence as an intrusion into

---

[2] The tradition of reliance on the militia to defend the nation can be clearly traced to the Anglo-
Saxons in early Britain. It was important for any number of English kings as a part of their
defensive system. Composed then, as in the colonial period, of ordinary freemen, the militia
was designed to be called up for short periods of time; at the conclusion of the campaign, the
militiamen were released to return to their farms and livelihoods.

an area to which the British claimed to have prior rights. As a consequence, after the Dutch had driven the Swedes out by force of arms (1655), the English mounted an expedition and in turn drove out the Dutch (1664), officially extending English authority into what is now the eastern part of the Commonwealth. Subsequently, a deputy governor and a military commander were appointed, but laws specific to the new territory were not immediately imposed on the newly conquered land, a part of which would become Pennsylvania.[3] In 1676, however, the laws of the Duke of York and Albany were officially imposed on what would become Pennsylvania by order of Governor Edmund Andros.[4] These laws were originally designed for New York, a colony granted to the brother of King Charles II, the Duke of York, and promulgated for that area in 1664. It was the extension of these laws into what would become Pennsylvania that provided the area with its first militia obligation.[5]

According to the laws of the Duke of York's jurisdiction, every male citizen over the age of 16 was required to attend local military exercises; towns were required to provide powder magazines; and forts were to be maintained. Standards for this organization and its soldiers were included in the provisions. In short, they required:

> *Every male within this government from sixteen to sixty years of age . . .*
> *be furnished with Armes and other Suitable Provision hereafter mentioned,*
> *under the Penalty of Five Schillings for the least default there in Namely,*

---

[3] Colonel Richard Nichols, who had commanded the expedition to defeat the Dutch, was initially appointed as the deputy for the newly acquired province. Captain Robert Needham became acting military commander. While militia laws were not immediately put into place for the newly acquired territory, the colonies were in fact still under English law, and thus militia obligations were still in effect for all free white male citizens.

[4] At the time this was done, Andros was governor of New York, although later in 1686 he would become governor of the United Royal Colony. Like his non-Quaker peers in Pennsylvania, he would have many problems in enlisting the cooperation of the leading Quakers in his colony, particularly in Rhode Island. See Rufus M. Jones, *The Quakers in the American Colonies* (London: MacMillan and Co., 1911), pp. 187-194. Cited hereafter as Jones, *Quakers in the American Colonies*.

[5] While these laws were the first officially applied to Pennsylvania on September 22, 1676, it should be noted that once English authority was extended into the eastern areas of Pennsylvania, the settlers there were in fact under English law. Thus, some type of militia obligation was implied and, according to early records, exercised. See John B. Linn and William H. Egle, eds., *Pennsylvania Archives: Provincial Affairs in Pennsylvania: Papers Relating to the Dutch and Swedish Settlements on the Delaware, 1682-1750*, second series, vol. VII (Harrisburg, E. K. Meyers, State Printer, 1890), pp. 835-837. Cited hereafter as Linn and Egle, *Papers Relating to the Dutch and Swedish Settlements*.

*a Good Serviceable Gun (allowed sufficient by his Military Order) to be
kept in Constant Fitness for present Service with a good Sword, Bandeleers
or Horne, a Worme, a Scowerer, a Priming wyre, Shott Badge and
Charger, one pound of Good Powder, foure pounds of Pistol Bullets or
Twenty Foure Bullets fitted for the gunne, foure at home or Serviceable
Match for a match locke, Foure Good Flints fitted for a Fire Lock Gunn.
And all Captains or Military Officers are hereby required to give or send
an Accompt yearly to the Gov[erno]r and councill how the Inhabitants are
furnished and provided, that due Supply may be Ordered.*[6]

Even though the population density was extremely low and the threat
of war was slight, documents from the period show that the early pre-
Commonwealth settlers were concerned with establishing a dependable
defense, even before the official imposition of the laws of the Duke of York.
In the wake of an insurrection on the Delaware and the rape of a white woman

**Perhaps the earliest colonial defensive structure in what is
now Pennsylvania was built by the Swedes. Several older
histories of the Commonwealth show the Old Swede Blockhouse at Wicaco in Philadelphia.**

---

[6] Gail M. Beckman, *The Statutes at Large of Pennsylvania at the Time of William Penn, 1680-1700*,
vol. I (New York: Vantage Press, 1976), p. 71. Cited hereafter as Beckman, *Statutes at Large of
Pennsylvania.* See also, *Pennsylvania Military Regulation No. 80, March 1, 1937* (Harrisburg: Adjutant
General's Office, 1937), p. 3.

by an Indian, in 1669 a resident who called himself Captain John Carr proposed to the government in New York that a blockhouse should be constructed in New-Castle to defend the area. The council approved this proposal and directed citizens of the area to advance funds and choose the best location for the blockhouse.[7] Correspondence continued for several years about this blockhouse and its condition, but most intriguing for the militia's history are several citations that refer to militia in the area.[8] Granted, the militia mentioned was being governed under the authority of the Duke of York in what is now Delaware. From the chartering of the Commonwealth in 1681 until the beginning of the American Revolution, however, the Delaware area was part of Pennsylvania. Thus, the earliest known militia in what would become English-ruled Pennsylvania dates from 1669.

That the militia was necessary from the inception of the Commonwealth would become even more obvious in the next few decades. The British government was heavily involved in rivalries with other colonial powers, particularly Spain and France. With few regular British troops, settlers had to play a major role in their own defense.[9] Consequently, as settlements were established, colonists found it necessary to organize militia forces quickly in order to defend against the general lawlessness of the frontier and the potential for attacks by the Indians, who disliked the intrusion of the settlers into their pristine wilderness.

Even though the territory that would become Pennsylvania had specific authorization for military forces as early as 1676, the period from 1664 to 1681 is best described as a transitional phase in the Commonwealth's history. This transition from control of eastern Pennsylvania by non-English powers to the status of a chartered English colony took a unique turn in 1681. When Pennsylvania was organized as a proprietary colony in March of 1681, the militia provisions from the laws of the Duke of York became invalid. The military or militia provisions in the proprietor's charter were not implemented by the newly chartered proprietary colony. This was so because the charter for

---

[7] Linn and Egle, *Papers Relating to the Dutch and Swedish Settlements*, pp. 781-782.

[8] Governor Andros mentioned the militia in a letter to Captain Cantwell at New-Castle in 1674, including reference to the captain's "Ensigne" and his sergeant. A letter dated August 14, 1677, also shows the continued existence of the militia, with Andros appointing Captain Billop to relieve Captain Collier and "bee Commander of the Militia and fforces in the River and Bay." Ibid., pp. 815, 841-842.

[9] In the early years of the Commonwealth, only during Queen Anne's War, 1704-1713, did the Crown send a substantial body of troops to the colonies. At that time some 5,000 regulars were employed in a thrust into Quebec.

Pennsylvania was given to William Penn, a leading spokesman for the Society of Friends, more commonly known as the Quakers. The decision by Charles II to grant Penn the proprietary charter for the Commonwealth would result in Pennsylvania having a unique character regarding military matters, compared with the other twelve original English-speaking colonies.

Penn and other leading Quakers had a distinct vision for Pennsylvania. They dreamed of establishing a colony that would function philosophically according to the beliefs promoted by the Society of Friends. Thus, the Commonwealth was to be a colony where the Christian concepts of love, peace and harmony were totally integrated into the everyday workings of the government and where violence and aggression toward the colony's citizenry, its would-be enemies or the American Indian population would be scorned.[10] The Friends sought to implement the prophet Isaiah's concept of a "Peaceable Kingdom" in which "the wolf shall also lie down with the lamb." Through practical application of these Christian principles, the citizenry of the newly established Commonwealth could both follow the Quaker traditions of peace and nonviolence and, at the same time, be saved from the horrors of war.

As an additional and practical motivating factor, William Penn and other members of the Society (along with virtually all other non-conformists) had experienced severe persecution during the Puritan Commonwealth period and from the Stuarts, the reigning British royal family in the late 1600s. Because of these experiences, Penn was interested in finding a place of refuge for members of the persecuted sect and other like-minded dissenters. The Quaker dream was realized on March 4, 1681, when Charles II granted Penn a proprietary charter for the new colony that would be called Pennsylvania.

As Charles granted the proprietary charter to Penn, he clearly intended that the Commonwealth be protected from danger through the force of arms and assumed that the colonists, Quakers or not, would share in the colony's defense. Thus, the charter given to Penn provided the Commonwealth and its leadership with military powers. The proprietor was given the authority:

---

[10] The Quakers were unusual for their time since they promoted toleration and peaceful dealings with all people, despite their political or religious beliefs. The right of the individual to seek truth and the toleration of society to allow him to do so were important parts of their theology. For example, Penn, after returning from a trip to Germany and Holland in 1677, published a plea for liberty for all dissenters, even "papists" (Catholics). In this period of English history, a call for liberty for Catholics required tremendous courage and caused some of Penn's detractors to regard him as an agent of the Jesuits (even though Penn had previously called for a restriction of Catholic freedoms). See Melvin V. Eddy Jr., *William Penn and Early Quakerism* (Princeton: University Press, 1973), pp. 314-316.

*to Levy, muster and traine all sorts of men of what condicion or whereso-
ever borne in the said p[ro]vince of Pensilvania for the time being and to
make warr and pursue the enemies and Robbers aforesaid as well by Sea
as by Land, yea even without the Limits of the said p[ro]vince and by
Gods assistance to vanquish and take them and being taken to put them to
death by the Law of Warr or save them att theire pleasure and to doe all
and every other Act and thing which to the charge and office of a Captaine
Generall of any Army hath ever had the same.*[11]

The powers mentioned in the latter portion of the quotation, in the
experience of the other English colonies, were intended to provide a method
to organize military forces, commission officers and even command Commonwealth troops. All of these responsibilities, to include the necessity of having
a military force, were objectionable to many Quakers. Military duties and, for
some, the mere existence of the military were in contradiction to the basic
beliefs of many citizens affiliated with the Society of Friends.

Considering the religious beliefs of the founder, it is not surprising that
the frame of government approved by William Penn on April 20, 1682, implementing his authority in the new colony did not contain provisions for a militia
to defend the colony. "The Frame of the Government of the Province of
Pennsylvania" approved by Penn on that date and the "Laws agreed upon in
England" did not include any references to the creation of a militia. Granted,
the frame of government gave the governor and his Provincial Council the
responsibility to "have the care of the peace and safety of the province and that
nothing be by any person attempted to the subversion of this frame of government."[12] But while the peace and safety of the Commonwealth were responsibilities of the government, military forces were not authorized, due to the
beliefs of the Quaker leadership.

Penn might have possessed the knowledge to engage in military affairs,
for while he is remembered today as a leading pacifist, he was no stranger to the
profession of arms. The son of a British admiral, he served briefly with his
father (Admiral Sir William Penn) as a volunteer in 1665 and spent his early
years in a military household. But Penn, the preeminent Quaker in the
American experience and proprietor of the colony, did not personally govern
Pennsylvania. Instead, he chose to delegate this task to deputy governors who

---

[11] Charter of the Commonwealth of Pennsylvania, as reproduced in Beckman, *Statutes at Large
of Pennsylvania,* p. 115.
[12] Ibid., p. 4.

were usually not Quakers. Using non-Quakers in this role was important to Penn because he sincerely believed in political privilege for all, to include non-Quakers. Indeed, he selected men for political office who were not Quakers to promote diversity and balance in the Commonwealth. This was a logical tactic because non-Quakers, many of whom had some type of military experience, could exercise the military function and other governmental duties that might cause conflicts of conscience for a practicing Quaker.[13]

Penn seemed to recognize from the onset of his "holy experiment" that both political and military power would have to be wielded by the executive branch of the government. Due to religious convictions, Quakers would often be unable to perform at least part of those governmental functions. Thus, Penn was willing to allow non-Quakers to perform in such roles so long as he personally did not have to engage in activities that were in contradiction to his religious beliefs. This willingness to allow others to perform tasks that were counter to Quaker beliefs should not be regarded as hypocrisy, but rather as a measure of Penn's political pragmatism and genuine commitment to pluralism. Penn's firm belief in tolerance for the ideals and convictions of others and his belief in promoting political and religious liberty for Pennsylvania's other citizens made the Commonwealth's political system unique.

These compromises by the proprietor, however, caused a series of conflicts within the Commonwealth's government, almost from its inception. Penn pledged to build a society that would be a model of tolerance and peace. Yet an integral aspect of governing this new province was providing protection: defense for the citizenry. Penn's government provided the Commonwealth's citizens with tolerance – a scarce commodity in the 18th century – but defending the Commonwealth was a difficult task, considering Quaker beliefs. The defense issue was made even more difficult by the lack of consensus within the leadership of the Quaker movement concerning the extent to which a believer could stretch individual beliefs in order to provide protection for the citizenry. Not all Quakers were as tolerant as Penn and, perhaps more important, not all were as politically astute.[14] While some were not averse to military operations conducted by others within the Commonwealth, their beliefs prevented them

---

[13] For example, in 1681 Penn appointed his cousin William Markham, a captain in the British army, as deputy governor and commander in chief of the province. Captain John Blackwell, a serious and sober former Cromwellian soldier, served as deputy governor in 1688-90, although he was not a Quaker. Frederic A. Godcharles, *Pennsylvania: Political, Governmental, Military and Civil*, governmental volume (New York: American Historical Society, 1933), pp. 66-100.

[14] Some Quakers worried that allowing non-Quakers to participate could result in their taking control of the government and instituting persecution against the Society of Friends, much as

from taking part in military activity themselves or voting to expend funds for military purposes.

Problems for the defense of the Commonwealth and for the growth of the militia almost immediately emerged because, as noted previously, English traditions were the basis for Pennsylvania government, even under the Quakers. While the deputy governor had military powers, giving him the ability to authorize and field military forces, he had to request funds from the Provincial Assembly. This chamber was heavily dominated by the Quakers, many of whom regarded voting for military appropriations as tantamount to participating in or condoning military action.

The dominance of members of the Society of Friends in the Provincial Council and the Assembly resulted in more than a failure to authorize a Pennsylvania militia in the early years of the Commonwealth's existence. Quaker dominance also meant the Commonwealth was unable to adequately answer royal requests for either troops or funds to support the wars that occurred in British America. A review of the Commonwealth's records shows members of the Society of Friends retained numerical superiority on the Provincial Council for the first 20 years of the Commonwealth's existence and wielded a controlling influence over the state Assembly until 1756.[15] Thus, for the first 75 years of its history as a proprietary colony, Pennsylvania was unable to field a state military force of any size through the militia concept, which required a universal military obligation by its citizens.

The world that the Quakers envisioned – a world of peace, tolerance and harmony – was in stark contrast to 17th- and 18th-century Pennsylvania. Both centuries were plagued by a series of interlocking wars involving, among others, the armies of Britain, France and Spain, on both the continent and in the colonies. These major-power rivalries, complicated (in the mid-18th century) by difficulties with the Indian population, ultimately made it imperative for the Commonwealth to have a defensive capability. The need for a strong defense was initially felt by the lower counties of the Commonwealth, now the state of Delaware. These coastal areas, largely non-Quaker, felt threatened by French naval elements and, desiring to protect their families and investments, requested that the provincial government exercise the proprietor's military

---

they had to suffer in England. Some of this faction were decidedly opposed to allowing "papists" any role in the government. Quakers and non-Quakers alike concurred on one point: there was no place in the government for atheists.

[15] Isaac Sharpless, *A History of Quaker Government in Pennsylvania: The Quakers in the Revolution*, vol. II (Philadelphia: T. S. Leach and Co., 1899), pp. 2-6.

authority and create a militia. The Quaker-dominated Assembly, in keeping with their conscience, logically refused.

In many respects, it was the displeasure of the Crown, rather than pressure from the early settlers, that drove the late 17th-century debate over how to defend Pennsylvania. The Crown quickly tired of the Quakers' unwillingness to field troops or pay for costs incurred in the defense of British America. Although the royal government was willing to allow the Quaker dissenters a haven where their beliefs could be practiced, this unusual royal tolerance did not extend to absolving the Commonwealth of the responsibility to provide for its defense.

Open conflict on the defense issue began in 1689 with the outbreak of what the colonists called King William's War. Since few British regulars were stationed in the colonies, the Crown suggested that Pennsylvania form a militia. The Friends in the council staunchly rejected this request, noting that the governor had the power to create a militia if he so desired. They further stated they would not interfere with his prerogative to raise a militia unless it offended their conscience. In 1693, the unresolved defense issue again emerged due to a request from New York for Pennsylvania to supply either 80 armed men or funds to assist in the defense of New York from French and Indian attack.[16] When action on this request failed to occur promptly, the royal advisory body, the Lords of Trade and Plantations, recommended that Pennsylvania's charter be voided and the colony be re-chartered with a new government willing to actively assist with the defense of the colonies. William, the new British sovereign, only recently crowned after the Glorious Revolution, was already uneasy with Penn due to the latter's friendship with the former sovereign James II.[17] Consequently, the Lords' advice was followed, and Penn's charter was revoked. In Penn's place William appointed a soldier, Colonel Benjamin Fletcher, as "Captain Generall and Governor in Chief of the Province of New Yorke, province of Pennsilvania, countrey of New Castle and the Territories and tracts of land depending theron." This appointment meant that Fletcher was the military commander of British colonies from Massachusetts Bay to Maryland.[18] Fletcher's appointment as governor of a unified New York and Pennsylvania

[16] Isaac Sharpless, *A Quaker Experiment in Government: A History of Quaker Government in Pennsylvania, 1682-1783* (Philadelphia: Ferris and Leach, 1920), pp. 190-196.

[17] Actually, Penn's close relationship to James caused his arrest, because Penn was regarded as a strong Stuart supporter by William and his key advisors. It would require several years for Penn to again establish royal trust. See Vincent Buranelli, *The King and the Quaker: A Study of William Penn and James I* (Philadelphia: University of Pennsylvania Press, 1962).

[18] *Pennsylvania Archives: Colonial Records of Pennsylvania, Minutes of the Provincial Council of*

clearly indicated the Crown's displeasure with the Quaker government.

Arriving in the colonies in April 1693, Fletcher attempted to both negate what he perceived to be the anti-military bent of the Penn government and form a new Assembly that would be amenable to supporting the defense of the colonies. In a meeting with the Provinial Council in Philadelphia on May 16, 1693, the new governor noted the burden of war on New York and urged the Council to place the Commonwealth in an active role of assisting with the defense of this neighboring colony. The governor was cognizant of the sensitivities within the Commonwealth on the defense issue. In his first speech Fletcher gave assurances stating that the money provided by the Assembly would be used to provide for "officers Sallaries and other Charges" and would be "converted to these uses and shall not be dipt in blood."[19] Reacting to strong pressure from the Crown and aware of Penn's recent removal from office, the Assembly began the process of raising funds and even drafted a bill concerning the creation of a militia. The impetus for a militia, however, was short-lived, and by the time the bill had its third reading, it was soundly defeated. Since militia legislation had failed, the only possible method for Pennsylvania to assist the Crown with defense was by raising funds.

The Assembly initially seemed willing to consider the new governor's requests. Once the initial pressure relaxed, however, they adopted a stalling tactic on the funding bill and attempted to gain key concessions from the governor as a prerequisite for action. Specifically, they sought recognition of the Assembly as having the sole appropriation power for the Commonwealth. Due to the Assembly's delays, by the end of May Fletcher was furious. He demanded an answer from the Assembly as to whether or not they would comply with the Crown's appropriation request. Recognizing the significance of the governor's ultimatum and realizing that a positive or negative response was required, the Assembly retreated and approved Fletcher's supply bill.

This direct confrontation between the Crown and the Quaker-dominated Assembly, which resulted in a Quaker retreat, did not appear to damage the Quakers' power base. Even though the number of their detractors was slowly increasing, they were not unpopular with the majority of the Commonwealth's citizens, despite the growing percentage of the populace who were Anglicans or Germans of various religious denominations. The Quakers maintained their power base because they had proven themselves to be astute politicians in the

Pennsylvania from the Organization to the Termination of the Proprietary Government, vol. I (Philadelphia: Joseph Severns and Co., 1852), p. 352.
[19] Ibid., p. 400.

struggle with the new colonial governor. Furthermore, their resistance to the Commonwealth's direct participation in the Crown's wars won them many friends.

Those who opposed the Quakers received a definite setback when Penn's ouster proved to be brief and the charter was returned to him in 1694. Penn's charm had convinced William and his royal bureaucracy that he was a valuable asset in governing the diverse elements in the Commonwealth.[20]

There were no further crises regarding the military issue for the remainder of the 1690s, but Colonel Fletcher had been unable to overcome the Assembly's reluctance to fund military forces. Fletcher's only real accomplishment in this sphere of activity was the passage of an appropriations act. Passed on November 7, 1696, this act failed to provide direct military appropriations but supplied £300 "for ye supply & relief of those Indians of the five Nations yt are in friendship with ye English with necessaries of food and raymt."[21] Through this circuitous path the Assembly provided the Crown with the necessary funds but assuaged its own conscience by not labeling the money as military appropriations.[22]

King William's War ended in 1697 without any resolution to the question of how or whether Pennsylvania would defend itself. In many respects, however, the Assembly's provision of funds which were not specifically allocated for military purposes but could be used at the government's discretion served as a precedent. Through this device the Quakers found a method to retain their role as British America's prime promoter of peace and harmony and, at the same time, deal with the odious task of providing military appropriations for the Crown. Their compromise, an action which some might regard as subterfuge, was perhaps the best that could be accepted by both sides, given the totally different views of the Quakers and the royal government.

Such stopgap measures were, however, only a brief respite from the conflict between the ruling Quaker oligarchy and those who wanted some

---

[20] To regain the colony, Penn promised "to see that the Pennsylvania Council and Assembly received the King's commands, that he would insist that they all give due respect to royal wishes, and that he would do all he could to make sure that the legislators acted properly." Harry E. Wildes, *William Penn* (New York: Macmillan Co., 1974), pp. 264-265.
[21] Russell F. Weigley, "The Colonial Militia," in *The First Century: A History of the 28th Infantry Division*, prepared under the direction of Col. Uzal W. Ent (Harrisburg, Pa.: Stackpole Books, 1979), p. 18. Cited hereafter as Weigley, "The Colonial Militia."
[22] As mentioned previously in the text, Fletcher alleviated some Quaker opposition by assuring the members that the appropriation would be used for other purposes and not "dipt in blood." This was obviously dodging the issue, but the Quakers appeared to be satisfied with this assurance. See Jones, *Quakers in the American Colonies*, p. 488.

method to defend the Commonwealth. As the 18th century began, Britain and her colonies would increasingly find themselves involved in a series of wars that would last for most of the century. Logic dictated that Pennsylvania, a geographically large and populous colony, could not be exempted for long from the responsibility to defend itself or the interests of the Crown.

The War of Spanish Succession began in 1702 with Britain and France as the primary antagonists. This conflict quickly spread to the colonies, where it was more commonly known as Queen Anne's War. The conflict had a direct and immediate effect on Pennsylvania because the French had successfully negotiated a treaty with the Iroquois, a formidable five-nation confederation that had suzerainty of most of eastern Pennsylvania's Indian tribes. The threat to the Commonwealth was potentially so serious that the deputy governor, a non-Quaker named Andrew Hamilton, asked the Assembly to create a militia.[23]

The Assembly, which had actually increased its powers since 1693, refused to grant this request, which the deputy governor expected. To counter the Assembly, Hamilton recruited, on his authority as Captain General of Pennsylvania, a militia force – an action that was totally within his powers. Drummers were sent throughout Philadelphia calling the citizenry to service. As was the custom, the recruiters often bolstered military ardor with strong spirits. Despite incentives, there was insufficient support for this venture among the citizens. Many Pennsylvanians simply saw no real threat to the Commonwealth. In addition, some of the Anglican population purportedly ignored the call to arms, hoping to provoke such a crisis over defense that the Quaker-led government would fall. Thus the initiative came to naught. With Hamilton's death in 1703, the question of how Pennsylvania should defend itself, within the confines of Quaker conscience, remained unresolved.

Some of Penn's non-Quaker enemies were certain this latest military crisis would bring about the Quaker's demise, but again Penn demonstrated his resilience. When the new deputy governor, John Evans, arrived in Philadelphia on February 2, 1704, he brought with him specific authorization from Penn to raise a militia.[24] Of course, Penn's decisions did not always have the concurrence

---

[23] Hamilton's logic to the council was: "For if those who profess themselves under a Scruple to bear arms would think it a hardship to be fforced to it, so (I hope) they'll also think it one to Invade the principles of others by Disabling them to Effect what they in Conscience ought to do wch is to Provide under God for ye Defense." *Pennsylvania Archives: Colonial Records of Pennsylvania, Minutes of the Provincial Council of Pennsylvania from Organization to the Termination of the Proprietary Government*, vol. II (Philadelphia: Joseph Severns and Co., 1857), pp. 78-79. Cited hereafter as *Minutes of the Provincial Council*, vol. II.

[24] According to Russell Weigley, when Evans arrived in Pennsylvania on February 2, 1704, he

of all Quakers, a factor that Evans would soon come to appreciate. When settled in his new position, Evans presented to the Provincial Assembly the urgent need to establish a militia, in order to provide for an adequate method to defend the Commonwealth. True to their beliefs, the Assembly, still heavily dominated by the Quakers and following their own consciences (rather than Penn's), refused. Similar to his ill-fated predecessor Andrew Hamilton, Evans began the process of recruiting a militia on his authority as governor and without the Assembly's support. He called this force, recruited in Philadelphia, the Governor's Guard and offered the citizens who were interested a relief from the ward and watch duty which the corporation of Philadelphia imposed on its citizens.[25]

At first the governor seemed to have found the formula for success, for he soon claimed to have ten companies in service. His fortunes were also bolstered by the participation of Penn's son, also named William. Evans' opponents, however, claimed that there were never ten companies, but rather only "some forty bedraggled men."[26] Whatever the true number, the Governor's Guard was a short-lived experiment. Although they supposedly were exempt from watch duty, militiamen who refused their watch duties were reported to the Mayor's Court by constables. Such punitive actions by the city government, coupled with the lack of pay or any type of official recognition, rapidly caused citizen interest in the militia to wane.[27]

Evans, however, was not to be dissuaded from his goal. When the Quakers would not allow a militia and the growing non-Quaker element would not back a governor's militia, Evans resorted to subterfuge. On May 14, 1704, a courier arrived in Philadelphia, bringing news of a purported sighting of a French fleet, lying off the coast of the mid-Atlantic states. The letter, suppos-

---

had specific authorization from Penn to raise a militia. That Penn did not oppose this initiative is underscored by his son's active participation in drilling the Governor's Guard on Society Hill in Philadelphia. Weigley, "The Colonial Militia," p. 18.

[25] The minutes of the Provincial Council in the spring of 1704 refer to publishing the commission of officers of the militia who should be exempted from watch, which clearly shows an intent to carry out the governor's pledge. See *Minutes of the Provincial Council*, vol. II, May 11, 1704, pp. 151-152.

[26] Weigley, "The Colonial Militia," p. 18.

[27] It is also important to remember that attempts by royal officials to create some type of militia centered on Philadelphia. There was a growing resentment in the hinterlands by village and rural citizens who felt they were defenseless due to the inaction of those who were comfortable and safe within the environs of the city. Major William P. Clarke, *Official History of the Militia and National Guard of Pennsylvania from the Earliest Period of Record to the Present Time* (Philadelphia: Charles J. Hendler, 1909), pp. 7-8. Cited hereafter as Clarke, *Official History of the Pennsylvania Militia*.

edly from Maryland's John Seymour, seemed to officially confirm that war was directly threatening Quaker Pennsylvania. Having what appeared to be just cause, Evans called the Provincial Council together, and the non-Quaker members heartily agreed with the necessity of calling Pennsylvania to arms. During the next few days, the governor – his cause bolstered by the purported French fleet – pushed military preparedness, fueling the crisis with additional updates of French naval activity. The supposed crisis was exacerbated on May 16 when the sheriff of New Castle County rushed into Philadelphia to inform the citizens that six French privateers were in the bay and had bombarded Lewes into ruins. Evans capitalized on this report and called on all able-bodied men of Philadelphia to become members of the Governor's Militia.

A number of Quakers, however, gradually became suspicious. Despite the reported disasters, French sails did not appear on the horizon, nor were any refugees appearing in Philadelphia as a result of bombardment from the ships or pillaging by French forces. James Logan, a respected leader in the community and in the Provincial Council, traveled south into the reported war zone and quickly confirmed there was no unusual French naval activity in the region. In fact, the whole episode had been manufactured by the governor to goad Pennsylvania into developing a militia. Rather than improving the Commonwealth's military preparedness, Evans had only succeeded in discrediting the militia movement and ensuring his recall as governor, an action that occurred in 1708. Obviously, these antics made it impossible for Evans to make any progress in fielding a militia or determining any other suitable method for obtaining the Assembly's assistance in defending the Commonwealth.

This is not to say, however, that defense was a dead issue for the remainder of Evans' time in office. England remained at war with France from 1702 until 1714. This war ultimately spilled over into the northern regions of the Commonwealth, again highlighting the military unpreparedness of Pennsylvania. As a result of the war and the legacy of Evans' tenure, the tasks confronting Charles Gookin, the Commonwealth's next governor, were daunting. Shortly after assuming office, Gookin was required to request funds for defense. In 1709 the Crown planned to counter French presence in North America by launching an attack to retake Newfoundland and conquer Canada. The colonial governors were asked to supply troops and funds for the expedition, and 150 men of the 1,500-man expeditionary force were to come from Pennsylvania. The other colonies slated to participate in the attack were New Jersey, New York and Connecticut. Gookin, well aware of the experiences of his predecessors, wisely decided not to renew attempts to organize a militia and instead requested the Assembly to provide £4,000 to support the war effort.[28]

To protect the Quaker conscience, he allowed the appointment of a committee from their number to oversee the expenditures. The Assembly did not at first agree with this proposed compromise, for they did not wish to provide money so men could be hired to kill other men. Instead, they offered to provide £500 in revenue, a gift to the queen, and if she wanted to use it for military purposes, that would be her prerogative. This initial gift was augmented by an additional £300 from the Assembly a short time later. Much like his predecessor, Gookin was furious with the Quaker-led Assembly, for they had not selected either of the options he had placed before them and showed little willingness to compromise.[29]

Despite the governor's displeasure, royal pressure for compliance with the Crown's request for support was lacking. Consequently the issue would simmer unresolved for several months. It was not until 1711, in response to yet another call for Pennsylvania to contribute troops or funds for a proposed expedition into French Canada, that an agreement was reached. It called for the Commonwealth to provide £2,000 for equipment and supplies, rather than the requested 150 soldiers.[30] Originally, these funds were earmarked for the queen's use, but when the governor insisted the money be given to his office, a compromise was made for half the money to be sent to New York and the remainder retained for the expedition's supplies.[31]

It is interesting to note that, even though the Quaker leadership worded their actions to appear as though they did not officially provide military funding for the queen's wars, they knew full well the intended purpose of these funds. They were military appropriations. According to one critic, the Quakers justified what was an obvious contradiction to their Peace Testimony by stating the obligation to render unto Caesar what was Caesar's – the biblical require-

---

[28] In a message to the Assembly on June 2, 1709, Gookin noted it would not be difficult for a colony as populous as Pennsylvania to raise this many men except "in a country where most of the inhabitants are of such principles as will not allow them the use of arms." George E. Reed, ed., *Pennsylvania Archives: Papers of the Governors, 1681-1747*, fourth series, vol. I (Harrisburg: State of Pennsylvania, 1900), pp. 300-301. Cited hereafter as Reed, *Papers of the Governors*, vol. I.

[29] Gookin stated on June 11, 1709, that the sum the Quakers were willing to give – £500 rather than £4,000 – was not worthy of "Her [the Queen's] royal acceptance" and that they had an opportunity to show themselves to be "truly dutiful subjects; words alone I assure you Gent. are not much valued by the ministry at home and £500 from Pennsylvania will add to 'em doubt but very little weight." Ibid., pp. 301-302.

[30] Clarke, *Official History of the Pennsylvania Militia*, pp. 7-8.

[31] Hermann Wellenreuther, "The Political Dilemma of the Quakers in Pennsylvania," *Pennsylvania Magazine of History and Biography* (April 1970), p. 154.

ment of the Christian citizen to support government.[32] Before additional crises over appropriations could occur, Queen Anne's War ended in 1713. The appropriations earmarked for military use, which had been allocated by a reluctant Assembly, were never actually turned over to the governor. Again, the Assembly had been successful in eluding the Crown's call for any meaningful support for Pennsylvania's defense.

Although the pacifism of the Quakers is by far the primary reason for the impasse on the defense issue, it is not the only one. As the decades elapsed between the beginning of the defense debate in the early 1690s and 1740, the Quakers steadily diminished in number. However, despite their numerical decline, they were able to preserve their influence in legislative matters. An unofficial alliance had evolved between the Quakers, opposed to the exercise of military force, and other diverse elements in Pennsylvania society who perceived little threat from the Indians and virtually no immediate danger from the other continental powers. In fact, a number of Pennsylvania's colonial citizens were not at all interested in contributing, in any fashion, to the frequent wars in which the British Empire became embroiled. So, while the Quakers are generally chastised by innumerable writers for their key role in blocking defense enactments, their actions or lack thereof on the military issue could not have occurred without the tacit approval of a number of non-Quaker inhabitants. Some non-Quaker citizens also viewed the issue of fielding military forces with deep suspicion.[33]

In time, however, neither the anti-war convictions of the Quakers nor the reticence of those who supported their cause could prevent the creation of military forces by and for the Commonwealth. Continental-power rivalry continued in the intervening years, and the peace treaty that ended Queen Anne's War in 1714 provided Europe and the colonies only a brief respite, not a lasting peace. In the years following the peace, Pennsylvania expended considerable effort in improving relations with the Indians, who fortunately had not

---

[32] A tract was printed which registered at least some opposition to such compromises within the Society of Friends. Written by Thomas Maule, it was entitled *Tribute to Caesar, now paid by the best Christians, and to what purpose. With some remarks on the late vigorous expedition against Canada. Of civil Government, how inconsistent it is with the Government of Christ in his Church, compared with the ancient just and righteous principles of the Quakers, and their modern practice and doctrine. With some notes upon the discipline of their Church in this province, especially at Philadelphia.*

[33] This border dispute emerged in the early 1730s and continued for the next three decades. Papers that relate to the particulars of the dispute can be found in John P. Linn and William H. Egle, eds., *Pennsylvania Archives: Provincial Affairs in Pennsylvania: Papers Relating to the Boundary Dispute between Pennsylvania and Maryland, 1734-1760*, second series, vol. VII (Harrisburg: E. K. Meyers, State Printer, 1890), pp. 319-425.

added to the Commonwealth's problems with any hostile actions, despite many grievances. Interwar security problems did not emerge due to difficulties with the Indians or the European powers, but rather as the result of a border dispute with Maryland.

The peace enjoyed by the Commonwealth's citizens was broken when in September 1736 a force of 300 armed Marylanders invaded Lancaster County and pressured the inhabitants to leave so the land could be claimed for Maryland. Although there was some skirmishing between the citizens, the dispute was by and large waged between the governments of the two colonies. Again, Pennsylvania's citizens were at a decided disadvantage in such border disputes, because they did not have any type of militia troops to defend their homes.[34] The controversy would not be settled by force of arms but rather by agreements between the heirs of Lord Baltimore and Penn, which resulted in the survey line started by Mason and Dixon in 1764.[35]

The dispute with Maryland, however, was a minor issue, because while it was transpiring, Britain and British America were again moving to the brink of war. The seeds of the next war were sown in 1739 when British sea captain William Jenkins appeared before Parliament with a grisly illustration of the Spanish intent to regulate commerce with Spanish America: his severed ear. The War of Jenkins' Ear, which began that same year, would expand beyond a dispute between the British and Spanish empires and would, within a few short years, include France. The colonies, to include the Commonwealth, were quickly drawn into this early Spanish phase and thus became active participants almost from the outset. Once again the Pennsylvania Assembly was faced with the challenge of balancing Quaker conscience and belief with the Crown's request to contribute to the common defense.

Initially, it seemed that in the 25 years that had passed since the end of Queen Anne's War the opportunities for creating a militia force in Pennsylvania should have substantially improved. Even though members of various German sects, who shared the Quaker aversion to bearing arms, had settled in the

---

[34] Reed, *Papers of the Governors*, vol. I, pp. 657-658. The papers of James Logan, president of the Council, who served briefly as governor (1736-1738) due to the untimely death of his predecessor, are dominated by the correspondence between him and Maryland's lieutenant governor.
[35] The boundary dispute between the two proprietary colonies had its origins at the beginning of the Commonwealth's existence because the drafter of Pennsylvania's charter was apparently unfamiliar with earlier patents and uncertain about the geography of the New World. This, together with vague language in the charters, caused disputes with Virginia, Maryland and Connecticut. The dispute with Maryland was settled by surveyors Charles Mason and Jeremiah Dixon, who set the southern border of Pennsylvania 19 miles south of the 40th parallel.

Commonwealth, so had a substantial number of Presbyterians, Lutherans and Anglicans. Thus, as noted earlier, in the years between the wars, the Quakers had become a minority faction in the Commonwealth.[36] Furthermore, by this time some of the Quaker families had lost the intensity of their convictions regarding the defense issue – and were at best nominal members of the movement – and no longer opposed military service with any fervor. In fact, by 1739 the majority of the colony's population no longer opposed military service, even though they still questioned the necessity of fielding military forces. Still, a sufficient number of influential and traditional Quakers retained seats in the Assembly, and they were astute enough to wield a disproportionate influence in the deliberations of that body. In short, despite their decreasing percentage of the population, the Quakers were still able to block military enactments desired by the Crown and its colonial governor.

Quaker influence became obvious when a renewed debate flared in the early stages of the War of Jenkins' Ear. Some of the Commonwealth's leadership had actually attempted to preempt the traditional fight over military appropriations. Indeed, in 1739 John Penn advised recently appointed Governor George Thomas that a militia should be formed.[37] Given the experiences of his predecessors, the governor expected this to be a contentious proposal because "a number of people are principled against fighting" and would contend that a law which would "oblige them to carry arms, would be persecuting them."[38] Both Penn and Thomas recognized the difficulty of forming a militia, regardless of the actual dangers facing the colony. Penn suggested following the example of Governor Evans who, during Queen Anne's War, had organized a militia through his executive powers and without the support of the Assembly.

---

[36] It might seem that various German pietistic groups, with their anti-militaristic bent, would reinforce the Quaker attitudes, but the Germans were a divided group that did not function as a coherent voting bloc. Splintering among the pietists undermined their political influence. See Robert L. Brunhouse, *The Counter-Revolution in Pennsylvania, 1776-1790* (Harrisburg: Pennsylvania Historical and Museum Commission, 1971), pp. 1-3.

[37] After William Penn's death the Penn family drifted away from the Quaker faith and returned to the Church of England. Even so, John Penn's advice to the governor was not totally out of character for the Penn family. William Penn had occasionally endorsed military service, and his son Billy had actually drilled one of the ill-fated early and unrecognized militias. Russell Weigley best sums it up by stating that the Penn family had an "on again off again martial tradition." See Weigley, "The Colonial Militia," p. 18.

[38] Penn was practical because, as he noted, "No Government can be Supported without being capable to defend it's self." John Penn, in a letter to George Thomas, dated August 2, 1739, in "The Pennsylvania Manuscripts: Thomas Penn Letterbook," microfilm roll 1, Letterbooks, January 19, 1729-August 1742 (Philadelphia: Historical Society of Pennsylvania), pp. 306-307.

Although in the end this initiative was unsuccessful, it remained a possibility. Under this concept, the governor would offer commissions to gentlemen within the Commonwealth, and they in turn would raise volunteer units. The Assembly could then be requested to purchase weapons for the volunteer militia and even supply a small stipend for the volunteers each time they attended military training.[39]

Thomas did not immediately attempt to implement such a plan. Instead, recognizing the imminent spread of war from Europe to the colonies, on October 16, 1739, he gave a speech to the Assembly concerning the likelihood of war coming to the Commonwealth.[40] There is little evidence that the traditional Quakers, who still dominated the Assembly, were at all moved by the governor's warning or were willing to permit the members who were concerned about the issue of military preparedness to act in accordance with their consciences. In fact, at the September 1739 Yearly Meeting of Pennsylvania Quakers, a circular was approved which demanded strict adherence to the Peace Testimony, an action which set the stage for another major confrontation between the Quakers and the Crown.

Thomas seemed most perturbed that the Quakers, "they who profess conscience, will not allow others to act agreeable to theirs."[41] Conversely, though Thomas and those desiring the passage of some method of defense for Pennsylvania expected inaction on any defense measure sent to the Assembly, they apparently were willing to bide their time until it was certain that the Assembly would not pass any type of military legislation. They also hoped the elections of 1740 would result in a more favorable legislative body.

As Thomas had predicted, the call for colonial troops came in 1740. The governor announced with a proclamation on April 14, 1740, that the king had declared war on Spain and intended to send an expedition to the West Indies. The Crown requested the American colonies to supply 3,500 soldiers to form an American regiment to engage in military operations, not on Pennsylvania soil, but against the Spanish in the Caribbean. When this call

---

[39] Ibid. This concept of paying militiamen for their training was far ahead of its time. In 1791 George Washington would propose a National Militia act which included the idea among its provisions. When the act passed in 1792, militia pay was one of the many provisions excised. It would not be until the 20th century that federal legislation mandated payment for National Guardsmen – the lineal descendants of the militia – for training duty.

[40] George Thomas, in a speech to the Assembly concerning the hostilities with Spain, in Reed, *Papers of the Governors*, vol. I, pp. 688-689.

[41] Sally Schwartz, *A Mixed Multitude: The Struggle for Toleration in Colonial Pennsylvania* (New York: University Press, 1987), p. 165. Cited hereafter as Schwartz, *A Mixed Multitude*.

came, Pennsylvania had neither a militia act nor an Assembly that was willing to vote for military preparedness. Of the quota requested by the Crown, Pennsylvania was asked to provide eight companies of 50 men each. The plan was that once Pennsylvania had raised the troops and transported them to their area of employment in the Caribbean, the British government would assume all responsibility for their care.[42] Rather than engaging in a lengthy debate with the Assembly, and considering the likely end result, Thomas, who had holdings in the Caribbean region, used his executive authority to raise the requested force (as had been suggested by John Penn).

The results of his initiative were surprising. Pennsylvania exceeded the quota set by the government, with between 450 and 700 men (depending on which source is used) volunteering to serve.[43] Citizens of the Empire from this area of the Atlantic seaboard, including these Pennsylvanians, were enlisted in His Majesty's American Regiment of Foot, also known as the American Regiment. This regiment was not a regiment in the traditional sense, because it consisted of four battalions of nine companies each, for a total of 36 companies.[44] According to a report from the period, on September 8, 1740, seven companies were prepared to sail within the next few days. Shortly after their departure, they were scheduled to stop in New Castle, in the lower counties, and pick up two additional companies that were raised in that area.[45] Evidence indicates that recruitment for the American Regiment did not cease once the companies sailed. In the spring of 1742 an officer from one of the New Jersey companies stationed in the West Indies was in Pennsylvania recruiting additional soldiers.[46]

While on the surface it would seem that the Pennsylvania military problem had been resolved, objections to these enlistments emerged almost immediately from some of Pennsylvania's established citizens. A number of the enlistees were indentured servants who had enlisted without the consent or knowledge of their owners. They had been promised their freedom in exchange for their military service. By allowing recruiters to make such prom-

---

[42] George Thomas, in a speech to the Assembly concerning "the Province's Contribution to Publick Defense," July 2, 1740, in Reed, *Papers of the Governors*, vol. I, pp. 727-729. See also Weigley, "The Colonial Militia," pp. 19, 20.

[43] Douglas E. Leach, *Roots of Conflict* (Chapel Hill, N.C.: University of North Carolina Press, 1986), p. 52.

[44] "Four Independent Companies of Foot, May 1746-November 1747," paper prepared for the author by Joseph Seymour, December 22, 1998.

[45] *The Pennsylvania Gazette*, September 8, 1740.

[46] *The Pennsylvania Gazette*, April 8, 1742.

ises, the governor had antagonized the Assembly, a body that had never been keen on the military enterprises of the Crown or the executive's singular exercise of military power.[47] The governor had also antagonized the Quaker faction by pursuing a military venture outside the authority of the Assembly. And to compound his problems, he had antagonized the proprietary faction, which was opposed, for their own economic reasons, to emancipating indentured servants in exchange for military service.[48]

The crisis between the governor and the Assembly reached a new height on July 2, 1740, when the governor presented the Assembly with the necessary request to provide funds for transportation, food and other supplies for provincial troops.[49] The Assembly responded with a unique bill which provided military funds for the Commonwealth but would not allow the funds to be released until all of the indentured servants in the governor's companies were returned to their legal owners. In addition, the governor's recruiters were required to pledge not to recruit any additional indentured servants. The Assembly also took steps to prosecute recruiters for depriving the masters of their property without due process of law.

For Thomas, the Assembly's actions were the last straw. Incensed, he wrote a sharp letter to the British government recommending the exclusion of Quakers from office. If this was not done, in his opinion, Pennsylvania would be indefensible. Once the Assembly heard of the governor's action, they retaliated by denouncing Thomas as an "enemy of the people."

Obviously, by this stage the controversy had become so bitter that any type of compromise was impossible, given the polarization of Pennsylvania politics. In fact, the defense controversy had led to the emergence of two political factions in preparation for the elections of 1740: those who supported the governor and proprietary interests and an opposing faction led by the Quakers and in loose confederation with some of the German elements. The governor and his faction attempted to portray the Quakers as unfit for office, asserting

---

[47] Thomas sent a letter to the Assembly dated August 5, 1740, telling them his instructions to the officers raising the companies were to "engage as many Freemen (and Freemen only) as they could." He stated that in the future he had instructed the officers to avoid recruiting indentures, but as for those already recruited, he could not release them despite the anger of their owners. Reed, *Papers of the Governors*, vol. I, pp. 750-751. The recruitment of indentures would again emerge as an issue during the French and Indian War.

[48] Philip S. Klein and Ari Hoogenboom, *A History of Pennsylvania* (New York: McGraw-Hill Co., 1973), p. 50.

[49] An introductory speech to the Assembly by Governor George Thomas in Reed, *Papers of the Governors*, vol. I, pp. 727-729.

that as long as they dominated colonial politics the Commonwealth would be unable to defend itself. The Quakers played on the fears of the Common-wealth's German elements, reminding them of the horrors of war experienced by the inhabitants of central Europe and the potential loss of freedom if the governor's faction prevailed. In spite of the accusations lodged against the Quakers and their backers, the elections of 1740 returned most of the incumbents to office, with broad backing across the political and religious spectrum. The bullying of constituents by a succession of royal governors had not swayed the electorate toward the king's view.

The hesitancy to oust the Quakers was likely due to the reluctance of some of the citizenry to back policies that might involve the Commonwealth in various British military operations. It was not that the colonials opposed defending their portion of the New World; rather, they wanted to avoid involvement in the Crown's military ventures throughout the colonies. Nor did the colonists want to bear the expense of building forts and maintaining troops to defend the king's domain. Thus, in spite of organized opposition, the elections of 1740 found the Quakers still able to wield substantial power in the Assembly.

In this emotion-charged debate, there was at least one rational voice consistently urging a reasonable and pragmatic approach. James Logan, a respected leader within the Quaker community, believed the Quakers would be wise to compromise and not hold strictly to all political and religious principles. He reasoned that if they, as a minority group, ignored too long the wishes and beliefs of other citizens, they could conceivably lose their power and influence in Pennsylvania.[50]

To promote his call for a reconsideration of Quaker strategy, Logan in 1741 published a pamphlet which emphasized that even though offensive warfare was wrong, defending one's property was a legitimate act. He stated that Quakers who strictly adhered to their beliefs and could not, according to their consciences, compromise their beliefs should not participate in government. Furthermore, he reminded his fellow Quakers that they had been fortunate to have the Crown grant them tolerance in Pennsylvania, and thus they should act

---

[50] James Logan was assuredly one of the best appointments to any position of power that Penn made. Politically astute, this Scots-Irish Quaker backed Penn and his policies even when other Quakers criticized the proprietor and attempted to undermine his plans and policies. Logan was convinced that the Quakers had to show tolerance toward the political beliefs of the non-Quaker majority, but he was totally opposed to underhanded political maneuvering such as Governor Evans' manufactured crisis of 1704, which Logan personally exposed.

responsibly in retaining these privileges. Although today the logic of his arguments seems reasonable, Logan's essay, presented at a 1741 meeting, was not
well received by his peers. The heated atmosphere resulting from the bitter
debates over the defense issue would not allow logic a role in the deliberations.
The Crown and the Friends remained on a collision course, and given the
demographics of the state, it was a confrontation the Quakers could not win.[51]

After all the rhetoric, charges and counter-charges over the issue of
defense in general and the governor's nine companies in particular, the Pennsylvania companies prepared to embark at Philadelphia on September 8, 1740, for
the Windward Passage and Jamaica. An additional company from the lower
counties (now Delaware) embarked from New Castle a short time later.[52] The
companies still included the contentious indentured servants. They were scheduled to rendezvous with regular British troops which made up the remainder of
the Caribbean expedition. The Pennsylvania troops and the entire American
Regiment were under the command of William Gooch. This Virginian served
the Crown in several capacities, including lieutenant governor of Virginia, captain general of that colony's military forces and commander-in-chief of His
Majesty's forces in North America. These first Pennsylvania troops to be used
in an expedition outside the colonies served in the American Regiment with
companies recruited in Virginia and New Jersey.

From the outset the expedition went awry. The regular British troops
that were to be an important part of the expedition did not arrive until winter,
forcing the colonial troops to wait for the Crown's regular army units. Even
though the British had succeeded in creating a credible force to attack Spanish
bases in the Caribbean, they had failed to provide a solid logistical base for the
expedition. Nonetheless, the British regulars and the colonials, after lengthy
delays, laid siege to Cartagena, Spain's key seaport on the northern coast of
South America. The siege was a miserable affair, and the entire expedition a
monument to poor planning and poor leadership. To further complicate matters, tropical diseases such as yellow fever struck the expeditionary force hard.[53]
The siege lasted from March 9 to April 11, 1741, and the troops, badly deplet-

[51] For additional information on Logan, see William Hanna, *Benjamin Franklin and Pennsylvania Politics* (Stanford, Calif.: Stanford University Press, 1965), pp. 12-13 and Schwartz, *A Mixed Multitude*, pp. 171-173.
[52] The report in *The Pennsylvania Gazette*, September 8, 1740, stated, "Tis said the Transports will sail in a few Days, the Companies are all full, and the men chearful and in good Heart."
[53] Summarizations of the ill-fated expedition are included in Weigley's "The Colonial Militia," p. 20, and Douglas E. Leach's *Arms for the Empire: A Military History of the British Colonies in North America, 1607-1763* (New York: Macmillan Co., 1972), pp. 217-219.

ed by disease, had to be withdrawn.

Records in the Commonwealth indicate that, despite this initial failure, Spanish fortifications at Cartagena were eventually destroyed. The news of this ultimate success prompted celebrations in Philadelphia. According to a news article on May 14, 1741:

> *Two Companies of Gentlemen met, under Arms, at the State House and from thence, with his honor the Governor, in the center, accompanied with our Honorable Proprieter, the Council and the Mayor and Corporation, by a long march through the City, during the continual firing of the great Guns from the Ships and Wharffs came to the Court House where they discharged three Volleys.*[54]

The American Regiment remained in the West Indies into 1742. A contemporary report in April 1742 indicates that two officers from the regiment were in the Commonwealth on a recruiting expedition. Some Pennsylvanians may have served with British garrisons or the fleet even longer.[55]

The Caribbean expedition was not a glorious campaign for the Pennsylvania military tradition, but it was a beginning nevertheless. Troops had been raised without a militia law, and they had fought in support of the interests of the Crown. There was additional evidence that the stalemate in the Assembly was slowly being eroded in favor of a more realistic attitude. A softening of attitudes by elements in the Assembly was evidenced by its action in 1741. Cognizant of the displeasure of the governor and the sovereign over their recent inaction, the Assembly voted £3,000 for the Crown's use – money which was designed to support the Crown's military needs, though it was not specifically identified as a military appropriation. With at least some funds appropriated and Pennsylvanians organized as troops raised to defend the interests of the British sovereign, it seemed as though Pennsylvania might be on the threshold of shedding its anti-military image.[56]

---

[54] *The Pennsylvania Gazette*, May 14, 1741. This report mentions great guns being fired from the "Wharffs," and a report from July 3, 1740, in the same periodical refers to a number of guns being fired from the hill, in honor of William Gooch's visit to Philadelphia. Whether these field pieces were part of a royal battery or some as-yet unidentified local effort is not known. The existence of troops and guns in the harbor at this time in the Commonwealth is, to say the least, intriguing.

[55] The April 8, 1742 issue of *The Pennsylvania Gazette* indicated Captain Robert Farmar (who raised a company in New Jersey) and Lieutenant Palmer were recruiting in Pennsylvania.

[56] Caution in interpreting these events is warranted, because the provision of funds which were

Acknowledging that some measure of progress had been made, there were still some major issues that had to be addressed. Preeminent among them was the fact that Pennsylvania, unlike its neighboring colonies, had a powerfully established and articulate group in the Assembly that was totally opposed to military service and any form of military preparedness for the Commonwealth. While the Quakers had shown some willingness to compromise, their philosophy, based on strong religious convictions, remained essentially unchanged. As a consequence, small amounts – virtually tidbits – of military enactments were given to the governor. By so doing, a complete break between the royal government, which sought Pennsylvania's contribution to the defense of the colonies, and the Assembly, which sought to avoid the involvement of Pennsylvania in royal military ventures, could perhaps be avoided.

What the Crown sought from Pennsylvania was legislation providing for a militia force to defend the Commonwealth and royal interests within the Western Hemisphere. This type of legislation, however, was unlikely as long as the Quakers dominated the Assembly. A militia law offended Quaker tradition because it placed a military obligation on the Commonwealth's citizens and, in a sense, implied an obligation by the Assembly to fund them when called to duty. This the Quakers and their allies were unwilling to do.

An intriguing issue: even though the Quakers held the power to block military legislation, in all likelihood they could not have accomplished their delaying actions without support from the non-Quaker citizenry. Even though a change in the politics of the Commonwealth seemed to be looming by 1742, Quakers were still being elected to office. What was not yet obvious in Pennsylvania was a serious threat to the average citizen. Many of the Commonwealth's citizens did not feel any danger to life, home or property and did not have any interest in supporting Britain's imperial wars. Thus, many of the citizens were willing to endorse Quaker foot-dragging on defense issues. Their antipathy toward military service could be seen both in this willingesss and in the fact that it was much easier for Thomas' recruiters to enlist indentures rather than free citizens.

Still, this most recent war had brought military action to the colonies that comprised British America and caused some of the rising non-Quaker merchant and artisan class, most notably in Philadelphia, to have some concern

---

obviously military but not stipulated as such was the compromise first reached for Queen Anne's War. By this time the Assembly was more willing to entertain military appropriations, but the tradition of dealing with the issue by vague identification of the appropriations' purpose continued.

about the defense of the Commonwealth. This class continued to support the Quakers, but they would only be convinced of the wisdom of Quaker policies as long as they felt no immediate threats to person, property or their rapidly expanding businesses. Faced with an obvious enemy, rather than a mere imperial venture, they could and did easily turn their backs on the Quaker leadership. In the early 1740s, the only thing lacking was an actual threat to home and family and a leader wise and articulate enough to force the change. Both would emerge in 1744, when the War of Jenkins' Ear would expand to include France and become known by the colonists as King George's War.

CHAPTER 2

Pennsylvania Fields a Force:
The Associators

*I determined to try what might be done by a voluntary
association of the people.*

– Benjamin Franklin, 1747

The War of Jenkins' Ear, which began in 1739, was an outgrowth of Spain's attempt to reassert its former preeminence in several areas of the world, including the Caribbean. To undermine the British presence in the region, the Spanish and their agents launched a campaign of intimidation and harassment of British shipping. They did this by engaging in privateering activities against British merchant ships and boarding and searching their vessels. This practice annoyed the Crown because it threatened to interrupt the free flow of British trade.

At first glance, a war with Spain, centered in the Caribbean, did not seem to pose a serious threat to many inhabitants of Pennsylvania. When, however, the French joined the fight as allies of the Spanish in 1744, a more direct threat to a broad spectrum of the citizenry emerged. French belligerence caused a more immediate danger because the French had holdings both in what is now Canada and in the Caribbean. Holding positions on both the northern and southern flanks of the Atlantic colonies gave the French the opportunity to raid mid-Atlantic commerce. Hostile French intent, including their raids on British colonial commerce, brought the first direct military threat to the Commonwealth since its initial chartering. War was about to become a reality for Quaker-led Pennsylvania.

When the French joined the war against the British Empire, the enlarged conflict came to be known in the colonies as King George's War. As the war expanded, the Pennsylvania Assembly was unable to address the crisis promptly since it was not in session. Instead, on June 11, 1744, Governor George Thomas reacted and exercised his authority as Captain General of

Pennsylvania by unilaterally declaring that a state of war existed between the Commonwealth and France. Following at least in spirit the advice John Penn provided in 1739, Thomas called for:

> *all His Majesty's Subjects in this Province capable of bearing Arms, forth to provide themselves with a Good Firelock, Bayonet and Cartouch Box, and with a sufficient Quantity of Powder and Ball that they may be prepared not only to defend this his Majesty's Province and their own Persons, Families, and Estates, but to annoy the Enemy in case it Shall be thought proper to attack them.*[1]

He also began the process of preparing a list of the most qualified men in each county, who could, upon demand, organize troops. Apparently, he planned to offer commissions to the most likely leaders.[2] In addition, to meet the demands of defending the Commonwealth, Thomas asked the Assembly to provide a magazine of arms and ammunition for the troops he hoped to raise.[3] Of greater significance, he also asked for the enactment of a militia law. As could have been predicted from earlier experiences, the Assembly declined to do either.

There were those within the Quaker leadership who sought to minimize the continual struggles between the Assembly and the governor. For example, John Kinsey, perhaps the most prominent politician from the Society of Friends, approached Thomas as early as 1743, in hopes of finding some method to avert the persistent bickering between the governor and the Assembly. While some progress was made in easing the problem, the Assembly remained sluggish and often uncooperative regarding military appropriations.

The Crown's growing displeasure with the Assembly and its Quaker leadership, the increasing number of non-Quakers in the Commonwealth, and the "falling away" of some later-generation Quakers did, however, provide a climate for potential change. The Mayor and the Common Council of Philadel-

---

[1] George E. Reed, ed., *Pennsylvania Archives: Papers of the Governors, 1681-1747*, fourth series, vol. I (Harrisburg: State of Pennsylvania, 1900), pp. 838-839.

[2] The Assembly acknowledged this in a message to the governor which stated that, since he had issued a proclamation requiring all persons under his government able to bear arms to be prepared to do so "and was preparing lists of able bodied in the counties and was preparing to give commissions, a militia was raised within this province and as it seems to be warranted by our charter of privilege, it will, we hope, excuse us from preparing a Bill to this end." Gertrude MacKinney, ed., *Pennsylvania Archives: Votes of the Assembly, October 14, 1741-September 11, 1753*, eighth series, vol. IV (Harrisburg: State Printer, 1931), pp. 2942-2944.

[3] Ibid., pp. 2934-2938.

phia, which was by this time under non-Quaker leadership, also exerted significant pressure for change.   This Philadelphia leadership, weary of the
Assembly's delays, sent a petition to the king that described the obvious dangers
that a rich and affluent city like Philadelphia faced in a wartime environment.
Specifically, the Philadelphians noted that there was no legal obligation for the
citizens to defend the city or the Commonwealth. In addition, the city did not
possess any fortifications or military stores. Worse yet, according to the petition, attempts by the citizens or the Assembly to address these problems were
always blocked by elements with firm religious principles – the Quakers. Thus,
the Philadelphia leadership felt it had no choice but to appeal directly to the
Crown to redress these serious grievances.[4]

The king failed to respond to Philadelphia's leaders with any type of
direct action, but, if nothing else, the petition did indicate the growing concern
among non-Quakers about the defense issue. Conversely, the Assembly's anti-
military stance meant that, for at least the immediate future, the Commonwealth would have to utilize the stopgap method that had evolved to assist in
its defense. As in the past, the Commonwealth would supply funds to the
Crown in lieu of supplying troops, a method which for the most part seemed
acceptable to some of the royal representatives.

By the 1740s, the practice of supplying military funds through innovative budget categories was being accomplished with a reduced number of
objections from the Quaker assemblymen. The tactic was again exercised with
the onset of King George's War, when Governor Thomas requested funds to
support an attack against the French fortress of Louisbourg in present-day
Nova Scotia.   The governors of Massachusetts, New Hampshire and
Connecticut had proposed this venture and were seeking Pennsylvania's assistance.[5] In keeping with what had become their normal practice, the Assembly
in January 1745, after considerable debate, provided £4,000 for beef, pork,
flour, wheat and other grain to support the request. Though Thomas was genuinely disgusted with the Assembly's tactics, he saw an opportunity in the wording of the Assembly's actions. He conveniently determined that "other grain"
could be interpreted as grains of powder and, with this liberal interpretation,
purchased gunpowder rather than foodstuffs with some of the funds.[6]

---

[4] Mayor and Common Council of Philadelphia to the King, October 23, 1744, in *Minutes of the
Common Council of Philadelphia, 1704-1776* (Philadelphia: N.P., 1847), pp. 440-441.
[5] Sally Schwartz, *A Mixed Multitude: The Struggle for Toleration in Colonial Pennsylvania* (New York:
University Press, 1987), p. 177.
[6] Carl Van Doren, ed., *Benjamin Franklin's Autobiographical Writings* (New York: Viking Press,
1945), p. 719. Cited hereafter as Van Doren, *Franklin's Autobiographical Writings*. One author

It was during the debates on the Commonwealth's defense that a community leader from Philadelphia began to assert his influence in the Assembly. Benjamin Franklin – printer, inventor and politician – recognized the problems and dangers resulting from the lack of a militia force. While debating the issue of providing funds to answer the Crown's request and how such monies could be used, Franklin, annoyed with the Quakers and determined to secure an adequate defense for the Commonwealth, clearly stated his resolve to purchase military stores. He told his colleagues:

> *If we fail, let us purchase a fire engine with the money; the Quakers can have no objection to that: and then if you nominate me and I you, as a committee for that purpose, we will buy a great gun, which is certainly a Fire Engine.*[7]

Thus, Franklin was more than willing to use a creative interpretation of language to subvert the Quaker Assembly's leadership. Still, neither Franklin nor the governor had by the end of 1745 succeeded in devising a method to gain the desired result: a dependable method to defend the Commonwealth.

In a move that seemed even more indicative of the demands for change pressuring the Assembly, the Crown in May 1746 instructed Governor Thomas to raise troops for the conquest of Canada. The Assembly, in its tradition, delayed action on this request but ultimately voted £5,000 for military appropriations.[8] The governor further enhanced Pennsylvania's contribution by raising four companies, referred to as Independent Companies of Foot, each consisting of more than 100 men. Captains William Trent, John Shannon, Samuel Perry and John Deimer commanded the troops raised for this expedition.[9] They left Philadelphia on September 4, 1746, and began their march to Albany,

cites an error by some writers who give Franklin the credit for developing this novel interpretation of how grain could be defined. Franklin, however, attributes the creative definition to Thomas who, he says, when questioned about this definition stated, "I shall take the money for I understand very well their meaning; other grain is gunpowder." See Henry Albert Smyth, *The Writings of Benjamin Franklin: The Autobiography of Benjamin Franklin* (New York: Macmillan Co., 1905), p. 368.

[7] Van Doren, *Franklin's Autobiographical Writings*, p. 719.

[8] After five months of debate the Assembly voted another £5,000 "for the King's use." The preamble to the bill justified the action by stating the Assembly's desire "of demonstrating our Obedience to our present Sovereign King George II, by yielding a ready and Cheerful Compliance with his Commands, so far as our religious principle will admit."

[9] Frederic A. Godcharles, *Pennsylvania: Political, Governmental, Military and Civil*, military volume (New York: American Historical Society, 1933), p. 16.

New York to prepare for the invasion.[10]

The invasion of Canada, however, was postponed; the expedition was "laid aside for the present" by His Majesty.[11] Still, the Pennsylvania troops were retained on active duty for almost 18 months. They stayed in winter quarters in Albany in 1746-1747 and were not finally discharged until November 19, 1747. A combination of poor rations, bad weather and substandard equipment resulted in high rates of desertion. Desertions were noted as early as July 1746, with rewards being posted for the return of the errant soldiers.[12] In addition, the commanders of the companies jointly announced on June 9, 1747, that deserters had until August 10 to return to their units, and if they did so, they would be pardoned and receive full pay. How successful this amnesty was is not known.[13] Ironically, the intended use of these troops, the siege of Louisbourg, actually occurred, but it lasted only seven weeks. The siege and surrender of the French fort was a result of the efforts of militiamen from New England, rather than from Pennsylvania.[14]

That Pennsylvania was experimenting with militias, without a militia law and without funding by the Assembly, is evident through records in the Pennsylvania Archives that show the appointment of provincial officers and soldiers. Effective December 1, 1744, Captain Thomas Edwards, Captain William Maxwell, Lieutenant Reece Morgan and Ensign James Wilkins are listed as provincial officers and soldiers. Additionally, Thomas appointed William Moore as colonel of the Red Regiment of Militia of Foot in that part of Chester County between Brandywine Creek and the Schuylkill River. Reece Morgan was commissioned as a company commander and James Wilkins as ensign.[15] Subsequent entries in the records of these early companies show

---

[10] The actual membership of these companies can be found in Thomas Lynch Montgomery, ed., *Pennsylvania Archives: Officers and Soldiers in the Service of the Province of Pennsylvania, 1744-1765*, fifth series, vol. I (Harrisburg: Harrisburg Publishing Co., 1906), pp. 6-16. Cited hereafter as Montgomery, *Officers and Soldiers of Pennsylvania, 1744-1765*.

[11] Ibid., p. 5.

[12] *The Pennsylvania Gazette*, July 31, 1746.

[13] A paper by Joseph Seymour for the author entitled "Four Independent Companies of Foot, May 1746-November 1747," December 22, 1998. See also *The Pennsylvania Gazette*, July 2, 1747.

[14] The irony of this is that some scholars question whether the Assembly ever paid these soldiers for their services. Much correspondence from 1747 indicates these men did not receive their pay. A letter from Anthony Palmer noted that their pay from June 25 through October 31 was due and that the veterans were very discontented. See Anthony Palmer to the Assembly, in George E. Reed, ed., *Pennsylvania Archives: Papers of the Governors, 1747-1759*, fourth series, vol. II (Harrisburg: State of Pennsylvania, 1900). Cited hereafter as Reed, *Papers of the Governors, 1747-1759*. At this stage I am uncertain if the soldiers' pay was ever resolved.

[15] Montgomery, *Officers and Soldiers of Pennsylvania, 1744-1765*, p. 3.

names of soldiers and, in many cases, their occupations.[16]

At least some of these events show an increasing awareness by Pennsylvanians that military preparedness would have to be improved and seemed to indicate some degree of flexibility among those who held the Peace Testimony. There remained, however, strong opposition in the General Assembly to institutionalizing a military presence in the Commonwealth. Many of the Quaker leaders were willing to consider military requests on a case-by-case basis, but they were totally unwilling to pass a militia act which would provide a standing military structure in Pennsylvania. The emerging leaders in the Assembly – like Franklin, a non-Quaker, and Logan, a pragmatic though devout Quaker – were certain that the European wars of empire would soon pose a direct threat to Pennsylvania. As late as 1747, however, they were unable to convince the necessary number of their peers of the impending danger.[17]

Their fears were not ill-founded. In July 1747, French privateers entered the Delaware and landed parties at two plantations below New Castle. For the first time since its founding, Philadelphia was in serious danger of being attacked. Alone among the major coastal cities of British America, Philadelphia had no means of defending itself. Any logical reaction to this threat would have been difficult under the best of circumstances, for logical responses were blocked by the Quaker control of 20 of 36 seats in the Assembly.[18] The problem was further exacerbated by the absence of the governor, who had left June 1, returning to London due to ill health. Even if they had been willing to do so, without the proprietor's representative, the Assembly would be unable to enact any legislation.

Despite the inability to conduct an official session, leaders of the Assembly were called in for discussions by the Provincial Council – even though the council did not favor immediate action, if any at all, to prepare for French incursions. Anthony Palmer, president of the Provincial Council, repeatedly pressed for some type of action by the Assembly, but the latter was not to be moved by either the events or his pleas.[19]

[16] Ibid., pp. 6-16.

[17] Anthony Palmer, president of the Provincial Council, in a letter dated March 5, 1748, was clear as he described the situation to the commander in chief at Cape Breton. He told of the attempts of the government to provide for the defense of the Commonwealth but stated that "we have the misfortune to have an Assembly consisting chiefly of Quakers." Reed, *Papers of the Governors, 1747-1759*, p. 411.

[18] Major William P. Clarke, *Official History of the Militia and National Guard of Pennsylvania from the Earliest Period of Record to the Present Time* (Philadelphia: Charles J. Hendler, 1909), p. 8. Cited hereafter as Clarke, *Official History of the Pennsylvania Militia*.

[19] Sally F. Griffith, "'Order, Discipline, and a Few Cannon': Benjamin Franklin, the Association,

The Assembly met for its regular session in mid-August and devoted some of its time to the defense issue. It acknowledged the occurrence of raids against outlying plantations, but since there had been no direct attack on Philadelphia, it discounted any danger to the city and politely scolded the Council for publicizing the city's lack of defense and raising public fears about French provocations. Indeed, the Assembly criticized the Council for its calls to action, making it abundantly clear that despite the real threats to the safety of coastal Pennsylvania, it was not willing to provide for any method of defense.[20]

French provocations not only continued but in fact increased. In September, three more French privateers appeared in the bay, and rumors circulated that at least six more ships were mustering in the West Indies to raid the Commonwealth. Of particular concern, the leaders of the raiding party had supposedly mentioned Philadelphia as an easy target due to its total absence of defenses. When the impending danger was again brought to the Assembly's attention, it exhibited little concern. The Provincial Council, totally exasperated with the Assembly and its Quaker leadership, wrote to the proprietor in London requesting speedy assistance in providing for the defense of Philadelphia.[21]

The immediate answer to the problem, however, did not lay with the systems sanctioned through the Commonwealth's charter or any particular legal structure. Since the approved governmental system had failed to provide for defense, the solution would have to be found outside the government, by some extralegal method. Furthermore, with the governor absent, the legally appointed executive was not present to lead further attempts to subvert the Quakers.

With the Commonwealth faced by an apparently unsolvable stalemate,

---

and the Rhetoric and Practice of Boosterism," *Pennsylvania Magazine of History and Biography* (April 1992), p. 134. Cited hereafter as Griffith, "Order, Discipline, and a Few Cannon."

[20] The Assembly's logic in this matter is curious. They indicated that the visibility given by the Council, particularly a speech on the defenseless nature of Philadelphia, would encourage invasion. They stated, "Besides as this speech from the president and council may be sent beyond the sea, if it should fall into the hand of our enemies it may possibly induce them to make an attempt they otherwise would not have thought of." *Pennsylvania Archives: Colonial Records of Pennsylvania, Minutes of the Provincial Council of Pennsylvania from Organization to the Termination of the Proprietary Government*, vol. V (Harrisburg: Theo. Fenn & Co., 1851), pp. 101-104. Cited hereafter as *Minutes of the Provincial Council*.

[21] At the time this letter was written, the proprietorship had passed from William Penn to his son Thomas. While he came from Quaker stock, he, like his brother "Billy," was most willing to supply the necessary measures for the colony to defend itself. For that matter, William Penn had agreed to the militia concept some 40 years earlier.

Benjamin Franklin conceived a plan to develop a solution. Concern about issues which faced Pennsylvania was not new to Franklin for, according to his writings, he was at this time vitally interested in the need for fire companies and institutions of higher learning.[22] At 41, Franklin was not only a leader in the community, he was innovative and inventive in approach. These were the exact qualities needed to break the defense logjam in Pennsylvania politics.

The Quakers were a major cause of this logjam, but they were not the sole cause, only the most influential element that remained unconvinced of the need to provide for the Commonwealth's defense. Some of Philadelphia's citizenry did see the need for a militia. The mercantile classes, particularly in the Philadelphia area, were clearly concerned about the absence of fortifications. It should not be assumed, however, that all or even most citizens shared their concern. This is not to say that dangers to the Pennsylvania seaboard were manufactured or imagined, for they were not. A substantial number of citizens, both rural and urban, simply felt no particular urgency for creating defense forces because the issue of defense had no direct bearing on them.

It is also significant to note that, even though defense-conscious citizens complained about the power the Quakers wielded in the Assembly, the Quakers achieved their majority in the Assembly through the democratic process. In 1754 they were again elected as the majority faction. In short, while the Quakers no longer made up most of the population, they could still represent and articulate the misgivings of a large and diverse body of Pennsylvanians unconvinced that the Commonwealth needed a military establishment. These dissenters were either concerned about colonial involvement in imperial wars or could not perceive a valid threat requiring a military force. Thus, Franklin and his colleagues needed to both find a method to undermine Quaker power in the Assembly and, at the same time, convince more of the citizenry that Pennsylvania was in need of a method to defend itself. The privateering incursions into the lower counties and a threat to the city of Philadelphia would not be sufficient to change the general attitude in the colony.

Herein lies Franklin's contribution. As a printer, writer and publicist he had considerable ability to affect public opinion. After discussing potential tactics with other dissidents, such as Trench Francis, Pennsylvania's attorney gen-

---

[22] Franklin stated in the early 1740s that, in his opinion, there were several problems in the Commonwealth that were in need of resolution. He noted the lack of provision for defense or the "compleat education of youth" – no militia, no college. He would ultimately attempt to solve both issues, in addition to providing fire companies for Philadelphia. See Van Doren, *Franklin's Autobiographical Writings*, p. 715.

eral, and Thomas Hopkinson (who became the first president of the American Philosophical Society), it was decided that an anonymous tradesman should write a pamphlet decrying the inaction of both the Council and the Assembly. This would serve as a vehicle to attempt a mobilization of the people to provide for the defense of the Commonwealth.

The anonymous tradesman was, of course, Franklin. On November 17, 1747, there appeared a pamphlet entitled *Plain Truth: or, Serious Considerations on the Present State of the City of Philadelphia, and Province of Pennsylvania.* The publi-

---

PLAIN TRUTH:

O R,

SERIOUS CONSIDERATIONS

On the PRESENT STATE of the

CITY of *PHILADELPHIA,*

A N D

PROVINCE of *PENNSYLVANIA.*

By a TRADESMAN of *Philadelphia.*

Capta urbe; nihil fit reliqui victis. Sed, per Deos immortales, vos ego appello, qui semper domos, villas, signa, tabulas vestras, tantæ æstimationis fecistis; si ista, cujuscumque modi sint, quæ amplexamini, retinere, si voluptatibus vestris otium præbere vultis; expergiscimini aliquando, & capessite rempublicam. Non agitur nunc de sociorum injuriis; LIBERTAS & ANIMA nostra in dubio est. Dux hostium cum exercitu supra caput est. Vos cunctamini etiam nunc, & dubitatis quid faciatis?. Scilicet, res ipsa aspera est, sed vos non timetis eam. Ima vero maxume; sed inertiâ & mollitiâ animi, alius alium expectantes, cunctamini; videlicet, Diis immortalibus confisi, qui hanc rempublicam in maxumis periculis servavere. NON VOTIS, NEQUE SUPPLICIIS MULIEBRIBUS, AUXILIA DEORUM PARANTUR: vigilando, agendo; bene consulendo, prospere omnia cedunt. Ubi socordiæ ttte atque ignaviæ tradideris, nequicquam Deos implores; irati, infestique sunt. M. POR. CAT. *in* SALUST.

Printed in the YEAR MDCCXLVII.

Cover of *Plain Truth,* Franklin's pamphlet that documented the need for the Commonwealth's defense and resulted in the creation of the Associators.

cation was free, and the first printing of 2,000 copies was quickly exhausted, necessitating a second printing in December. Franklin's goal was to convince the citizenry of a bona fide emergency, requiring them to work together outside the structure of government to address it. Offering a graphic depiction of privateers entering Philadelphia and sacking and burning the city, Franklin used his well-known literary skills to paint a bleak picture of what would happen unless the citizens took immediate action.[23] To avoid such a disaster, Franklin planned to lay before his fellow citizens a proposal for the organization of an association for defense, which would supply volunteer militia companies.

Franklin's proposal to develop a voluntary association was not, for him, a new concept. Eleven years earlier, in 1736, he had proposed and successfully established Articles of Association for the Union Fire Company in Philadelphia, using the volunteer concept to resolve an issue that had previously concerned him greatly, the city's fires. Defensive associations were a logical extension of this approach.[24] According to Franklin, his pamphlet had a significant impact, stirring popular reaction that was both immediate and enthusiastic. Even James Logan, an influential and pragmatic Quaker, approved of Franklin's proposal.[25] A short time after the first edition of *Plain Truth* was published, Franklin, William Allen and Richard Peters met and drafted a proposal for a military association.

On November 21, 1747, Franklin then outlined the proposal to some 150 tradesmen and mechanics at Walton's schoolhouse. Pulling the text from his pocket, Franklin spoke of a voluntary citizens' militia that would be organized into companies based in each of Philadelphia's wards, each company led

[23] In Franklin's words, "On the first Alarm, Terror will spread over all; and no man can know with Certainty that another will stand by him ... Sacking the City will be first, and Burning it, in all probability, the last act of the enemy ... Confined to your houses you will have nothing to trust to but the Enemy's Mercy." A Tradesman of Philadelphia, *Plain Truth: or, Serious Considerations on the Present State of the City of Philadelphia, and Province of Pennsylvania* (Philadelphia: 1747), pp. 7-8.
[24] Leonard W. Larabee, ed., *The Papers of Benjamin Franklin, January 1, 1735-December 31, 1744*, vol. 2 (New Haven: Yale University Press, 1960), pp. 150-153. According to this source, Franklin may have patterned his Union Fire Company after Boston's Fire Society, founded in 1717. (The names and occupations of those who signed this voluntary association appears on pp. 153-54.) Whether any continuity exists in the membership of the early volunteer fire associations and the Philadelphia Associators has not been researched, but it would make an interesting study.
[25] Logan was also not hesitant to compliment Franklin and recognize his accomplishment. On November 24, 1749, he stated, "He it was by publishing a small piece in the year 1747 with his further private contrivances occasioned the raising of ten Companies of near one hundred men each in Philadelphia and above one hundred companies in the Province and Counties, of which I have a list. He it was who set on foot two Lotteries for Erecting of Batteries, purchasing great

by officers elected by its soldiers. Franklin did not seek a vote or attempt to sign up any volunteers at this meeting. Wisely, as a next step, he sought the support of another, more influential class of citizens. He decided to present the association plan to the principal gentlemen and merchants of the city for their support. This was done on November 23 at Robert's Coffee House, with Franklin supplying the group with advance copies of his proposal. Franklin addressed what he described as "a pretty full house," and the assemblage endorsed the proposal. The following evening, Franklin scheduled yet another meeting at the New Building, focusing his appeal on a target group of trades-men, shopkeepers and farmers. In what could only be described as an enor-mous success, some 500 men of all ranks signed their names to an agreement calling for the creation of a voluntary association.[26]

In the days that followed, the association concept was circulated in other parts of Philadelphia and printed in the December 3, 1747, *Pennsylvania Gazette*. Within a few days more than 1,000 signatures had been collected. Despite his unqualified success, Franklin did not rest on his laurels but contin-ued his campaign, using both his persuasive skills and the columns of his news-paper to promote the Associator concept. In his issue of December 3, he reprinted the full text of the Articles of Association, placed in the section nor-mally reserved for government proclamations. Through this tactic he gave the Associator concept what appeared to be official status as well as publicizing its basic tenets.

It is significant to note that the Associators actually received official recognition, even though it was not authorized by any enabling legislation. This approval came after some 600 of these volunteer soldiers met at the State House in Philadelphia and marched to the Philadelphia Court House, where they divided themselves into companies according to wards and townships. On December 7, 1747, the Associators who had enrolled in this unique organiza-tion met as a group at the Court House and were told by Council President

guns and to dispatch which he went himself to New York and borrowed there 14 – which were brought thro' New Jersey by land, and here mounted till such Time as there could be others had from England, and in which thy assistance is in some measure expected; and all this without much appearing in any part of it himself, unless in his going to New York himself in Company with others of whose going he was the occasion, for he is the principal Mover and very Soul of the Whole." Leonard W. Larabee, ed., *The Papers of Benjamin Franklin, January 1, 1745-June 30, 1750*, vol. 3 (New Haven: Yale University Press, 1961), p. 185. Cited hereafter as Larabee, *Papers of Benjamin Franklin*, vol. 3.

[26] Ibid., pp. 184-186. Note that at the November 23 meeting Franklin was prepared to sign up supporters. Following the meeting he wrote, "I had prepared a Number of printed Copies and provided Pens and Ink dispersed all over the Room." See p. 205.

Anthony Palmer that their efforts were not disapproved and that he would commission the officers they elected.[27] With this deft statement, the Associators had the approval of the Council and its president.[28] Obviously, approval by the Assembly would be too much to expect, but through the efforts of Benjamin Franklin and a few like-minded citizens, a method to defend the Commonwealth was born.

The voluntary association of citizens was a uniquely American creation. It was acknowledged by the government but not directly supported or sanctioned by it. The Articles of Association drafted by Franklin provided Pennsylvania with a basic structure for some of its first recognized military units. According to Franklin's articles, companies of 50 to 100 men were to be formed. At the first meeting each company was to elect a captain, a lieutenant and an ensign, whose names were to be submitted to the governor for commissioning. Once the companies formed, leaders elected from each county were to meet and establish one or more regiments, depending on their population base. These regiments were to elect colonels, lieutenant colonels and majors. Provisions were also made to elect representatives from each county and from the associations to form a General Military Council, designed to be the Commonwealth's coordinating and policy-making agency for military affairs.

Although members of Pennsylvania's volunteer associations were called Associators, they followed militia concepts as practiced in other colonies. Thus, as was the militia tradition, the basic soldier's equipment was the individual's responsibility. Each Associator was to supply himself with:

> a good Firelock, Cartouche-box [flintlock and cartridge box], at least 12 Charges of Powder and Ball, and as Many of us as conveniently can, a good Sword, Cutlass or Hanger, to be kept always in our respective Dwellings in Readiness and good Order.[29]

[27] Russell Weigley notes the extralegal nature of the Associators, since Palmer chose to say their efforts were not disapproved, rather than approving their efforts. Russell F. Weigley, "The Colonial Militia," in *The First Century: A History of the 28th Infantry Division*, Uzal W. Ent, ed. (Harrisburg: Stackpole Books, 1979), p. 21. Cited hereafter as Weigley, "The Colonial Militia."
[28] It should be noted, however, that Thomas Penn opposed Franklin's association. In a letter to Provincial Secretary Richard Peters, Penn objected both to the association and to Franklin as a leader of this movement. He stated, "I am sure the people of America are too often ready to act in defiance of the government they live in, without associating for that purpose." Of Franklin he said, "He is a dangerous Man and I should be very Glad he inhabited any other Country as I believe him to be a very uneasy spirit." "The Pennsylvania Manuscripts: Thomas Penn Letterbook II," June 9, 1748 (Philadelphia: Historical Society of Pennsylvania), p. 232.

Philadelphia was the birthplace of the Associator movement, and it led in the formation of these units. One regiment of twelve companies, commanded by Colonel Abraham taylor, was called the Associated Regiment of Foot of Philadelphia. That the Friends were already finding defections from the Peace Testimony is evident from the records of the Associated Regiment of Foot. Among the elected officers of the regiment was Lieutenant Richard Renshaw, clearly identified in the roster as a Quaker. Records from the period show nine regimental commands scattered throughout the Commonwealth and the command structure spread through several counties.[30]

Even though the origins of the Associator movement are traced to Franklin and Philadelphia, the appeal of the Associator concept went far beyond the boundaries of the city. It spread from Philadelphia throughout the Commonwealth and even extended to some non-English citizens. The Commonwealth's Germans had originally been regarded as allies of the Quakers, for some strongly supported the Peace Testimony, based on their own religious convictions. Other Germans, though not pietists, had been initially swayed by the Quakers, who sought to convince them that military involvement by the Commonwealth would bring to Pennsylvania the horrors of war which they had experienced in Europe. *Plain Truth* was translated into German, and one of the first companies formed was composed of Germans, indicating that Quaker influence over this ethnic group was far from complete.[31]

Lancaster County would ultimately boast 33 companies, divided into the Associated Regiment of the East End of the County, the Associated Regiment of the West End of the County, and the Associated Regiment of Lancaster County proper (composing the remainder). Bucks County was able to organize 19 known Associator companies, the majority of which came from the northern townships, particularly Northhampton. Clearly, at the outset the source of Associator strength was the Philadelphia area. The city of Philadelphia itself had a total of 12 companies which were reinforced by Philadelphia County's additional eight companies. As a primary force in the movement to found an association, Franklin was offered the colonelcy of one of the regiments. Wisely and graciously he declined, leaving the command for someone more fit for the task. Chester County had 26 companies which, in 1748-1749, were divided into two battalions. By whatever criteria one chooses, Franklin's

---

[29] Larabee, *Papers of Benjamin Franklin*, vol. 3, pp. 205-207. See also *The Pennsylvania Gazette*, December 3, 1747.
[30] Montgomery, *Officers and Soldiers of Pennsylvania, 1744-1765*, pp. 17-18.
[31] Clarke, *Official History of the Pennsylvania Militia*, p. 65.

Associator concept was a great success.

In Philadelphia, in the days following the approval of the Associator companies, there was a flurry of activity as the merchants and artisans of the area sought to answer the sudden demand for weapons and military accouterments. Associators were having such difficulty finding weapons that a plea was sent out to the other colonies for help. It stated, "If there are any Quantities of Small Arms to spare in the neighboring Governments, they would meet here with a ready Market."[32] Franklin himself sought to offer some wares to the prospective soldiers, advertising "a parcel of good Muskets, all well fitted with Bayonets, Belts and Cartouch Boxes, and Buff slings to cast over the shoulder, very useful to such as have Occasion to ride with their Arms."[33] Arms were procured, and the Associators in Philadelphia followed the articles to which they had subscribed, meeting and drilling weekly. The foot soldiers were attempting to become a dependable force, and from the perspective of infantry, Philadelphia was no longer defenseless.

It should not be forgotten, however, that the initial danger that prompted the organization of the Associators was a threat by sea, rather than by land. Some means had to be provided to defend Philadelphia from marauding French privateers. Exploiting the flexibility that was a hallmark of the Associator concept, the merchants of Philadelphia committed £1,500 to buy cannon for fortifications. Through the efforts of Franklin, William Allen and Thomas Hopkinson, a lottery was organized to raise an additional £3,000 to buy cannon and construct fortified batteries to defend the Delaware.[34] The lottery was limited to 10,000 tickets, which were sold out in short order.[35]

With the newly available funds, the Associators were able to purchase 39 cannon from Boston and order additional artillery pieces from England. Since such an order would take time, and the danger on the Delaware was imminent, Franklin and other community leaders called on Governor George Clinton of New York to lend the Commonwealth a few cannon until all their equipment arrived. The governor of New York, after some initial hesitancy, loaned Pennsylvania 18 cannon complete with their carriages. With this loan and the purchases in Boston, the Commonwealth was beginning to develop a

---

[32] *The Philadelphia Gazette*, January 9, 1748.

[33] *The Philadelphia Gazette*, March 8, 1748.

[34] Before purchasing cannon, the lottery managers took an inventory of cannon available in Philadelphia. They found a total of 70 of various types but apparently determined that was insufficient. See Larabee, *Papers of Benjamin Franklin*, vol. 3, p. 221.

[35] Griffith, "Order, Discipline, and a Few Cannon," p. 137.

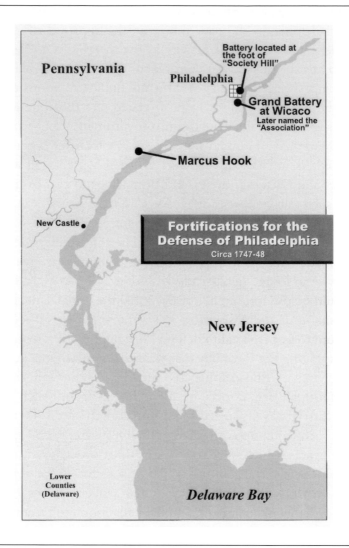

Battery located at
the foot of
"Society Hill"

Pennsylvania

Philadelphia

Grand Battery
at Wicaco
Later named the
"Association"

Marcus Hook

New Castle

**Fortifications for the
Defense of Philadelphia**
Circa 1747-48

New Jersey

Lower
Counties
(Delaware)

Delaware Bay

defensive capability.[36]

By April 1748 two batteries had been completed, the first at the foot of Philadelphia's Society Hill and a second, called the Grand Battery, below the city at Wicaco. The latter initially held 14 of the cannon lent to Pennsylvania by

[36] According to Franklin, "He [Governor Clinton] first refus'd us peremptorily but at dinner with his council where there was great drinking of Madeira wine, as the custom of that place then was, he softened by degrees, and said he would lend us six. After a few more bumpers he advanc'd to ten; and at length he very good naturedly conceded eighteen." Weigley, "The Colonial Militia," p. 21. *Minutes of the Provincial Council,* May 26, 1748, p. 249 indicates the New York guns were mounted in the Grand Battery.

Governor Clinton. Franklin recorded the status of both fortifications on April 28, 1748. He noted that the Grand Battery at Wicaco was near completion and it would likely be ready at the beginning of "next week" when the heavy cannon borrowed from New York were mounted. The previous week, the fortifications constructed below Society Hill, on William Atwood Wharf (named for the mayor of Philadelphia), had been completed. Franklin described them, stating, "The Breastwork is 8 or 10 Foot thick, compos'd of Timber and Plank, filled with Earth rammed down."[37] Due to the growing defense expenditures, a second lottery had to be organized in June 1748. Even this additional requirement for funds did not cool the enthusiasm of the city. The Grand Battery continued to grow throughout 1748. In August, a new "large cannon" purchased in England arrived, and the Associators in Philadelphia met under arms and marched to the Grand Battery where they were greeted by a 21-gun salute. The Grand Battery was subsequently named the Association Battery.[38]

Even though King George's War ended in April 1748, preparation of fortifications for Philadelphia continued. September 1750 found 14 additional cannon arriving from England, all 18-pounders. By 1750 the Grand Battery consisted of upwards of 50 cannon: 18-, 24-, and 32-pounders. Of particular interest, one of the 32-pounders had been presented by the Schuylkill Associator Company. This cannon, massive by the standards of the day, was called the Schuylkill Gun. It was distinctively inscribed with "Kawanio che keeteru" (Unami Lenape for "This is my right, I will defend it") and the initials W. P. in honor of the original proprietor.[39] Through these efforts Philadelphia now had the capability to defend itself.

While the creation of the associations was an admirable endeavor and marked a watershed in the debate on defense, no serious hostile action ever occurred during King George's War to test the Associators. A Spanish vessel did approach New Castle during the summer of 1748 and was driven off by the guns mounted there. By the time the Associators were fully organized, however, King George's War was virtually over. The peace treaty of Aix-la-Chapelle

[37] Larabee, *Papers of Benjamin Franklin*, vol. 3, p. 312.

[38] *The Pennsylvania Gazette*, September 1, 1748.

[39] Ibid. See also "The Restoration of the Schuylkill Gun to the State in Schuylkill," *Pennsylvania Magazine of History and Biography* (April 1884), pp. 198-215. As a result of the research for this book, the Schuylkill Gun has been rediscovered by the historical community. It was found at Fort Mifflin in 1884 and was given to the private organization known as the State in Schuylkill, where it remains today. This significant piece from Pennsylvania's early military history had been spiked, had both of the trunions and cascabel broken off and had been hit in the muzzle area. Likely it was disabled by the Continentals when they evacuated the fort or by the British when they left.

was signed on April 19, 1748. Communication, slow as it was in those days, pre-vented the news from reaching Philadelphia until August 24.

During the next few years, with no obvious danger to the Commonwealth, Associator organizations received less emphasis than in their peak period in 1747. But even when the war ended in 1748 they were never officially disbanded as military organizations. Because the Associators were never a legally constituted part of the Commonwealth's defense, there was no formal need to demobilize them. Besides, in the Philadelphia region there were still perceived threats to the harbor facilities. In some instances, the momen-tum of developing methods to better defend Pennsylvania continued. For example, as noted previously, the Grand Battery at Wicaco was retained, manned and even improved.[40] On May 26, 1748, Colonel Abraham Taylor was appointed colonel of the Associated Regiment of Philadelphia, and the Provincial Council charged him with the responsibility of "tak[ing] the batter-ies and guns into Your Charge & Care, and to give such Orders & Directions for mounting, fitting & preparing them for service and to appoint such Officers and Men of your Regiment as a Guard."[41]

Even as late as 1750, two years after King George's War had ended, a ship arrived from England bringing fourteen 18-pounders from England, a gift from the Quaker proprietors. This shipment is interesting for it not only shows the continuance of an Associator battery, it also demonstrates that the propri-etors recognized the importance of defense. By this gesture, they gave more than tacit approval to attempts at defending Pennsylvania. For certain, the pro-prietors were much more flexible than their Quaker brethren in the Pennsyl-vania Assembly.

It would be difficult to overestimate the significance of Franklin's accomplishment in devising defensive associations. Granted, a militia law still did not exist for the Commonwealth, and thus, unlike other colonies, there still was no legally constituted standing military force for Pennsylvania. Furthermore, despite their dwindling numbers, the Quakers still held control of the Assembly, which meant that the passage of any military appropriations on their watch could be a significant challenge and the passage of a militia act an impossibility. Still, despite these acknowledged problems, a group of political-ly astute citizens had, in cooperation with the Provincial Council, bypassed the Assembly and provided a method of defending the Commonwealth. Since these associations were voluntary, the Assembly could not repeal their legal

[40] *The Pennsylvania Gazette*, September 1, 1748.
[41] *Minutes of the Provincial Council*, May 26, 1748, p. 251.

standing; nor could they cut off funding, for the organizations funded themselves. Furthermore, the creation of military associations provided Franklin with political leverage, since he now had additional allies to contest the control of the Quaker elite who had for so long dominated the legislative process in the Commonwealth. Through the creation of the Associators, the Quaker imposition of their beliefs on the defense of the Commonwealth had been decisively eroded.

Of equal significance, once the Peace of Aix-la-Chapelle was in effect, the Associator organizations were retained, though the intensity of the movement slackened. The maintenance of these groups would be very important beginning in 1754, when war would again come to colonial America and Pennsylvania would still be without a militia law. Beginning in 1754, the Associators would again be required to defend the Commonwealth.

CHAPTER 3

French Designs on the Ohio River Valley: A Catalyst for Change

*The Government at home will take some method to oblige
'em to act for the future as becomes the duty of his
majesty's Subjects.*

– General Edward Braddock, 1755

In the wake of the Treaty of Aix-la-Chapelle, which proved to be only a brief respite from war, it became obvious that many attitudes and policies in the Commonwealth remained constant, at least on the defense issue. For example, while Pennsylvania had been in existence for more than 75 years, it still did not have a militia law establishig a permanent defense force. Even though wars were beginning to impact the lives of Pennsylvania's citizens, the Quakers continued to control the Assembly and remained opposed to enacting legislation requiring the creation of a military force in Pennsylvania. The Commonwealth had to continue its dependence on those Associator companies which remained in reduced numbers after the war's end.

Despite the impasse with the Quakers on a militia law, the process of fortifying the Philadelphia area to protect it from the dangers of seaborne attack progressed through the late 1740s. The Quakers did not oppose this initiative because it was accomplished through Associator auspices and thus required no permanent or statutory commitment for defense from the government. Still, it was troubling to some of the Commonwealth's leadership that Pennsylvania was unable to proceed beyond the Associator concept. The proprietor, in particular, was very uncomfortable having to rely on the Associators. In a letter to the Provincial Council, Thomas Penn stated:

> *If the People had desired to unite for their defense, they should have applyed
> to you, their legal Governors for License to do, when you would have formed
> them into Bodys proper for Service & issue such Orders as would be from*

time to time necessary.[1]

Penn went on to state that, since the necessary laws had not been passed, he was concerned that the men and the Grand Battery would be quickly neglected and Pennsylvania would again find itself without any dependable method of defense.

Within the Commonwealth, however, it was generally accepted that even though the Associators were a stopgap measure, the concept worked. Associators were recognized, and their existence was not opposed by those who promoted the Peace Testimony.[2] This stymied any movement to devise a true legal method to provide for a permanent defense for the Commonwealth.

The absence of a statutory means of defending Pennsylvania continued to trouble Benjamin Franklin. Franklin was also concerned about a related issue, the demographic changes occurring in Pennsylvania in the wake of King George's War. In the late 1740s, thousands of German-speaking immigrants, primarily from the Rhineland Palatinate, settled in what was then the western frontier of Pennsylvania, a region roughly running from north of Easton to Carlisle. This exodus was primarily due to the destruction of large sections of the Palatinate by marauding armies during King George's War. With no real end in sight for continental power rivalry, large numbers of Rhinelanders decided to leave Europe and emigrate to British America. By the early 1750s, Pennsylvania's population was about 33 percent English, 30 percent German and 30 percent Scots-Irish. The rest were Swedes, Dutch, Finns, Africans and others, resulting in close to 40 percent of the population having non-British roots.[3]

This sudden influx of Germans concerned Franklin, who questioned:

---

[1] Thomas Penn, in a letter to the Council on March 30, 1749, in George E. Reed, ed., *Pennsylvania Archives: Papers of the Governors, 1747-1759*, fourth series, vol. II (Harrisburg: State of Pennsylvania, 1900), pp. 676-679. Cited hereafter as Reed, *Papers of the Governors, 1747-1759*.

[2] As mentioned previously, Thomas Penn opposed the Associators – "Franklin's Army" – because they provided only a temporary solution to the problem of how to defend the Commonwealth. His opposition was due to a perceived erosion of his proprietary authority and his desire for an obligatory and thus dependable militia. It is ironic that Penn, the current proprietor and the founder's son, whose name epitomizes the Quaker movement in America, was in the position of pressing for military preparedness in the face of opposition from the Quaker leadership in the Assembly.

[3] The demographics of Pennsylvania would not change radically during the century. A modern study of the 1790 census found the populace to be 35.3 percent English, 33.3 percent German, and 23.1 percent Scots-Irish. See Robert L. Brunhouse, *The Counter-Revolution in Pennsylvania, 1776-1790* (Harrisburg: Pennsylvania Historical and Museum Commission, 1971), p. 2.

Why should the Palatine Boors [German farmers] be [allowed] to swarm into our Settlements and by herding together establish their Language and Manners to the Exclusion of ours? Why should Pennsylvania founded by the English become a Colony of Aliens who will shortly be so numerous as to Germanize us instead of our anglicizing them?[4]

Franklin's objections, however, went beyond the issues of language and custom and related directly to the defense issue. He was troubled because members of the various German pietistic sects had a tendency to support the Quaker Peace Testimony. As he noted to Peter Collinson, a scientific protégé in London:

Indeed in the last war our Germans showed a general disposition that seems to bode us no good; for when the English who were not Quakers, alarmed by the dangers arising from the defenceless state of our country entered unanimously into an Association within this Government and the lower Countries [counties], raised armed and disciplined [near] 10,000 men, the Germans except a very few in proportion to their numbers refused to engage in it giving out one among another, and even in print, that if they were quiet the French, should they take the Country, would not molest them.[5]

In reality, Franklin's fears about the new immigrants proved to be unfounded, because many of the new wave of Germans were members of mainline denominations rather than sects which would support Quaker beliefs on the defense issue. While they were not enamored of war, neither did they follow the peace testimony. Within the next few years, Franklin would find these new German immigrants to be allies, rather than enemies, when it became necessary to contest the Quaker control of the Assembly.

The change in demographics which concerned Franklin was not the most significant issue facing British America in the post-war period. For the Commonwealth, far more important were the emergence of claims and counterclaims to the western part of Pennsylvania and their potential impact on the desired domestic tranquility. The proprietors had initially laid claim to the trans-Appalachia area, to include the Ohio Territory, in their grand design for the Commonwealth. In the latter part of the 1740s, however, Pennsylvania was

---

[4] Leonard W. Larabee, ed., *The Papers of Benjamin Franklin, July 1, 1750-June 30, 1753*, vol. 4 (New Haven: Yale University Press, 1961), p. 234.
[5] Ibid., p. 485.

faced with counterclaims from two major sources: the Ohio Company of Virginia and the French. The French seemed to pose the greatest threat, because their claims were bolstered by their presence in the area stretching from the Great Lakes to the Ohio River Valley and as far west as the Mississippi River Valley. Moreover, French interest in moving south from Canada had been evident for a number of years. These counterclaims to the Ohio Valley, from both sources, began to reach dangerous proportions in the early 1750s and would finally result in a culminating crisis with Pennsylvania's Quakers.

The French actually began to contest British presence and influence in the Ohio Valley within a year of the signing of the Treaty of Aix-la-Chapelle. The challenges began in 1749 with a French expedition out of Montreal, led by Captain Pierre-Joseph Cèleron de Blainville. The captain's force of 230 men and 23 canoes covered some 3,000 miles, traveling south to underscore the French plan to hold the territory all the way to New Orleans. While Cèleron de Blainville admitted that the regions he traveled were "badly disposed towards the French and entirely devoted to the English,"[6] his trip was successful in that it asserted the French determination to establish a strong presence in the Ohio River Valley.

Unlike the English, the French were not as much interested in building a network of large permanent settlements and clearing large tracts of land for agriculture as they were in creating a network of armed posts to maintain control of the river system and its lucrative fur trade, driving English traders out of the region and dominating the native population in the process. This quest brought the French into western Pennsylvania and into yet another conflict with Britain and its colonies.

The French push to regain control of the Ohio Territory, an area they had previously claimed, began in earnest in 1753. They planned to build a series of forts from Lake Erie to the Ohio River in order to secure the Ohio Valley for their Canadian provinces.[7] It was ultimately their desire to develop a system

[6] J. Martin West, ed., *War for Empire in Western Pennsylvania* (Fort Ligonier, Pa.: Fort Ligonier Association, 1993), p. 10. Cited hereafter as West, *War for Empire*. During his expedition, Captain Cèleron de Blainville reported that he expelled English traders from the Ohio, but after giving a speech to the Indians at Logstown, encouraging them not to trade with the English, the Indians replied "that while there was any Indians in those Parts they would trade with their Brother the English." John B. Linn and William H. Egle, eds., *Pennsylvania Archives: Papers Relating to the French Occupation in Western Pennsylvania, 1631-1764,* second series, vol. VI (Harrisburg: State Printer, 1891), pp. 78-79. Cited hereafter as Linn and Egle, *Papers Relating to the French Occupation.*

[7] A French report in the Pennsylvania Archives, dated December 1750, speaks to the necessity of securing Canada and Louisiana, countering the aggression of the English and in essence

of strongpoints in a crescent configuration from the Great Lakes to the
Mississippi, blocking any British penetration into this rich heartland of the
American continent. In support of their strategy, the Marquis de Duquesne,
Governor General of New France, dispatched an expedition of considerable
strength in 1753.[8] The expedition departed with two advance detachments, the
first leaving Montreal on February 1 and the second on April 15. The main
body did not leave until April 26. Initially, French forces were successful, for
they were able to build two forts, Fort de la Presqu'isle (present-day Erie) and
Fort de la Rivière au Boeuf (now Waterford). The French planned to build
three additional forts, Fort Anjou at Venango (present-day Franklin), Duquesne
at Chininque (Logstown) and Sonihoto (Scioto). While they met their basic
goal, shortages of provisions and sickness in the ranks caused their garrison
strength to be considerably less than planned.[9] Still, by fall of the same year,
they could claim success in reasserting their claims to the Ohio Valley, including western Pennsylvania.

Immediately prior to this French expansion, the English had also
attempted to strengthen their presence in the area. For example, in 1749
Thomas McKee, one of the early traders and explorers affiliated with the
British, constructed a trading post at the Lenape Indian town of Venango (present-day Franklin).[10] The French, however, regarded this as an intrusion, for they
had other plans for the site. They subsequently evicted McKee and built a
stockade around the old trading post. This fort, in addition to those previously mentioned, provided the beginnings of France's plan to block British expansion into the Ohio region.

Building this system was an arduous task. As winter arrived, the French
expedition, no longer able to transport the necessary men and supplies to con-

anchoring the French empire from Canada, Detroit, Niagara, Illinois and Louisiana. The river
systems in this area were key, as was control of the Great Lakes. English presence in western
Pennsylvania threatened this design because of their intrusions into the Ohio River Valley.
Ibid., pp. 97-113.

[8] Instructions were given to M. Duquesne in April 1752 to consider the plan developed by the
Marquis de la Jonquière to drive the English from the "River Ohio," which the French often
called the "Beautiful River." The end desired was "to drive the English from our territory and
to prevent them from coming there to trade." Ibid., pp. 133-137.

[9] To build and garrison these forts, the French had planned for a force of 1,800. By October
1753 their force had been reduced to 900 men, half the desired strength. William A. Hunter,
Forts on the Pennsylvania Frontier, 1753-1758 (Harrisburg: Pennsylvania Historical and Museum
Commission, 1960), pp. 21-23. Cited hereafter as Hunter, *Forts on the Pennsylvania Frontier.*

[10] In addition to McKee, other notable traders sympathetic to the English and active in the
region were Jacques Le Tort, Pierre Basillion and George Croghan.

tinue the construction, withdrew – but not before leaving garrisons behind and laying plans to return in the spring for another campaign to strengthen their position. French presence on the western frontier brought about renewed debate in Pennsylvania about how or whether to defend the Commonwealth. The danger posed by French expansion was presented to the Assembly, but they replied that the French forts in question were not within the legal boundaries of the Commonwealth. Thus, a response to French aggression was not needed.[11] Thomas Penn, son of the original proprietor, strongly disagreed and insisted that the Assembly take the necessary steps to defend the proprietor's claims to the land beyond the Appalachian Mountains. In fact, as early as 1749, Penn sought to construct a fort in western Pennsylvania to bolster the proprietor's claims.[12] The proprietor and the Proprietary Party, together with active community leaders like Franklin, pressed for action but were still faced by that unique political factor in Pennsylvania, Quaker dominance in the Assembly.

The proprietor, concerned about the threat to his interests, had first proposed to supply funds to help build a fort on the Ohio.[13] Franklin, in support of the proprietary interests, had also proposed in 1750 to protect the lucrative trading network of western Pennsylvania and eastern Ohio through the construction of a fort. The Assembly refused to cooperate with Franklin's plans, much as they had refused to cooperate with Penn the previous year. Again, the Quakers were willing to tolerate the Associators and provide some funding for defense-related expenditures, but the construction of a fort exceeded Quaker tolerance. Building it with Assembly approval would establish a permanent military presence in Pennsylvania, which the Quakers strongly and consistently opposed.

Still, despite the Assembly's traditional attitude on matters of defense, Pennsylvania was not totally without a method to defend its citizenry. Even though the Associator movement had declined since its peak in 1748, at least some groups of Associators were still active. This was particularly true in Philadelphia, where threats to the harbor had been a concern since the early part of the 18th century. Reports in *The Pennsylvania Gazette* show artillery units practicing in 1754 and a sergeant and corporal in each of several companies ordered to recruit for the artillery during the same year.[14] The continuance of

[11] Hunter, *Forts on the Pennsylvania Frontier*, p. 184.
[12] The proprietor offered £400 toward the expense of building a fort or blockhouse and £100 annually for the maintenance of a garrison. Part of this letter is included in *Pennsylvania Archives: Minutes of the Provincial Council*, vol. V (Philadelphia: Joseph Severns and Co., 1840), p. 515.
[13] Ibid.
[14] *The Pennsylvania Gazette*, June 27, 1754, and October 15, 1754.

Associators in the harbor area was logical due to the permanent fortifications established for the Grand Battery. The existence and manning of Associator fortifications was mentioned in a 1755 report by William Smith, who stated:

> *In Pennsylvania we have but one small Fortification and that raised and supported at the Expense of private People. The Proprietors, indeed, generously made us a Present of twelve large Cannon, part of the twenty-six we have mounted, and they have also given the Gunner of the Fort a Salary of £twenty per Annum toward his Support.*[15]

Associators would become increasingly active throughout the period 1754-1756, with units expanding between 1755 and 1756.

The resilience of Quaker power and influence, despite their shrinking percentage of the population, remains an intriguing factor in Pennsylvania politics. By 1750, only one of every six Pennsylvanians was a Quaker. As late as 1754, however, Quakers still filled 27 of the 36 seats in the Pennsylvania Assembly.[16] Their political success was possible because, even in the 1750s, they still had non-Quaker partisans willing to assist them in maintaining their power. Some Pennsylvania Anglicans were found to be among their supporters. The majority of the Anglicans in Pennsylvania had favored a stronger defense during the past war, and many had joined the Associator movement. But when the war was over, a significant number found it advantageous to back the Quakers against the western settlers who, due to their perceived "imperialist designs" on western territory, were thought to be a group capable of pushing the colonies into an unnecessary conflict. Besides, as Isaac Norris, the leader of the Quaker faction, noted, the Anglicans "dread the Presbyterians [mostly Scots-Irish] and Germans ... the Church of England knows they must keep in with the Quakers, to keep the others out."[17]

For a number of years, the Quaker position on defense issues had been opposed by an organized faction known as the Proprietary Party, a coalition of several religious and national groups. Among their supporters were the majority of Pennsylvania's Presbyterians, who by this time could claim more than 20 percent of the population, and the majority of the Anglican urban-dwelling merchant class, who sought vigorous prosecution of the wars against Britain's

---

[15] William Smith, *A Brief State of the Province of Pennsylvania* (London: NP, 1755), pp. 11-12.
[16] Marc Egnal, *A Mighty Empire: The Origins of the American Revolution* (Ithaca, N.Y.: Cornell University Press, 1988), p. 70.
[17] Ibid., p. 71.

imperial enemies.

Franklin, though he tended to be in support of the Proprietary faction, did not officially affiliate with any faction because, as he stated, "An Appearance of Impartiality in general, gives a Man sometimes much more Weight when he would serve in particular Instances."[18] Franklin was a known advocate of military preparedness, but in spite of his stance, he remained on good terms with Quaker legislators, who were pleased to befriend the best-known publisher and propagandist of the colony. They also knew Franklin as the author of the Associator concept, an idea with which they seemed comfortable, due to its voluntary nature and the fact it did not require a permanent military presence. Franklin cooperated with the Quakers when non-defense interests were at stake, and they in turn felt comfortable with Franklin representing the Commonwealth at significant conferences at Carlisle (1753) and Albany (1754).[19]

Grand or Association Battery at Wicaco, on the site of the old Navy Yard in Philadelphia, circa 1754. This drawing shows a permanent structure which served the defensive needs of the Commonwealth in the mid-18th century.

[18] A letter from Benjamin Franklin to Peter Collison, December 29, 1754, in Larabee, Leonard W., *The Papers of Benjamin Franklin, July 1, 1753–March 31, 1755*, vol. 5 (New Haven: Yale University Press, 1961), p. 453.

[19] The Carlisle conference was called in an attempt to retain the friendship of the western Indians. The Assembly supported Franklin's attendance and provided gifts which it was hoped would help persuade the Indians to remain loyal to Britain. Russell F. Weigley, "The Colonial Militia," in *The First Century: A History of the 28th Infantry Division*, Uzal W. Ent, ed. (Harrisburg: Stackpole Books, 1979), p. 22.

Given the crisis that was emerging, the proprietor Thomas Penn and Governor James Hamilton proposed defenses for western Pennsylvania but were predictably met with traditional Quaker devices. Always politically astute, the Assembly added justification for its reluctance to provide military funds by citing the Crown's recent instructions "not to be the aggressor" in the Ohio country.[20] Rather than provide a militia law or forts for the western region, the Assembly, as usual, supplied funds for several activities they could claim were defense-related. Monies were provided to present gifts to the Indians at a 1753 conference. This conference was held at Carlisle at the urging of the Commonwealth's key Indian agent, George Croghan, to encourage the pro-British sentiments of the western Indian tribes. When the French push to take the Ohio region became undeniable, the Assembly voted £20,000 for the "King's use."[21] The concern expressed by western settlers about obvious French incursions and the safety of their families and properties could not shake the belief of the Quaker-dominated Assembly that military force should not be contemplated.

What the Quaker leadership in the Assembly failed to recognize was that by 1753 the security environment in Pennsylvania was rapidly changing. A bona fide threat to the citizens of the Commonwealth was becoming evident. In previous wars, threats had come from the sea, had been against mercantile interests, and in one instance had been contrived rather than actual. The new French threat came from a hostile land force that threatened a much broader spectrum of British citizens. Furthermore, French presence promised to block further westward expansion of British America. Aggressive French designs directly affected the future settlement intentions of two significant British colonies, Pennsylvania and Virginia. While the Quaker-controlled Assembly in Philadelphia could stall action by Pennsylvania, the colonial government in Virginia was unhampered by Quaker sensitivities and power plays. When it became evident to the leadership in Williamsburg that the French were seizing land claimed by Virginia, that colony's leadership acted.

In December 1753, Virginia's Lieutenant Governor Robert Dinwiddie sent 21-year-old George Washington, then a major in the Virginia militia, to deliver a message to the small French garrisons at Fort Machault and Fort de la Rivière au Boeuf.[22] Reaching Fort le Boeuf, Washington delivered Dinwiddie's

---

[20] Sally Schwartz, *A Mixed Multitude: The Struggle for Toleration in Colonial Pennsylvania* (New York: University Press, 1987), p. 206. Cited hereafter as Schwartz, *A Mixed Multitude*.
[21] Ibid., p. 209.
[22] Washington's role in these events, in his own words, is recounted in *The Journal of Major George*

message, which stated, "By whose authority [have the French] invaded the King of Great Britain's territories? It becomes my duty to require your peaceable departure."[23] The French politely refused Washington's demand and immediately began reinforcing their settlements in the region. In the first few months of 1754, despite the incivility of the weather, the French succeeded in bringing additional supplies over the frozen Great Lakes so they could proceed with their plans to construct a band of forts.

The Virginians began increasing their military preparedness during the same period. The refusal of Washington's offer caused Dinwiddie to send a militia company to build a Virginia fort at the forks of the Ohio. As the Virginia contingent of some 40 men was hurriedly throwing up a small stock-

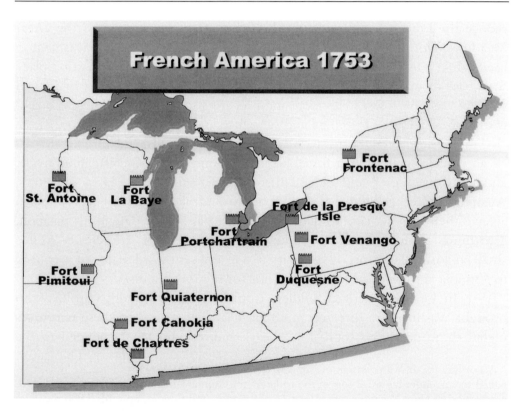

Map of French America showing the major fortifications in the area between the Mississippi, the Great Lakes and the Ohio.

Washington; An Account of His First Official Mission, October 1753-January 1754 (New York: Dominion Books, 1963).
[23] West, *War for Empire*, p. 16.

ade, the French force arrived on April 16, 1754. Intending to stake their claim to the forks of the Ohio, the French committed a total of 360 canoes and bateaux (flat-bottomed boats) and 500 to 1,000 men for the task. Badly out-numbered and outgunned, the Virginians capitulated on the 17th, but they were allowed to leave the stockade in good order and with their arms.[24] With the departure of the Virginians, the French began in earnest to construct a major fort on the site that they would name Fort Duquesne.

The Virginians were not so easily dissuaded. Desiring to recapture control of the forks, they dispatched now-Lieutenant Colonel Washington with a militia force of 132 soldiers. The French, recognizing the increasing threat posed by the Virginians, were in the process of building their strength at this valuable site. When Washington and his men reached the Monongahela area, they decided to wait for reinforcements and artillery before attempting to reduce the French fortifications at the forks. On what he termed the Great Meadows, not far from present-day Uniontown, Pennsylvania, Washington established a temporary camp, determining that this clearing was a good place for a base of operations. Friendly Indians informed him that a party of French soldiers was only a few miles away and preparing to attack. Washington quickly organized a force of 40 men and set out to attack the French.

In the ensuing skirmish, Washington, supported by Indian allies, defeated an equally small French force, killed its commander, Monsieur Jumonville, and ten of his soldiers and took 22 prisoners. Returning to the Great Meadows, Washington, recognizing that the French would likely send a larger force to avenge their loss, set about building a circular palisade to defend his position. Two thirds of this palisade was to be covered by trenches. He referred to this small enclosure as a "fort of necessity."[25] He also sent word of his victory back to Virginia and appealed to the governor for reinforcements.

In June they arrived, soldiers from Virginia and South Carolina who brought Washington's force up to about 400. The arrival of these reinforcements came none too soon, for as expected, the French responded to the

---

[24] According to Mr. Ward, ensign of Captain Trent's company of Virginia militia, he "was compelled to surrender his small fort in the forks of the Monongahela to the French on the 17th past, who fell from Venango with a fleet of 360 Batoes and Canoes, upwards 1,000 men and 18 pieces of Artillery ... Mr. Ward having but 44 men and no Cannon, to make a proper defense was obliged to surrender on Summons, capitulating to march out with their Arms etc." Mr. Partridge's enclosure, May 8, 1754, as cited in Major William P. Clarke, *Official History of the Militia and National Guard of Pennsylvania from the Earliest Period of Record to the Present Time* (Philadelphia: Charles J. Hendler, 1909), pp. 104-105.

[25] West, *War for Empire*, p. 20. See also William B. Hindman, "The Great Meadows and the Climaxing Battle at Fort Necessity," *West Virginia Historical Review*, vol. 16 (1954-55), pp. 65-89.

English presence.   About 600 French troops, supported by a contingent of some 100 Indians, left Fort Duquesne on June 28 and advanced on Fort Necessity. The French opened fire on the fort on July 3, with Washington's men still attempting to finish their preparations. Throughout the day, the French directed fire against the temporary fort, better described as a stockade. After some nine hours of battle, the Virginians were in desperate straits, due to short-ages of food and ammunition. The French commander, Coulon de Villiers, noting the plight of the Virginians, called for a conference, and surrender terms were arranged. Washington was allowed to withdraw and even take his military stores for what he regarded as an honorable surrender.[26] The surrender was signed on July 4, 1754. By the terms of this agreement, the Virginians prom-ised to stay east of the mountains for a year. Thus, virtually a year would elapse while British America organized to pose another challenge to the French pres-ence in the Ohio River Valley and western Pennsylvania.

As was evident from the fate of Washington's expedition, the Virginians alone did not possess the strength to evict the French without assistance from Pennsylvania. Ironically, this first significant land battle against an enemy of England on Pennsylvania soil was fought and lost by Virginians, with the help of a few South Carolinians.[27] Pennsylvania, still hobbled militarily by the Quakers, was unable to field a military force.

London had long depended on militia forces from the various colonies to guarantee their security, but with the severity of the French threat, the British government decided to send regular soldiers. In 1755 Major General Edward Braddock was sent to Virginia with the 44th and 48th Regiments of Foot. Braddock's task was to recruit these two regiments to strength, using colonials, and serve as commander of all British forces in North America. With assis-tance from colonial militias, his overall goal was to expel the French from ter-ritories claimed by the British.[28]

---

[26] According to one author, Washington thought the terms were honorable, based on an imper-fect translation of the French document provided by a certain Jacob van Braun. See Frederic A. Godcharles, *Pennsylvania: Political, Governmental, Military and Civil,* military volume (New York: American Historical Society, 1933), p. 48. Cited hereafter as Godcharles, *Pennsylvania: Political, Governmental, Military and Civil,* military volume. In truth, Washington had little choice, for the day's fighting had left him with 31 dead and 70 wounded. A steady rain had made the inside of the stockade a muddy morass and soaked the powder supply. Thus, as he and a Captain Mckay were given a second parley, they had few if any options.

[27] Ibid., p. 51. William Thackery states, "It was strange that in a savage forest of Pennsylvania, a young Virginia officer should fire a shot and waken up a war which was to last for sixty years."

[28] Instructions were given to General Braddock on November 25, 1754, requiring him to "drive the French from their posts upon the Ohio." See "Secret Instructions to General Braddock,"

The Pennsylvania Assembly, still under Quaker control, was unwilling to defend the western settlers or claims to that region by the proprietor. Ever astute to political realities, the Quakers continued to meet the defense issue with their standard devices of delaying and offering funds to the Crown rather than troops. They were aware that Braddock had a strong aversion to the Quakers and their politics.[29] As a result, they sent Benjamin Franklin to meet with Braddock at Frederick, Maryland, to determine what the Commonwealth could do to assist him – as long as this did not mean creating a military force. Franklin quickly determined that Braddock was quite displeased with the lack of support from the colonies and, in particular, was having difficulties obtaining the necessary equipment and supplies for his campaign. Responding to the general's needs and at the same time gaining favor for Pennsylvania, Franklin obtained 150 wagons (each with four horses) and 259 pack animals to transport the planned expedition into western Pennsylvania. In addition, Franklin supplied a touch of class by providing every British officer with a horse, along with such luxuries as Jamaica spirits, two dozen bottles of Madeira, Gloucester cheese and two well-cured hams.[30] Braddock commented that Pennsylvania had "promised nothing and performed everything" while the other colonies had "promised everything and performed nothing."[31]

Braddock may have moderated his opinions about Pennsylvania and its

in Linn and Egle, *Papers Relating to the French Occupation*, pp. 223-225.

[29] Braddock was briefed on the issues by Thomas Penn and thus from the outset had some prejudices against the Quaker-dominated Assembly. Still, he was genuinely disgusted with Quaker complaints that the Assembly was in error for its "absolute refusal to supply either men, money, or provisions for their own defense while they furnish the Enemy [i.e., the Ohio Indians who still wanted ties with the British Empire] with provision" and threatened to "repair by unpleasant methods," even including the quartering of troops, "what for the character and Honnour of the Assemblies I should be happier to see chearfully supplied." Edward Braddock to Robert Morris, February 28, 1755, as cited in Francis Jennings, *Empire of Fortune* (New York: W. W. Norton and Co., 1988), p. 142.

[30] The wagon accounts and Franklin's letter to the inhabitants of Lancaster, York and Cumberland counties are found in Leonard W. Larabee, ed., *The Papers of Benjamin Franklin, April 1, 1755-September 30, 1756*, vol. 6 (New Haven: Yale University Press, 1963), pp. 13-22. Cited hereafter as Larabee, *Papers of Benjamin Franklin*, vol. 6. The actual package supplied by Franklin included not only the luxuries mentioned but also items such as six pounds of loaf sugar, 20 pounds of good butter, six pounds of ground coffee and six pounds of chocolate.

[31] West, *War for Empire*, p. 31. Not everyone was pleased with Franklin's innovative solutions. Governor Morris, for example, was displeased because he had hoped to find a way to pressure the Assembly to build a war chest for military operations in the Commonwealth. Franklin's actions had relieved the pressure on the defense issue and, as a result, prevented him from getting the funding he sought. See Ralph L. Ketcham, "Conscience, War and Politics in Pennsylvania, 1755-1757," *William and Mary Quarterly*, vol. XX (1963), pp. 418-419.

Quaker-dominated Assembly, but the logistical support given him through Franklin's efforts could not avert the tragedy that ended his campaign: the Battle of the Monongahela. Braddock had begun his campaign with the departure of his army from Fort Cumberland on June 9, 1755. With the assistance of a capable Virginian named George Washington, Braddock's troops advanced into Pennsylvania. Their immediate goals were the capture of Fort Duquesne and the building of a British fort at the forks of the river. Attaining these objectives, Braddock planned to move north, driving the French from those territories claimed by British America. By July 9 the British force, composed of regulars and some independent companies from Virginia, Maryland, New York and both Carolinas,[32] was able to reach the banks of the Monongahela and cross before the French reached their position. On the same day, before Braddock's force could contemplate an attack on the French fort, British and French collided in what should be regarded as a classic meeting engagement.

In the ensuing battle, the French initially encountered a major disadvantage: they faced an enemy that essentially outnumbered them two-to-one.[33] Nevertheless, the French rebounded and in two hours of fighting inflicted a major defeat on the British. Even General Braddock became one of the many British casualties.[34] Braddock's army had advanced in two parts, with the second and slower column, commanded by Colonel Thomas Dunbar, naturally lagging behind because it incorporated the supply trains. The British rout soon included Dunbar's troops who, due to the defeat of Braddock, became demor-

[32] The multi-colonial composition of the force resulted from the overlapping and duplicative claims the colonies had filed in the Ohio area. The Virginia Ohio Company, formed in 1748, was probably the most aggressive. The interest in the western territories could be seen through the Council of Governors meeting held at Alexandria, Virginia on April 14, 1755, when representatives from New York, Massachusetts, Pennsylvania, Maryland, Virginia and North Carolina met at Braddock's camp to finalize plans for the general's campaign. See Frederic A. Godcharles, *Pennsylvania: Political, Governmental, Military and Civil*, governmental volume (New York: American Historical Society, 1933), p. 165.

[33] According to reports from the period, the French force consisted of three captains, ten subalterns, 23 cadets, 72 regulars, 146 militia and 637 Indians. Franklin Thayer Nichols, in "The Organization of Braddock's Army," *William and Mary Quarterly*, vol. IV (1947), pp. 125-147, describes the English force as having more than 2,000 men, far larger than any army the French could form on the frontier.

[34] The battle could have gone either way because the French lost Captain Lienard de Beaujeau, the head of their column, in one of the first volleys, and the column began to sag. But Captain Jean-Daniel Dumas reorganized the column in a half-moon formation and, by so doing, was able to flank the British troops. As the British column began to waver, General Braddock received a mortal wound, and the British fell apart. The British suffered nearly 1,000 casualties, including 60 officers and Braddock, who had four horses shot out from under him. See West, *War for Empire*, pp. 34-35.

alized. Dunbar and his soldiers, rather than develop a defensive position for western Pennsylvania, moved east toward Philadelphia, where they "took up preparations for winter quarters." The English would not muster the strength to contest French control of western Pennsylvania for another three years.[35]

The failure of Braddock's expedition was an additional reason for a spirit of gloom to spread over the frontier regions of Pennsylvania. Even as Washington had begun his military venture to the forks in 1754, the defense debate had begun anew in Pennsylvania. Governor James Hamilton, a native-born Pennsylvanian, wanted to resolve the defense issue but was caught in a predicament. Frontier elements were exerting pressure on the Assembly to authorize and fund a militia. The Assembly, however, refused to pass a law requiring military service by all citizens. Instead, the Assembly proposed the creation of a voluntary military association, patterned after Franklin's association of 1747-1748, to better serve Pennsylvania's needs. Hamilton, though, was loyal to the proprietor, Thomas Penn. Penn was originally cool to creating associations and by this time was decidedly opposed to what he called Franklin's "private army." In Penn's opinion, the Associators merely offered a "safety valve" against the pressure building for a regulated militia. Penn felt that Pennsylvania should have a permanent state-sanctioned militia or nothing at all. The political infighting and constant bickering between the governor and the Assembly on this and other issues was too much strain for Hamilton. He offered his resignation, and it was accepted.

Penn quickly chose Robert Hunter Morris, former Chief Justice of New Jersey, as a replacement. Morris arrived in Philadelphia in the autumn of 1754 and soon echoed the former governor's demands to the Assembly for supporting military actions against the French. Morris told the Assembly:

> *I think it is my duty to remind you that this province is still without a militia or the necessary means of Defense. I do therefore in his Majesty's name call upon you, gentlemen, to put this province into a posture of Defense by establishing a Militia (in doing which you will have a due Regard to scrupulous Conscience) that this plentiful country, situate in the middle of the British Colonies, may no longer be open to the enemy.*[36]

---

[35] A French account of the battle shows their elation at defeating a numerically superior force. They also recognized that the soldiers of the other column, which had not been engaged, were equally panic-stricken and abandoned provisions and ammunition along the way. The French report concluded that "the English had left 1,000 men on the field of battle ... a great portion of the artillery and ammunition, provisions and also their General, whose name was M. Braddock." Linn and Egle, *Papers Relating to the French Occupation*, pp. 270-271.

As could be expected, the Assembly initially delayed any action, for they were awaiting royal demands for support, which they knew from experience would come. Those demands from the Crown arrived in December 1754. As discussed earlier in the chapter, they required support from Pennsylvania, for the Crown planned to commit regular British troops to push the French out of the Ohio River area.

To support the British initiative, the proprietor directed the new governor to petition the Assembly to:

> *provide at this time for the Defense and safety of the province . . . by estab-lishing a regular militia . . . and providing Arms and stores of war, and building proper magazines in the most convenient places.*[37]

Despite the gravity of the situation developing on the western frontier, the Assembly declined the proprietor's request. The Assembly was cognizant of the significance of dispatching British regulars to the colonies, commanded by a British major general. Conversely, the Assembly figured they could weather the crisis using established tactics. Accordingly, early in 1755 the Pennsylvania Assembly voted £20,000 for the king's use to counter this latest military threat. The funds were to be raised by issuing paper money, which the Assembly planned to redeem in ten years. The plan was in some respects controversial, because then-Royal Governor Robert H. Morris feared that too much reliance on paper money might irritate the British government and cause another attempt to change Pennsylvania from a proprietary colony to a royal colony.[38] Given this concern, the governor attempted to change the period of redemption from ten years to five. This proposal set off another round of bickering between the governor and the proprietors and the governor and the Assembly, which meant there was little chance of the Commonwealth's government immediately resolving the defense issue.

Pressure from several sources continued to build for the Assembly to

[36] Robert Hunter Morris to the Provincial Assembly, August 9, 1755, in Reed, *Papers of the Governors, 1747-1759*, p. 456.

[37] Hunter, *Forts on the Pennsylvania Frontier*, p. 183.

[38] Almost from the founding of the Commonwealth, those who disliked Penn or his Quaker experiment tried to take the colony, which belonged to the proprietor William Penn, and place it under the Crown where its policies could be directly controlled by the king. A royal colony could be required to provide for the king's defense, and furthermore, the large tracts of land controlled by the Penn family could then be taxed and redistributed to those who better supported the Crown.

act. For example, Cumberland County presented a petition dated July 15, 1754, signed by 75 persons who expressed concern over "the late defeat of the Virginia Forces." Another petition from Paxton, Derry and Hanover townships (then Lancaster County, now Dauphin County), dated July 31, was received by the Provincial Council:

> *setting forth the great danger they apprehended themselves to be in since the late defeat of the Forces under General Braddock and praying that this house would furnish them with Arms and ammunition for the defense of their houses and Families.*[39]

The governor clearly recognized the seriousness of the situation and pressed the Assembly to supply additional funds to bolster the defense effort. The Assembly, however, simply reverted to time-worn devices and began discussing the possibility of raising £50,000 through a direct tax. This only started more squabbles, because about two thirds of the province consisted of proprietary estates, and under this proposal these properties, formerly non-taxable, would be taxed. Because the proprietor was opposed to this, so was his governor, Robert Morris. Thus, positions had been taken which pitted the proprietor and the governor against the Assembly and virtually guaranteed that little would be accomplished in passing defense-related legislation.

The politically charged atmosphere in Commonwealth government was reflected in the elections of October 1754, which became extremely bitter. Those exasperated with the Quakers called on Quaker legislators to either vote the necessary funds for defense or relinquish their offices. As one advertisement stated:

> *Many "current delegates" were bound, [by] their religious scruples . . . not to afford the necessary supplies at this important and critical Conjuncture required for defeating the province's inveterate Enemies, it was hoped that they would be replaced by men who would act to preserve "our Country Fortunes and Families."*[40]

The Quakers and their defenders resented their negative image in this debate. They noted that other provincial assemblies had in fact reacted in a comparable fashion and had refused to grant funds to the government when

---

[39] Hunter, *Forts on the Pennsylvania Frontier*, p. 173.
[40] Schwartz, *A Mixed Multitude*, p. 208.

their governors had attempted to dictate terms on funding, which in England was a legislative prerogative. By guarding the legislative "power of the purse," the Quakers and their supporters claimed to be guardians of the people's liberties, a tradition developed over centuries of experience in England. In a move that seemed to affirm Franklin's earlier concerns about the Commonwealth's German community, the Germans were advised by Christopher Sauer's newspaper *Pennsylvanische Berichte* to return the Quakers to office since they had a record of representing the general good.[41] In spite of the deteriorating situation on the western frontier and the stubborn refusal of the Assembly to provide for defense, the October elections saw most of the incumbents re-elected. In Lancaster County, with "scarcely one hundred" Quakers among the citizenry and the majority being German or English (and in terms of religious persuasion Anglicans, Presbyterians and various independents), four Quakers were elected to represent the county. It seemed that many who lived in eastern Pennsylvania were not dissatisfied with the Assembly and its policies. The outcome of the elections may also have indicated a concern about the encroachment of executive and centralized power. Furthermore, there was another message in the results: frontier inhabitants could or should defend themselves through a proven device – voluntary associations.[42]

The proprietary faction and its supporters were, to say the least, perturbed about their inability to convince the non-Quaker majority that Quaker domination of the Assembly must be replaced by representatives who were not opposed to providing for the common defense. Additionally, even though the call for an established militia had become increasingly strong over the previous ten years, voters from the more stable, settled eastern part of Pennsylvania seemed unable to see the need to provide for greater military preparedness. That realization appeared to exist largely in the frontier areas. To those in the more established portions of the Commonwealth, the threats on the western frontier were far removed from their everyday consideration. If they were directly menaced by an enemy, as they had been in 1745-1747, they could again use the Associators to provide for their defense. But while the proprietary faction ranted and fumed about the Quakers, the fact remains the populace had

---

[41] *Pennsylvanische Berichte (The Pennsylvania Reporter)*, which appropriately originated in Germantown, told the German settlers that the Provincial Council intended to virtually enslave them, making soldiers of them and burdening them with oppressive taxes. They were encouraged to come to Philadelphia to vote in the elections and support a Quaker slate. Morton L. Montgomery, *History of Berks County in Pennsylvania* (Philadelphia: Everts, Peck & Richards, 1889), p. 107.

[42] Schwartz, *A Mixed Multitude,* note 42, p. 212.

John Harris' home in Harrisburg, showing its dual purpose as a fort.

again placed their trust in them.

These perceptions were to quickly change, however, for the war that began in western Pennsylvania almost overnight moved eastward. On October 16, 1755, a series of attacks were initiated not by French regulars but by French allies, Indians from the Algonquin tribes.[43] As noted earlier, the French had decidedly seized the initiative from the English on the western frontier. However, once the French had initial success in the Ohio Valley, they seemed content to consolidate their gains and provide leadership and encouragement to allied Indians who began raiding the English settlements. The Indians, rather than stage direct attacks and extended sieges, used raids against outlying settlers and small settlements. These tactics posed a major problem for the Common-wealth, since British regulars had withdrawn to the safety of Philadelphia and no militia forces existed to provide for defense. Raiding parties burned, looted and scalped throughout the frontier, forcing many colonists to withdraw from their forward settlements.

The crisis began with a raid by the Delaware on October 16 at Penn's

[43] The Algonquin Indians lived between the Ohio River and the Great Lakes and were by this time French allies. Included in this grouping were the Delaware, Shawnee, Ottawa, Miami, Kickapoo, Illinois, Sauk-Fox, Potawatomie and Ojibwa.

Creek, near Shamokin.[44] Following the so-called Penn's Creek Massacre, John Harris, owner and operator of Harris Ferry, organized a group of about 40 men who went to the scene, recovered the bodies and proceeded to Shamokin in an attempt to persuade the local Indians to remain friendly.[45] But Indian attacks continued throughout the month and into November. On November 1, a party of Delaware Indians led by Shingas and "Captain Jacobs"[46] attacked and wiped out some 20 families in Cumberland County. This raid was followed by a second attack into Cumberland County which resulted in that county being termed the "most needful part of the Frontiers."[47]

The absence of a militia and the lack of resources and training for the Associator companies left the Pennsylvania frontier virtually defenseless to handle the Indian hit-and-run tactics. To resolve this problem, on November 2 John Armstrong of Carlisle presented the governor with a plan to defend the Pennsylvania backcountry. He proposed a chain of blockhouses along or near the south side of Kittatinny Mountain, from the Susquehanna River to the so-called temporary line. The concept of building blockhouses was accepted not only on the state level but on the individual level as well. John Harris, for example, given his recent experiences, cut loopholes into his house and prepared to fend off attacks by French-inspired Indians. Many citizens who lived in the backcountry region followed his example.

In addition, Associator companies, dormant after 1748, again emerged as a method of defense. Documents show that Associator companies continued to exist and train after 1747 in the Philadelphia area, and additional research would likely show continuance elsewhere.[48] With the danger now facing the

---

[44] As Franklin reported to a friend, "We have this Day the bad News that the Enemy [Delawares] have last Week supriz'd and cut off eight Families in this Province. 13 grown Persons were killed and scalped and 12 Children, carried away." Benjamin Franklin to Richard Partridge, October 25, 1755, in Larabee, *Papers of Benjamin Franklin*, vol. 6, p. 231.

[45] This was unsuccessful, however. Harris later reported to the governor that on October 28 his party was attacked, four of his men killed and four more drowned. Harris himself had his horse shot out from under him. See Harris' report in Godcharles, *Pennsylvania: Political, Governmental, Military and Civil*, military volume, p. 68.

[46] "King" Shingas and Captain Jacobs were Delaware leaders who would spearhead many of the raids on frontier Pennsylvania. In 1747 Shingas was recognized "king" of the Ohio Delawares. Although the Delawares had been friends of the English between 1753 and 1755, he led them into the French camp. Captain Jacobs was one of his aggressive war chiefs who led many raids in the Cumberland Valley until his death in 1756 during the attack on Kittanning.

[47] Hunter, *Forts on the Pennsylvania Frontier*, pp. 176-177.

[48] As mentioned earlier in this chapter, two permanent batteries existed in the harbor of Philadelphia in the early 1750s. Both were manned by Associators and continued to practice throughout the interwar period. Records clearly show that the Association Battery at Wicaco

Commonwealth, Associators began to organize or reorganize in communities like Lancaster, Reading and Heidelburg Township. Although the Associator movement was an admirable stopgap for defending Pennsylvania, its limitations quickly became evident. For example, as Edward Shippen noted on November 4, 1755:

> *The people of this county are very willing to join in repelling the Invadres, but are without order and many want Arms. There are five companies in this town from the lower end of this county and the upper end of Chester County, besides the three companies belonging to the town.*[49]

He also noted with alarm that "a number of families but 35 miles from us are entirely cut-off." He went on to recount:

> *An alarm last night about twelve o'clock; we assembled in the square, say about three hundred, but with fifty guns; it was shocking to hear at such a moment, when in expectation of the savages, we had neither the sufficiency of guns, nor ammunition.*[50]

Due to the scattered nature of the Associator units, Morris tried to add some organization to the movement by commissioning Conrad Weiser of Berks County as colonel of the forces east of the Susquehanna River and John Armstrong of Cumberland County colonel of all Associators west of the river.

While attempts were in progress to fortify the frontier settlements and better organize the Associator companies, on November 3, 1755, Morris again asked the legislature to do what was clearly needed: raise a fully regulated and disciplined militia. Despite the obvious danger facing the Commonwealth, the Assembly refused because, by this time in the Commonwealth's history, the defense issue had also become a factor in a political power struggle between the Assembly and the proprietor. This development, plus the traditional Quaker aversion to military legislation, meant that progress toward establishing a militia was still going to be exceedingly difficult. The Assembly did vote to provide the beleaguered inhabitants of the frontier region with the store of flour and

---

was a permanent structure that was maintained and even improved. By 1754 it was an imposing structure, well constructed, well armed and with trained crew available.
[49] Hunter, *Forts on the Pennsylvania Frontier*, pp. 175-176.
[50] Franklin Ellis and Samuel Evans, *History of Lancaster County Pennsylvania with Biographical Sketches of Many Pioneers and Prominent Men*, vol. II (Philadelphia: Everts and Peck, 1883), p. 566.

cattle in Cumberland County originally intended for Braddock's army. Beyond this, however, they were unwilling to proceed.

The Indian attacks continued, heightening concerns of the outlying settlers. On November 15 a platoon of Lancaster Associators standing watch in present-day Dauphin County were attacked by Indians. In the ensuing fight, six Associators were killed, and in the days afterward additional settlers were killed and their homes burned.[51]

While this crisis was transpiring, the German elements in the Commonwealth became exasperated. Many of Pennsylvania's Germans had come to America to escape the ravages of war which had swept their homeland in the first half of the 18th century. Initially, this seemed to make them natural allies of those who promoted the Peace Testimony. Now in the New World, where they hoped to find peace, they faced attacks from French-inspired Indians, with virtually no means of countering this new enemy. As these attacks swept into Cumberland, Lancaster and Berks counties, the Germans decided to act. A number of them gathered at the home of Conrad Weiser in Womelsdorf and demanded that Weiser, a prominent German in the Commonwealth, lead them in a confrontation with the government. Subsequently, on November 25, 1755, hundreds of German farmers marched on Philadelphia to emphasize their demand that the government do something to remedy the helpless state of the Pennsylvania frontier. Their numbers, variously estimated at between 500 and 1,000, were referred to as the "Dutch mob" because many of the members preferred or had to speak German rather than English.[52]

Governor Morris refused to speak with a mob. Instead he agreed to meet with a small delegation, a committee of two, headed by Weiser. The governor discussed the defenseless state of the Commonwealth and attributed the problems facing the western settlements to the Assembly, which consistently refused to provide for the Commonwealth's defense. Accepting this explanation, the mob marched to the State House where the Assembly was in session. The speaker, John Kinsey, told them the Assembly was doing everything it could to assist them, without abridging their rights. He also reminded them that the Assembly had voted funds for defense on numerous occasions, and much like Governor Morris, Kinsey blamed the problems on the other branches of government. Whether confused, satisfied, exasperated or simply weary, the

---

[51] Hunter, *Forts on the Pennsylvania Frontier*, p. 179.
[52] The Pennsylvania Germans have long been referred to as "Pennsylvania Dutch." The error results from a corruption of the German word *deutsch*, which means "German." This misconception exists even today.

German mob dispersed and went home, having at least vented their frustrations.

In the midst of this dissension on the issue of defense, Franklin introduced a militia bill in the Assembly. This was the first time since 1693 that any assemblyman had seriously offered a bill to create a militia. Franklin, as noted earlier, had in the past shown considerable political skill on the militia issue and had not specifically allied himself with either faction in the dispute. Now, however, with his introduction of a serious militia bill, he was clearly in opposition to the Quaker leadership of the Assembly. Yet Franklin was a realist. He knew the bill would have to be a compromise if it were to have any chance of passing. Above all, it would have to recognize the special sensitivities of the Quakers.

His bill – entitled "An Act for Better Ordering and Regulating Such as are Willing and Desirous to be United for Military Purposes Within this Province" – received additional impetus from an event which occurred at essentially the same time and further galvanized public opinion in favor of implementing new defensive measures for the Commonwealth. On November 24, 1755, even while the militia bill was being debated, a Shawnee war party with French assistance attacked a Moravian mission settlement at Gnaddenhuetten in present-day Carbon County. The Moravians posed no threat to the Indians who lived nearby. As a devout, pious group they were widely known and respected for their kindness and consideration toward all people. Still, the Indians burned the mission to the ground and killed 11 of the inhabitants.[53]

In the wake of the Gnaddenhuetten massacre, on November 25, 1755, Franklin's defense act was passed by the Assembly. Passage was possible because, under substantial pressure from a number of sources, Quaker solidarity in the Assembly broke down. The "principled" Friends abstained, and the more pragmatic Friends followed Isaac Norris and his faction, voting with the rest of the Assembly in support of the militia act.[54]

Compared with militia laws in the other colonies, the Pennsylvania act was unique. For example, militia service was not compulsory but voluntary.

---

[53] William H. Rice, "The Gnadenhutten Massacres: A Brief History of Two Historic Tragedies," *The Pennsylvania German: A Popular Magazine of Biography, History, Genealogy, Folklore, Literature, etc.,* vol. 7, no. 1 (January 1906), pp. 26-31.

[54] This summary of Quaker actions during this crisis is too brief to do justice to the quandary that faced many sincere, public service-minded Quakers. Some of these men were proud of the 75 years of stability Quaker leadership had brought to Pennsylvania. Although they had by their policies forced their views – specifically on the defense issue – on many Pennsylvanians, they had provided the Commonwealth with decades of honest and tolerant governance. There

Those who objected to military service would not be forced to serve. No militiaman would have to spend more than three days away from his home, and none would be kept on duty for more than three weeks unless through special arrangements.[55] The militia established by Franklin's act was in many respects little different from his Associators, since it was a volunteer force with limited responsibilities. It was significant, however, because it was an officially sanctioned organization, not merely one permitted or tolerated by the Assembly.[56]

Franklin's leadership, the furor on the frontier and the recent pressure exerted by the Germans (whose assistance in defense matters Franklin had originally questioned) had resulted in the passage of the militia act. Afterward, a companion act, called the Supply Act of November 27, 1755, was passed. It called for, among other things, the construction of a series of frontier forts which would bolster the defense of the Commonwealth. Creating a system of forts, however, stretched the newly created Pennsylvania militia beyond its limited potential. In particular, the limitations on terms of service imposed by the statute made the militia an unlikely organization for the type of garrison duty required. Instead, the Supply Act provided for raising a full-time regiment for this purpose. This force would be known as the Pennsylvania Provincial Regiment.[57]

The actual size of provincial forces from 1756 until the end of the French and Indian War shows that the demand for troops constantly changed. In December 1755 it was anticipated that Pennsylvania would need approximately 550 men. By the time an additional Supply Act was passed on March 23, 1757, however, the number had grown to well over a thousand. By March 1759, the Assembly had authorized a provincial force of 2,700. At the outset,

---

were those among the Friends who still believed all must hold fast to their basic religious principles without compromise; there were others who, like James Logan, firmly believed a strong defense would have to be devised. Finally, there were those in the middle variously pulled by the arguments from the two opposing poles. See Isaac Sharpless, *A Quaker Experiment in Government: A History of Quaker Government in Pennsylvania, 1682-1783*, vol. I (Philadelphia: T. S. Leach and Co., 1899), pp. 212-272.

[55] *Statutes at Large of Pennsylvania, 1682-1801*, vol. V, 1744-1759 (Harrisburg: State Printer, 1898), pp. 197-201.

[56] On March 13, 1756, Governor Robert Morris issued regulations recognizing that companies had been formed and specifying how they were to be formed into regiments. Reed, *Papers of the Governors, 1747-1759*, pp. 589-590.

[57] Even though militia troops were not the most likely resource for regular garrison duty, pressure to cover the contingencies caused them to be used in this capacity. On June 24, 1757, Governor William Denny wrote a letter to Colonel John Stanwix telling him that lower county regiments of militia would be sent to the forts on this side of the Susquehanna so that Stanwix could move provincial troops to join up with his forces. Ibid., p. 832.

Pennsylvania's provincial forces were divided into two regiments: the First Pennsylvania, also known as the Augusta Regiment, and the Second Pennsylvania. The First consisted of William Clapham's battalion of eight companies, and the Second had two battalions commanded by Lieutenant Colonel John Armstrong. Initially, two methods were used to recruit the Provincial Regiment. In some cases, militia companies, most of them formerly Associator companies, were placed on paid status to become the necessary garrison forces. But there were problems with using militia companies to build up the strength of the Provincial Regiment. They did not have discipline and training that was up to the standards sought by the government, and, as was their practice, they chose their own officers. Consequently, some leaders preferred to adopt other methods of recruitment. They also wanted officers to be commissioned by the governor and these newly commissioned officers authorized to recruit new companies.

Garrisoning the forts was an expensive proposition. The Assembly provided £60,000 for their first year of operation, 1756. However, this was hardly sufficient to defend the Commonwealth from French and Indian attacks. As a consequence, after this initial appropriation, additional funds had to be supplied annually for defense. In some respects, the financial burden was ameliorated by a British policy decision in 1758. It stated that when Commonwealth troops were serving under British command, Pennsylvania was only required to provide the soldiers with pay and uniforms. The Crown would be responsible for arms, munitions, tents and provisions. If the Commonwealth had to act before royal monies were available, the Crown pledged to reimburse Pennsylvania for these expenditures.[58]

Through this new legislation, Pennsylvania now had the ability to field military forces and defend itself against French and Indian incursions. This happened none too soon, for the war that had started on the frontier of Pennsylvania was rapidly spreading. By 1756 it would merge into a larger war known in history as the Seven Years War.

---

[58] Details on these arrangements are found in correspondence from William Pitt to Governor Denny on December 30, 1757, in *Pennsylvania Archives: Colonial Records of Pennsylvania, Minutes of the Provincial Council from Organization to the Termination of the Proprietary Government*, vol. VIII (Harrisburg: Theo. Fenn & Co., 1852), p. 28. See also correspondence between the same on December 29, 1758, p. 288, and Pitt to Governor Hamilton on January 7, 1760, pp. 451-452.

A 1666 portrait of William Penn, 22, in armor, by an unknown
artist. This is one of several copies of the missing original
(reproduced by permission of the Historical Society of
Pennsylvania).

James Logan, a leading Quaker and voice of moderation in the militia debate (portrait by Gustavus Hesselius, reproduced by permission of the Historical Society of Pennsylvania).

Benjamin Franklin, founder of Pennsylvania's unique voluntary defense force, the Associators (portrait by Charles Wilson Peale, reproduced by permission of the Historical Society of Pennsylvania).

The Schuylkill Gun, an original artillery piece manufactured for the Association Battery which was located at Wicaco. This gun apparently was disabled during the American Revolution at Fort Mifflin (a major fortification in the Philadelphia area) by either colonial or British troops during one of the evacuations of Philadelphia (photo courtesy of the State in Schuylkill).

George Washington as a Virginia provincial officer in 1758, during his period of service in the French and Indian War (portrait by Charles Wilson Peale, Washington/Curtis/Peale Collection, Washington and Lee University).

Fort Ligonier, the only colonial fort in Pennsylvania to be restored on its original foundations. This photo depicts the fort as it appeared during the French and Indian War (photo courtesy of the Fort Ligonier Association).

Conrad Weiser, leader of the Pennsylvania German community. No known portrait of Weiser exists, but a visual depiction of Weiser was created in stained glass at Muhlenberg
College Chapel (photo courtesy of Muhlenberg College).

Colonel Henry Bouquet, soldier for the King and commander of British forces at the Battle of Bushey Run in 1763 (portrait by John Wollaston, reproduced by permission of the
Historical Society of Pennsylvania).

Color used by the Philadelphia Light Horse, 1775. This flag is in the
possession of Troop A, 1st Squadron, 104th Cavalry in Philadelphia,
the unit's lineal descendant (courtesy of First Troop Museum, Philadelphia City Cavalry).

Color used by Thompson's Rifle Battalion, an early Associator unit and perhaps the most famous element of the Pennsylvania Line. This photo shows the preserved color with the letters from the reverse side showing through the thin material (reproduced by permission of the State Museum of Pennsylvania, Pennsylvania Historical and Museum Commission).

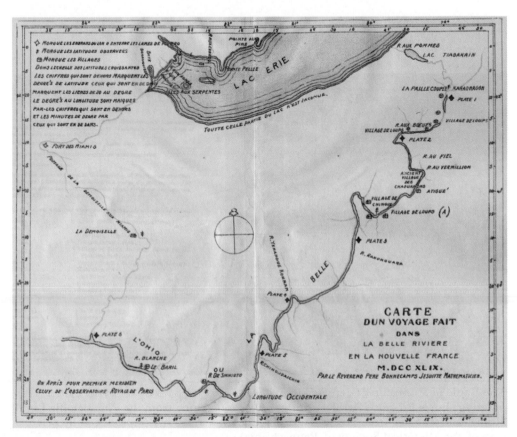

Copy of a map drawn by Father Pere Bonnecamps depicting Captain Pierre-Joseph Cèleron de Blainville's expedition, from George Dallas Albert's *The Frontier Forts of Western Pennsylvania*. Note in particular the red diamond-shaped markers where leaden plates were buried, indicating French claims to the area.

The Battle of Princeton as depicted by William Mercer, a participant in the battle. This painting shows Proctor's Artillery firing, several horsemen from the Philadelphia Light Horse, and infantry from Cadwallader's Pennsylvania Troops (reproduced by permission of the Historical Society of Pennsylvania).

The brig *Niagara,* from which Commodore Oliver Hazzard Perry concluded his famous Battle of Lake Erie on September 10, 1813. The vessel was subsequently raised and restored in 1913.

FORT McINTOSH.—SITE OF TOWN OF BEAVER.

Fort in western Pennsylvania constructed by the Westmoreland Militia in 1778 (from George Dallas Albert's *The Frontier Forts of Western Pennsylvania*).

Color designed for the Hanover Associators in 1775, one of the earlier units reorganized to protect the rights of the Pennsylvania colonists (reproduced by permission of the State Museum of Pennsylvania, Pennsylvania Historical and Museum Commission).

FORT LE BOEUF (1796) AT WATERFORD, ERIE COUNTY, PA.

Fort le Boeuf as depicted in a painting in 1796 (from George Dallas Albert's *The Frontier Forts of Western Pennsylvania*). This fort, at New Waterford, Erie County, was one of a series of forts that the French constructed in 1753 and intended to stretch from Lake Erie to the Ohio River.

CHAPTER 4

The French and Indian War

*The provincials appear to have done well and their good
men are better in this war than the regular troops.*

– Colonel Henri Bouquet, 1758

As related in the previous chapter, the Pennsylvania militia was finally born out of a bona fide military threat resulting from French and Indian agitation across large areas of the Commonwealth. This agitation, which lasted throughout the first half of the 1750s, continued to build in intensity and expanded into a full-scale war known appropriately in the colonies as the French and Indian War. The war would not, however, remain a colonial conflict. In 1756 it spread to the European continent, where it was referred to as the Seven Years War.[1]

The Seven Years War seriously tested the mettle of the major European nations that were fighting for hegemony on the continent as well as in their colonies. The test would be particularly difficult for the Commonwealth of Pennsylvania, which at the beginning of the decade was still without the statutory authority to provide for a military force. Granted, the enactment of the first Militia Act seemed to indicate that Pennsylvania had finally taken the first step in defending itself – even though the authorization provided by this initial legislation, passed on November 25, 1755, was short-lived. On July 7, 1756, the king vetoed the act, stating that it was "rather calculated to exempt persons from militia service than to encourage and prompt them."[2]

With the militia problem unresolved, as Indian raiding parties descended on the largely undefended frontier, Associator companies were at first the

---

[1] The war would not be limited to a British-French confrontation but would be a coalition war with Prussia, Russia, Austria and Spain becoming involved. The war even expanded to India, where both Britain and France had commercial interests.
[2] Russell F. Weigley, "The Colonial Militia," *The First Century: A History of the 28th Infantry Division*, Uzal W. Ent, ed. (Harrisburg, Stackpole Press, 1979), p. 25. Cited hereafter as Weigley, "The Colonial Militia."

only local force available to meet the crisis. Some of these companies had been inactive since the late 1740s, while others, such as the Philadelphia Artillerists, had continued to function even after the end of King George's War. These Associator companies were locally based, and the Militia Act did little to change their nature, even though logic would seem to dictate that the militia, a more inclusive organization, would supplant Associator companies. However, the militia created by the 1755 act was limited even as the Associators were, since they could not be required to move more than three days beyond the Commonwealth's settled parts or stay in garrison for more than three weeks.[3] Because they were locals, close to their homes, both Associators and militia companies were plagued with absenteeism in this early period of the war, as the citizen-soldiers attempted to keep their farms and businesses operating despite their military duties.[4]

Recognizing the weaknesses exhibited among both Associators and militia units, first Governor Robert Hunter Morris and later Governor William Denny pursued additional methods of defending Pennsylvania even as they were attempting to resolve the militia logjam. The executives began creating provincial troops who were enlisted in the pay of the Commonwealth for specific periods of time and were not constrained by geographical limitations. These troops were authorized on November 17, 1755, when the Assembly voted funds to establish provincial forces and construct forts.[5] Since provincials enlisted for longer periods of time and were paid for their services, it was assumed they would be more dependable than either Associators or militia.

This assumption was, at least at the outset, erroneous, because as provincial companies were formed, existing Associators or militiamen often transferred into provincial status. Thus, although the units were different, the personnel were often similar if not identical. Companies with Associator or militia status had at least some experience and military structure, an obvious asset for a Commonwealth under attack. In addition, with pay provided to soldiers for provincial service, the economic hardship resulting from military obli-

[3] *Statutes at Large of Pennsylvania, 1682-1801*, vol. V (Harrisburg: State Printer, 1898), pp. 197-212. Cited hereafter as *Statutes at Large of Pennsylvania, 1682-1801.*
[4] As noted in a recent periodical, "The pull of domestic concerns made citizen soldiers difficult to keep in the field, for untended animals and crops, idle forges, tanneries and work benches threatened the economic fabric of domestic local and regional economies." R. S. Stephenson, "Pennsylvania Provincial Soldiers in the Seven Years War," *Pennsylvania Magazine of History and Biography*, vol. LXII, no. 2 (Spring 1995), pp. 199-200.
[5] Of these troops Franklin stated, "Those men posted on the Frontier are not militia, but what we call our provincial troops, being regularly enlisted to serve a term, and in the pay of the province." Ibid., p. 200.

gations was alleviated. For these reasons, Associator/militia/provincial companies were some of the earliest to man the new system of forts.

Another problem emerged for provincial forces, reminiscent of an earlier issue regarding state units during King George's War. As soldiers were recruited to form provincial regiments (and even the British Army's Royal American Regiment), criticism mounted because indentured servants were being enlisted, much to the consternation of their owners. Before his untimely demise, General Braddock told his officers, who were pressed to fill out their regiments, that it was their "duty to take all Volunteers that offer, without considering whether they are Servants or not."[6] Apparently they heeded his advice, as did provincial regiment recruiters. The Commonwealth's pay of one pistole and one shilling and six pence per day further induced many indentures and new immigrants to enlist. A study of the backgrounds of soldiers in the Pennsylvania Regiment has led one scholar to conclude that as many as two thirds of its foreign-born recruits were servants or former servants. Furthermore, possibly half the troops in the Pennsylvania Regiment may have been servants or former servants who were foreign-born and only a few years in the colony.[7] Thus, it seems likely that provincial regiments, although they included many former Associators and militiamen, were also composed of a surprising number of indentures and recent immigrants. In any event, the shortage of manpower for both British army regiments and provincial forces meant that pressure for militia legislation would continue.

The sovereign's veto of the first Militia Act of 1755 looked like a serious reversal in the push to obtain military legislation in the Commonwealth. However, the king's veto of the act did not become known in Pennsylvania until October 15, 1756, a mere 15 days before it was due to expire. The natural lag in communications during this period meant that the act was virtually allowed to live out its natural life. With the gravity of direct military threats facing British America, additional acts would be forthcoming and would clearly indicate a changed attitude on the defense issue by the Commonwealth's elected representatives.

Of particular note was an act passed on March 29, 1757 entitled "Forming and Regulating the Militia of the Province of Pennsylvania."[8] Unlike

---

[6] *Pennsylvania Archives: Colonial Records of Pennsylvania*, eighth series, vol. VII (Philadelphia: Joseph Severns and Co., 1852), pp. 39-40.

[7] Matthew C. Ward, "An Army of Servants: The Pennsylvania Regiment during the Seven Years War," *The Pennsylvania Magazine of History and Biography*, vol. CXIX (January/April 1995), pp. 79-93.

[8] *Statutes at Large of Pennsylvania, 1682-1801*, p. 609.

its predecessor, which had been carefully crafted by Benjamin Franklin to avoid unnecessarily offending Quaker sensitivities, the new act required military service of Pennsylvania's citizens. All males (except servants and apprentices) within every township, borough and ward were to be listed by the sheriff. Each county was to be subsequently subdivided and was required to supply a company of male citizens capable of bearing arms.[9] The act further specified officer qualifications and appointment procedures and provided for regular meetings even when the Commonwealth was not on a wartime footing. Specifically, the new act mandated that each company assemble on the first Monday in June, August, November and March for a company muster and on the second Monday of each October for a regimental muster. By law, citizens who were "not conscientiously scrupling the use of Arms" also were required to be:

> *sufficiently armed with one good musket, fuzee or other fire lock well fixed, a cutlass, bayonet or tomahawk, a cartouch box, filled with twelve or more cartridges of powder, twelve or more sizable bullets and three good flints.*[10]

All this was a far cry from the proprietary colony which, only a decade earlier, had been unable to pass a militia law. This progress was possible in part because of the increased awareness of the threats facing the Commonwealth. More significant, however, were the changes that had recently occurred in the Pennsylvania Assembly. The demands placed on Pennsylvania by a widespread ground war caused the final demise of Quaker influence in the Assembly.

Between 1745 and 1755 the controversy over the need to find a method of defending the Commonwealth's citizenry had helped erode Quaker influence. The ability of Quaker assemblymen to block legislative action, however, was well understood by their opposition. This was again evident when the governor and the proprietors were unable to comply with a request from their sister colony of Massachusetts for the participation of Pennsylvania in an expedition against Fort Duquesne, the major French fortress in what is now western Pennsylvania. The request came from Major General William Shirley, who was both the governor of Massachusetts Bay and the commander in chief in British

---

[9] Males exempted from this requirement were "religious societies or congregations whose tenets and principles are against bearing arms" and "all papists and reputed papists." Thus, Quakers and like-minded citizens were exempted, but in addition, Catholics were specifically exempted due to their supposed loyalties to another realm, that of St. Peter. British America, like the home islands, was apparently still too close to the Reformation and religion-based warfare, which had only ended in 1648, to trust Catholics. Ibid., p. 610.

[10] Ibid., p. 612.

North America. Shirley's request was not well received by the other neighboring colonies, and due to continued Quaker control of the Assembly, Pennsylvania, which was vitally affected by the French presence, could not favorably respond.

After appealing in vain for the Assembly to stop blocking action on defense issues, and recognizing that voters had shown an unwillingness to vote Quakers out of office, the British government proposed another method to end their obstructionism.[11] A bill would be submitted, sponsored by the British government, which would compel all provincial officeholders and legislators to swear an oath to support the government. Although innocuous by today's standards, this proposal, had it been enacted, would have forced all practicing Quakers to leave political office, since their beliefs forbade them to swear oaths.

The Society of Friends in England, recognizing the long-term implications of this proposal – particularly the danger of such a law to all members of the Society – proposed a compromise. Rather than have a bill enacted which would make it impossible for any practicing Quaker to hold office, in March 1756 a delegation of English Friends met with a high-ranking member of the British government to defuse the crisis. The leadership of the English Quakers pledged to persuade the colonial Friends to resign from the Assembly, rather than have this restrictive law on the statute books. Subsequently, both letters and emissaries were sent to the principled Friends in Pennsylvania urging them to retire from politics. In June 1756, six experienced Quaker members of the Assembly resigned their positions. Their statement was in keeping with their basic beliefs:

> *As many of our constituents seem of opinion that the present situation of public affairs calls upon us for services in a military way which from a conviction of judgment after mature deliberation we cannot comply with, we conclude it most conducive to the peace of our minds, and the reputation of our religious profession to persist in our resolution of resigning our seats,*

[11] This proposal caused a major crisis of conscience for Pennsylvania Quakers because repeated challenges were threatening their cardinal principles. Specifically, the Society renounced war, because the Quakers were a peaceable people who depended on the protection of God alone. For those who depended on Him, His protection was far superior to that which could be provided by man. Still, the defense debate which had raged throughout the first half of the 18th century had already caused some Quakers to alter their beliefs to allow for defensive war – as distinguished from offensive war. But to swear allegiance to a secular government was something that simply could not be accommodated. For an excellent statement of Quaker faith see excerpts from the letters of James Logan in Isaac Sharpless, *A Quaker Experiment in Government* (Philadelphia: Ferris and Leach, 1902), pp. 224-230.

which we now accordingly do.[12]

In the following months, additional Quakers declined re-election, and after the new Assembly met, four more Quakers left the Assembly and three others refused to run for re-election. By the end of 1756, Quaker control of the Assembly had ended, and only six of the 36 assemblymen were members of the Society of Friends. Once the Quakers surrendered control of the Assembly, to which they had been legally elected by the citizenry, they would never attempt to regain it. The Quaker-imposed deadlock on militia and defense appropriations had finally been broken.

While the struggle was being waged over who would control the Assembly, and particularly whether military bills could be passed by that body, Pennsylvania still found it necessary to field troops. Authorization came not through the first or second militia acts but rather through the Supply Act, noted earlier, which had been passed to construct and supply a system of forts for the Commonwealth. This act allocated funds for defense, which were to be dispensed by an independent commission led by James Hamilton and John Mifflin of the Provincial Council and Isaac Norris, Benjamin Franklin, John Hughes and Evan Morgan from the Assembly.[13] The Independent Commission first focused its energies on building forts and providing for Pennsylvania troops to garrison them.

Even though the commission was designed to be an administrative entity, the crises facing Pennsylvania were so pressing that the commission was required to take an active role in the defense of the Commonwealth. In fact, according to Benjamin Franklin:

> *The Governor prevail'd with me to take charge of our North-western Frontier, which was infested by the Enemy, and provide for the Defence of the Inhabitants by raising Troops, and building a line of Forts. I undertook this military Business tho' I did not consider myself well qualified for it.*[14]

---

[12] The resignation of the six Quakers and the statement they signed are included in Gertrude MacKinney, ed., *Pennsylvania Archives: Votes of the Assembly, October 15, 1753-September 24, 1756*, eighth series, vol. V (Harrisburg: State Printer, 1931), p. 564.

[13] William A. Hunter, *Forts on the Pennsylvania Frontier, 1753-1758* (Harrisburg: Pennsylvania Historical and Museum Commission, 1960), p. 198. Cited hereafter as Hunter, *Forts on the Pennsylvania Frontier.*

[14] Carl Van Doren, ed., *Benjamin Franklin's Autobiographical Writings* (New York: Viking Press, 1945), p. 743.

To implement the governor's request, an expedition was organized to provide some security for the frontier settlements. The expedition was to be led by commission member James Hamilton. Franklin and Joseph Fox, chairmen of the important Committee of Accounts, were to accompany it. A newly commissioned provincial captain, James McLaughlin, actually commanded the military force. Obviously, military experience was missing, with the exception of Franklin's son William. He had served as a provincial lieutenant in the previous war and became his father's aide-de-camp during the expedition. As Franklin stated, he was "of great use to me."[15]

The commission's expedition left Philadelphia on December 18, 1755. Its mission lasted about 50 days and was successful in establishing a defense for the frontier regions without encountering any military misfortune. The commission's first task was to organize the defenses of Easton, which included setting up a militia and improving the existing crude stockade that had been erected around the town. In the process, Franklin himself organized a town guard of 24 men, led by a major.[16] Ten days later the expedition proceeded to Reading for a prearranged rendezvous with Governor Morris. He discussed with the commissioners his plan to build a fort at Shamokin and recruit 500 men to either garrison the fort or serve as rangers to protect the area. Franklin, however, suggested a more comprehensive approach to defending the frontier. He proposed adoption of the plan authored earlier by John Armstrong of Cumberland County. According to Armstrong's plan, a chain of forts was to be built to protect the frontier. Morris agreed to this concept, including the siting of one of the forts, as originally planned, at Shamokin. Before the conference could finish its business of planning for Pennsylvania's defense, the Indians struck again.

When the commissioners departed from Easton, they had left instructions for Captain William Hay's company to build a blockhouse or fort at the site of an earlier disaster, Gnaddenhuetten. On New Year's Day, however, a portion of Hay's company was lured into a trap and ambushed. The remainder of the garrison retreated to Bethlehem, and the Indians burned what existed of the new stockade, some of the area houses and the Moravian Brother's Mills.[17]

---

[15] Ibid.

[16] Franklin's role in the defense of the Commonwealth is discussed in Hunter, *Forts on the Pennsylvania Frontier*, pp. 230-240. See also Leonard W. Larabee, ed, *The Papers of Benjamin Franklin, July 1, 1753-March 31, 1755*, vol. 5 (New Haven: Yale University Press, 1962).

[17] According to one author, some of the troops were having fun skating on the river and observed some Indians at a distance. Thinking they could easily capture them, the troops took off in pursuit, chasing the bait right into a well-laid Indian trap. After this group was dispensed

The governor acted quickly and with obvious anger, offering a bounty of 40 pieces of eight for every Indian scalp brought in.[18] On January 5, Franklin, whose duties on the commission had been largely administrative, was commissioned a colonel. He was sent back to Northhampton County to raise troops and reorganize the area's defenses. Specifically, the governor gave him power to:

> *take into your Charge the County of Northampton, to dismiss all Persons who have been commissioned by me to any Military Command, and to put others in their Places and to fill up the Blank Commissions with the Names of such Persons as you judge fit for his Majesties Service.*[19]

With rather broad authority, Franklin placed several local Associator companies under provincial status and put them under the command of William Parsons. With troops now available, Franklin moved to Bethlehem, where he encountered numerous refugees and a general feeling of despair over the Indian successes. Franklin established himself at Gnaddenhuetten and supervised the construction of Fort Allen and three other forts in the county: Fort Franklin, Fort Norris and Fort Hamilton. In addition, Franklin continued to recruit troops and, through the authority given to him by the governor, commissioned officers. He commissioned William Parsons as a major with responsibilities for the defense of Northhampton County and George Croghan as captain with authorization to organize the defenses of Cumberland County. Having assisted with the military preparedness of two counties, he departed for Bethlehem on January 7, finally returning to Philadelphia on February 5. By January 26, 1756, he had 552 troops in Northampton County alone, a noteworthy accomplishment considering the lack of forces before his arrival. Through his efforts, two key frontier areas had some measure of defense. Only a few months before, the Commonwealth had no paid troops. Furthermore, Franklin's recruitment in many respects marks the origins of the First

---

with, the Indians again moved on Gnaddenhuetten, and the troops and citizens, terrified, withdrew. See Frederic A. Godcharles, *Pennsylvania: Political, Governmental, Military and Civil*, military volume (New York: American Historical Society, 1933), p. 73.

[18] Governor Morris' response to the Indian attack was offensive to the Assembly and to inhabitants in settled areas such as Philadelphia. Offering bounties for scalps of males or females above 12 years of age was thought to be as barbaric as some of the atrocities perpetrated by the Indians.

[19] Robert Morris, Lieutenant Governor and Commander-in-Chief, Commission to Benjamin Franklin, January 5, 1756, in Leonard W. Larabee, ed., *The Papers of Benjamin Franklin, April 1, 1755-September 30, 1756*, vol. 6 (New Haven: Yale University Press, 1963), pp. 347-348.

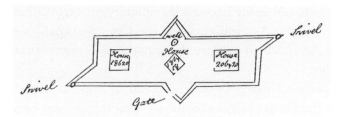

Benjamin Franklin's drawing of his plan for Fort Allen, drawn while he was in the field with troops during the French and Indian War. It was sent with a letter to an unknown recipient, who forwarded it to Governor Robert Morris.

Pennsylvania Battalion.[20]

The Indian raids, which had occurred with regular frequency in the last three months of 1755, gave rise to a plan to provide a significant defensive system for Pennsylvania, as outlined in the Supply Act. This system, backed by Governor Morris, called for the construction of a line of defenses roughly following the Blue Mountains from Easton to Mercersburg. These fortifications were to consist of stockades and blockhouses, with the former large enough to hold a militia company. The forts were to be positioned at intervals of 20 miles, with the smaller blockhouses located at five-mile intervals. As noted earlier, the force developed to garrison these facilities was the Pennsylvania Provincial Regiment, the first official Pennsylvania military force.[21]

Planning and building these fortifications took place in the early part of 1756, and these actions and the recruitment of troops had to be accomplished through the first Militia Act and the Supply Act. The inadequacy of the laws spelled difficulty for Pennsylvania's troops from the very beginning. No system for procuring and distributing adequate supplies existed, and the pay for troops

[20] In this expedition Franklin records one of the earliest known examples of the chaplaincy in the Pennsylvania militia. Franklin's troops were accompanied by a Presbyterian minister, the Reverend Charles Beatty. During the course of the expedition, Beatty complained to Franklin about lagging attendance at his services. Franklin, ever innovative, solved the chaplain's problem by giving him the responsibility of distributing the rum ration, following his scheduled prayer sessions. In Colonel Franklin's own words, "Never were prayers more generally and more punctually attended." Ibid., p. 363.

[21] A historian usually hesitates to identify the first or last of any organizational structure in this period, but as noted in Weigley, "The Colonial Militia," p. 24, "The militia force founded upon the Militia Act of 1755 is the most direct colonial ancestor of the Pennsylvania National Guard and the 28th Division."

was often late and certainly irregular.[22] Troops without proper supplies and regular pay, of course, can easily become disciplinary problems. Recognizing this, on April 15, 1756, the Assembly passed the Commonwealth's version of the British Mutiny Act,[23] which subjected Pennsylvania's nascent military force to military discipline.

Attempts were made as early as 1756 to impose some organizational standards over the Pennsylvania companies which had been organized at various localities on the frontier. When these units were first organized in the spring of 1756, three battalions were formed. The first was commanded by Lieutenant Colonel Conrad Weiser, the second by Lieutenant Colonel John Armstrong and the third by Colonel William Clapham. The three battalions were then organized into the Pennsylvania Regiment. This one regiment was subsequently divided into two, with the First or Augusta Regiment initially commanded by Clapham. The second, a two-battalion force, did not have a regimental commander. Command instead was split between Weiser and Armstrong.[24]

This initial scheme was altered in 1758 when Pennsylvania troops were reorganized again into a single Pennsylvania Regiment and the governor, William Denny, became its colonel. The title of colonel was largely honorific; in actuality Pennsylvania's troops served under the command of General John Forbes.[25] For the remainder of the war Pennsylvania would have a single regiment, although strength of provincial troops would vary considerably.[26]

---

[22] Early Pennsylvania records reveal numerous occasions when provincial troops were not paid promptly. In fact, the Commonwealth was often months in arrears on payment of accounts. This was due to the rather chaotic method the Commonwealth used to finance the war. Commissioners from the Assembly, or sometimes the Provincial Council, were responsible for disbursing funds, but when they had done so, all too often political infighting prevented the prompt passage of new legislation to pay the troops.

[23] The Commonwealth's version of the mutiny act was necessary because colonial troops suffered from two problems: the lack of organization and the inability of the commander to discipline them. By mid-1756 the organizational issue was not a major concern for company-size units, and manning had been fairly well standardized. The Mutiny Act provided the legal structure to allow commanders to place their troops under military discipline.

[24] The structure of the early provincial forces can be found in Thomas Lynch Montgomery, ed., *Pennsylvania Archives: Officers and Soldiers in the Service of the Province of Pennsylvania, 1744-1765*, fifth series, vol. I (Harrisburg: Harrisburg Publishing Co., 1906), pp. 44-47. Cited hereafter as Montgomery, *Officers and Soldiers of Pennsylvania*.

[25] Correspondence from John Forbes to Henry Bouquet on June 6, 1758, noted that provincial troops would be in three regiments. See Louis M. Waddell, John L. Tottenham and Donald H. Kent, eds., *The Papers of Henry Bouquet*, vol. II (Harrisburg: Pennsylvania Historical and Museum Commission, 1978), p. 39.

[26] The diverse backgrounds of some of the early Pennsylvania units is intriguing. For example,

For those who seek to find campaign and battle honors for these Pennsylvania troops, it must be remembered that for the first few years these provisional troops were largely occupied with garrison duties. The battle streamers desired by units and their sponsoring states do not exist. Other than the raid staged by John Armstrong against the Indian settlement at Kittanning, most Pennsylvania forces were engaged in defensive efforts.

It seems possible, even likely, that some Associators, perhaps recognized for what they really were – militia – served in various capacities along the frontier either as militia or provincial forces. A case in point is the Kensington Artillerists. Records indicate that in May 1760, Jehu Eyre, from the Kensington section of Philadelphia, led a party of shipbuilders to Fort Pitt to build bateaux for the British forces. These men were both artillerists and shipbuilders. Following the completion of his work there, Eyre led his men north to Presqu'Isle, present-day Erie, and made oars and bateaux for Major Robert Rodgers. Eyre's daybook does not indicate in what capacity he and his men performed these duties – as Associators, militia or provincials. Records do show that Captain Jehu Eyre was appointed chief engineer and director of artillery for the Associator facilities in Philadelphia on March 18, 1756. They also show that Eyre's company of Associator artillerists was mustered into the service of the Crown in May 1756.[27] That they were Associators can be documented, but exactly how they were serving is difficult to ascertain.[28]

The reader should remember that Pennsylvanians served the Crown in

Francis Harback, who enlisted July 1, 1758, is listed as a mulatto. He served in John Bull's company in the 3rd Battalion, Pennsylvania Regiment of Foot. Andrew McGill, who was from Maryland and served in John Wright's company, was an Indian. The provincial ship *Pennsylvania* lists a Negro seaman named Cuff. Despite the position of the Society of Friends, Lieutenant Richard Renshaw, a Quaker, is listed as an officer in the Associated Regiment of Foot of Philadelphia. Montgomery, *Officers and Soldiers of Pennsylvania*, pp. 18, 87, 236, 279.

[27] In recent years, some excellent original work has been done on the Philadelphia Artillerists. In 1976 Michael Benson wrote a paper entitled "The Early History of the Artillery Battalion of Philadelphia, 1760-1777" and was able to use Jehu Eyre's daybook. Recently, Joseph Seymour wrote "Soldiers of the Quaker City: The Story of the Philadelphia Artillery, 1747-1783" (1997) using Benjamin Loxley's daybook.

[28] Continuity in terms of location and personnel in Associator units exists in areas other than Philadelphia and in some instances extends into the Revolutionary period. For example, the Reading Associator unit was organized in 1754 by Conrad Weiser and had among its officers Captain Jack Morgan, who commanded a unit at Fort Lebanon. His ensign was George Nagle. Weiser's Associator units served throughout the French and Indian War, and when the Revolutionary War began, the local company was commanded by now-Captain George Nagle. Jacob Morgan, a company commander in the French and Indian War, was still a captain but was serving as Lieutenant of the County – in essence, the local officer who issued the call for Associator volunteers. This continuity in location and membership was discovered by Sergeant

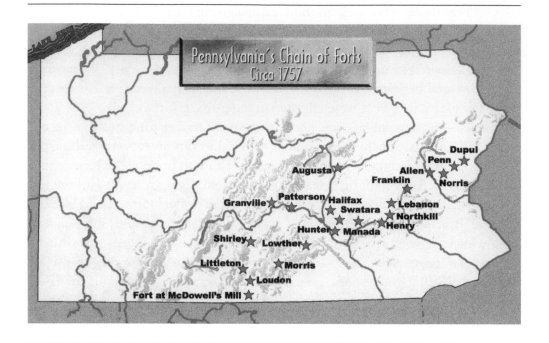

several capacities.   In British mainline regiments (for example, Braddock's army), colonials filled out strengths by enlisting as regular soldiers. In addition, they served in militia companies initially formed under the 1755 act and later the 1757 act. They also served as members of provincial regiments and as Associators, which fed soldiers into all these various military units. In short, in the French and Indian War Pennsylvanians took up an active role in participating in the defense of the Commonwealth.

Pennsylvania troops were almost immediately pressed into building and garrisoning facilities because, by the early part of 1756, the frontier fort system had essentially been completed, all along the Blue Mountain line. This at least gave the Commonwealth a static means of defense against French and Indian incursions.

By spring of the same year, troops were available to man the fortifications. Initially, one battalion was headquartered at Fort Augusta, and two battalions of the Pennsylvania Regiment were given specified geographical responsibilities.   The first battalion had the preponderance of posts east of the Susquehanna River, and the second was responsible for the fortifications west

Thomas L. Stout, a member of the Pennsylvania Army National Guard, while doing research at the Historical Society of Berks County.

of the river.

The static defense provided by this system could blunt but not permanently end French and Indian advances. The folly of depending on a lightly garrisoned line became obvious by the summer of 1756. In July of that year, a French and Indian force led by the Delaware war chief Captain Jacobs laid siege to Fort Granville and on July 30 took the fort. Thirty-one inhabitants, including five or six children, were taken prisoner, and the fort was burned. Among the dead was Lieutenant Edward Armstrong, whose brother, Lieutenant Colonel John Armstrong, commanded the second battalion's companies west of the Susquehanna.

The fall of Fort Granville was a psychological blow for the Commonwealth, for it showed that the emerging initiatives on defense were not sufficient. This disaster resulted in the natural charges and countercharges from those seeking to fix responsibility, but far more important than pinning blame was the need for Pennsylvania to stage a counterblow. Indeed, a plan for doing that existed. In June 1756, Lieutenant Colonel John Armstrong from Carlisle had proposed to the governor to organize an expedition for an attack on the Delaware settlements along the Allegheny River at Kittanning and at Chinclackmoose on the Western Branch of the Susquehanna.[29] Approval was received from Morris on July 31, a day after the fall of Fort Granville, but poor communications meant that when this approval was given, news of the disaster still had not reached the governor.

Kittanning was a significant objective for several reasons. It was not only a center of Delaware strength, it was also a location where the Delaware housed captives, including those taken at Fort Granville. In addition, this village served as the major base in western Pennsylvania for staging raids on forts and settlements along the frontier. To accomplish the destruction of the Delaware stronghold, Armstrong formed a special task force out of his battalion (while half stayed behind to garrison the forts). The task force, consisting of between 250 and 300 men, used Fort Shirley (now Shirleysburg) as a base. They left in two phases beginning on August 29-30. The two groups joined together near Hollidaysburg and reached the vicinity of Kittanning on September 7. It was fortunate that the expedition was organized and executed at this time and place, because Indians captured on that date informed Armstrong that within a few days a French and Indian raiding party was to

[29] A good summary of John Armstrong's service during this period can be found in J. W. Kings' "Colonel John Armstrong: His Place in the History of Southwestern Pennsylvania," *Western Pennsylvania Historical Magazine*, vol. 10 (1927), pp. 129-145.

attack Fort Shirley.

The attack on Kittanning began in the early morning of September 8. Kittanning was not one large village but rather a series of settlements, and Armstrong's attack focused on the main settlement where Captain Jacob's home was located. By noon the battle was over, and Captain Jacobs and about 40 Indians were dead. In addition, eleven prisoners were liberated, and stockpiles of supplies and ammunition, the logistical base for Delaware raids, were destroyed. However, the raid by no means meant the end of the Delaware threat in western Pennsylvania. Abandoning Kittanning, the Delawares moved their main settlement further west to Logstown, which placed them under the protective umbrella of the French at Fort Duquesne.[30]

Because French presence remained in the Ohio region and western Pennsylvania, French and Indian raids would continue to devastate portions of western Pennsylvania. Still, Armstrong's raid was important. For morale purposes it was a tremendous success, boosting spirits throughout the frontier and even resulting in Philadelphia striking a commemorative silver coin recognizing Armstrong's victory.[31] Most significant for the history of the Pennsylvania National Guard, Armstrong's raid was the first successful military expedition mounted by Pennsylvania, using Pennsylvania troops under the command of a Pennsylvanian. In short, with Kittanning the long tradition of military prowess by Pennsylvanians began to emerge.

Even though the raid against Kittanning was a clear victory for British America in general and the Commonwealth in particular, the major irritant that had caused the war on the frontier to erupt remained. As long as France sought to control the Ohio River Valley, peace would remain elusive. Indeed, French presence in the region was assured as long as Fort Duquesne remained in French hands. This became obvious in the spring and summer of 1757 when Indians, inspired by the French, again began their raids across the Commonwealth's frontier. These raids forced the three battalions of Pennsylvania troops to again attempt to stem the tide with their prepared defenses.[32] Peace in west-

---

[30] For an excellent account of the raid on Kittanning, see William A. Hunter, "Victory at Kittanning," *Pennsylvania History: Quarterly Journal of the Pennsylvania Historical Association*, vol. 23, no. 3 (1956), pp. 376-407.

[31] According to an article in the February 17, 1757, *Pennsylvania Gazette*, Colonel Armstrong was told "the corporation of the City of Philadelphia greatly approve your conduct and publick Spirit in the late expedition against the Town of Kittanning, and are highly pleased with the signal Proofs of Courage and personal br[av]ery given by you, and the Officers and soldiers in your command in the Demolishing of that place. I am therefore ordered ... by the corporation to present you with a Piece of Plate and a Silver Medal and each of your commissioned officers with a medal."

ern Pennsylvania could only come through a successful expedition against Fort Duquesne and the eradication of French influence in the Ohio Valley.

Fortunes for British America began to rapidly improve in 1757 as a result of new leadership in London. In late 1757, William Pitt became First Minister and tackled the problem of Britain's poor wartime performance with characteristic energy and enthusiasm. Pitt's influence was felt almost immediately in military affairs. With the assistance of his military advisor, General Sir John Ligonier, who had long experience as a British soldier, Pitt developed plans to take British America out of the defensive mode. He devised an aggressive strategy to destroy French ambitions in North America. It called for British expeditions to strike three major centers of French strength: Louisbourg, at the mouth of the St. Lawrence River; Fort Ticonderoga, on Lake Champlain; and most important for this narrative, Fort Duquesne. Given past experience, to successfully contest the French presence at Fort Duquesne, British reinforcements would have to be committed. The task of taking Fort Duquesne was given to Brigadier General (in North America) John Forbes, a Scot and a competent professional who had Ligonier's confidence as a result of having served on his staff. Forbes arrived in Philadelphia in April 1758 and immediately began to plan his operation. As a basic strategy, Forbes planned to use what was known as a "protected advance."[33] This concept required a deliberate advance into enemy country, leaving nothing to chance and consolidating gains by periodically building posts and supply depots at appropriate intervals.

Although this was an agonizingly slow strategy, it meant the French would face a well-supplied and properly reinforced column when it eventually reached Fort Duquesne. The route of advance was carefully chosen to make the most effective use of this strategy. Initially, Forbes planned to proceed from Carlisle and pick up the old Braddock Road which would take him to the French fort. After consultation with some of his engineers and officers, however, he decided to abandon the Braddock route and take the old Raystown Indian path. This path would take him through some fairly rugged terrain but would save him 40 miles and provide excellent forage for his animals.

To accomplish his assigned mission of taking Fort Duquesne, Forbes had more than ample forces. He was able to field an expeditionary force that

[32] For British America the situation was even worse. Pennsylvania had to contend with French-inspired raids – "petits guerres" (little wars) – by Indian forces. Along the Canadian border, sieges and battles were fought with some unsatisfactory results in the early part of the war. For example, in 1756 Oswego fell to the French, and in July 1757 Fort William Henry followed.

[33] This concept was outlined in a 1754 book entitled *Essai sur l'Art de la Guerre*, or *Essay on the Art of War*, written by Lancelot, Comte Turpin de Crissé.

was roughly twice the size of Braddock's ill-fated army, at least in part due to participation by Commonwealth troops. His army consisted of about 1,300 men of the First Highland Regiment, several companies from the First Battalion of the Royal American Regiment (commanded by Colonel Henry Bouquet); the Pennsylvania Regiment, consisting of three battalions; and two Virginia regiments. In addition, 40 artillerymen from the Royal Regiment of Artillery and various militia detachments from Maryland, Delaware and North Carolina were included.

The change in the political climate in Pennsylvania allowed for a much stronger level of popular and legislative support for the Forbes expedition, compared with that afforded Braddock. With Quaker obstruction no longer present in the Assembly, the new governor of the Commonwealth, William Denny, who was also an army officer, offered to raise a force of close to 3,000 men to properly contribute Pennsylvania's share of support for the expedition. In addition, to adequately supply and pay this force, the Assembly voted to appropriate £100,000 for the king's use. All of this was in sharp contrast to previous attempts, prior to 1756, to organize and finance military operations.

The various elements of the expeditionary force gathered in Carlisle in late May 1758. Two Pennsylvania battalions, one commanded by Lieutenant Colonel John Armstrong, hero of Kittanning, and the other by Lieutenant Colonel James Burd, joined the royal forces nominally commanded by John Forbes but actually led by Colonel Henry Bouquet. Forbes, though a competent and professional soldier, was relegated by personal circumstances to the role of expedition planner and organizer, while Bouquet served as actual commander in the field. Forbes would have preferred a more active role, but he was prevented by ill health from the beginning of the campaign. That this illness was serious is now obvious because, after returning to Philadelphia in early 1759, he died that spring.

The tasks facing Bouquet were daunting because he was responsible for taking a French stronghold that had already destroyed the career and life of one royal officer, General Braddock. In addition, the troops at his disposal were not prepared for the task. They were in dire need of training. The Americans were particularly a problem. Bouquet, a European officer who had fought in previous continental wars, found the American troops poorly armed and lacking in experience. Consequently, despite having the luxury of a relatively large force, he could not depart from Carlisle until arms were issued and some of the troops provided with rudimentary training. It was not until late June that Bouquet left Carlisle and led the first elements of the army westward. They

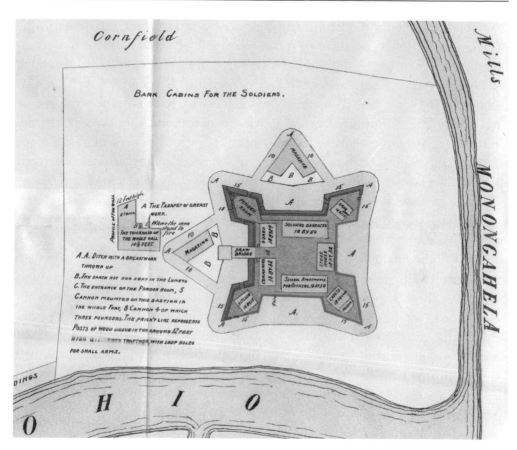

Fort Duquesne in 1754, as depicted in George Dallas Albert's *The Frontier Forts of Western Pennsylvania.*

pushed ahead about 80 miles to Raystown where, according to the strategy selected by Forbes, they began building Fort Bedford. Bouquet had gathered a substantial number of wagons and horses to haul the supplies westward for the meticulous, well-supplied advance. With a first fort — actually a strongpoint — completed in late July, Bouquet sent 1,200 soldiers into the Allegheny Mountains. Their mission was to begin the task of building Forbes Road, which was to take them to the gates of Fort Duquesne. The mountains and heavy forests made this a daunting task, but by September 3 part of the force had reached Loyalhanna, which placed them within 50 miles of Fort Duquesne. Here again they built a fortified camp with ample storehouses, surrounded by a stockaded fort. This fort was later named Fort Ligonier, after General John

Ligonier, Pitt's commander in chief and military advisor.

     To this point, the British had followed the strategy of their command-
er very closely, being attentive to the requirement of building forts and assuring the existence of adequate supplies. Now, however, so close to the goal,
Bouquet became either careless or overconfident. On September 9 he sent
Major James Grant and 850 soldiers to conduct a reconnaissance-in-force of
Fort Duquesne. Purportedly, Grant was to determine the strength of the
French fort, attempt to take some prisoners and, with the presence of a force
of this size, deter any French raids against Ligonier. The missions were not
illogical, but in many respects the force itself was – far too large for a reconnaissance mission but not large enough to properly defend itself from a determined attack should the French decide to contest this intrusion so close to their
major fortress.[34]

     On the final heights before Fort Duquesne, Grant and his soldiers were
surrounded. Altogether his force suffered about 300 casualties, and Grant too
became a French prisoner. The remainder of his troops retreated to
Loyalhanna. Forbes properly reprimanded Bouquet for jeopardizing the success of the expedition through this foray. If there was any reason for Pennsylvanians to feel fortunate about this near-disaster, it was because the 300
Pennsylvanians with Grant's reconnaissance force were not among the casualties. They sensed that something was wrong, pulled back before the envelop-
ment was complete, and thus survived.

     Despite this French success, the commander of Fort Duquesne,
Francois-Marie le Marchand, had good reason to be concerned. The "protected advance" adopted by Forbes was the tactic he could least afford to counter.
While he was faced by a well-organized and well-supplied attacking army, the
French logistical system, never the strongest, was eroding. French sources of
strength in New France were in Canada and the Illinois-Louisiana area. The
most logical supply line, and the shortest, came from the Canada-Great Lakes
region. Pitt's strategy dramatically affected this area, for it called for an advance
in three prongs, two of them focused on Canada. At the same time that Forbes

---

[34] An account of the period has Major Grant doing much more than scouting and deterring a
French attack. According to a report written in Annapolis on October 5, 1756, Grant believed
there were only 200 men in the fort, including Indian allies. Grant sought to draw the soldiers
out of the fort and ambush them. Although he drew them out, it was a larger force than anticipated, which led to his defeat. John B. Linn and William H. Egle, *Pennsylvania Archives: Papers
Relating to the French Occupation in Western Pennsylvania, 1631-1764*, second series, vol. VI
(Harrisburg: State Printer, 1891), pp. 453-454. Cited hereafter as Linn and Egle, *Papers Relating
to the French Occupation*.

was advancing westward, the British took Fort Frontenac (now Kingston, Ontario). At Frontenac the British destroyed a substantial French supply depot, along with military stores that could not be immediately replaced. Thus, while the British supply and communication systems were improving, the French ability to sustain its force was withering, with no real prospects for recovery.

The mounting strength of the British was evident to both the French and their Indian allies. The situation was made even more serious by non-military initiatives, run through non-governmental auspices, to woo the Indians away from the French and return them to their earlier allegiance to the British Crown. During the summer, diplomatic efforts were initiated through a respected Quaker, Israel Pemberton Jr., with the full support and encouragement of General Forbes. Pemberton's task was to reestablish friendly relations with the western Indians and attempt to separate them from their allegiance to the French. Christian Frederic Post, a Moravian missionary, was recruited to support this effort by carrying messages of friendship and a desire for peace from Governor Denny and General Forbes to the Ohio Valley tribes.[35]

With the good services of these two Pennsylvanians – whose religious beliefs prevented them from assisting the Commonwealth in any other way but diplomacy – formal negotiations were initiated with the western tribes. Taking part were the governors of New Jersey and Pennsylvania, George Croghan and Conrad Weiser, and a group called The Friendly Association for Regaining and Preserving Peace with the Indians by Pacific Measures. Their efforts resulted in the Treaty of Easton, negotiated October 8-26, 1758. This treaty pacified the Indians for a time by ceding back to them a considerable amount of the territory drained by the Ohio River system. Through this and other promises, the Ohio Valley tribes were effectively separated from the French.

The French recognized the gravity of the rapidly developing situation, and as the British diplomatic initiatives were proceeding, they advanced on Loyalhanna on October 12. With about 600 French and Indian troops, the French hoped to stage a raid that would pose a serious enough threat to delay any further British military advance until spring. If this were successful, the lull might give the French time to rebuild their tattered logistical base and prepare for the British attack on Fort Duquesne, which would certainly occur in the

---

[35] The mission of Christian Frederic Post is a fascinating story. Taking wampum, messages from the governor and copies of treaties with Tedyuskung, the Delaware king, Post – who had lived 17 years among the Indians – worked among them and succeeded in setting up a council meeting in October 1758. The French watched and attempted to entrap him, but through his efforts the loyalty of Indians to the French cause was severed.

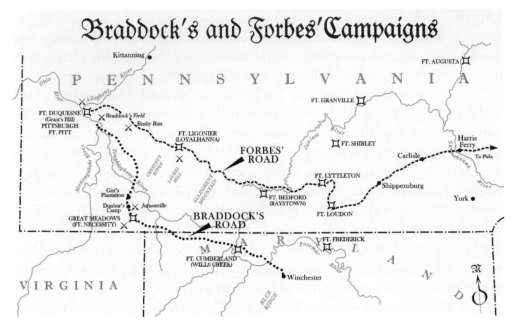

Braddock's and Forbes' Campaigns

The Forbes and Braddock campaigns against Fort Dusquene, from *Guns at the Forks*, by Walter O'Meara, ©1979 (map by Jim Kistler).

spring. When the French appeared, Colonel Bouquet was not at Loyalhanna because he was leading yet another reconnaissance force. As a result, Colonel Burd took charge of the defense. The engagement lasted a total of three hours, and once again the performance of British forces left something to be desired. The British lost 12 killed, 18 wounded and 31 missing, and most of their horses were driven off. The French reported only two killed and seven wounded and could claim some measure of success because they forced the British to retire from the field and seek refuge in their prepared defenses. Both Bouquet and Forbes were highly displeased that their superior force had been badly handled by a numerically inferior French expedition.

The French plan, however, was unsuccessful. Rather than wait for the spring and summer campaigning season, the British decided to act. Key in this decision was the presence of General Forbes. Enduring considerable personal discomfort, the ailing Forbes reached Loyalhanna on November 2. On November 11 a council of war was held, and it was decided that the campaign was over until spring. On November 12, however, when the interrogation of a prisoner revealed that the French garrison had shrunk considerably, as it usually did in the winter months, the decision was reversed. Forbes decided to push ahead, even though winter was rapidly approaching. Although there were still 50 miles of road to be built, Forbes began moving a 2,500-man force, complete with artillery, toward the French fort. By November 24, the British reached Turtle Creek. At this point they heard large explosions. Scouts were sent out, and when they returned they reported that Fort Duquesne was burning. Forbes reached the fort on November 25, finding only the smoldering remains of the once powerful French fortress. Duquesne had been abandoned by the French, who realized they did not have the resources to hold it.[36]

Forbes and his troops remained for a brief period at Fort Duquesne but then left for Philadelphia. But the site, long coveted by both the French and the British, was not abandoned, despite the coming of winter and the lack of suitable shelter. Colonel Hugh Mercer and 200 troops were left behind to guard the forks of the Ohio so that in the spring a new fort, which Forbes named Pittsburgh, could be constructed. The main body of British troops withdrew for the winter, establishing themselves in prepared strongpoints such as Fort Ligonier.[37] A stockade, appropriately named Mercer's Fort, was thrown up by January 1759, but it was a temporary expedient. A new fort would have to be built to guard the critical juncture of the river.

Forbes, commander of this successful expedition, undertook the journey back to Philadelphia. The trip took 43 days and was likely the final straw for his precarious health. Forbes died in Philadelphia in March 1759. His successor in command was Brigadier General John Stanwix.

Without the French presence at Fort Duquesne, the frontier was much safer. However, the Seven Years War lasted until 1763, and neither French nor Indian threats were completely over, despite military successes and the mission of Frederic Post. The French still held Fort Machault (now Franklin, Pennsylvania) and from this base could stage another expedition down the Allegheny to Mercer's Fort. The potential attack never occurred, but only good fortune prevented it. The French did in fact mount an expedition to regain their lost ground. This expedition, sent in the spring of 1759, consisted of 700 soldiers,

[36] Forbes sent a glowing report from the site of Fort Duquesne (in his own words "now Pittsburg") to Governor Denny, dated November 26, 1758, in which he claimed "success of his Majesty's Troops over all his Enemies on the Ohio, by having obliged them to Burn and abandon their Fort Duquesne," though he also noted "the Enemy having made their escape down the River part in boats and part by Land." Linn and Egle, *Papers Relating to the French Occupation*, pp. 457-458.

[37] Colonel Mercer's task was a difficult one. He had a limited force, and furthermore, both the French and the Indians remained a threat. In addition, winter had set in, supplies were limited and initially there were no fortifications. To make matters even worse, at the outset his men had the unpleasant task of cleaning up the scattered and mutilated bodies at Grant's Hill.

complete with artillery, and 800 still-loyal Indians. It reached the vicinity of Pittsburgh but was called back to assist with the defense of Fort Niagara. On the banks of the Niagara River, the expedition took substantial casualties in action against British troops, and it was never reconstituted for the retaking of the forks. The French subsequently began their withdrawal from the Ohio River area.

Taking into consideration the potential of the French and their remaining allies to retake this critical terrain, William Pitt ordered the construction of Fort Pitt, which would become the largest and most elaborate fortress in British North America. Fort Pitt, a well-designed and well-constructed five-sided fortress, was an 18-acre facility that dwarfed both of its predecessors, Fort Duquesne and Fort Mercer. Although it was never tested by a French assault and was in many ways unnecessary by the time of its completion, it accomplished one very important thing. It underscored the determination of the British to hold the critical juncture of the Ohio and maintain the safety of the citizenry in the western part of the Commonwealth.

The Seven Years War would not be officially over until the signing of the Treaty of Paris in 1763, but for all practical purposes the French threat to Pennsylvania virtually disappeared after 1760. The fall of Fort Niagara and Quebec in 1759 and the fall of Montreal the next year doomed New France. But while the French threat had ended, hostile actions against the Commonwealth had not. The Indian population of western Pennsylvania had one additional campaign to wage.

Although the Delaware had agreed to peaceably settle their differences with the English, the westward expansion of British America almost immediately began unraveling both the diplomacy of Frederic Post and the agreements made at the Treaty of Easton by George Croghan and Conrad Weiser in 1758. Through this treaty, Pennsylvania had relinquished claim to a substantial block of land in the Ohio River region, at least on paper returning it to Indian control. This agreement removed a major irritant between the tribes and British America: the relentless westward march of the settlers, with their insatiable appetite for Indian land. Once the French threat faded in 1760, settlers began to move back into these lands. In addition, the British presence in the former French forts, plus their desire to build additional military facilities in the area drained by the Ohio River system, caused considerable disillusionment among the Delaware.

The bitterness harbored by the Delaware resided not only in the Ohio Valley but also among Indians in the Great Lakes region, who had just lost their chief European ally, the French. The catalyst for an Indian war came through the activities of a charismatic Ottawa chief named Pontiac. Beginning in the early 1760s, Pontiac urged the Ohio Valley tribes to join in a war against the British settlers – the hated enemy who consistently broke agreements, sold Indian land and destroyed the Indian way of life. While the Ottawa were not native to the Commonwealth, Guyasuta and Custaloga, Seneca and Delaware chiefs who answered Pontiac's call, lived in the Ohio Valley areas of the Commonwealth.

In early May 1763 the Indians struck across the frontier. In rapid succession, Fort Presqu'Isle (present-day Erie), Fort le Boeuf (Waterford) and Fort Venango (Franklin), all held by small garrisons, fell to marauding Indian bands.

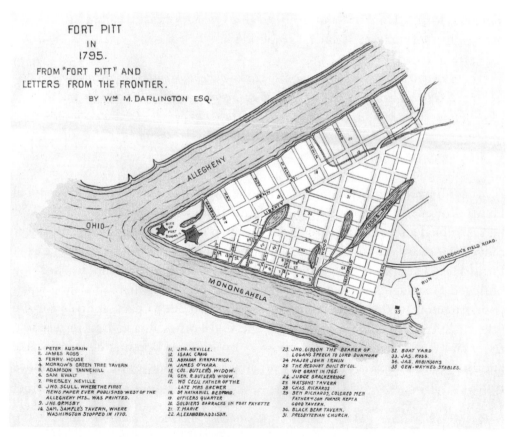

Map showing the location of Fort Duquesne and Fort Pitt at the confluence of the Allegheny and Monongahela Rivers, as depicted in George Dallas Albert's *The Frontier Forts of Western Pennsylvania.*

In addition, Forts Pitt, Ligonier and Bedford were under siege, and Fort Augusta seemed close to falling. Within a month of the initial attack, Indian war parties were again active as far east as Cumberland County. Key to holding western Pennsylvania was retaining control of Fort Pitt, garrisoned by just 125 soldiers under the command of Captain Simeon Ecuyer of the Royal American Regiment. To complicate problems for the defenders, once Indian attacks began, close to 600 refugees crowded into the protective environment offered by this modern fortification. A relief force had to be organized.

The commander in chief of British forces in North America was Sir Jeffery Amherst. To meet the rapidly developing crisis, Sir Jeffery wanted Pennsylvania to raise troops to turn back the Indian tide and asked Governor James Hamilton to provide the Crown with 1,000 soldiers. The Assembly, however, no longer under Quaker control, responded with a bill to provide 700 soldiers not for the king's use but, to borrow a Quaker phrase, to guard their own homes. In exasperation, Amherst responded:

> *I cannot help repeating my surprise at the infatuation of the people in your province, who tamely look on while their brethren are being butchered by the savages, when without doubt, it is in their power by exerting the proper spirit not only to protect the settlements, but to punish the Indians that are hardy enough to disturb them.*[38]

The relief mission for the frontier was ultimately given to Colonel Henry Bouquet.[39] Receiving little assistance from Pennsylvanians, east or west, he assembled a force of about 500 men, drawn from three regiments. Bouquet moved westward on July 19, 1763, with both supplies and troops to relieve Fort Pitt. He picked up a few additional men at Fort Bedford and reached the besieged Fort Ligonier on August 2, relieving the troops there at a time when their situation was perilous. Shifting the supply train to pack animals for the sake of speed, his force moved along the Old Forbes Road. Before reaching the vicinity of the abandoned outpost at Bushy Run, Bouquet elected to take another route in hopes of avoiding an attack by Indians aware of his advance route.

[38] *Pennsylvania Archives: Colonial Records of Pennsylvania, Minutes of the Provincial Council of Pennsylvania from Organization to the Termination of the Proprietary Government*, vol. I (Philadelphia: Joseph Severns and Co., 1852), p. 62.
[39] A good survey of Bouquet's life can be found in Donald H. Kent's "Henry Bouquet," *American Heritage*, vol. 4, no. 3 (1952-53), pp. 43, and Douglas E. Branch, "Henry Bouquet: Professional Soldier," *Pennsylvania Magazine of History and Biography*, vol. LXII (1939), pp. 41-51.

This tactic proved unsuccessful, for on August 5 at Edge Hill, near Bushy Run, a well-prepared force of Indians ambushed Bouquet. The engagement began around noon and lasted into the evening, with attack and counterattack occurring on several occasions. Being under fire, the British troops could not shift their positions and find favorable defensive terrain, nor could they, in the hot August sun, find a source of water. While Bushy Run could have been a replay of the fate which befell Braddock's force, Bouquet's troops met the challenge with discipline and courage. Casualties were significant, but officers and men performed admirably. When evening came, Bouquet moved among his men, encouraging them to resist to the end of their resources. On the morning of the 6th, the Indians moved in for what they thought was the final attack. At this juncture Bouquet demonstrated his ability as a tactician. Once the Indian attack started, two of his companies feigned a retreat. When the Indians rushed in to follow up on what they saw as their success, they were met by organized fire on both sides and a reserve force which blocked their advance. Following this carefully planned ruse, a bayonet charge broke their attack, and the Indians fled the field in defeat. Although he suffered more than 100 casualties, roughly a fifth of his force, Bouquet successfully reached and relieved Fort Pitt on August 10.[40]

The war against the Indians did not end in 1763 with the Treaty of Paris, but continued into 1764. In the concluding campaigns, Bouquet again made his presence felt. Basing himself in Carlisle, he led additional forays against the Indians. In October 1764 his campaigns extended into the Ohio Valley, where he campaigned along the Muskingum River.[41] For the Commonwealth, however, the greatest impact he had on the war remained the stunning victory at Bushy Run.

It is appropriate to reflect on the significance of the period 1754-1763 for the Commonwealth and its nascent military forces. Pennsylvania had begun these troubled years without a militia law and with only scattered and minimally trained Associator units to defend its citizenry. This years from 1754 to 1763, however, saw an almost uninterrupted demand for defense along the frontier, against both the French and their Indian allies. Threats posed by both meant that Quaker obstructionism on defense matters – a phenomenon for almost 75

---

[40] See Niles Anderson, "Bushy Run: Decisive Battle in the Wilderness," *Western Pennsylvania Historical Magazine*, vol. 46 (1963), pp. 211-245.
[41] An interesting source available on this expedition is Edward G. Williams' "The Orderly Book of Colonel Henry Bouquet's Expedition against the Ohio Indians," *Western Pennsylvania Historical Magazine*, vol. 43 (1959), pp. 179-206, 283-302.

years – would likely come to an end, one way or another. The Crown could ill afford to have a colony as large and strategically positioned as Pennsylvania contributing so minimally to the defense of British America.

Leaders within the Commonwealth, including some Quakers, recognized the gravity of the situation. As a result, in the mid-1750s long-sought changes regarding military matters occurred. For the remainder of the Seven Years War, Pennsylvania would be a full participant in the defense of the New World. Although squabbles would continue between the populous east and the frontier and between the proprietor and the citizens of the Commonwealth, the decades of the 1740s and 1750s brought about substantial changes in the Commonwealth. In this period of political and military tribulation, the origins of Pennsylvania's military tradition began.

CHAPTER 5

The Interwar Years

Our frontier people are yet greater barbarians than the
Indians and continue to murder them in time of peace.

— Benjamin Franklin, 1764

For Pennsylvania, the period after the conclusion of the Seven Years War was a time of relative peace. During the first part of this period, the Commonwealth was governed by John Penn (1763-1771), son of Richard Penn and grandson of the Commonwealth's founder. Pennsylvania was, however, a colony on the edge of the frontier, and its relative peace was interrupted by several contingencies that required the use of military force. Indeed, among the years that passed between the end of the French and Indian War in 1763 and the beginning of the American Revolution in 1774, only a few passed without at least limited military activity. These actions centered on three issues: finishing Pennsylvania's wars with the Indians along the frontier; suppressing civil disorder within the Commonwealth; and resolving conflicting claims by other colonies to Commonwealth land. Each of these issues posed significant difficulties, because the legislation authorizing the creation of a militia, passed during the Seven Years War, had expired.[1]

An initial problem facing the post-war Commonwealth, a least in the eyes of many frontier inhabitants, was the Indian population. Although the French and their Indian allies had been defeated in 1763, some of the tribes that had aggressively supported the French throughout the war were still present in the Commonwealth. Worse yet, they seemed unrepentant. The British government was also concerned about the danger from Indians and, like the fron-

---

[1] Pennsylvania's first functional militia act, passed in 1757, expired with the end of the French and Indian War. See *Statutes at Large of Pennsylvania, 1682-1801*, vol. V, 1744-1759 (Harrisburg: State Printer, 1898), p. 609. The reader should remember, however, that the Commonwealth could still raise and fund provincial troops to support the general defense, and it could allow the creation of Associator units. Pennsylvania was thus not defenseless.

tier population, was determined to wage war against them. The British desire to continue this campaign had, during the Pontiac rebellion, resulted in a request for 1,000 troops from the Commonwealth. With diminished Quaker influence, the Assembly supported plans to field additional troops but bickered with the royal government about how they would be employed. Plans to raise troops also caused the Assembly to run afoul of the proprietary interests.

Throughout the greater part of the 18th century, the proprietor had carefully monitored the status of revenue-producing bills introduced into the Assembly, because of the Penn family's substantial holdings throughout the Commonwealth. Acts requiring any new revenue-generating measures meant that the proprietor, without a specific exemption, could likely be required to provide a healthy sum in taxes. In the 1760s proposals to levy taxes did not result in bitter standoffs between the supporters of proprietary interests and those who opposed them, as they had in the early 1700s. In 1763 the Assembly reached a compromise on the taxation issue. Before it did so, however, a resolution was passed condemning the proprietor, essentially for his conflict of interest on the issue.

That the concern over Pennsylvania's Indians, together with the requirement to suppress the ongoing Pontiac rebellion, caused Pennsylvania to maintain troops past the 1763 Peace of Paris is evident through records of that period. They show, for example, that Colonel James Burd's company was on garrison duty and being paid by the Commonwealth at Fort Augusta from November 1, 1763 until June 1, 1764.[2] Troops commanded by Major Asher Clayton were posted on the frontiers of Lancaster, Berks and Northampton counties (with some of his command at Fort Henry) as late as June 1, 1764.[3] Mentioned as well in colonial records are three companies on the northern frontier, commanded by Captains John Little, George Miller and Samuel Postlewaite, all of which were in existence as late as October 2, 1764.[4]

For some citizens, however, these scattered military units were insufficient to provide security for Pennsylvania. In the 1750s citizens living on the frontier had come to feel that settled, "civilized" easterners had not shown enough interest in the frontier's defense nor had they realized the seriousness of the threat posed by the Indians. All too often, in the opinion of the fron-

---

[2] Thomas Lynch Montgomery, ed., *Pennsylvania Archives: Officers and Soldiers in the Service of the Province of Pennsylvania, 1744-1765*, fifth series, vol. I (Harrisburg: Harrisburg Publishing Co., 1906), p. 326.

[3] Ibid., p. 334-338.

[4] Ibid., p. 338.

tier citizenry, laws enacted represented the interests of easterners or people of wealth. Anger was also directed against the Quakers, who had consistently resisted any attempts to pass defense legislation.[5] The resentment of two decades of frustration erupted into anger when representatives from the frontier pleaded with the Assembly, during the Pontiac War, to provide for their defense.[6]

Since many on the frontier felt that apathy and inaction were consistently the Assembly's response, in the wake of the Pontiac War some frontiersmen decided to act on their own. They felt that the Indians – even the settled and often christianized ones – were simply not trustworthy and would have to be evicted in order to assure peace for the Commonwealth.

The ire of the citizenry was particularly directed against the Moravian Indians and those at Conestoga, Pennsylvania, who purportedly had aided hostile Indians during the French and Indian War or were guilty of complicity in some of the raids during the Pontiac War.[7] In December 1763, Matthew Smith and some associates in the Paxton area decided to investigate reports of hostile Indians around Conestoga. He and a group of about 50 men advanced on Conestoga and killed six Indians, even though their intentions had not yet been determined. At the end of December, Smith and his supporters raided a Lancaster workhouse, where the 14 survivors from the Conestoga settlement had been housed for their protection by sympathetic settlers, and killed them all. These irregulars, called the Paxtang or Paxton Boys, attacked defenseless Conestoga Indians in what amounted to outright murder. To many frontiersmen, however, the Paxton Boys were regarded as heroes. Elements in the fron-

---

[5] Hugh Williamson, writing at the time, perhaps summed up the feelings of many when he stated, "For God's sake, are we always to be slaves, must we groan forever beneath the yoke of three Quaker counties?" Hugh Williamson, *The Plain Dealer or Remarks on Quaker Politicks in Pennsylvania* (Philadelphia: 1764), p. 22.

[6] As was too often the case in American politics, policy toward the Indians was mired in conflicting interests. The governor, for example, sought to meet royal requests for troops, which would seem a much easier task with diminished Quaker influence. The Assembly, however, used the British request for 1,000 troops to bargain with the proprietor for the ability to tax proprietary estates. The Quakers sought to promote better relations with the Indians by gifts and basic kindness, but the Indians were under relentless pressure by settlers who were constantly seizing their traditional lands. Finally, the settlers sought protection from the Indians whose lands and interests they were violating. See Brook Hindle, "The March of the Paxton Boys," *William and Mary Quarterly*, vol. 3 (1946), pp. 463-464. Cited hereafter as Hindle, "The March of the Paxton Boys."

[7] The feelings toward the Indians are reported in John W. Jordan, "Biographical Sketch of Reverend Bernhard Adam Grube," *Pennsylvania Magazine of History and Biography*, vol. XXV (1901), p. 17. Cited hereafter as Jordan, "Biographical Sketch of Reverend Grube."

tier communities felt these irregulars were finally settling what they perceived as the Indian problem – a defense issue that neither the Crown nor the proprietary government had been willing or able to address.

The Paxton Boys' activities, however, caused a furor in Philadelphia among those in the Assembly who were either sympathetic to the Indians' plight or found the raids of the Paxton Boys to be little different from those of the hostile natives. The Assembly finally authorized the 1,000 soldiers previously requested by General Jeffrey Amherst, and the governor set about the task of suppressing the Paxton Boys – whose activities were, in his opinion, tantamount to an insurrection.

In so doing, he faced a major problem. Since Pennsylvania was without a militia law, it had no official way to raise troops. Acting with the strong support of the proprietor, John Penn, Benjamin Franklin called for the Assembly to pass a new militia law. When this did not happen, Franklin used the only logical option: he called for a new Association.[8] The citizens in the eastern areas responded, and before the Paxton episode was over, about 1,000 citizens joined the Associators. They were subsequently organized into six companies of foot, two companies of horse and one artillery battery.[9]

It did not prove necessary, however, to use these newly organized troops against their frontier counterparts. The Paxton Boys staged their final foray by planning a raid on Philadelphia. Their purpose was to dispose of a group of Indians being held there in protective custody.[10] Hoping to avert a

---

[8] What was happening to the Indians was of great concern to Benjamin Franklin. He wrote a letter to Richard Jackson, a member of the British Parliament, stating, "The spirit of killing Indians, Friends and Foes, spread amazingly thro' the whole Country. The Action was almost universally approved by the common People; and the Rioters thence receiv'd such Encouragement, that they projected coming down to this City, 1000 in Number, arm'd to destroy 140 Moravian and Quaker Indians under Protection of the Government." He counted the willingness of some of the citizens of Philadelphia to take up arms as critical, saying, "the Fighting Face we put on made them more willing to hear Reason." Benjamin Franklin in a letter to Richard Jackson, January 16, 1764, as reproduced in Thomas Fleming, ed., *Benjamin Franklin: A Biography in His Own Words* (New York: Harper and Row, 1943), pp. 182-183. See also *The Pennsylvania Gazette*, February 9, 1764.

[9] As reported in *The Pennsylvania Gazette*, February 9, 1764. Franklin said he took this action because "I formed an Association at the Governor's request ... we having no Militia." See also Carl Van Doren, ed., *Franklin's Autobiographical Writings* (New York: Viking Press, 1945), p. 149.

[10] Various threatened Indian groups had been moved from place to place during this troubled period; some were saved from their tormentors, others unfortunately were not. Consistently, the safety of the friendly or christianized Indians was championed by both Franklin and the Quakers, who abhorred the actions of the Paxton Boys. In Philadelphia the specific objective of the Paxton Boys was the group of 127 Indians who had been taken there. When the citizens of that city exhibited hostility toward them, they were moved to Province Island at the

confrontation, Franklin left Philadelphia with a small delegation and met the insurgents at Germantown. After several hours of discussion, the Paxton Boys turned back with the understanding that their grievances would be speedily heard.[11]

Although there would be later threats by Paxton forces to march on Philadelphia, the movement they represented had peaked, and the threat of insurrection passed – fortunately, without open hostilities among the people of the Commonwealth. The Paxton episode remains an interesting part of Commonwealth history. Depending on one's perspective, it represents either the end phase of the French and Indian War or the nascent beginnings of the Revolution.[12] At the very least, the march of the Paxton Boys shows the decidedly different perspectives of the frontier people and those in the cities about the effectiveness of the defense provided by the government for its citizens.

Equally intriguing about the Paxton episode is that, when insurrection faced the Commonwealth, Franklin called for a new militia act – but even though the Quaker bloc had been dismantled, parliamentary politics prevented speedy passage of such an act. With a bona fide need for a military force, Pennsylvania quickly fell back on the device of 1747, the Associators, to provide for the Commonwealth's defense. With this extralegal device, legislation did not have to be passed, and the necessary units were quickly raised and organized. The Associator tradition again proved to be flexible, acceptable to the people, and then as now, a mark of the distinctive heritage of the Commonwealth.

Since the response to the Paxton Boys had been based on the Associators and since a militia act was not in existence, when the threat of Indian attacks – real or imagined – clearly declined, there was a brief period after the mid-1760s when military units were substantially reduced in number throughout the Commonwealth. However, two disputes erupted with Pennsylvania's neighbors which marred the generally peaceful situation. The first began in early 1769 in the Wyoming Valley.

The Wyoming Valley controversy, much like a similar dispute with the Commonwealth of Virginia, is best understood by studying the map on page 107. Many of the original colonies had ill-defined western borders at best; some claimed substantial territory as far west as the Mississippi River.

mouth of the Schuylkill. See Jordan, "Biographical Sketch of Reverend Grube," p. 17.

[11] *Collections of the Historical Society of Pennsylvania*, vol. I (Philadelphia: N.P., 1853), p. 73-75.

[12] See James Kirby, "The Return of the Paxton Boys and the Historical State of Pennsylvania, 1764-1774," *Pennsylvania History: Quarterly Journal of the Pennsylvania Historical Association*, vol. 38 (1971), pp. 117-133, and Hindle, "The March of the Paxton Boys," pp. 461-486.

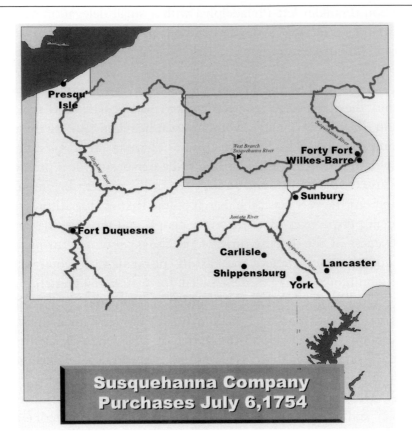

Susquehanna Company Purchases July 6, 1754

Map showing the extent of the Susquehanna Company's Wyoming Valley purchase.

Connecticut claimed considerable lands westward, with its southern boundary entering Pennsylvania in the Stroudsburg area and proceeding west through Bloomsburg, Clearfield and New Castle. In short, Connecticut claimed the northern half of the Commonwealth. Penn's charter, however, fixed the northern boundary much further north, at the 42nd degree of latitude. Conflicting claims to this area were not a problem until settlement became a realistic possibility in the 1750s.

The seeds for conflict were sown in July 1753 when a group of men met in Windham, Connecticut to organize the Susquehanna Company. Like many of Connecticut's citizens, they felt constrained by the limited land available to them and, with the consent of the colony's government, had determined to establish a settlement west of what we now recognize as Connecticut. American Indians still had active settlements in the Wyoming Valley into the

1750s, and thus it was not considered open for white settlement. At a June 1754 meeting with the Indian tribes at Albany, New York, where delegates of all of the colonies were assembled, representatives from Connecticut persuaded representatives from the Six Nations to cede a tract of land in the Commonwealth's charter to the Susquehanna Company. At another meeting in November 1768 at Fort Stanwix, New York, the Commonwealth also made agreements with the Six Nations reaffirming its claim to a substantial tract of land in present-day Pennsylvania, including the Wyoming Valley. The final irritant which set the stage for conflict occurred in December 1768, when advertisements were published in both Pennsylvania and Connecticut announcing a meeting of the Susquehanna Company in Hartford, Connecticut to discuss settlement of the area.

The desire of the citizens of both colonies to settle the area led to a series of clashes referred to as the first and second Pennamite wars.[13] Governor Penn asserted a strong claim to the region despite the aggressive claims advanced from Hartford. While attempts were begun to resolve the dispute through the political process, in December 1768 Pennsylvania sent a group of settlers into the Wyoming Valley. Led by Captain Amos Ogden, the Pennsylvanians established a settlement on Mill Creek and built a small fort or blockhouse. At virtually the same time, Connecticut sent an advance party of 40 settlers to establish a physical presence in the valley. The Connecticut group arrived on February 8, 1769, and quickly erected a small fort or blockhouse named the Forty Fort, after their number. A second and larger group of settlers sponsored by Connecticut arrived on May 12 and within a short time began establishing a permanent settlement. After some 25 cabins were constructed, this group, led by Major John Durkee, began enclosing their dwellings with a stockade. They called this fortified area Fort Durkee.

These two groups had strong bonds to their sponsoring colonies, and neither could tolerate the presence of the other. From 1769 to 1771 there occurred the First Yankee-Pennamite War, which is best described as a series of skirmishes between partisans from the two colonies. The Yankee settlers were on five separate occasions evicted from their fortifications, and in each case Pennsylvania briefly reasserted control over the Wyoming Valley. In July 1771, however, the Yankees, led by Captain Zebulon Butler and Lazarus Stewart, raised forces and moved once again to secure the Wyoming Valley for

[13] The reader should not perceive the Pennamite or Yankee-Pennamite Wars as major wars but rather as a series of skirmishes and sieges that ran intermittently from 1769 to 1784. As these were occurring, the two colonies were trying to resolve the issue through the political process.

Forty Fort, one of the fortifications built in 1770 by Connecticut settlers during the Yankee Pennamite Wars. It was purportedly named for the number of settlers that garrisoned it (from George Dallas Albert's *The Frontier Forts of Western Pennsylvania*).

Connecticut. The Pennamite adherents of the Pennsylvania cause fortified their area and named it Fort Wyoming. Besieged by the Yankees and cut off from resupply, they were literally starved out, surrendering on August 15, 1771. For the next four years the Connecticut settlers held the area and proceeded with its consolidation into Litchfield County, Connecticut. Wilkes-Barre was laid out, and five additional townships were organized, all as a part of Litchfield.

Up to this point, the skirmishes caused minimal loss of life. They resulted from the actions of pseudo-military formations or civil authorities. Leadership of both the Yankee and Pennamite factions used military rank but were not part of any officially organized military forces.[14] Pennsylvania's situation was unique because, while the proprietor had no intention of relinquishing claim to the Wyoming Valley, he did not have enough military forces on hand to firmly hold the area. Calling for a new Association was always a possibility, but it is unlikely, at this stage, that sufficient enthusiasm could have been

[14] There are, however, some intriguing exceptions. An older history of Wilkes-Barre notes that, at the onset of the controversy, "Colonel Turbut Francis, commanding a fine company from the city [Philadelphia] in full military array, with colors streaming and martial music descended into the plain and sat before Fort Durkee about June 20, 1769. Colonel Francis informed the Connecticut settlers he had orders from the Governor to remove Connecticut settlers." See Charles Minor, *History of Wyoming* (Philadelphia: J. Drissy, 1845), p. 67.

whipped up for this contingency on the frontier. Thus, much of the Pennsylvania response was actually civil, through the provisions of a Riot Act, and was carried out through the Sheriff of Northampton County, John Jennings, rather than military commanders.[15] Posses rather than militia or Associators were involved. On the Connecticut side, both Major John Durkee and Captain Zebulon Butler repeatedly led expeditions into the Wyoming Valley, but neither appears to have had any official military connections. Both languished for a period of time in irons in Philadelphia, arrested under civil provisions rather than military. Another prominent Yankee irregular in Pennsylvania records was Lazarus Stewart, who did not carry any rank but whose successful raids caused him to be sought by Pennsylvania authorities.[16]

The final phase of the First Yankee-Pennamite War occurred in 1775 when Yankee elements continued establishing settlements along the West Branch of the Susquehanna. Judge William Plunket, commandant of Fort Augusta (also referred to as Colonel Plunket), called together militia – or a posse composed of some militia – and prepared to stop the advance of settlers loyal to Connecticut.[17] Commanding a force of about 500 men, Plunket was successful in breaking up the West Branch settlements, but when he tried to take Fort Wyoming in December 1775, either the Yankee force was too strong or his military talents were insufficient. The year ended, the Revolutionary War was beginning, and partisans of the Connecticut cause were still in control of

[15] James Hamilton, lieutenant governor of the Commonwealth, as early as February 10, 1761, framed the response by expressing concern about the intrusions of Connecticut into the Wyoming Valley. He said, "I immediately dispatched the Sheriff and some of the Magistrates of that county to go thither, to warn the Intruders off, to claim those lands for our proprietaries, and fully apprize them of the mischievous Consequences that must attend their attempting to make settlements there." Even at that time the sheriff reported there were about 20 families from Connecticut settled there. George E. Reed, ed., *Pennsylvania Archives: Papers of the Governors, 1759-1785*, fourth series, vol. III (Harrisburg: State of Pennsylvania, 1900), pp. 52-54. Cited hereafter as Reed, *Papers of the Governors, 1759-1785*. On September 18, 1771, Hamilton stated that in response to the violence in the Wyoming Valley the government at great expense "Raise(d) a Sufficient Posse to enforce the Execution of the Riot Act." Ibid., pp. 229-231.

[16] Several publications on the Wyoming Valley refer to Lazarus Stewart and his "Paxtang Boys." See Frederic A. Godcharles, *Pennsylvania: Political, Governmental, Military and Civil*, military volume (New York: American Historical Society, 1933), pp. 312-314. In addition, in a proclamation on February 11, 1771, the actions of Lazarus Stewart were condemned, and it was noted he was joined by "a number of other lawless People from Hanover, in Lancaster county, and other places." Reed, *Papers of the Governors, 1759-1785*, p. 434-436.

[17] Whether this force was actually militia or a posse drawn from former militia companies is difficult to ascertain. While former militia companies existed in the area, the expiration of the militia law made it unlikely that they could be called as militia. The only legal way to field a force was through a posse or an Association.

the Wyoming Valley. The adjudication of this problem would have to await the end of the American Revolution and a second Yankee-Pennamite War.

That the Wyoming Valley remained under Connecticut's control in this critical period of American history led to a unique circumstance in the history of the Pennsylvania militia. With the Revolution rapidly approaching, on May 11, 1775, elements of the 24th Regiment, Connecticut Militia, were organized in the Wyoming Valley. When this area finally reverted to Pennsylvania's jurisdiction in 1782, the lineage of the local militia was carried into the Pennsylvania militia. As a result, today's Headquarters and Headquarters Battery, 109th Field Artillery in Wilkes-Barre traces its roots back to Connecticut's 24th Regiment.[18]

Governor John Penn wanted to resolve this intrusion from the outset but lacked military force to solidify his hold on the area. He bemoaned the absence of militia which potentially could have settled Pennsylvania's claim, but to no avail. Despite the absence of the Quakers, Pensylvanians saw no immediate need for a militia. With state resources, Penn requested the assistance of British regulars from Major General Gage to help settle the dispute. Since it was an internal matter between two colonies, Gage declined to supply troops.[19] In reality, a second reason likely prevented Gage's intervention. Records from the period indicate that Gage was having difficulties in maintaining British military forces in the colonies. This was evident as early as 1770, when the Earl of Hillsborough informed Governor Penn of the Crown's intent to augment its units with levies from the colonies and requested the assistance of the Commonwealth's government in raising the necessary recruits.[20] Of particular relevance, on November 2, 1772, Gage informed Governor Penn that royal troops were abandoning Fort Pitt, despite the concerns of Pennsylvanians that this might put them in danger. All military stores contributed to this fort by the Commonwealth were to be returned to it.[21] Thus, even if Gage had been inter-

---

[18] The Connecticut lineage is shown in the official lineage certificate of Headquarters and Headquarters Battery, 109th Field Artillery, as published by the U.S. Center of Military History. Even in the Revolutionary period, CMH shows the 24th Regiment, Connecticut Militia organized on May 11, 1775.

[19] *Pennsylvania Archives: Colonial Records of Pennsylvania, Minutes of the Provincial Council from Organization to the Termination of the Proprietary Government*, vol. IX (Harrisburg: Theo. Fenn & Co., 1852), p. 664.

[20] A letter from the Earl of Hillsborough to Governor Penn December 1, 1770, in Samuel Hazard, ed., *Pennsylvania Archives: Selected and Arranged from Original Documents in the Office of the Secretary of the Commonwealth Conformably to the Acts of the General Assembly, Commencing 1760*, vol. IV (Philadelphia: Joseph Severns and Co., 1853), p. 382. Cited hereafter as Hazard, *Pennsylvania Archives Commencing 1760*, vol. IV.

[21] Major General Gage to Governor Penn on November 2, 1772, ibid., p. 457.

ested in supporting the Commonwealth, it is unlikely that he would have supplied forces in this straincd atmosphere.

Connecticut was not the only territorial issue facing the Commonwealth. In 1774 Virginia pressed its claim to western Pennsylvania. As mentioned in the previous chapter, throughout the 1750s Virginia troops had been prominent in the French and Indian campaigns in the western part of Pennsylvania. Their interest in the lands traditionally claimed by the Commonwealth resulted from Virginia's counterclaims to a vast tract of land north and

west of its present borders, including the vicinity of Pittsburgh. The French and Indian War had not settled this territorial dispute – nor had it intended to – and in the latter part of 1773 a conflict called Lord Dunmore's war erupted. This so-called war was precipitated when Virginia, which had contributed significantly to the fighting in western Pennsylvania during the French and Indian War, vigorously pressed its claims to the western part of the Commonwealth, some of the Ohio Valley and even part of Kentucky.

Virginia, through its governor John Murray, the Earl of Dunmore, sought to assert its claim to all of southwestern Pennsylvania that lay south of the Ohio River. In the summer of 1773, a surveying company in the employ of Virginia proceeded down the Ohio and up the Kentucky River, laying out the town of Louisville in the process.[22] Murray subsequently asserted with confidence that Pittsburgh was outside the jurisdiction of the Commonwealth and thus belonged to Virginia.[23]

In late 1773 Virginia's governor appointed Dr. John Connolly, a Pennsylvanian whose loyalty was to Virginia, as commandant of the militia in Pittsburgh.[24] Connolly seized Fort Pitt, which had been abandoned by royal order, refurbished it and changed its name to Fort Dunmore. A government loyal to Virginia was subsequently set up in what the Virginians called the District of West Augusta, with Pittsburgh as the county seat. Pennsylvania countered by supporting a 100-man unit in the area of Westmoreland County and having one of its local officials, Arthur St. Clair, arrest Connolly and have him bound over for trial. There ensued a game of tit-for-tat, with arrests and counter arrests. As Virginians and their supporters settled on lands claimed by local tribes and recognized as theirs by treaty, relations with the Shawnees and the Delaware brought the area to the brink of war with the Indian tribes. It was not until 1779, well into the American Revolution, that the two commonwealths agreed to a settlement which gave the disputed Pittsburgh area to Pennsylvania.[25]

---

[22] George P. Donehoo, *Pennsylvania: A History*, vol. II (New York: Lewis Historical Publications, 1926), p. 944.

[23] His contention was supported by George Croghan, a prominent figure in the early history of the western portion of the Commonwealth. Croghan believed that five degrees longitude marked Pennsylvania's western border, a position also taken by the governor of Virginia. This placed Pittsburgh on the land claimed by Virginia. Croghan's nephew was Dr. John Connolly, who would be a leading figure in Lord Dunmore's War.

[24] A proclamation by Lord Dunmore on April 25, 1774, stated that he had appointed a militia and needed to have a significant number of men to repel any insults to this area. Hazard, *Pennsylvania Archives Commencing 1760*, vol. IV, pp. 490-491.

[25] In short, they first agreed to the extension of the now-famous Mason-Dixon Line westward

The border squabbles such as Lord Dunmore's War and the Pennamite wars are interesting if for no other reason than that they validate the existence of state military units during the interwar period – a fact that some authorities have questioned.[26] Ample evidence exists in the wake of the Seven Years War indicating the continuance of units in these border disputes and in the Philadelphia area. That a military presence would have continued to exist in Philadelphia seems obvious, because the need to defend the harbor was a major motivating factor that caused the creation of Associator units. Thus, although a general war did not occur in the 1760s or in the first half of the following decade, Associators continued to practice their military skills, some in the permanent defensive facilities that were constructed beginning in the late 1740s.

As an example, when the Paxton Boys episode occurred, the February 9, 1764, *Pennsylvania Gazette* reported that six companies of foot, one of artillery and troops of horse were formed and paraded in Philadelphia. Two years later, a report in the *Pennsylvania Gazette* dated June 12, 1766, stated that a salute was fired by the city artillery. The Artillery Association was active in the early 1770s as well. Benjamin Loxley's Daybook, in the collections of the Historical Society of Pennsylvania, includes a memorandum to supplement the previous Articles of Association between Benjamin Loxley and Jehu Eyre, both Associators in the Philadelphia Artillery. An entry in the daybook dated February 17, 1773, includes an invoice for the construction of cannon. An entry of October 1, 1773, records the clearing and cleaning of an 18-pounder for the governor. Clearly the Artillery Associators in Philadelphia remained active.[27]

Granted, once the military demands of the Seven Years War were over and the Pennsylvania militia law had expired, the militia decreased in size,

---

to its five-degree limit. A meridian was then drawn northward as far as the Ohio. In 1784, with Virginia no longer interested in the area, Pennsylvania extended the meridian to Lake Erie, finalizing its western boundary.

[26] For example, in "From Revolution to Whiskey Rebellion," a chapter in Uzal W. Ent, ed., *The First Century: A History of the 28th Infantry Division* (Harrisburg: Stackpole Books, 1979), Colonel (Ret.) John B. B. Trussell stated, "The approach of the Revolutionary War found Pennsylvania with a precedent for military organization but, alone among the British colonies in America, with no military units actually in being." He further said, "The province had never had a militia in the strict sense of the term (that is, an organization in which enrollment was mandatory)." In part Trussell is correct, for as previously noted, Pennsylvania had never instituted a law which imposed a universal military obligation on its free white male population. However, Pennsylvania was not without militia units. Indeed, the conflict with the Quaker-dominated Assembly had given the Commonwealth a unique military tradition. The fact that some militia units continued to exist is well documented in Pennsylvania's archival material.

[27] For the information mentioned see "Benjamin Loxley's Daybook, 1771-1785," in the Historical Society of Pennsylvania, pp. 36, 100, 143.

provincial troops faded away, and many Associators returned to civilian pursuits and ignored their assumed military responsibilities. Despite the absence of a militia law, however, a unique military tradition had developed – a tradition based on the Associators. This tradition continued to prosper because Franklin's Associator concept continued to be exercised. Beginning with the creation of the Associators in 1747, Pennsylvania had an alternative method of defending its citizens. While not as desirable as a militia law requiring obligatory service of all free white males,[28] it was still a method that allowed the mustering of military units in times of emergency. It would serve the Commonwealth beginning in 1748, it continued into the French and Indian War, and it would be the basis of Pennsylvania's initial contribution to the Revolutionary War. As a result of the Associators, as the American Revolution approached, military units and martial spirit were readily resurrected.

This spirit was soon required. While in the popular mind the origins of the American Revolution center in New England and in particular Boston, Pennsylvania was heavily involved in the politics of the Revolution. In fact, a basic issue that prompted the Revolution – the need by the British government to raise funds for the common defense – affected all the colonies. Few were more vocal about the problem than Pennsylvania.[29] Indeed, the preeminence of Pennsylvania and its leaders in the politics of protest meant that the Commonwealth, despite its weaknesses in militia legislation, would play a major role in the Revolution from the outset.

When the Stamp Act was passed on March 22, 1765, requiring official stamps on legal documents such as deeds, bonds and notes, crowds formed in Philadelphia to object. Between the spring of 1765 and the spring of 1766 there were a total of five Stamp Act crowd actions, none of which would constitute a riotous mob. Although there was a lack of rioter's frenzy, on September 16, 1765, a crowd did surround the building in Philadelphia where Stamp Commissioner John Hughes had his office. Their actions were menac-

---

[28] This distinction, free white males, was common for militia service in this period. Those who had indentured servants obviously did not want to lose their investment to military service. The idea of women serving would have been absurd to the society of the day, and black soldiers, while not unheard of, as the Revolution would show, would not be acceptable for another hundred years.

[29] Pennsylvanians were vocal on this issue, although as Sally Schwartz noted in her book, *A Mixed Multitude: The Struggle for Toleration in Colonial Pennsylvania* (New York: University Press, 1987), p. 268, "Many observers perceived Pennsylvanians as somewhat more moderate in resistance to this law than people in other provinces." Thus, though feeling on the Stamp Act ran deep in Pennsylvania, there were no riots in the streets. Pennsylvanians made their objections known through other methods.

ing, but they in no way threatened him.[30] Resentment was so high in the Commonwealth that when a shipment of official stamps for Delaware, Maryland, New Jersey and Pennsylvania was sent to the middle colonies, the ship found it necessary to lay off the coast at New Castle until it could be escorted into Philadelphia by a British man-of-war. The Pennsylvania Assembly proposed that the colonies unite and present a unified petition to the king opposing this parliamentary taxation and appointed Benjamin Franklin to represent the Commonwealth's interest in the endeavor.

Even after the Stamp Act was repealed, Pennsylvania continued to seethe with resentment over the various attempts of Parliament and the Crown to institute new revenue-producing measures. John Dickinson's "Letters From A Farmer in Pennsylvania To The Inhabitants of the British Colonies" (November 10, 1767) were read throughout the American colonies and were regarded as an eloquent statement of the American position that taxation without representation was wrong. Philadelphia rapidly became the center of revolutionary activity and by 1776 eclipsed the early revolutionary events that occurred in Boston. And as the public fervor turned from political rhetoric to actual revolution, Pennsylvania was thrust into a leadership role.

---

[30] Steven Rosswurm, *Arms, Country and Class: The Philadelphia Militia and the "Lower Sort" during the American Revolution* (New Brunswick, N.J.: Rutgers University Press, 1987), pp. 29-31.

CHAPTER 6

The Commonwealth and the Revolutionary War

Twelve companies of riflemen [from Pennsylvania] reported near Boston, some of them having marched a distance of 800 miles. These were the first troops raised upon authority of the Continental Congress and were soon recognized as the six best corps in the Army. In spite of cold and starvation and suffering they fought throughout the war and formed the backbone of those gallant troops which finally achieved our independence.

– Harrison Dickson
Early 20th century historian

As the crisis between the colonies and the British government deepened and armed conflict appeared likely, Pennsylvania found itself in a predicament unlike any of its sister colonies. Due to the legacy of the Quaker years, the Commonwealth still lacked the necessary legislation to adequately contribute troops for the War of Independence. As mentioned in the previous chapter, Pennsylvania's militia law had expired, and there was no means of imposing obligatory service on the male inhabitants of the Commonwealth. Pennsylvania could and did organize additional Associator units, but the use of volunteers mustered through this system had two notable drawbacks. Associations could not supply the numbers of troops needed for a major conflict, nor could they stay in active service for long periods of time. Despite these limitations, when troops were needed, Pennsylvania initially had no choice but to call for more Associators.

Problems with Pennsylvania's lack of enabling legislation for "official" military formations – i.e., militia – had not, however, prevented some residual military units from fulfilling many roles after the end of the Seven Years War. As noted earlier, Associator units were organized for the Paxton Boys' raids, and elements from militia units indirectly contributed to the Wyoming Valley episodes. The importance of Philadelphia's harbor area caused Associators to continue practicing their military skills in permanent facilities that had been built in the late 1740s.[1] But the existing legal structure did not allow the Commonwealth to impose a military obligation on all male citizens nor raise the necessary number of troops for extended periods and thus contribute adequately to the Revolution.

In spite of these shortcomings, the willingness of the citizens to support the Revolution can be seen through the actions of many who met in numerous localities in Pennsylvania in 1774 to express their concern about British policies. As an example, in Hanover Township, Lancaster County, a citizens' group met on June 4, 1774. They passed a series of resolutions or resolves that officially opposed recent British acts they deemed oppressive.[2] The actions taken at Hanover were replicated in a number of other communities in Lancaster County. Middletown followed with comparable resolves on June 8, and Lancaster on July 9. The Lancaster County group during their July 9 meeting decried the oppression of the British Parliament and set up a relief system to aid their besieged "brethren of Boston."[3] Subsequently, many of these local organizations, both in Lancaster County and throughout the Commonwealth, began establishing military units. Within the Pennsylvania tradition, this meant that Associator organizations were created, revived or strengthened.

Citizens in Hanover began organizing Associators, and a flag was designed for the unit to be fielded from the area.[4] A group in Philadelphia began meeting in Carpenters Hall to discuss the city's defense even as the newly formed Continental Congress was meeting in another part of the building. On November 17, 1774, they too began organizing for military purposes and cre-

---

[1] The most obvious example of this is the artillery Associators who guarded the harbor area, discussed in the previous two chapters. According to Loxley's Daybook, sheds existed at the State House, the Gaol and the Court House for the purpose of storing ordnance. Joseph Seymour, "Soldiers of the Quaker City: The Story of the Philadelphia Artillery, 1747-1783," an unpublished manuscript written in 1997. Cited hereafter as Seymour, "Story of the Philadelphia Artillery."

[2] William H. Egle, *Pennsylvania Archives: Pennsylvania in the War of the Revolution: Associated Battalions and Militia, 1775-1783*, second series, vol. I (Harrisburg: Clarence M. Busch: State Printer, 1896), p. 271. Cited hereafter as Egle, *Pennsylvania in the Revolution*, vol. I.

[3] Ibid., p. 273.

[4] William H. Egle, *Pennsylvania Archives: Pennsylvania in the War of the Revolution: Associated Battalions and Militia, 1775-1783*, second series, vol. II (Harrisburg: Clarence M. Busch, State Printer, 1896), p. 756. Cited hereafter as Egle, *Pennsylvania in the Revolution*, vol II.

ated the Philadelphia Troop of Light Horse. This unit would later become the First Troop Philadelphia City Cavalry. Initially composed of 28 of the city's gentlemen, the Philadelphia Troop was destined to become one of the oldest units in continuous service in Pennsylvania.[5] Like many other Pennsylvania units, the First Troop would also participate in numerous actions in the Philadelphia region during the Revolutionary War.

A review of the Revolutionary period, 1774-1783, shows that Pennsylvania used a number of distinct methods to raise the troops necessary to support the war. As noted above, the first was Pennsylvania's proven method of mobilizing forces: voluntary defensive associations. Throughout the last quarter of 1774, local communities across the Commonwealth revived or reorganized their associations. Despite the rapid approach of the Revolution, there was no immediate impetus in the government to pass a militia law. Instead, on June 30, 1775, legislation was passed by the Assembly to provide legal authorization for defensive associations.[6] It permitted "the Association entered into by the good people of this Province for the Defense of their Lives, Liberty and Property."[7] On August 19 of the same year, this law was strengthened by the passage of a set of rules and regulations for the governance and discipline of the associations.

The Assembly's act officially recognized associations and established a Committee of Safety for the colony which was given the responsibility:

> *for calling forth such and so many of the Associators into actual service, when necessity requires, as the said committee shall judge proper, for paying and supplying them with the necessities, while in actual service, for providing for the defense against invasion and insurrection and for encouraging and promoting the manufacture of saltpeter.*[8]

---

[5] The color of this historic unit, which still exists in Philadelphia as Troop A, 104th Cavalry, is described in Egle, *Pennsylvania in the Revolution*, vol. II, p. iv and is pictured among the color illustrations in this volume.

[6] *Pennsylvania Archives: Votes of the Assembly, January 7, 1771-September 26, 1776*, eighth series, vol. VIII (Harrisburg: State Library, 1935), p. 7245. Cited hereafter as *Votes of the Assembly*, vol. VIII. This action is interesting because on December 7, 1747, the original Associators met with Council President Anthony Palmer at the courthouse in Philadelphia and were informed that their efforts were *not disapproved*. Thus, tacit approval was given to an extralegal group to serve the Commonwealth's defense. Twenty-seven years later, associations – the stopgap measure developed by Franklin – were officially approved by the Provincial Assembly, in preference to passing a new militia act.

[7] Ibid., p. 7247.

[8] Ibid. The Committee of Safety which was subsequently organized began meeting in mid-sum-

The Assembly specified membership to include ten citizens from Philadelphia, four from the county, two from Chester County and one from each of the other counties. The Assembly formally legitimized the defensive organizations that had spontaneously come into being throughout the Commonwealth through local initiatives. They also passed a resolution approving them and recommending that all counties that had not yet done so provide weapons, ammunition and equipment for their use. In the following months, officers were commissioned and 53 Associator battalions were authorized.

The Assembly also recommended that the Board of Commissioners of the city of Philadelphia and each county in the Commonwealth make provision for the defense of their area. They recommended that each county supply its citizenry with:

> a proper Number of good new Firelocks [muskets] with Bayonets fitted to them, Cartridge Boxes, twenty-three Rounds of Cartridges in every Box, and Knapsacks . . . that the Firelocks were to be provided as aforesaid be of one size and bore and were to come complete with steel rammers well fitted to the same; and that Patterns of the said Firelocks, rammers and Bayonets be immediately made in the City of Philadelphia and sent to the various Counties.[9]

Joining an Associator company was a popular move, one which involved a large number of citizens of all socioeconomic groups. As related by one author:

> Gentlemen, Merchants, tradesmen, old, young, English, Irish, German,

mer. The list of its membership reads like a "who's who" in the American Revolution. Included were John Dickinson, Anthony Wayne, William Thompson, Benjamin Franklin, Edward Biddle and Robert Morris. At its July 3, 1775, organizational meeting Benjamin Franklin became president. This committee was significant because it would have authority over Pennsylvania's military forces until the fall of 1777. The Committee of Safety was not unique to Pennsylvania. The first such organization was created on October 26, 1774, by the Provincial Congress of Massachusetts Bay. With the degeneration of relations with the British government, they thought a committee with the power to collect military stores and call out the militia was necessary.

[9] *Votes of the Assembly*, vol. VIII, p. 7246. The supplies recommended are as follows: Not less than 1,500 of each article for the city and county of Philadelphia; 500 for the county of Chester; 300 for the county of Bucks; 600 for the county of Lancaster; 300 for the county of York; 300 for the county of Cumberland, 400 for the county of Berks; 300 for the county of Northampton; 100 for the county of Bedford; 100 for the county of Northumberland; and 100 for the county of Westmoreland.

Dutch etc. are [drilling?] and stand shoulder to shoulder. One company, composed of "young gentlemen only" earned the nicknames "silk stocking company" and the "Lady's light Infantry." Some Quakers turned out; by the beginning of August about one hundred had taken up arms.[10]

Due to this broad support, in this early period of the Revolution, the organization and power of the Associators and the county structure which served as their base is striking. Each county had its own Committee of Safety, which was an organized political faction, and the task of administering the Associator units was given to these committees. They even allowed Associator units to exercise disciplinary authority over non-Associators. As a further sign of their power, on November 26, 1775, the Assembly passed a requirement for assessors of the several townships, boroughs, wards and districts of Pennsylvania to deliver an exact list of names of "every Male white person, capable of bearing Arms, between the age of sixteen and Fifty years." Those able-bodied free men who refused to sign up in an Associator unit were to be fined two pounds ten schillings by the commissioners.[11] The reliance on Associators as soldiers to fulfill the military needs of the Commonwealth was also evidenced by the passage of a law in May 1776 that required all non-Associators to surrender their weapons.[12] In the face of such punitive measures, the ranks of the Associator battalions expanded, although with less popular enthusiasm than their 1747 counterparts.

It is significant to note that the hesitancy of some citizens to enlist in Associator companies may have been in part class-based. Simply put, some citizens from the lower classes could not realistically afford to join an Associator company. For example, every officer and every private in a rifle company was required to "furnish himself with a good Rifle-Gun and Powder Horn, a Charger, a Bullet Screw, Twelve Flints, a strong Pouch or Bag that will hold four Pounds of Ball, and such other Accouterments as may be proper for a Rifleman."[13] The average citizen of lesser means, regardless of his level of

---

[10] Steven Rosswurm, *Arms, Country and Class: The Philadelphia Militia and the "Lower Sort" during the American Revolution, 1775-1783* (New Brunswick, N.J.: Rutgers University Press, 1987), p. 50.
[11] *Votes of the Assembly*, vol. VIII, pp. 7380-7382.
[12] Egle, *Pennsylvania in the Revolution*, vol. I, pp. 526-527. In a letter from William Atlee of Lancaster to Benjamin Franklin, president of the Convention of Pennsylvania, on July 23, 1776, Atlee acknowledges this ordinance by the convention to disarm non-Associators. He then discusses the Commonwealth forces in his area and the poor state of their supplies but expresses optimism that they will be agreeable to the orders of the convention.
[13] *Votes of the Assembly*, vol. VIII, p. 7371.

patriotism, could not afford the £10-12 needed to buy this equipment. The working man also had difficulty attending drill or exercise sessions because they conflicted with his work obligations.

Despite the inherent limitations of the Associator concept, Pennsylvania's first response to the need for troops had to come through Associator units. They were, so to speak, a bargain for the Commonwealth. They could be raised through the existing state structure without additional legislation; the concept was accepted by diverse elements in the Commonwealth; and some Associator units offered a depth of experience that was sorely needed.

Although today the associations are regarded by some as a weak and temporary expedient for defense, compared with an obligatory militia, in the period 1754-1775 they actually had more permanence than most people realize. This was particularly true in the Philadelphia area, where Associators provided a military tradition that is often overlooked. A prime example of this can be seen through artillery Associator units in Philadelphia. Both experience and continuity of personnel were particularly important in artillery units because 18th-century crews required specialized skills and regular practice. At least some of the artillery crew needed to have a rudimentary understanding of mathematics and a good knowledge of explosives.[14] Evidence shows that the Grand Battery – The Association – was maintained after 1763, and sheds stood at the State House, Gaol and Court House to store ordnance. Perhaps most important, the artillerists continued to practice their military craft.[15]

Good artillery crews logically came from the Philadelphia area. Since the early part of the 18th century, this leading colonial port had pressed the Assembly for a dependable method to defend its harbor. This need led to the founding of the Associators in 1747 and the subsequent establishment of batteries in Philadelphia at the foot of Society Hill and the Grand Battery at Wicaco. The artillery Associators of Philadelphia could not afford to disband as they were the harbor's main source of defense.[16] This continuity, crucial for artillery crews, may have existed in other Associator units as well.

---

[14] As Steven Rosswurm noted in *Arms, Country and Class*, p. 174, previously cited, "The most widely read manual contained square root tables, a section on the theory of powder and chapters on the construction of artillery pieces." The manual he refers to was John Muller's *A Treatise of Artillery* (Philadelphia: 1779).

[15] Seymour, "Story of the Philadelphia Artillery," p. 5.

[16] In fact, they had never really been able to disband after any of the conflicts. After the end of King George's War, for which they were originally founded, they continued to function. An entry in the June 27, 1754, *Pennsylvania Gazette* indicates that militia (likely Associators since there was no militia law in effect) were being regularly drawn up, and artillery was firing from

While artillery elements are currently acknowledged as Associator units for the early Revolutionary period, additional research would likely indicate the existence of other Associator units in the Commonwealth immediately prior to the Revolutionary War. In Philadelphia, for example, in 1774 Captain John Cadwalader had an Associator unit known as the "Philadelphia Greens," and Captain Joseph Cowperthwaite commanded a unit known as the "Quaker Blues."

One interesting category of early units were those composed of Pennsylvania Germans. Since the early history of the Commonwealth, Pennsylvania had a strong German element in its population. When Pennsylvania fought the French and Indian War, it used the assistance of the German community and its leadership – notably Conrad Weiser – to muster this ethnic bloc and defend areas such as Berks County. When the Commonwealth moved toward revolution, the German community followed the practices of the "English" and formed German Associator units. Colonel Nicholas Lutz, for example, formed a battalion of German-American Associators from Berks County. Colonel Kichlein, whose home was in Easton, also formed a battalion of German-American Associators. Two companies of Samuel Atlee's Battalion were composed of German-Americans. Much like similar non-German battalions and companies throughout the Commonwealth, when the fighting started these German units served as part of the "Flying Camp," and with the passage of a militia act some of these units transitioned to official militia status.[17] A German Regiment was ultimately created which served the cause of American independence throughout most of the war.

The purpose of noting this level of detail on Associator officers and lineage is to reinforce the unique military tradition that had developed in the Commonwealth by this time. For some 30 years, whenever military units were needed, Associators – militia in fact if not in name – stood up to defend the Commonwealth. In the French and Indian War, Associators organized and then transitioned into provincial or militia troops. In the Revolutionary War,

---

several blockhouses. An October 15, 1754, story states that a sergeant and corporal of each company in the train of artillery were ordered to go recruiting. An August 21, 1755, story refers to a meeting of the managers of the association in which they resolved to repair their battery. After taking part in the French and Indian War, the Philadelphia Artillery continued its service.
[17] Henry M. M. Richards, *The Pennsylvania-German in the Revolutionary War, 1775-1783* (Lancaster, Pa.: Pennsylvania German Society, 1908), pp.43-45. Nicholas Lutz is a good example of an Associator who made the transition to the militia. Although initially an Associator battalion commander, in May 1777 he was commander of the Fourth Battalion, Berks County Militia. Egle, *Pennsylvania in the Revolution*, vol. II, p. 267.

PROCTOR'S ARTILLERY

December 7, 1747	Associators founded in Philadelphia.
December 29, 1747	Artillery Companies of the Associated Regiment of Foot of Philadelphia are organized.
June 18, 1748	Captain John Siebold commissioned as an artillery officer commanding fortifications in Philadelphia.
October 15, 1754	Train of Artillery mentioned in area records, indicating the continued existence of more than one company.
January 1, 1756	Multiple artillery companies are in existence, including Artillery company at the Fort, Association battery at Wicaco, Artillery company of the city.
March 18, 1756	Captain Jehu Eyre appointed chief engineer and director of artillery.
May 1756	Jehu Eyre's company, Associator Artillery of Northern Liberties, mustered into British service for the French and Indian War.
October 2, 1760	Captain Eyre's company at Fort Pitt and Presqu'Isle.
1775	Associators of the City and Liberties of Philadelphia reorganized to consist of six battalions, one of which was artillery; companies identified (by commanders) were Captain Jehu Eyre, Captain James Biddle, Captain Benjamin Loxley, Captain Thomas Proctor, Captain Joseph Moulder.
October 27, 1775	Captain Thomas Proctor's company designated as the Pennsylvania State Artillery Company.
August 14, 1776	Company expanded and designated as the Pennsylvania Artillery Battalion.
September 23, 1776	Mustered into federal service as Proctor's Continental Artillery.
June 19, 1777	Elements constituted in the militia as the Artillery Battalion, Colonel Jehu Eyre commanding.
November 15, 1783	Proctor's Artillery demobilized at Philadelphia; personnel enter Artillery Battalion, Pennsylvania Militia.
1794	Militia force expanded into a regiment of artillery of the City of Philadelphia, Colonel Thomas Proctor commanding.

Lineage of the Philadelphia Artillery, showing the continuity of the unit and its personnel in one geographical area during the 18th century.

some Associator units became Continental units or served the Commonwealth in some other capacity.[18] Thompson's Rifle Battalion originated in the Associator movement in the Cumberland Valley before it became part of the Pennsylvania Line in the Continental Army. The Berks County Militia began in 1775 when many of the eligible residents subscribed to the Articles of Association and were assigned to various companies in the Fifth Battalion of Associators. In 1776-1777 companies still existed in the area, but by this time they were militia.[19] The contribution of the Associator concept to the defense of Pennsylvania can also be seen through the records of a number of officers who served in Pennsylvania's units. Anthony Wayne, Samuel and Thomas Mifflin, Arthur Saint Clair, Edward Hand and Daniel Brodhead, to name a few, were all Associators before they became Continental officers.

A second method used by Pennsylvania to provide troops for the Revolution was the creation of state regiments with specified responsibilities only to the Commonwealth, not to the Continental Army. This type of unit was necessary because, when the Continental Congress called on the newly formed states to contribute troops, a number of Associators from the Commonwealth were ordered to proceed north to perform duties in the New York-New England area. This left Pennsylvania without adequate forces to defend itself, because in 1775-76 it still did not have legislation permitting a militia. Furthermore, the number of Associators available for this duty was considerably reduced because they were fulfilling the manpower quotas established by Congress for Pennsylvania.

This posed a significant problem because an attack by British forces, particularly in the Philadelphia area, was a distinct possibility. With its port facilities and its status as a center of the Revolution, Philadelphia was a lucrative military objective. In addition, not all citizens of the Commonwealth supported the Revolution. Some of these "loyalists" (colonists loyal to Britain) might even take direct military action to restore British control. To counter

---

[18] As a sidelight, the Associators contributed to the creation of another important military formation, the U.S. Marine Corps. According to Allan R. Millet, when the senior captain of the newly authorized Continental Marines began recruiting members, he was "accompanied by drummers, presumably borrowed from the Philadelphia Associators (city militia) as they scoured the city for recruits in December 1775." *"Semper Fidelis": The History of the United States Marine Corps* (New York: Free Press, 1980), p. 8.

[19] Clyde S. Stine, "A Former Berks Militia Unit, Company C, 103rd Quartermaster Regiment," *Historical Review of Berks County* (October 1940), p. 18. While I call these units militia by 1776-1777, writers at that time and in the present do not always discriminate between actual militia companies and Associators. Sometimes the terms are used interchangeably.

these threats, the Committee of Safety took steps to raise troops for the defense of the Commonwealth against any British incursions. These state military units were referred to as "State Regulars" and were enlisted for longer terms of duty, in the official service of the Commonwealth rather than the Continental Congress. In many instances they were former Associators.

The need to provide for the Commonwealth's defense always had to be balanced against the quotas established by the Continental Congress. Soldiers were soon desperately needed from the middle colonies for Continental service because, after the April 19, 1775, engagements at Lexington and Concord, the military focus shifted to the siege of Boston by colonial forces. The demand for troops to block any movement of British troops from Boston caused Congress on June 14, 1775, to call for ten companies of riflemen for 12 months' service. Initially, six of these companies were to be from Pennsylvania. The support given to the government's call was so great that the number of companies was increased to nine. The Pennsylvania companies in total comprised the Pennsylvania Battalion of Riflemen, better known as Thompson's Rifle Battalion. After its arrival in Cambridge, Massachusetts, the battalion was designated as a federal unit called the 2nd Continental Regiment; it was renamed the 1st Continental Regiment on the first of the following year. Like other Pennsylvania units, Thompson's Rifle Battalion clearly had its origins in the Associator movement.[20] It would be the first Pennsylvania unit to contribute significantly to the defense of the colonies; although not a traditional militia unit, it was certainly a unit with solid roots in the Commonwealth's defensive system.

Thompson's Battalion proceeded north in the late summer of 1775 to assist forces in the Boston area. They arrived August 18 and were almost immediately assigned to man the outpost line. Even though their deployment destined them for early action, their record in the latter part of 1775 is mixed. For example, Company H, recruited in Lancaster County, became unruly and ultimately mutinous. The two ringleaders of the mutiny were arrested and court martialed on September 12. On the other hand, more than half the battalion saw action when the British attacked American positions on August 27. From that point on, elements of the battalion were regularly involved in skirmishes with British troops. A notable action occurred on November 9, 1775 when the British, supported by naval guns and artillery, landed troops on

---

[20] A list of colonels of associated battalions included in the Articles of Association dated August 19, 1775, in state archival records shows William Thompson of Cumberland County, initially a colonel, made brigadier general. See Egle, *Pennsylvania in the Revolution*, vol. I, pp. 257-258.

Lechmere's Point. Thompson's Battalion was sent forward to repel the invasion, and despite the need for infantry to move through deep water, the Pennsylvanians repelled the British force.

Analogous to present practices with federalized National Guard units in 20th century wars, some Pennsylvania troops were pulled out of Thompson's Battalion and employed for other purposes. For example, on August 5, 1775, Captain Matthew Smith's company, which had been recruited in what is now Harrisburg and Dauphin County, was detached from the battalion and assigned to an expedition which was to invade Canada. It was joined by Captain William Hendrix's company, recruited in Cumberland County.[21] The two Pennsylvania companies were part of Captain Benedict Arnold's expedition which proceeded through Maine and reached the fortress of Quebec. The expedition laid siege to the fortress early in December. A full-scale attack was launched on December 31, which ended in defeat for the Continental force. Captain Hendrix, one of the Pennsylvania officers on the field, was killed, and a considerable number of the attacking force perished. Many troops in the two Pennsylvania companies were killed in action or taken prisoner.[22] Once the Arnold expedition failed to capture Quebec, its remnants joined up with another force from New York which attempted to push the British out of Canada.

Thompson's Rifle Battalion would only be the first of many units formed in Pennsylvania and employed in Continental service during the early years of the Revolution. Before the end of 1775 a second, third, fourth, fifth and sixth Pennsylvania battalion were organized. Although some of these units would draw their initial strength from Associator membership, they, like Thompson's Rifle Battalion, ultimately belong to the Pennsylvania Line.

Another example of a unit which made the transition from Associator status to the Continental Army was a Philadelphia artillery company. On October 16, 1775, the Pennsylvania Committee of Public Safety conferred official status on a unit known as Proctor's Artillery Company. Proctor's Artillery

---

[21] The sojourn of Captain William Smith is detailed in Robert Grant Crist, *Captain William Hendricks and the March to Quebec, 1775* (Carlisle: Hamilton Library and Cumberland County Historical Society, 1960).

[22] Two Pennsylvania women accompanied their husbands on this campaign. In Matthew Smith's company, Private James Warner's wife Jemima marched with her husband until he became ill. After his death, she took his place in the company and marched with the other soldiers to Quebec. She was killed by enemy fire on December 11, 1775, when she was apparently helping deliver mortar fire against the fortress of Quebec. In Captain William Hendrix's company, Sergeant Joseph Greer's wife Susanna (or Ann) marched with her husband to Quebec and endured the siege of the fortress. She was killed by friendly fire on April 18, 1776.

was one of a number of companies first organized to protect the Philadelphia harbor and its Delaware River approaches. At the beginning of the Revolution, a City Artillery Battalion already existed, commanded by Colonel Samuel Mifflin. Mifflin had a longstanding affiliation with Associators as captain of the Association Battery at Wicaco in 1756. In 1775 the Associators of the City and Liberties of Philadelphia were organized, consisting of six battalions, one of them artillery. The October 16 action by the Committee of Public Safety moved Proctor's Artillery Company from Associator status to that of a Pennsylvania state artillery company, officially charged with defending the Commonwealth.[23] Proctor's Artillery expanded and became the Pennsylvania Artillery Battalion on August 14, 1776. It was mustered into Continental service on September 23, 1776, as Proctor's Continental Artillery (the 4th Continental Artillery) and remained a Continental unit until mustering out in Philadelphia on November 15, 1783.[24]

Many additional Associators or Associator units made the transition to Continental service, playing a major role in the early phases of the Revolution. They also provided Pennsylvania troops in a fashion similar to what would be expected of militia.[25] In addition to becoming Continental Army units, Associators became a part of what was termed the "Flying Camp." The Flying Camp was created by Congress in July 1776 to provide a pool of men or units which would serve as a reserve force for emergencies facing the Continental Army. To man this force, in June 1776 Congress requested Delaware, New Jersey,

---

[23] John B. Linn and William H. Egle, eds., *Pennsylvania Archives: Pennsylvania in the War of the Revolution, Battalions and Line, 1775-1783*, second series, vol. II. (Harrisburg: Lane S. Hart, State Printer, 1880).

[24] Proctor's Artillery served with distinction throughout the war. Its most famous member, however, was not Thomas Proctor but the wife of one of his artillerymen. John Caspar Hays had been with Proctor since December 1, 1775. His wife, like many spouses, accompanied her husband and assisted in the camp, tending the wounded and serving water. Molly Hays became known as Molly Pitcher. During the Battle of Monmouth, New Jersey, her husband fell in action, and she seized the rammer for the field piece and took his place on the gun crew. In 1822 her veteran status was recognized when Pennsylvania began paying her a veteran's annuity. Chadwick Allen Harp, "Remember the Ladies: Women in the American Revolution," *Pennsylvania Heritage: Quarterly of the Pennsylvania Historical and Museum Commission*, vol. XX (Spring 1994), pp. 33-37. Cited hereafter as Harp, "Remember the Ladies."

[25] While the tracking of unit personnel and activities has been well documented with the Philadelphia Artillerists, Associator infantry battalions also played a significant role in this stage of the Revolution. They were also involved in the Trenton-Princeton campaign and the subsequent actions at Brandywine and Germantown. On March 17, 1777, elements of the Infantry Associators, part of the original Associators of the City and Liberties of Philadelphia, were reorganized as the Philadelphia Brigade of Militia. The current 111th Infantry of the Pennsylvania Army National Guard carries their lineage and the title "The Associators."

Artist's version of Molly Pitcher at the Battle of Monmouth, New Jersey.

Maryland and Pennsylvania to supply 10,000 men to be drawn from local or militia-type units. As a large and populous state, Pennsylvania's share of this call was 6,000 soldiers. Since Pennsylvania did not have a militia in a traditional sense, most of the troops – some 4,500 – would have to be drawn from Associator auspices. The remainder would come from Colonel Samuel Miles' Pennsylvania State Regiment of Riflemen and Colonel Samuel Atlee's Pennsylvania State Battalion of Musketry. Employing Associators in the Flying Camp again highlighted their disadvantages. As voluntary short-term enlistees, they could not be committed to extended periods of service with the Continental Army under existing laws. Thus, their enlistment in support of the Flying Camp only lasted until November 30.

Even the selection of soldiers to fill the quota posed a problem. The method for selecting the requested 4,500 Associators involved convening representatives from Associator units at Lancaster on July 4, 1776. Delegations consisting of two officers and two privates from each Associator battalion represented their group's interests at the meeting. A total of 53 battalions of

Associators were represented, clearly indicating the strength of the movement as late as 1776. Although they were responsible to the wishes of the Assembly, the delegates on their own took considerable initiative. They assigned quotas to the counties; authorized the Associators who were organized for state purposes to serve outside Pennsylvania; and elected two senior officers, a "first brigadier" (Daniel Roberdeau) and a "second brigadier" (James Ewing), who were to command the total Pennsylvania contingent of 6,000 men.[26] The state troops commanded by Colonels Miles and Atlee, as non-Associators, were not represented at the Lancaster gathering. As a result, they would not serve under the command of Brigadiers Roberdeau and Ewing. When the Pennsylvania troops moved toward New York, their two units were attached to a Continental brigade on Long Island.[27]

The highest priority for the 6,000 Pennsylvania soldiers in service with the Flying Camp was the defense of New York. British regulars on Nova Scotia had been reinforced and were preparing for a campaign to suppress the rebellion. Reports indicated loyalists in New York were organizing forces to assist the British. This crisis resulted in the dispatch of Pennsylvania's Flying Camp elements to New Jersey to reinforce General Washington's army as it prepared to counter any attempt by Britain's General Howe to invade New York.

Even though Pennsylvania was able to throw in these Associator and state troops to assist Washington, the shortcomings of the Associator method quickly became evident. Each of the individual units was required to serve 60 days of active duty and, following this period of service, provide soldiers to fill a previously established quota to maintain the strength of the Flying Camp. Therefore a curious mix existed among Pennsylvania's troops on the field. Some of the soldiers left in 60 days, while others who were drafted to fill these quotas stayed behind and were formed into regiments. Thus, at any one time the Commonwealth had two types of units serving side by side which had their origins in the same Associator base. Service away from home and dissatisfaction with Continental service in general made desertions a major problem — one that necessitated the posting of reliable guards at key locations to keep soldiers from returning to Pennsylvania.

In spite of the low morale afflicting some of the troops, the Flying

[26] Minutes of the Convention of Delegates from the Associated Battalions at Lancaster, July 4, 1776, in Egle, *Pennsylvania in the Revolution*, vol. I, pp. 260-268.
[27] Both the regiment and the battalion were attached to the Continental Army and participated in the Battle of Long Island on August 27, 1776. They met an inglorious end, since both units were defeated and their commanders taken prisoner.

Camp with its sizable Pennsylvania component did in fact make a significant contribution. The fact that the New York campaign was ultimately a disaster for Washington's army should not diminish the role of Pennsylvania soldiers. The mere existence of this body posted in New York and New Jersey disrupted the British army, making it impossible for them to carry out their planned operations. Beyond the impact of simply providing additional soldiers to the resource-poor Continental Army, the Pennsylvania contingent of the Flying Camp actually participated in some of the war's early military engagements. For example, elements of one of the York County battalions were used as part of a Continental force that raided British units on Staten Island on October 15, 1776. Elements of the Philadelphia artillery also contributed to the fighting in the New York-New Jersey Campaign. Colonel Samuel Mifflin took three companies to Amboy in northern New Jersey to build fortifications and observe British shipping. Other artillerists remained behind to provide some of Pennsylvania's quotas for the Flying Camp.[28]

When the Hessians staged an attack on Fort Washington on Manhattan Island on November 16, 1776, Pennsylvania units were present and gave a good account of themselves.[29] Associator units continued their support of Washington's army throughout the rest of the year. Despite their short-term enlistments, the end of the year found 1,173 Pennsylvania Flying Camp soldiers from five different battalions still with Washington's army.[30] These soldiers, together with 3,000 other Associators, also took part in the attack on Trenton, New Jersey on December 26, 1776.[31] When Washington fought the Battle of Princeton on January 2-3, 1777, some 1,700 Associators were still with the Continental forces. While patriotism undoubtedly caused some of these troops to stay in service, the Assembly assisted by providing financial incentives. On

---

[28] Seymour, "Story of the Philadelphia Artillery," p. 6.

[29] Among the units present for the Fort Washington action was the Pennsylvania Artillery. A soldier in the first company, John Corbin, was accompanied by his wife Mary Cochran Corbin, who brought water to the artillery crews. When her husband was mortally wounded, she took his place on the crew until she was severely wounded by Hessian artillery fire. She recuperated after the battle and served for a period in an invalid regiment. Toward the end of the war she was pensioned and after her death was buried in the post cemetery at the United States Military Academy. Harp, "Remember the Ladies," pp. 33-37.

[30] John B. B. Trussell, "Revolution to Whiskey Rebellion," in *The First Century: A History of the 28th Infantry Division*, Uzal W. Ent, ed. (Harrisburg: Stackpole Books, 1979), p. 33.

[31] The First Battalion and the Third Battalion of Associators were present on the field, although they had trouble crossing the river due to ice and winds of gale force. See Michael R. Benson, "The Early History of the Artillery Battalion of Philadelphia, 1760-1777," unpublished paper, March 19, 1976, p. 6. Cited hereafter as Benson, "Artillery Battalion of Philadelphia."

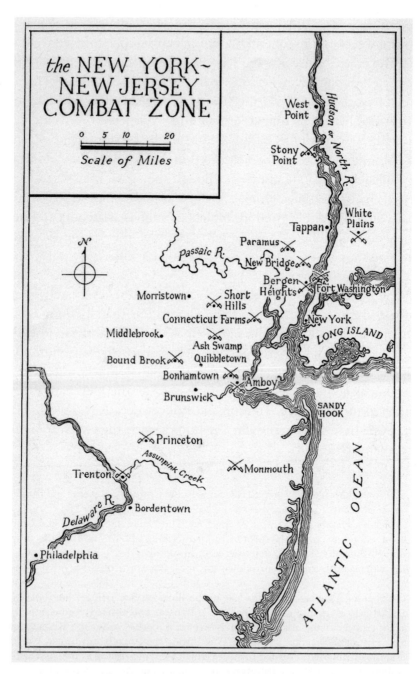

Map of the New York-New Jersey Theater of Operations, from *The Pennsylvania Line: Regimental Organization and Operations, 1775-1783* (published by the Pennsylvania Historical and Museum Commission).

December 12, 1776, the Assembly authorized bonuses of $5-10, depending on the speed of response, for those Associators who volunteered to stay on duty for six more weeks. Consequently, a number of Associators were still in service for Trenton and the early 1777 Battle of Princeton. As the Continental Army retreated through New Jersey, across the Delaware and into Pennsylvania, among the Associators still on the field was Brigadier General Hugh Mercer. This officer had begun his military career in the Associator movement and had contacts with Associators as early as 1760 in the western Pennsylvania campaigns.[32] Among the Associator units used in the Trenton-Princeton campaign was the Philadelphia City Cavalry. Although they gave reliable service to the Continental Army, the Philadelphia Cavalry was not employed to full advantage as a cavalry unit but rather used in driblets of individual scouts and headquarters guards and messengers. This poor usage was due to the lack of cavalry experience on the part of Washington – the infantry officer – not to any shortcomings of the Philadelphia Troop.[33]

        When the Battle of Princeton occurred, the estimated strength of Associator companies on the field had fallen to less than 1,700 men. Despite this precipitous drop, Associators participated significantly in the Battle of Trenton. Soldiers of Jehu Eyre's Second Company of the City and Liberties of Philadelphia, part of the Philadelphia Artillery Battalion, showed their versatility by serving as boatsmen in the night crossing of the Delaware River and as artillerymen in the battles of Trenton and Princeton.[34] A few weeks afterward, however, even Eyre's company left for home, since their term of enlistment expired on January 25, 1777.[35]

[32] Ibid., p. 2. General Mercer was able to remain with the Continental Army and the Associators until the Battle of Princeton, where he was killed.

[33] Russell F. Weigley, *History of the United States Army*, The Macmillan Wars of the United States, Louis Morton, ed. (New York: Macmillan Company, 1967), pp. 70-71. It is also interesting to note that the Philadelphia Light Horse was used in October 1779, augmented by artillery, to restore order when a mob tried to burn down the homes of some of the area's unpopular political figures.

[34] Eyre's record as an Associator and his role in the Philadelphia Artillery are well documented in Benson, "Artillery Battalion of Philadelphia." Benson notes that Eyre began working as a shipwright apprentice in the mid-1750s at Northern Liberties, now the Kensington area of Philadelphia. His military career started in 1756 during the French and Indian War. After the war he and some of his men returned to their civilian jobs and drilled as the Associators of the Northern Liberties. Eyre remained a motivating force for the Associators for the next 14 years, and in 1775 he formed his men into a company for the Revolution in which he would serve as a captain.

[35] Eyre and his artillerists would, like most Associators, be drawn back into the conflict in another capacity. Records show Eyre in command of an artillery battalion in the Pennsylvania Militia

Eyre's departure was part of a larger trend within the Associator ranks. Associator strength fell after the end of 1776, for several reasons. First, the conversion of Associator units into Continental Army elements in 1775-1776 obviously decreased the number of soldiers available for the Associator ranks. Second, the demands of the Revolution pushed Associators beyond their original purpose: voluntary defense of a local area, usually for brief periods of time. The Revolution required Pennsylvania Associators to serve in New York, New Jersey and even on the border with Canada. For some soldiers, the demands of the Revolution were far more than they had anticipated. The need for Pennsylvania troops to serve outside the Commonwealth and the extended periods of service involved simply stretched the Associator concept beyond its intent.

The problems with meeting the demands of longer and geographically extended wars had clearly shown the Associator concept to be in dire need of replacement. Still, the year 1776 passed without enactment of a law to impose mandatory military obligations on the citizenry. In fact, as late as November 25, 1776, the Assembly passed new Articles of Association to standardize the structure and administration of Associator companies. According to these rules, an Associator battalion of riflemen would consist of six companies of not less than 40 nor more than 56 privates; the officer structure would consist of a captain, two first lieutenants, a fifer or horn blower, and as many sergeants and corporals as were necessary. The battalion officers were a colonel, lieutenant colonel, two majors, a standard bearer, an adjutant, a sergeant major and a drum and fife major. Thus, as 1776 closed, Associators remained as Pennsylvania's unique militia force, despite their serious shortcomings.

One often overlooked part of Pennsylvania's defense force in the early phases of the Revolution is the Pennsylvania Navy. This naval element was in essence a "brown water" force, authorized by the Committee of Safety on June 30, 1775, through a resolution providing for the defense of the Delaware River. Key leaders in the movement to ensure that a state navy was created to protect Pennsylvania's harbor facilities were Robert Whyte (or White) and Owen Biddle. These two men became an executive committee, and on July 7, 1775, they asked John Wharton to purchase materials to build a "boat or claevat." Wharton responded on July 8 by presenting a model of his vessel. The boats, to be designed and built in Philadelphia, were to be river gunboats. On the following day, Emmanuel Eyre, part of the Philadelphia artillerist family, presented a model of a second vessel. Although two vessels were a modest beginning,

on June 19, 1777, with his old company under the command of Captain Peter Browne.

in the following months thirteen galleys were built, equipped and manned for Pennsylvania's state navy.[36]

From mid-1775 until the war's end in 1783, the state navy grew to a total of 57 vessels.[37] Its period of greatest activity came in 1777, when it fought a number of engagements against the British navy. For example, on May 8-9, 1777, the Pennsylvania Navy assisted the Continental Navy in repelling the British frigate *Roebuck* and an accompanying sloop *Liverpool,* which were attempting to penetrate the defenses of the Delaware River. Later in the same year, the Pennsylvania Navy helped the Continental Navy stop another British attempt to push up the Delaware, which resulted in the loss or scuttling of several Pennsylvania ships.

Despite their contributions throughout 1777, by early the following year the Pennsylvania fleet had deteriorated badly. Funds to maintain the ships were in short supply. Noting the ships' condition, Washington wrote to the state Navy Board on March 2, 1778, recommending that most of the fleet be disbanded. In their state of disrepair, the British had the power to seize the ships and their supporting stores – an action that was clearly not in the best interests of Continental forces. Pennsylvania objected to the possible loss of its navy, but after a brief flurry of meetings and correspondence, the Pennsylvania Navy was cut to a token force. Reductions continued until December 20, 1781; at year's end only one officer, Captain Nathan Bays, remained in the state navy.[38]

Changes in the political complexion of Pennsylvania were occurring even before the year 1776 came to a close. The major change was highlighted by the adoption of a new state constitution on September 28, 1776. For the first time since the establishment of Penn's Peaceable Kingdom in 1681, the proprietary government officially ceased to exist. The new non-proprietary government guaranteed religious liberty in the Commonwealth, and except for selected classes of citizens, all had full rights accorded to participate in civil

---

[36] Emmanuel or Manuel Eyre was one of three brothers associated with the early defense of Philadelphia. Jehu, who was active in the French and Indian War, was an Associator captain by 1776. Emmanuel's firm built three ships, the *Bulldog, Franklin* and *Congress.* Emmanuel later served on the Pennsylvania Navy Board. The youngest of the Eyre brothers, Benjamin, served in the Army, where he reached the rank of colonel. He played key roles at Trenton and Princeton. Peter D. Keyser, "Memoirs of Colonel Jehu Eyre," *Pennsylvania Magazine of History and Biography,* vol. III (1879), pp. 296-307, 412-425.

[37] Various sources give different figures for the total number of ships. Edward W. Richardson, *Standards and Colors of the American Revolution* (Philadelphia: University of Pennsylvania Press, 1982), p. 111-112, gives the number of vessels as 42, served by 1,400 crewmen.

[38] An excellent overview of the Pennsylvania Navy is provided by John J. Jackson, *The Pennsylvania Navy, 1775-1781* (New Brunswick, N.J.: Rutgers University Press, 1974).

affairs.[39] With a new government controlled by the more radical political factions, a militia act was finally passed on March 17, 1777. It was entitled "An Act
for the Regulation of the Militia of the Commonwealth of Pennsylvania."

For the first time since the French and Indian War, the 1777 Militia Act
obligated military service for all white males between the ages of 18 and 53 able
to bear arms.[40] The basic unit for organizing militias was the county. In each
county a lieutenant was to be named to serve as the key militia official. He
required the constable of each township to furnish a list of all eligible men;
exempted were "delegates in congress, members of the executive council,
judges of the supreme court, masters and faculty of colleges, ministers of the
gospel of every denomination and servants purchased bona fide and for a valuable consideration." These lieutenants were responsible for dividing the counties into districts, and the eligible men listed were required to meet and elect
both field and line officers.[41]

The term of commission for all officers was three years. The artillery
companies and troops of light horse that were already in existence were recognized but not included in the militia structure at first. They were exempted by
special provision. Initially the new militia organization was focused on infantry
companies, with eight companies making up a battalion. Militia units were
obliged to train regularly, according to an established schedule, and when absenteeism became a problem, small fines were levied on members.

While inherently focused on local organizations, the Militia Act included a key provision for supplying manpower to the Commonwealth and the
newly formed nation. In the event of invasion or rebellion, the Executive
Council could call the militia into active service as individuals, rather than complete units. This section of the Militia Act may confuse the modern reader
because it refers to calling up militia by "classes." This term should not be
interpreted to mean social classes. Rather, it refers to a method to avoid taking
too many able-bodied men from one geographical area. The act provided for

---

[39] Members of Pennsylvania's small Jewish community were nominally excluded from full participation, but they were for the most part simply ignored. The real concern in the new government was non-believers and atheists. Sally Schwartz, *A Mixed Multitude: The Struggle for
Toleration in Colonial Pennsylvania* (New York: University Press, 1987), p. 386.

[40] A good summary of this act is included in Major William P. Clarke, *Official History of the Militia
and National Guard of Pennsylvania from the Earliest Period of Record to the Present Time* (Philadelphia:
Charles J. Hendler, 1909), pp. 21-25. Cited hereafter as Clarke, *Official History of the Pennsylvania
Militia*.

[41] Ibid. Section VII of this act, however, did provide for the field officers of each battalion to
nominate and appoint a surgeon and a chaplain.

a total of eight classes. When individuals were called up by class, they were organized into provisional companies for their period of national service, and a number of the provisional companies from a given county could then be organized into provisional battalions. From each county, classes were called up in numerical order. In an attempt to be equitable, no numerical class could be ordered up for another tour of service until all classes from the county had served. Assigning individuals to classes and calling them up by class allowed the local economy to function even during time of war and maintained a body of soldiers in each county in the event there was a local need. Obviously, this concept had merit, but the method of mobilizing militia as individuals rather than units meant that companies and battalions that had trained together would not fight together. The 1777 act did provide for training. Each year militiamen were to train a total of ten days in company configuration and two additional days in battalion. But since they were called up by class, mobilized militia would merely serve as a pool of manpower that would have to be organized and further trained to function as units. By law the period of active duty was limited to 60 days.[42]

Soon after the act was passed, the Commonwealth's officials recognized these problems and began strengthening the Militia Act through legislative action. On June 17, 1777, a method of collecting the penalty from those who neglected their mandatory militia meetings was instituted. On December 30, 1777, another act was passed by the Assembly giving the president of the Council the authority to call the militia into service – a detail that had been unclear in the original legislation.[43]

These acts which officially established a militia created a force that would be used for multiple missions in the remaining years of the war. Similar to the latter-day militia and National Guard, the mid-Revolutionary War militia was called on to defend the Commonwealth, assist in defending the nation and suppress civil disorder.[44] The pressure on the militia to fulfill these multiple

[42] A policy of assigning militia to class was repeatedly used in militia acts in Pennsylvania. The policy endured into the 19th century, and Pennsylvania had the same system in place for the War of 1812.

[43] The legislature passed a number of acts through March 21, 1783, amending and strengthening the Militia Act. The basic act through which the Commonwealth fought the war was still the act of March 17, 1777. See Clarke, *Official History of the Pennsylvania Militia*, p. 25.

[44] The militia was clearly intended to be used. According to a resolution of Congress dated September 4, 1777, sent to the Commonwealth, the Executive Council of Pennsylvania was to give orders "that all Militia of their State hold themselves in readiness to march at a moment's warning and that their arms be put in as good condition as possible." Samuel Hazard, ed.,

roles was considerable, because Pennsylvania was not only engaged in a war of independence against the British Empire, it was also faced with Indian incursions along the frontier.

From the establishment of the Commonwealth in 1681 until 1754, Pennsylvania had few difficulties with the Indian population – a credit to the wise policies of the Quakers. Beginning in 1754, however, the French encouraged the Indian resentments that had grown for 75 years and used the Indians to their advantage in the French and Indian War. With the coming of the American Revolution, the English as well exploited this resentment, the result of broken treaties, blatant land grabs and the relentless pressure of western expansion. As early as 1774, Indian wars began in the Ohio country with the Shawnees opposing the encroachment of Virginia's settlers. After brief clashes, an uneasy truce descended on the frontier, but in 1777 conflict again flared up. For Pennsylvania the greatest concern centered on the Indian attacks in New York and Pennsylvania. The Indian raids, encouraged and often supported by the British, split the Iroquois confederacy. The Oneidas and Tuscaroras remained loyal to the colonies, and the other four tribes supported the British. The Iroquois in particular posed a serious threat because they were led by a well-educated Mohawk named Joseph Brandt. In 1777 Indian raids struck various localities along the frontier. Some threats affecting Pennsylvania centered in the Ohio country, while others were more direct to the Commonwealth. Raids emanating from New York devastated the Wyoming Valley settlements, which were still in contention between Pennsylvania and Connecticut. Thus, the Commonwealth was required to counter the threat posed by British-inspired Indians as well as the British army itself.

In Westmoreland County, pressure from marauding Indians caused the militia to garrison local forts and react to the incursions without official calls. In October and November 1777, for example, there were numerous raids into Westmoreland County. Pressure from the British-backed Indians prompted a response. Discovering that there was a British magazine where Cleveland, Ohio, now stands, Brigadier General Edward Hand, commander of Fort Pitt, decided to organize an expedition to destroy the British supplies stored there. In February 1778, General Hand led some 500 militia from Westmoreland County to take the magazine. This largely militia operation ran into trouble almost from the outset because melting snows and rain delayed their march. In

Pennsylvania Archives: Selected and Arranged from Original Documents in the Office of the Secretary of the Commonwealth Conformably to Acts of the General Assembly, Commencing 1776, vol. V (Philadelphia: Joseph Severns & Co., 1853), p. 583.

the end they were unsuccessful in even reaching Ohio. The weather-imposed delay caused their commander to settle for a raid on an Indian village in the vicinity of present-day New Castle. When troops entered the village, they found only some women and children and one old man. Some of the inhabitants escaped, and Hand's soldiers had to be content with killing the man and one of the remaining women and taking a second woman captive. The prisoner told them that ten miles further along the Mahoning River there were ten additional Indians. A detachment of soldiers was dispatched; when they reached that site, they again found non-combatants. They shot two women and a boy and took another female captive. This heavily criticized episode became known as the "Squaw Campaign." While it had begun as a bona fide military expedition with a legitimate objective, frustration with slow progress and bad weather resulted only in the slaughter of women and children.[45]

Indian raids continued in various locations throughout the Commonwealth for the remainder of the decade. For the frontier, perhaps the worst episode was the attack by the British in concert with Tory Rangers – American loyalists – against the Wyoming Valley in the summer of 1778. In June a force of about 400 British soldiers and Tories and roughly 700 Indians advanced into the Wyoming Valley, which less than ten years earlier had been the scene of numerous skirmishes in the Yankee-Pennamite Wars. Forts or stockades had been constructed in this area, but they were neither strong enough nor were there sufficient militia to successfully defend against a force this size. In succession, one fort after another fell to the combined British-Tory-Indian attack. Fort Jenkins, Fort Wintermoot and Forty Fort all surrendered or were overrun. As news of the British-sponsored advance and innumerable Indian atrocities spread throughout the region (including both branches of the Susquehanna), a panic ensued which has become known as the "Great Runaway." In July 1778 the settlers thought this part of the frontier was too dangerous and evacuated their families in hopes of avoiding the marauding Indian bands. It was not until September that Colonel Thomas Hartley led an expedition composed of Continentals and militiamen to take the war to the Indians. In a campaign lasting several weeks, Hartley and his troops fought several engagements with the Indians and their Tory allies, initiating the process of making the Wyoming Valley and the western and northern branches of the Susquehanna safe again.

[45] A good account of Hand's expedition is found in Frederic A. Godcharles, *Pennsylvania: Political, Governmental, Military and Civil*, military volume (New York: American Historical Society, 1933), pp. 235-236.

Pressure at various points along the frontier resulted in the creation of a special type of militia unit called "ranging companies." They were formed for longer tours of frontier service, allowing them to react promptly to Indian incursions without the expected delay inherent in militia call-ups. Ranging companies were unique because of their flexibility. They could be enlisted for limited periods, for specific campaigns or "for the duration." Records from the period show the existence of any number of such companies, beginning in 1779, with some organized as late as 1782. Most were in the western areas of the Commonwealth, to include the counties of Northumberland, Bedford, Westmoreland and Washington, although at least one such company was organized in Lancaster County.[46]

Reports on the activities of these ranging companies, which were not always successful, exist in the Pennsylvania archives. One expedition which employed ranging companies was formed in 1781 by Colonel Archibald Lochry of Westmoreland County. Lochry was authorized to raise several companies of volunteers, which were to join with George Rogers Clark in a campaign against the Shawnees and other Indians along the Ohio. Ultimately the expedition was to proceed to the British post at Detroit. Lochry's soldiers rendezvoused at Carnahan's Block House (11 miles west of Hanna's Town) on July 24 and began their march on August 2. They failed to link up with General Clark's troops and were consequently several days behind the main body – a factor which was to spell disaster. Lochry tried to overtake Clark's column but only succeeded in apprehending deserters from Clark's unit. On August 24, short on supplies, Lochry's ranging companies camped near present-day Aurora, Indiana. While they were preparing a meal, they were attacked by Indians. Only a couple of the soldiers escaped, and Lochry, who had surrendered after the situation became hopeless, was tomahawked by an Indian as he sat on a log.[47]

In 1782, another comparable militia expedition was organized by Colonel William Crawford. About two thirds of the troops originated from Washington County, the rest from Westmoreland County. Their task was to stop the incursions of Indians into the frontier regions of Ohio and Pennsylvania. This so-called Sandusky Expedition began with a call for troops in April 1782. On May 10, 1782, 462 men were organized into 18 companies,

[46] Egle, *Pennsylvania in the Revolution*, vol. II, pp. 764-769.
[47] Ibid., pp. 681-683. According to this account, Brant, a Shawnee chief, reported that 36 of the company's strength, including five officers, were killed and 64 made prisoners. All the wounded who could not march were killed. An account of the privations suffered by the survivors, written by Lieutenant Isaac Anderson, can be found on pp. 685-689 of the same volume.

which then elected their captains. On May 25 they proceeded from their rendezvous point south of Fort Pitt on the west side of the Ohio River and began searching for the elusive Indians bands. On June 4 they reached Sandusky and shortly thereafter encountered Indians. In the fighting that followed, Colonel Crawford and about 60 of his men advanced against the Indians. They were cut off, then captured or killed. The remainder of the militia force under Lieutenant Colonel David Williamson were able to extricate themselves and succeeded in returning to Pennsylvania. Most of Crawford's group including the colonel perished.[48]

Militia units were not just used on the frontier but in a number of capacities from 1777 until the end of the war. With authorization now in hand, militia battalions were able to augment the Continental Army in key engagements at Brandywine, Germantown and Whitemarsh. The first major example of such use of the newly authorized militia occurred in September 1777 when Sir William Howe began an advance against Philadelphia, an important port and, in the eyes of the British, a center of sedition. Two Pennsylvania militia brigades with a strength of about 3,000 men were called up to assist Washington. The militia were prepared to support the Continentals as the Battle of Brandywine occurred on September 11, 1777. The militia's assigned role on the field was to guard a ford at the southern end of the battlefield. Washington assumed the main weight of the British attack would come through Chadds Ford, but the British surprised him by only staging a diversionary attack there and, instead, crossing the Brandywine a few miles upstream and driving south on his flank.[49] Although the commanders attempted to change their front to meet this threat, they were unsuccessful. As Washington's flank gave way, his position began to deteriorate. The Continental Army suffered a defeat, but a disaster was avoided by Washington's skillful handling of his troops as he withdrew. Through no fault of their own, the militia brigades took no part in this important engagement.

Following the defeat at Brandywine, General Howe divided his numerically superior force (Washington had approximately 11,000 at Brandywine vs. 30,000 with Howe) and tasked a substantial part of it with the mission of reduc-

---

[48] Ibid., pp. 708-727. To appreciate what happened to Crawford's Sandusky expedition, the narrative of Dr. John Knight, a surgeon with Crawford's force, can be found on pp. 708-717, and the narrative of John Slover, the guide, on pp. 717-727.

[49] Proctor's Artillery also took part in this battle, covering the high ground above the ford with its guns. It ultimately retreated, in less than orderly fashion. A black wagon train driver named Hector distinguished himself by retaining his equipment and gathering up muskets that had been discarded by retreating infantry.

ing the American fortifications on the Delaware River. He stationed the rest of his army in Germantown, where Washington surprised him. At the Battle of Germantown on October 3, 1777, Pennsylvania militia units again suffered a fate similar to Brandywine. In their assigned sector, they were on the fringe of the main battle. As a result, the Pennsylvania militia division was not involved in the heavy fighting that developed. The attached artillery did bring British forces under fire and helped to inhibit their freedom of movement in this area of the battlefield. Other Pennsylvania troops were on the field as well and played active combat roles. The Pennsylvania State Regiment, for example, was a part of Major General Nathaniel Greene's force whose role was to roll up the British right flank. Regrettably, this action was unsuccessful and resulted in some fratricide between Greene's column and Brigadier General Anthony Wayne's left brigade. In addition, the Pennsylvania German Regiment participated in the battle (as it had at Brandywine) as a part of Major General John Sullivan's division.[50]

In the following engagement at Whitemarsh, December 5-6, Pennsylvania militia were also involved in the fighting. The militia were positioned on the right flank of Washington's army, ready to counter the British probe on the 5th. In the brief battle that occurred, the militia took the brunt of the action, resulting in some 40-50 casualties, including Brigadier General James Irvine, wounded and captured by the British when he attempted to rally the militia. While the British were successful in their probes into Washington's position on that day, after some skirmishes at the outposts on the following day, Howe decided not to follow up and instead withdrew to Philadelphia. Washington would in turn take up his position at Valley Forge for the bitter winter of 1777-1778. Even at Valley Forge the militia were frequently employed to hinder British foraging expeditions and patrol the area between the British positions and Washington's cantonment.

It is not feasible within the confines of this book to trace all the uses of the Pennsylvania militia from 1777 to 1783. In covering these selected actions the author has attempted to show that the militia and its precursor, the Associators — who were often referred to as militia — served the Commonwealth in many ways during the Revolutionary War. Much like its lineal descendant the National Guard, the militia was used for internal security purposes, to defend the interests of the state, and most important to assist in the defense of

[50] John B. B. Trussell, *The Pennsylvania Line: Regimental Organization and Operations, 1776-1783* (Harrisburg: Pennsylvania Historical and Museum Commission, 1977), pp. 10-12, 205-207.

the nation. Moreover, the Associators contributed far more than is immediately evident, because in the period 1775-1777 numerous Associator units were converted into Continental units. Thus, their identity as Commonwealth units is sometimes difficult to ascertain. For certain, the militia in Pennsylvania was far more visible and, in its various forms described in this chapter, played a far larger role than its precursors in the French and Indian War.

The Revolutionary War drew to a close in September 1783, with the Peace of Paris officially ending the hostilities. At that time Pennsylvania still had some 2,210 troops in the field, including 1,760 rangers and 450 militia. The Militia Act, even with its shortcomings, had raised an estimated 60,000 men available for the Commonwealth's military purposes, many of whom were actually employed in the defense of both the Commonwealth and the new nation. In addition, some Continental units of the Pennsylvania Line still had former Associators in their ranks, and as a result, the total number of Associators or militia still serving the nation or the Commonwealth is difficult to determine. But this significant fact remains: the proprietary colony which once had the dubious distinction of refusing to contribute to the royal government's defense had redeemed itself by providing a large number of troops for the Revolution. In total, an estimated 120,514 Pennsylvanians served. Given this statistic, it is important to recognize the significance of the changes that had come to the Commonwealth's defensive system between 1775 and 1783.

As Pennsylvania transitioned from the French and Indian War to the Revolution, it initially reverted to the defensive system that had served it in the past: voluntary associations not unlike those initiated by Franklin in late 1747. Associators were Pennsylvania's only possible response under the laws in effect in 1775. As noted by one author, "During the revolution the Associators were the mainstay and support of Pennsylvania."[51] While this statement is certainly accurate for the early part of the Revolution, the colony which had shown no enthusiasm for defending Britain's interests at home or abroad eventually distinguished itself by supplying both troops and major leaders for the foundling American nation. Through the demands of the Revolution, the citizens and the new political leadership of the Commonwealth seemed to understand that voluntary associations, while a necessary compromise in the mid-18th century, were no longer an acceptable method of defense. The military burden had to be shouldered by a broader base of the population. Thus, as the Revolution ended, Pennsylvania witnessed the end of the Associator movement and the

---

[51] Clarke, *Official History of the Pennsylvania Militia*, p. 91.

beginning of a reliance on militias, which would last until the Civil War.

Although Associator units, as a means of defending the Commonwealth, would become a matter of history, the Associators as individuals would not. Many Associators, militiamen and Continental soldiers still felt a responsibility to defend their state and were unwilling to forget soldiering. The war was over, but the military tradition that arose in Pennsylvania had only begun to exert its positive influence.

CHAPTER 7

Defending the New Republic

*It will be universally acknowledged, that to guard a
republican government against internal encroachments, or
external violence, a well organized and a well disciplined
militia is the only safe and efficient instrument.*

– Governor Thomas Mifflin, 1793

D uring the mid-1700s, and specifically between 1757 and 1777, the
Commonwealth reached a watershed regarding its defense forces – a
fact few people in that time or now truly appreciate. For most of its
existence, Pennsylvania and its leaders had wrestled with the issue of how best
to defend the Commonwealth. The Quaker resistance to providing military
appropriations was part of the problem, but they alone should not be blamed
for the failure to provide for Pennsylvania's defense. As previous chapters have
shown, many of the Commonwealth's citizenry were hesitant to raise and support military forces and directly involve themselves in what they regarded as
British wars of empire. This reluctance began to erode when war, in the form
of a direct threat from the French and their Indian allies, came to Pennsylvania
in 1754. For a brief time, the Commonwealth fielded Associators, militia and
even provincial regiments. Although the demands of the French and Indian
War did not convince Pennsylvanians to provide for their defense permanently
by creating a standing militia based on mandatory membership, the logjam on
the defense issue was at last breaking up.

With the American Revolution, the final threshold was crossed.
Pennsylvania clearly recognized the need for a militia – a state military force –
requiring the obligatory membership of all free white male adults. The demand
for manpower to support the Revolutionary army demonstrated that Pennsylvania could no longer raise enough troops through Associator auspices. It had
to discard the voluntary associations, the device founded by Franklin in 1747,
in favor of a statutory militia. Thus, the Revolution resulted in the establish-

ment of permanent militia laws for the first time in the Commonwealth's history. The military tradition which had begun with the Associators reached its logical conclusion.

In some respects, Pennsylvania would have found it difficult to retain its former reticence regarding military matters after the Revolutionary War. In 1783 the thirteen colonies achieved their independence. As part of a newly independent nation, Pennsylvanians would have some defense responsibilities. These responsibilities were significant, because in 1783 the nation was affected by two traditions which would mold post-war Pennsylvania's defense posture. First, by the nature of their political and legal origins, the former colonies would follow the British tradition of dependence on militias to defend local communities. Second, within the colonies there had been a decided distrust of standing armies and a feeling by many that an army was or could be used as an instrument of tyranny.[1] Both of these factors meant that the newly independent nation would rely on a substantial non-federal contribution for defense. Even during the last two years of the war, support for a national army began to erode. The years 1782-1783 saw no major military operations by the Continental Army. Congress exhibited its now-familiar tendency to downsize the Army, even though a peace treaty had not been signed. As Washington accurately noted, the British army still had more Americans in its loyalist ranks than he had among his Continentals.[2]

As the Revolutionary War ended, the hesitancy of the colonies to retain a standing army of any size and the suspicion they bore toward it were recognized by Washington. He had the opportunity to express his views when a congressional committee, chaired by Alexander Hamilton, asked him to present his thoughts on how best to defend the fledgling nation. Basing his written response on his colonial experiences, the Revolutionary War and suggestions solicited from military colleagues, Washington submitted a treatise entitled "Sentiments on the Peace Establishment."[3] He recommended the maintenance of a small regular army and the establishment of a well-trained and regulated militia. According to his proposal, the militia was to have clear national respon-

---

[1] As one soldier-historian notes, in the early 1790s, as the constitutional government was newly established, there was much debate about the role of the military in the new republic and a fear that the military, despite its minuscule size, could be used for a coup. See David R. Palmer, *1794: America, Its Army and the Birth of the Nation* (Novato, Calif.: Presidio Press, 1994).
[2] Robert K. Wright Jr., *The Continental Army*, The Army Lineage Series (Washington, D.C.: Center of Military History, 1983), p. 171.
[3] Reproduced in appendix I, John McCauley Palmer, *Washington, Lincoln and Wilson* (New York: Doubleday, 1930), pp. 375-396.

sibilities and form a significant part of the new nation's defense. Washington understood the country's distrust of large standing armies. Together with his colleagues, he felt that a properly trained and equipped militia would be the most acceptable method for defending the country.[4]

As the post-war period emerged, Washington and other military leaders planned for the militia to have a strong role in the nation's defense. The nation, however, did not immediately take Washington's wise counsel. Instead, it drifted through a phase, from 1783 to 1787, in which it was governed by the Articles of Confederation, under which a central government of any strength seemed to be anathema. As a consequence, in the mid-1780s the Commonwealth of Pennsylvania was faced with an entirely new political environment. It was no longer a proprietary colony, but one of thirteen new states which retained significant powers. Each of these states had a degree of autonomy, but the citizens of each state had some responsibilities to the national government. In the Washingtonian concept, which soon would be accepted (with some notable exceptions), a major responsibility of the citizen and his state was the defense of the nation. Because the defense umbrella of the Crown no longer extended to this part of the New World, Pennsylvania did not appear to have the latitude it had in 1747 or 1763 to ignore defense responsibilities. The Commonwealth would have to do its part.

The defense issue facing Pennsylvania in 1783 was not nearly as daunting as it had been at the conclusion of other conflicts. For example, Pennsylvania did have on the books legislation that provided for its defense. In 1777 it had passed a wartime militia law and had amended it on several occasions during the war. When the act expired in 1780, it was renewed. In 1783, with the war over, Pennsylvania broke from the tradition established in the closing phases of the French and Indian War and renewed its Militia Act again instead of

---

[4] All too often critics of the militia and National Guard find it convenient to quote Washington's comments when he wrote in exasperation, "To place any dependence on the militia is assuredly resting upon a broken staff. Men just dragged from the tender scenes of domestic life, unaccustomed to the din of arms, totally unacquainted with every kind of military skill (which being followed by want of confidence in themselves when opposed to troops regularly trained, disciplined and appointed, superior in knowledge and superior in arms) makes them timid and ready to fly from their own shadows." Letter to Congress on September 24, 1776, reprinted in Major James B. Scott, ed., *The Militia, Senate Document 695, January 12, 1917* (Washington, D.C.: Government Printing Office, 1917), p. 23. Ignored by the selective use of Washington's comments is the fact that he was a militia officer from Virginia with over 20 years of service in that institution. A better understanding of his intent for the post-war defense force and his belief that a well-trained militia could indeed defend the country is clearly evident in his "Sentiments on the Peace Establishment."

allowing it to lapse.[5] This was despite the absence of any urgency regarding defense, since neither the Commonwealth nor the nation faced any direct threat of hostile action from a foreign power. The change in attitude was evident in 1786, when Charles Biddle, serving as the vice president of the Supreme Executive Council, informed the Assembly that Colonel Frances Mentges had been appointed as Inspector General of the Militia. His duties were to "encourage and direct this rising disposition, to mark out and establish a uniformity of appearance and discipline in the several corps, to examine into the state of arms and accouterments, and to notice and report all abuses of such public property as may fall within his care or observation."[6]

While no sovereign countries posed an immediate threat to Pennsylvania during the rest of the decade, the problem with the hostility of the Indians in western Pennsylvania and the Ohio region had not been resolved.[7] The potential for raids on the western counties remained a realistic possibility.[8] In 1788, Benjamin Franklin was serving as president of the Supreme Executive Council and noted, in a letter to the Assembly, a resolution of Congress dated August 12, 1788, referring to the necessity of "holding in readiness the militia

---

[5] There were actually three militia acts in 1783 – one passed on March 21, another on September 22, and the last on December 9. Major William P. Clarke, *Official History of the Militia and National Guard of Pennsylvania from the Earliest Period of Record to the Present Time* (Philadelphia: Charles J. Hendler, 1909), p. 25. Cited hereafter as Clarke, *Official History of the Pennsylvania Militia*.

[6] George E. Reed, ed., *Pennsylvania Archives: Papers of the Governors, 1785-1817*, fourth series, vol. IV (Harrisburg: State of Pennsylvania, 1900), p. 38. Cited hereafter as Reed, *Papers of the Governors, 1785-1817*.

[7] A number of incidents fueled these fears. For example, Council President John Dickinson was informed that in late March "savages" had taken a Washington County woman captive, had captured two men at "Weeling," and on April 1 had taken a Washington County family of eight prisoner." Samuel Hazard, ed., *Pennsylvania Archives: Selected and Arranged from Original Documents in the Office of the Secretary of the Commonwealth Conformably to Acts of the General Assembly, Commencing 1783*, vol. X (Philadelphia: Joseph Severns & Co., 1854), p. 6. Cited hereafter as Hazard, *Pennsylvania Archives Commencing 1783*, vol. X. In the same volume, additional reports exist about clashes with the western Pennsylvania Indians. See Lieutenant John Cummings' report to President Dickinson on March 29, 1783, p. 22, and a report to the president on March 26, 1783, by Captain Thomas Robinson of the Pennsylvania Rangers, pp. 14-15.

[8] Several attempts at negotiations and treaties are noted in the records of this period. For example, during the summer of 1783, Ephraim Douglass made an extended trip into the Ohio region to negotiate with the tribes there. On August 18, 1783, he reported to the Secretary of War on his trip. He had attempted to express to the Delaware, Huron and "Shauneze" tribes (and he ultimately visited a council where the chiefs of 11 nations were in attendance) the peaceful intentions of the new government toward the Indians. This officially sanctioned trip and the hope that he had clarified the peaceful intentions of the United States were included in records of the Pennsylvania Archives. Ibid., p. 6.

on the frontier to act in conjunction with the federal troops in defending the western country against Indian hostilities."[9]

The Indian problem was not the only contingency that might have required the use of military force. Shortly after the end of the Revolutionary War, the Wyoming Valley controversy erupted anew.

The First Pennamite War had ended in an uneasy truce shortly before the Revolution. During the war, Connecticut controlled the Wyoming Valley, and troops organized there for the Continental Army were recognized as Connecticut troops. The disputed claims to the valley, however, remained unsettled, and the Revolutionary War had only brought a pause in this controversy. Once the fighting came to an end, there was pressure by both Connecticut and Pennsylvania to legally settle the issue once and for all. In 1782 Pennsylvania asked the Continental Congress to do so. A special commission was appointed and, after examining the evidence on both sides, rendered its decision:

> that the Jurisdiction and Pre-emption of all the territory lying within the
> charter boundary of Pennsylvania and claimed by the state of Connecticut,
> do of right belong to Pennsylvania.[10]

The decree deeding the land to Pennsylvania was signed at the end of December 1782, but even this legal document did not end the controversy right away. Sporadic fighting broke out between the Yankees and the Pennamites in 1783 and lasted into the following year. Continental troops had been present in the Wyoming Valley during the Revolutionary War. When they were withdrawn in early 1783, two companies of Pennsylvania rangers were sent to replace them. Recognizing the sensitivities of the Connecticut adherents, the rangers were given specific instructions that "the Inhabitants settled at or near the Wyoming should be in all respects treated with kindness."[11]

The bitterness of the Wyoming settlers is clearly evident in a report to Pennsylvania's Council President John Dickinson on March 29, 1783, when he occupied Fort Wyoming (later called Fort Dickinson). He noted that "the Conduct and Behavior of the Inhabitants resembles that of a conquered

---

[9] Reed, *Papers of the Governors, 1785-1817*, p. 30.
[10] The language which provides the commissioners' decision is included in an act passed by the General Assembly on March 13, 1783. Hazard, *Pennsylvania Archives Commencing 1783*, vol. X, pp. 83-90.
[11] Ibid., pp. 167-168.

Nation very much."[12] Despite the presence of state forces, disturbances continued well into 1784. Finally, on August 10, 1784, Dickinson informed Lieutenant Colonel John Armstrong that insurgents in the Wyoming Valley should be convinced of the determination of Pennsylvania to retain the region. He further stated that all those responsible for disturbances should be held accountable for their actions and that the Wyoming fortifications should be leveled and the cannon removed to Sunbury.[13] Years would pass before the inhabitants of the area would finally accept the Commonwealth's authority, and the government of Connecticut was frequently guilty of encouraging the claims of their former citizens and attempting to act as their advocate in disputes. The insurgency requiring state troops to maintain order, however, would pass in the mid-1780s.[14]

Although local strife with the Indians and the internal conflict in the Wyoming Valley were the only real threats to Pennsylvania for the remainder of the decade, responsibilities assumed as part of a newly independent nation required the Commonwealth to maintain military forces. Throughout 1783-1784 troops that had been in Continental service were returned to state status and many promptly reorganized. Other Pennsylvania troops were still in service with the national government in 1784 and even 1785. The Commonwealth maintained a well-stocked state arsenal in Philadelphia. In the post-war era it even found it necessary to raise militia troops for contingencies with the Indians and in a few instances for the Wyoming insurrections.[15]

When America's constitutional government was established in 1790, the Commonwealth developed its Constitution of 1790 to serve as the legal basis for its own new government.[16] This Constitution had several significant military provisions. Article II, Section VII gave the governor the power to be

[12] Ibid., p. 23-24. Captain John Shrawder the following day noted, "The inhabitants are exceedingly reserved and to judge by their appearances the generality of them does not like the Pennsylvanians to an excess."

[13] Ibid., p. 307.

[14] It is important to remember that at the same time Pennsylvania was also attempting to settle the western territory dispute with Virginia – a dispute which had also required troops in the immediate pre-Revolutionary War period. Ibid., pp. 171-174.

[15] For example, a Major James Moore was given instructions on September 26, 1783, to recruit two companies of militia into Commonwealth service for a period of no more than two years. Ibid., pp. 127-128.

[16] A distinguished role for the post-war Pennsylvania militia was the assignment to escort the President of the United States through Philadelphia in 1789. Thomas Mifflin reported this honorific task to Richard Peters on March 13, 1789, with the cost estimate of 199 pounds, 7 shillings and 6 pence specie. Reed, *Papers of the Governors, 1785-1817*, p. 75.

"Commander in Chief of the Army and Navy of the Commonwealth, and of the Militia except when they be called into the actual service of the United States."[17] Article VI, Section II stated, "The Freemen of this Commonwealth shall be armed and disciplined for its defense." Conscientious objectors were exempted, and the appointment of militia officers was authorized in a manner and for the time specified by law.[18]

Although the Commonwealth had shown its willingness to maintain a peacetime military force, the necessity for the 1790 militia was driven by congressional action. The federal Constitution mandated the creation of militias, and in 1792 Congress passed legislation to implement the defense intent of the Constitution's framers. The Constitution had made provisions for the creation of an army, but its structure and size were dependent on what Congress was willing to authorize and fund. In addition, the Constitution required the thirteen new states to provide for militias. As noted above, George Washington – the commander of the Continental Army and the person who would soon be elected America's first President – recommended in 1782 that the nation's defense be militia-based. His intent was implemented in 1791, when he and Secretary of War Henry Knox drafted a militia act to establish the nation's defense posture. The resulting Militia Act of 1792, though emasculated by the compromises necessary to get it through a Congress wary of the power of the new central government, placed militia in a key role for the defense of the post-Revolutionary War nation.[19]

Pennsylvania responded with enabling legislation in 1793, establishing a new militia act to place it in compliance with the provisions of federal law. The Militia Act of 1793 created a requirement, in a peacetime environment, for a militia requiring the participation of male citizens. Although Pennsylvania had already shown its willingness to maintain a post-war militia, its militia had formerly been established according to its own needs and thus could have been dismantled by the whim of the state legislature. The Constitution and the 1792 Militia Act made the maintenance of the militia a federal requirement and

[17] Ibid., p. 120.
[18] Ibid., p. 126. The Constitution, Article IX, Section XXI also stated, "The right of the citizens to bear arms in defense of themselves and the State shall not be questioned."
[19] The 1792 Militia Act as conceived by Washington required a National Militia that would enroll all able-bodied free white males ages 18-60. As originally drafted, the federal government was to provide the equipment and pay militiamen for their training duty. This did not happen because a strong national force was not supported by the strong states' advocates, who regarded it as a potential instrument of tyranny. See *The Annals of Congress, 1789-1790, First Congress, Second Session*, vol. II (Washington, D.C.: Seaton and Gales, 1849), pp. 2142-2162.

helped ensure its permanence.

Pennsylvania's Militia Act of April 11, 1793, abolished all militia laws previously in force and created a new legal foundation for the Commonwealth's military establishment. The act required that all able-bodied white male citizens between the ages of 18 and 45, with the normal exceptions, were to serve the state and the nation through enrollment in the militia. As part of his military obligation, the militiaman had to own and maintain a weapon (with the obvious exception of artillery). The act also provided the basic structure for the militia. The Commonwealth was organized into nine divisions (not to be confused with modern divisions), each of which would have as commander a major general, with two aides-de-camp. There would be 22 brigades; each would have a brigadier general and a brigade inspector, who was to serve as the brigade major. There would also be 72 infantry regiments, each commanded by a lieutenant colonel. There would be one major in each of the battalions, along with a captain, a lieutenant, an ensign, four sergeants, four corporals, one clerk, one fifer, one drummer and a bugler. Regimental staff were also specified, as was the basic structure for artillery companies.[20]

Most important, the act provided for an adjutant general for the entire militia. This significant action had been preceeded in 1786 by Charles Biddle's appointment of an inspector general for the Commonwealth, which had given Pennsylvania a military commander with oversight on militia affairs. This position expanded in 1793, with duties specified for the adjutant general to distribute to the various commands all orders from the governor. The adjutant general was also charged with the responsibility to "attend all public reviews when the governor shall review the militia; to obey all orders from the commander-in-chief relating to carrying into effect and perfecting the military discipline established by the act."[21] The adoption of the 1793 act established the basic legal and organizational structure which would serve the Commonwealth for the remainder of the 18th century and even into the 19th. Even though the Commonwealth would no longer have to depend on defensive associations to protect its citizens, the heritage of these Associator units, and in some cases the actual membership, continued into the new era of constitutional government.

As mentioned earlier in this chapter, the primary defensive issue for Pennsylvania at this time was the unfinished business with the Indians. At the beginning of the 1790s, Thomas Mifflin, in a report to the Assembly, related

---

[20] Clarke, *Official History of the Pennsylvania Militia*, p. 26.
[21] Ibid.

Josiah Harmar, first commander of the peacetime American Army and Adjutant General of Pennsylvania, 1793-1799 (miniature by Raphael Peale, reproduced by permission of the U.S. Department of State).

the fears of the inhabitants of Pittsburgh about a potential Indian invasion.[22] Three companies of militia were maintained for the defense of the frontier during this period, and the Commonwealth continued to man fortifications in the Philadelphia harbor. Concerns about hostile Indians continued into 1793, although in his address to the Assembly that year the governor admitted that since the Assembly's adjournment the "fellow citizens on the frontier had been very little molested by the Indians."[23]

Permanently establishing a post-war militia in Pennsylvania and the other former colonies came none to soon, because the defense of the new

[22] Reed, *Papers of the Governors, 1785-1817*, pp. 214-215. This initial report came on December 22, 1791. On December 29 Mifflin transmitted another memorial from citizens of the western counties concerned about their protection. While he noted that federal help had been requested, he also noted that additional supplies of arms and ammunition were indispensable for the militia, for they would likely be called into service to defend the citizens. Ibid., pp. 214-217.

[23] Ibid., p. 258. Relations with the Indians during this period and throughout the 18th century are detailed in C. Hale Sipe's *The Indian Wars of Pennsylvania: An Account of Indian Events in Pennsylvania, of the French and Indian War, Pontiac's War, Lord Dunmore's War, the Revolutionary War, and the Indian Uprising from 1789 to 1795* (Harrisburg: Telegraph Press, 1931).

nation was soon to be tested. In 1794 the Commonwealth, some of its neighboring states and the federal government were faced by a rebellion in which a number of citizens contested the new government's authority. This conflict was known as the Whiskey Rebellion. The origins of the rebellion date to March 1791, when Congress passed an excise tax on whiskey over the opposition of representatives from the frontier areas of Pennsylvania, Maryland and Virginia. With strong support from the Atlantic seaboard, the bill was signed into law by President Washington. This excise tax, however, was strongly opposed by many residents from rural western America, including Kentucky, western Virginia and Ohio. The heart of the unrest was in Pennsylvania, specifically Bedford, Cumberland, Franklin, Northumberland, Allegheny, Fayette, Washington and Westmoreland counties. In both Pennsylvania and its neighboring states, the issue was the burden of the newly imposed federal tax on one of the major wage-earning products, whiskey.

Producing whiskey allowed rural residents to get most of their agricultural output to market easily. Shipping grain to the populous East posed a problem because it was bulky and susceptible to vermin and rot. Distilling it into a marketable liquid meant the best return for the farmers' labor. It is important to note that western Pennsylvania farmers essentially practiced subsistence agriculture. There was little profit in their operations, and any new tax was detrimental to their limited lifestyle and thus highly objectionable. To understand the significance of whiskey production in the early economy of Pennsylvania, records from this era show 36 Pennsylvania counties with a total of 3,594 distilleries. Of this number, 799 or 22 percent were in southwestern Pennsylvania, a lightly populated area.[24]

With this new tax cutting into farmers' profit margins, protests against it began before the year was out. The reaction on the frontier caused Congress, on the advice of Secretary of the Treasury Alexander Hamilton, to amend the law, lowering rates and permitting monthly payments instead of a lump-sum remittance. These changes did not placate the dissidents, however. Beginning in the summer of 1792 there were protest meetings and actual acts of hostility against tax collectors in the western regions of Pennsylvania, Maryland, Virginia, Ohio and Kentucky. Revenue agents were attacked, and residents who offered help, no matter how innocuous, became targets of local ire.[25] Without

---

[24] Jerry A. Clouse, *The Whiskey Rebellion: Southwestern Pennsylvania's Frontier People Test the American Constitution* (Harrisburg: Pennsylvania Historical and Museum Commission, 1994), p. 10. Cited hereafter as Clouse, *The Whiskey Rebellion*.

[25] For example, in early 1794 barns belonging to William Richmond and Robert Shawhan of St.

any immediate brake to slow it, the violence escalated. By 1794, the Whiskey Rebellion had proceeded beyond protest and become in fact a rebellion.

The acts of disobedience and the ensuing violence against the new government and its representatives concerned the new President. Washington believed the new excise tax, as a law, had to be obeyed. He was also concerned about the rebellion eroding federal authority and damaging the overall reputation of the new government. Yet crafting a response was a touchy situation for the first President. Actions that might be perceived as too punitive would likely be unpopular and would have an adverse effect on the fledgling government. Popular sentiment on this issue was significant because, although the rebellion was centered in western Pennsylvania, "Liberty Poles," a common expression of anti-excise sentiment, appeared in areas as far east as Carlisle, Reading and even Easton.[26] A measured response was also in order because – even though armed

A Liberty Pole, the standard expression of opposition to the excise tax (drawing by Taygety McNally).

Clair Township, Allegheny County were burned due to their owner's compliance with the new excise law. Ibid., p. 22.

[26] The "Liberty Pole" was a symbol erected by citizens opposed to tyranny. It was generally constructed of two spliced timbers – a flagpole in appearance – and often bound with iron bands or studded with nails. At its top flew a banner, often home-made, and a sign was affixed to the shaft which stated "Liberty and equality," "Liberty and no excise" or some comparable slogan.

mobs had committed violence against federal agents and their supporters, and Supreme Court Justice James Wilson confirmed that the judiciary could no longer compel obedience to the law in western Pennsylvania – no act of secession had occurred, and no real opposing army had been formed.[27] The western insurgents appealed to militia officers to muster on July 28, 1794, but this was not a direct appeal for rebellion.[28]

The west, however, moved to the verge of open rebellion in July 1794. This was prompted by the delivery by federal marshal David Lennox of a court summons on July 15 to an Allegheny County farmer and distiller named William Miller. Unfortunately, Lennox was accompanied by John Neville, who supervised excise collections in the area and, as the official charged with this task, was extremely unpopular.[29] In the process, they were harassed by David Phillips, farmer, preacher and local militia leader (who had received a similar summons earlier that day). Phillips was joined by a group of between 30 and 40 area citizens. On the following day about 100 men, some of them armed, returned to Neville's home and demanded his resignation and the surrender of all his tax records.[30] Neville was prepared for trouble, given his experience the day before, and had armed his slaves. In the fighting that ensued, five of the insurrectionists were wounded. One of them, Oliver Miller, died the following day. On July 17 an even larger group of about 600 Allegheny and Washington County militia, accompanied by drummers and thus functioning as a military unit, under the command of James MacFarlane (like Neville a Revolutionary War officer and local hero), returned to avenge the so-called murder of Oliver Miller. Sensing trouble, Neville had secured the services of his brother-in-law, Major Abraham Kirkpatrick, and ten soldiers from Fort Fayette north of

---

[27] The formation of a rebel army seemed to be occurring on the first of August through a military rally held on Braddock's field in western Pennsylvania. The leaders of the western Pennsylvania rebels organized this show of force, bringing onto the field 5,000-7,000 militiamen to highlight the bitter anti-excise sentiment. These errant militiamen followed this rally with a march on Pittsburgh – which the rebels referred to as Sodom – to demonstrate their strength to federal sympathizers there and coerce them into acquiescence or agreement. See the report of Jon Wilkins to General William Irvine in George E. Reed, ed., *Pennsylvania Archives: Papers Relating to What Is Known as the Whiskey Rebellion in Western Pennsylvania, 1794*, second series, vol. IV (Harrisburg: E. K. Meyers, State Printer, 1890), pp. 143-148. Cited hereafter as Reed, *Papers Relating to the Whiskey Rebellion*.

[28] Ibid., "Circular of the Western Insurgents to the Militia Officers," p. 67.

[29] Both these men were Revolutionary War veterans. Lennox had been a captain serving in the Pennsylvania Line, and John Neville had been a colonel-brevetted, a brigadier general in the Virginia Line.

[30] Jerry Clouse, in *The Whiskey Rebellion*, states there were 40 men in the group. However many were present, the group was referred to interestingly as the Mingo Creek Militia.

Pittsburgh. Another skirmish occurred, with MacFarlane becoming a casualty and the martyr of the rebellion. Neville was not captured nor did he resign, but his home and most of his outbuildings were burned. The refusal to obey federal law, coupled with attacks by local militia, functioning in an organized fashion against federal authorities and soldiers from Fort Pitt (four of whom were wounded), meant that an actual rebellion was in progress. This could not be tolerated by the new federal government.

Since the insurgents were American citizens, the government first tried to negotiate. On August 8 a peace commission was appointed and sent west by President Washington to reach an agreement with the western counties.[31] The commission proceeded to Pittsburgh and by the 20th decided, based on what they saw en route, that military force would be needed to quell the rebellion. Though many in the west appeared willing to bow to federal authority, particularly with the concessions the government was willing to make, the commissioners felt there was simply too much dissent. Federal terms were presented to the Insurrectionists' Committee of Sixty in Brownsville; 34 voted to submit to federal authority, and 23 voted for secession from the United States. Despite this victory for moderates, steps had already been initiated to use military force.

Washington faced two major hurdles in fashioning his response. First, the governor of Pennsylvania, Thomas Mifflin, himself a Revolutionary War hero, did not want to employ force until all judicial alternatives had been exercised.[32] While Washington wanted the governor's support and ultimately received it, he was intent on restoring federal authority in the region. The second problem facing the President was much more difficult. The United States had a largely militia-based defense, and as a result, the active-duty army was small. Most of this small army, under the command of a Pennsylvanian, General "Mad" Anthony Wayne, had moved west to Fort Recovery in the Ohio Territory (in present-day Indiana) to fight the Miami Indians, whose military prowess and aggressive actions caused Pennsylvanians considerable anxiety. Wayne's force was ultimately successful in the now-famous Battle of Fallen

---

[31] A copy of the appointment of James Ross, Jasper Yeates and William Randolph as commissioners and their instructions from Edmund Randolph, Secretary of State, are included in Reed, *Papers Relating to the Whiskey Rebellion*, pp. 116-118.

[32] In Governor Mifflin's message to President Washington he stated, "I, too, shall ever prefer the instruments of conciliation to those of coercion, and never, but in the last resort, countenance a dereliction of judicial authority, for the exertion of military force." At the end of his letter, however, he stated, "Whatever duty you may impose in pursuance of your constitutional and legal powers, will, on my part, be promptly undertaken and faithfully discharged." Ibid., pp. 88, 93.

Timbers, but they were not immediately available for Washington's use. A military response to the Whiskey Rebellion would have to be delivered by militia.

The President had to be careful. Some elements in the federal government wanted prompt military action, but others sought only a civil response. Thus, in a cabinet meeting on August 6, it was decided that preparations would be made for mobilizing troops, but the troops would not march until attempts were made to negotiate with the insurrectionists. On August 7 Washington ordered all insurgents to disperse and return to their homes and warned all citizens to avoid aiding and abetting, in any way, persons engaged in treasonable activity.[33] To ensure that order was restored, for the first time in the nation's history he called out the militia "to execute the laws of the Union" and "suppress insurrection" – roles which are clearly specified in the U.S. Constitution. On

General "Mad Anthony" Wayne – Associator, Continental officer and veteran of the post-Revolutionary War Indian campaigns (from a photo in the collection of the U.S. Army Military History Institute, Carlisle Barracks, Pa.

[33] Ibid., pp. 105-108. Governor Mifflin issued a similar proclamation to the citizens of the Commonwealth on the same date. Ibid., pp. 108-110.

Pennsylvania *in the* Whiskey Rebellion, *1794*

Pennsylvania in 1790

Pennsylvania Today
Seven Counties in the midst of the Whiskey Rebellion

August 8 the governor gave Pennsylvania's adjutant general instructions to mobilize to fill Pennsylvania's quota.[34] The quota was 5,200 militiamen, including enlisted soldiers and non-commissioned and commissioned officers. General Harmar planned to use his brigade inspectors to draft troops from numerous units by class, as required by law, rather than mobilize complete units. This plan was designed to produce a total of 5,196 men.[35]

These troops were to be organized into a provisional division under Major General William Irvine, with three provisional brigades under Brigadier Generals Thomas Proctor, Francis Murray and James Chambers.[36] The troops

[34] Major General Josiah Harmar was an officer with an impressive record. He had been in the First Pennsylvania Regiment in 1776 and had finished out the Revolutionary War as a lieutenant colonel. He served in Washington's army from 1778 to 1780 and with General Greene in the South from 1781 to 1782. At the end of the war he was made a brevet colonel in the United States Regiment but reverted to the permanent rank of lieutenant colonel in the Army of the Articles of Confederation. By 1789 he was a brevet brigadier general and General-in-Chief of the Army. He resigned from the Army on January 1, 1792, and at age 39 became Adjutant General of Pennsylvania.

[35] Note that the concept of drafting militia as individuals, rather than calling up units – a practice begun with Pennsylvania's 1777 act – had been retained in the 1793 law.

[36] The key leaders in the Commonwealth's response show a remarkable degree of continuity.

were to march west to Carlisle, where they would rendezvous with additional troops supplied by New Jersey to build a force of about 7,500 men. Marylanders were to gather in Williamsport and then move to Cumberland, Maryland. Virginia troops were to meet in Winchester and old Fort Pleasant and then move on to Cumberland. New Jersey forces were to assemble in Trenton, then proceed to Carlisle. Pennsylvania soldiers were ordered to meet at Carlisle and Chambersburg. Though both Carlisle and Cumberland were logical meeting places, their selection points to a show of force, since both locales had been sympathetic to the rebellion.

For the four states, use of the militia proved to be an interesting test of loyalty, because it required the use of militia against militia – citizens against their peers. There was little enthusiasm for the mobilization of the militia, and in some cases outright opposition. In Pennsylvania, despite the fact the force was being built with an inordinate number of easterners, there was little support from the citizens for an excursion against their western brethren. Thus, even though General Harmar issued orders for the building of a militia force, there was little immediate response from the lower echelons. On August 27 Governor Mifflin requested a status report from Harmar on the mobilization process, and the latter in turn appealed to the brigade inspectors on the same day, expressing confidence in them but clearly entreating them to move on the business at hand.[37] The lack of progress in raising troops to meet Pennsylvania's obligation caused the governor to instruct Harmar to cease efforts at drafting militiamen and instead fill out the remainder of Pennsylvania's quota with volunteers.[38] But while enthusiasm was lacking, at least Pennsylvania was spared the embarrassment of her neighboring states. The Maryland militia, at its draft muster in Hagerstown, refused to obey its officers, and there were several days of rioting and mob rule in the town.[39] Recognizing the problem, on

Governor Mifflin, General Harmar, General Irvine and Brigadiers Proctor, Murray and Chambers were all Revolutionary War veterans who were either in the Continental Army or the Pennsylvania Line.

[37] Reed, *Papers Relating to the Whiskey Rebellion*, p. 178.

[38] Reed, *Papers of the Governors, 1785-1817*, pp. 311-313. Governor Mifflin was clearly not pleased. He told General Harmar, "I have waited with the greatest anxiety, for the execution of the instructions that were issued, in order to organize a body of militia, to be employed in that service agreeably to the presidents requisition ... It is now with the utmost mortification, therefore, that I now discover, in the returns which you have communicated to me, so great an indisposition in some of the brigades, to comply with that call."

[39] Thomas P. Slaughter, "The Friends of Liberty, Order, and the Whiskey Rebellion," in Steven R. Boyd, ed., *The Whiskey Rebellion: Past and Present Perspectives* (Westport, Conn.: Greenwood Press, 1985), pp. 208-210.

September 10 Governor Mifflin toured parts of Pennsylvania and spoke to citizens' groups, explaining the need to support the federal government and clarifying that the Commonwealth had tried to reason with the insurgents. In the governor's message to the Assembly on September 17, he reported success with this personal appeal to his constituents.[40]

On September 25 President Washington issued his second proclamation, which actually called the militia troops into the field to suppress the rebellion.[41] As the troops moved west, their reception by the citizenry was mixed. A crowd in Myerstown heckled Pennsylvania troops, and in the confrontation, one of them was shot when a soldier's pistol accidentally discharged. Near Myerstown, a second heckler was bayoneted, reportedly by a soldier in the Philadelphia Light Horse. There was far greater public empathy for the insurrectionists than many realize.

The most significant act that brought the militia force and the citizenry together was the presence of the Commander in Chief himself. Washington left Philadelphia on September 30 and proceeded through Reading to Carlisle, arriving there on October 4. He stayed in Carlisle for the next week, inspecting troops and preparing to move westward into the heartland of the insurrection. While he served as commander in the field, Washington likely planned to return to Philadelphia rather than accompany his troops westward. Consequently, after a visit with Virginia troops mustered at Cumberland, Maryland, he left command of forces in the field with his friend and fellow military leader from the American Revolution, Governor Henry Lee of Virginia.

On October 10, with Washington still present, Governor Richard Howell of New Jersey departed from Carlisle with the first contingent of troops, which included the Philadelphia Cavalry (likely the First City Troop), a regiment of Pennsylvania infantry, a regiment of New Jersey infantry and some artillery. Among the Pennsylvania elements were the Philadelphia Blues, mounted on grey horses. A second column left Carlisle on the 11th led by Major General Mifflin. General William Irvine remained in Carlisle to receive and organize any late-arriving elements. Troops continued to arrive for the next few days, although as late as October 13, the contingents from Northhampton and Bucks counties had still not reached their full strength.

The activities of these troops could hardly be termed a traditional military campaign. The militia forces moved west in two wings. The right proceeded from Carlisle to Bedford, its final assembly area. The left column, under

[40] Reed, *Papers Relating to the Whiskey Rebellion*, pp. 263-264.
[41] Ibid., pp. 304-306.

General Lee, proceeded to Uniontown, and the right continued on until it reached Pittsburgh. Once the army had reached the heart of "rebel" territory, Lee camped in the vicinity of Parkinson's Ferry. On November 8 he appealed to the residents of the four-county area to accommodate troops and obey the laws of the land. The following day he provided General Irvine with a list of names and descriptions of area insurgents. On November 13 detachments of soldiers were ordered out into the countryside, to identify and arrest suspects and bring them back to temporary prisons. Once this was accomplished, and with no resistance offered by the citizens or their militias, on November 19 the Army began its march back. Some troops were retained in Pittsburgh and Parkinson's Ferry to monitor the situation, since there remained uncertainty whether the rebellion was actually over. The trial of the rebellion's leaders was yet to occur, but beginning with the departure of troops on November 19, the military's role in the Whiskey Rebellion was essentially complete.[42]

The Whiskey Rebellion is an interesting event in the history of the Commonwealth and the newly formed American republic. For the first time in its post-Revolutionary existence, the militia was called on to exercise a role defined by the Constitution, suppressing what the federal government deemed an insurrection. And the militia succeeded although a critic might note it had no real opposition. The militia mustered, though slowly, marched and returned home. This show of force, together with the rebels' disorganization, brought about the end of the rebellion. The success of the state-based militia as an instrument of national power can best be seen in the Commonwealth, where the governor was personally opposed to settling the disturbance with military force. Governor Mifflin, however, ultimately bowed to the national authority and actually led troops in this brief military excursion. The Whiskey Rebellion also offers the only example of the President of the United States taking to the field as Commander in Chief of the Army.

At the same time, the Whiskey Rebellion revealed problems with the militia which demanded resolution. It proved difficult to raise the necessary troops from existing militia units because some citizens sympathized with the rebels. Others failed to see a major threat to the country or their way of life, so they chose not to participate. And while in the end the militia was success-ful in defending the nation's interests, its excursion failed to test the mettle of the institution in which Washington had placed his trust. A true test of the mili-

[42] Altogether more than 40 men were arrested for their role, real or supposed, in the Whiskey Rebellion. Charged with crimes ranging from misdemeanor to treason, most were subsequent-ly pardoned.

tia's reliability would not come until the 1812, when an actual war against a foreign adversary occurred.

There would be, however, one additional employment of the militia to restore public order in 18th-century Pennsylvania. This was precipitated by the congressional enactment of another new federal tax in 1798. The tax was designed to help reduce the debts incurred by the United States in the Revolutionary War. It sought to produce revenue by taxing land, homes and slaves; it was promptly dubbed the "house tax," because the value of houses was determined by counting the number of windows and measuring their size. Almost immediately the new tax became unpopular in certain parts of the nation. For collection purposes, nine tax districts were created in Pennsylvania, and from these districts the Commonwealth was to collect $232,177.72. Five years earlier the opposition to the federal tax on whiskey, which prompted the Whiskey Rebellion, had centered in western Pennsylvania. Opposition to the "house tax" was based in Berks, Lehigh, Northampton and Montgomery counties. In these eastern areas, which had a sizable German population, understanding of the tax was at best limited, and opposition to its collection was significant and organized.

The opposition coalesced around John Fries, a Montgomery County resident who had served both in the American Revolution and in the force that suppressed the Whiskey Rebellion. Fries repeatedly denounced the tax and in February 1798 was prominent at a meeting held at the home of Jacob Kline. A paper was drafted at this meeting to oppose the tax, and Fries pledged to raise a force of 700 men to resist its collection. For the next few months Fries and 50 to 60 armed partisans harassed and intimidated federal tax collectors. Fries and his armed band also besieged the sheriff of Bethlehem and pressured him into releasing the tax protesters who were imprisoned there.

This rebellion was so serious that President John Adams issued a proclamation ordering the rioters to disperse and called on the governor of Pennsylvania and its militia to assist in maintaining order. On March 14, 1799, Governor Mifflin issued a proclamation, and on March 20 he called out forces from Philadelphia, Chester, Montgomery, Lancaster and Bucks counties to restore order. Fries was apprehended and brought to trial for treason against the government of the United States. He was convicted and sentenced to hang, but to soothe local feelings, he was wisely pardoned by President Adams.

The last decade of the 18th century had been important for the Pennsylvania militia. Once the federal Constitution had been adopted and Congress passed the Militia Act of 1792, the Commonwealth finally created a permanent state force like its neighboring states. Clearly established in both federal and state law was the concept that free white male citizens between the ages of 18 and 45 had the obligation to serve in the militia.[43] In addition, to provide the necessary command and control for the state's military forces, the Commonwealth created the Office of the Adjutant General, appointed the first adjutant general of Pennsylvania and, finally, provided a military structure for the Pennsylvania militia to fulfill its duties. That the Pennsylvania militia could muster and serve was proven in both the Whiskey Rebellion and the smaller but not insignificant Fries Rebellion. The Whiskey Rebellion in particular demonstrated problems with the militia system, but in fact in both rebellions the militia responded to an unpopular cause – suppressing fellow citizens and militiamen – and fulfilled its duties, even though the governor personally opposed the employment of military force and thus was at odds with the President. The last decade of the 18th century proved that Pennsylvania had a functioning militia that could be employed to support the nation's defense.

---

[43] According to the provisions of this act, every able-bodied white male citizen between the ages of 18 and 45, with a few exceptions, was to be enrolled in the militia. See Clarke, *Official History of the Pennsylvania Militia*, p. 26.

CHAPTER 8

Testing the Militia Concept

The preparation to qualify the citizens for the military service of their country should be encouraged, and enforced by every rational means . . . every freeman will cheerfully contribute a portion of his time and his property towards the personal expense to be incurred.

– Governor Thomas McKean, 1802

The first true challenge for Pennsylvania's militia and a national defense based on the militia came early in the 19th century, at a time when the new republic was woefully unprepared to defend itself or its interests. As noted in the previous chapter, America entrusted the national defense to the militia in the various states. This concept of a militia-based defense was authored by President George Washington, supported by his Secretary of War Henry Knox.[1] It might seem like a dubious concept, but Washington had few alternatives. The people were unwilling to accord the federal government any standing military presence, and even the national militia proposed by Washington was unacceptable. Thus, the first militia law, the Militia Act of 1792, was a mere shadow of what the President originally sought.

The federal act was implemented in Pennsylvania through the 1793 Militia Act, which allowed the Commonwealth to field troops to assist in suppressing the Whiskey Rebellion. Despite the success of the militia in this role, major flaws were evident in its structure from the outset. The basic problem was the federal act, which failed to provide funds or standards for the militia. It required states to provide for a militia and ensure that an annual muster was held – in short, to prove that soldiers existed and units could be assembled for

---

[1] According to one soldier-scholar, Brigadier General John McAuley Palmer, Washington considered the Militia Act as "his most important administration measure." Palmer, lecture entitled "The Military Policy of the United States," delivered at the U.S. Army War College, September 21, 1928 (p. 13 of his manuscript).

a state or national need. There was no real requirement, however, to organize and train militia forces. This responsibility was left to the states. It was presumed that each would provide some measure of structure and support for its militia. In most states, however, the enrolled militia was the epitome of an unstructured military force; little if any time was scheduled for training. By and large, militia acts were focused on a registration function: registering eligible citizens and enrolling them in the militia. Training and equipping them was not a part of this process. Thus, all eligible males had to belong to the militia, but they were not required to participate in an organized unit. The essential problem with the 1792 federal act was that, in the words of one scholar, it "imposed a duty on everyone with the result that it was discharged by no one."[2]

A few states, including Pennsylvania, devised a stronger structure for their militias. As early as 1793 the Commonwealth provided for a state commander, the adjutant general.[3] He was given the responsibilities of transmitting the governor's orders to the various corps, perfecting military discipline and attending all public reviews along with the commander in chief, the governor. In addition, some older units predated the Revolutionary War and maintained their organization due to pride and tradition, rather than the requirements of the militia act. For example, units had existed in eastern Pennsylvania prior to Franklin's drafting of the Articles of Association in 1747. Such units kept their strength despite the new militia law, rather than because of it.

Numerous examples could be cited of units which drilled in an organized fashion. The First Troop, Philadelphia City Cavalry functioned throughout this period as an organized unit. It assembled, trained and performed many important military and ceremonial duties. In the 1790s it escorted a number of significant guests to include General Lafayette, General Anthony Wayne and President Washington. On December 14, 1799, it participated in the funeral of the first President. It was also mobilized for the Whiskey Rebellion and for the suppression of the Fries Rebellion of 1798, a civil disturbance mentioned in the previous chapter.[4] The Artillery Associators of Philadelphia, with lineage back to 1747, also functioned in an organized fashion in the 1790s, serving as the

[2] Frederick B. Wiener, "The Militia Clause of the Constitution," *Harvard Law Review* (December 1940), p. 187.
[3] Even under the Articles of Confederation, Pennsylvania had an individual with at least some command or executive authority. In 1786 Charles Biddle appointed Colonel Francis Mentges as Inspector General of the Militia. See chapter 7.
[4] First Troop, Philadelphia City Cavalry, *History of the First Troop, Philadelphia City Cavalry, together with an Introductory Chapter Summarizing the Early History and the Rolls Complete from 1774* (Philadelphia: Winchell Company, 1991), p. 4.

Regiment of Artillery of the City of Philadelphia. They were commanded by a familiar figure in Pennsylvania military history, Colonel Thomas Proctor, an officer who certainly knew the value of training and organization. In fact, a thorough review of the records shows a higher degree of organization among the traditional units in the Commonwealth than was actually required by the militia act. Organized units in communities such as York, Reading and Pittsburgh functioned as volunteer militia, even though legislation recognizing volunteer militias would not be passed until the early 19th century.[5]

In the first decade of the 19th century Pennsylvania enacted laws to officially promote a more organized militia. Minor changes relating to militia structure were required by an act of the Assembly on April 6, 1802, but the major changes in the Pennsylvania militia system came through legislation passed on March 21, 1803.[6] This act authorized the creation of organized volunteer companies and exempted their members from attending the enrolled militia's regimental musters. Instead, they were permitted to meet for practice at a time and location mutually agreed to by the unit. The law also relieved members of volunteer regiments from being fined for failure to attend these musters. It should be noted, however, that this legislation merely allowed the organization of volunteer companies; it did not mandate it.[7] Statutes requiring citizen membership in the enrolled militia remained in force. Members of a volunteer militia company had to supply their own uniforms, individual equipment and weapons. As a result, considerable variety was the rule.

[5] For example, the Reading unit, organized on March 23, 1794, served in the suppression of the Whiskey Rebellion, during which they were known as the Reading Union Volunteers. They participated in the Reading reception for Washington, the Commander in Chief, and accompanied him westward to Carlisle, serving as his bodyguards. After the Whiskey Rebellion, the Reading company adopted the name Reading Washington Guard. This unit had the same company commander from 1794 to 1830, Captain Daniel DeB. Keim. W. J. Creed, *Historical Sketch and Souvenir, Reading Artillerists, Company A, Fourth Regiment Infantry, Third Brigade, NGP* (Reading, Pa.: B. F. Owen Publishers, 1894), p. 14.

[6] A significant change made by the Act of 1802 was how the regiments of the Commonwealth were numbered. Previously, a first regiment existed in each county, but with the passage of this act an entirely new numbering system was put in place. For a good review of changes in militia legislation, see William P. Clarke, *Official History of the Militia and National Guard of Pennsylvania from the Earliest Period of Record to the Present Time* (Philadelphia: Charles J. Hendler, 1909), pp. 167-169. Cited hereafter as Clarke, *Official History of the Pennsylvania Militia.*

[7] It did not, however, provide weapons for the volunteer units. As noted by Governor Simon Snyder in his 1811 annual address to the Assembly, "Frequent applications have been made by volunteer companies, for rifles; the applicants could not be gratified, because there are no rifles in the possession of the Commonwealth." George E. Reed, ed., *Pennsylvania Archives: Papers of the Governors, 1785-1817*, fourth series, vol. IV (Harrisburg: State of Pennsylvania, 1900), p. 748. Cited hereafter as Reed, *Papers of the Governors, 1785-1817.*

Throughout the first decade of the 19th century, legislation brought innumerable changes to the militia. In April 1805 an act was passed by the Assembly directing the governor to appoint a quartermaster general, and the state's numerous brigadier generals were given authority to appoint brigade quartermasters. In addition, authority was given to regimental commanders to appoint chaplains. Chaplains had existed in Pennsylvania units as early as the French and Indian War and in significant numbers in the Revolutionary War.[8] With the act of 1805, attending to the spiritual needs of men in uniform became official. Other changes were made through the 1807 Militia Act.[9] An act passed on March 26, 1808, further expanded the size and structure of the militia. New regulations for volunteer militia were required because these units were becoming more popular and more numerous. The 1808 act authorized the formation of volunteer companies of infantry and grenadiers for each battalion. It also authorized the governor to organize volunteer companies into battalions, regiments and brigades when they were called into active service. These provisions recognized the growing significance of volunteer units, as well as the fact that, in times of active service, volunteers could be organized into larger units rather than serving as an adjunct to enrolled militia units.

In the early 19th century, Pennsylvanians saw the emergence of two distinct types of militia forces: the enrolled militia and the volunteer militia. Legal provisions allowing a volunteer militia were important because they would be the primary force through which the United States waged its wars in the 19th century. The enrolled militia continued to exist for a time in some states, including Pennsylvania, but the lack of structure and meaningful training would

---

[8] As mentioned in a previous chapter, Benjamin Franklin was one of the earliest Pennsylvania military leaders to employ a chaplain in a military unit, during the French and Indian War. During the Revolution, numerous chaplains served as official members of Pennsylvania units, rather than as clergymen just accompanying them. In the Revolutionary War a Pennsylvania chaplain was the first to be killed in action: the Reverend John Rosbrugh, a Presbyterian minister who served with militia units at Trenton and Princeton. Perhaps the most famous Pennsylvania chaplain in this early period was David Jones, a Baptist. He served with a number of Pennsylvania units during the Revolution and in 1794 became chaplain of the United States Army. See Herman A. Norton, *Struggling for Recognition: The United States Army Chaplaincy, 1791-1865* (Washington, D.C.: Office of the Chief of Chaplains, 1977) and Roy J. Honeywell, *Chaplains of the United States Army* (Washington, D.C.: Department of the Army, 1958).

[9] By the act of 1807 the Assembly established the strength of a regiment at 500 to 1,000 men, a level that should be familiar to students of the Civil War. This act gave the same basic qualification for membership in the militia, i.e., that "every free able-bodied white male citizen of this or any other of the United States" had an obligation to serve. *An Act for the Regulation of the Militia of the Commonwealth of Pennsylvania* (Lancaster, Pa.: John R. Matthews, 1807), p. 4. Cited hereafter as *An Act for the Regulation of the Militia*.

ultimately relegate the enrolled militia to the role of a home guard or temporary emergency force.

As allowed by the 1803 act and reinforced through 1808 legislation, volunteer units were organized in many localities. Given the Associator tradition,
this is understandable. Some communities had units with a rich heritage which,
together with a broad base of local support, tended to promote the concept of
volunteer companies. Units in Philadelphia, such as the Regiment of Artillery
of the City of Philadelphia and the First Troop, Philadelphia City Cavalry have
already been mentioned. As the first decade of the century progressed, increasing numbers of volunteer companies adopted distinctive names. In Reading the
local militia unit retained the name Washington Guards, in remembrance of its
role in protecting the President during the Whiskey Rebellion. Some units
adopted geographically based names, like the Lancaster Phalanx or the
Wyoming Blues. "Blues" and "Grays" were popular appelations in the Keystone and neighboring states. Other units advertised their ethnic origins. A
growing element in Pennsylvania were the Irish, and the Commonwealth had a
regiment known as the Irish Volunteers.[10] In addition to distinctive names, the
volunteer companies continued the practice of adopting special uniforms and
headgear to distinguish themselves and feed the appetite for pomp and
pageantry so important to 19th-century America.

A better trained and more organized militia would have been more
advantageous than pomp and pageantry, because in the first decade of the 19th
century a national crisis developed that would require the exercise of military
power. It resulted in a war with Britain and required the Commonwealth to
activate and use its numerous but ill-prepared military forces. This crisis, the
War of 1812, had its origins in Europe. Beginning with the last decade of the
18th century, the major European powers were almost constantly at war. This
widespread strife resulted from Napoleon Bonaparte's expansive designs in
Europe. Great Britain consistently objected to the French emperor's revolutionary regime and led a variety of coalitions to oppose his revolutionary ideals.
As a consequence, Britain was intermittently at war with France from the last
part of the 18th century through the first decade and a half of the 19th.

The land campaigns fought in Europe did not at first directly affect the

---

[10] Of these early 19th-century units, unique in terms of history and lineage were the Wyoming
Guards of Luzerne County. The 3rd Regiment, Luzerne County has its origins with the 1st
Company, 5th Regiment, Connecticut Militia. At the time of the American Revolution, when
troops were organized from the Wyoming area, they were raised for Connecticut – a clear
reminder of the Yankee-Pennamite controversy.

newly formed United States or any of its limited interests. Since prosecution of the war involved control of the sea lanes, however, the nation was again brought into conflict with its mother country. The United States had only been independent since the Treaty of Paris in 1783, but in this brief period it had become a significant commercial power needing access to European markets. The importance of trans-Atlantic commerce put the United States on a collision course with the European powers, for both Britain and France sought to deny supplies to their respective adversaries. Both issued decrees asserting their right to restrict the commerce of neutral nations, thereby depriving their enemy of needed war materiel. Particularly odious to the new American republic was a British decree called Orders-in-Council which, among other things, claimed the right of crews from British warships to stop and search any nation's vessels on the high seas.[11] The most offensive aspect of British policy was their habit of removing seamen from U.S. ships and forcing them to serve in the British navy. President James Madison strongly contested these actions, and the U.S. government countered with its own embargoes, causing considerable damage to its commerce.[12]

With incidents on the high seas and confrontational decrees and policies inflaming national passions, it was only a matter of time before a clash occurred. On June 22, 1807, a British frigate named the *Leopard* attacked the *Chesapeake*, an American frigate. Not only did the *Leopard* fire on the American vessel, its crew boarded it and took four American sailors, alleged to be British deserters. The *Chesapeake* incident brought a significant protest from the United States, and the President called for militia troops to be mobilized for what seemed to be a rapidly approaching war. In July 1809 the United States was placed on a war footing in preparation for military action against the British.

Pennsylvania was given a quota for this activation consisting of 15,635

---

[11] Napoleon Bonaparte, emperor of France, had attempted to stop the British from engaging in commerce with the European continent through the establishment of what was called the "Continental System." The British countered with the Orders-in-Council, through which they established their right to monitor the flow of goods into Europe by searching and, if necessary, seizing vessels on the high seas. Since the United States had already become a major commercial power, this restriction of the free flow of goods could not be allowed. The conflict that arose in 1809, and again in 1812, was a result of the American insistence that the British did not have the right to stop and search American ships.

[12] This crisis and the effect it had on Pennsylvania were also highlighted by Governor Thomas McKean in his annual address to the Assembly in 1808. He noted, "The spirit of maritime enterprise has been restrained; the profits of trade for awhile surrendered ... the occupations of particular classes of citizens have been partially interrupted." Reed, *Papers of the Governors, 1785-1817*, p. 650.

officers and enlisted men. The governor, through Adjutant General Mahlon Dickerson, called the requisite number of troops by class. The activation specified that 781 of the soldiers were to be artillery, 1,563 cavalry. On July 13, 1807, troops were fielded from 15 of Pennsylvania's 16 divisions to meet the President's call. They mustered, ready to defend the nation, but the so-called "Chesapeake War" only lasted until August 5. Hostilities never even arose. The crisis was solved – or more accurately postponed – through diplomacy. For now, Pennsylvania militia would see no active service in the defense of the country.[13]

Even though the crisis had passed, the root cause – the restriction of American commerce – had not been resolved. For the next two years the British practice of searching U. S. vessels and seizing crewmen remained an irritant. Some American political leaders promoted additional negotiations to resolve the problem, while others encouraged settling the issue through force of arms. Finally, when five years of diplomacy failed to persuade the British to lift their Orders-in-Council, on June 18, 1812, the United States declared war on Great Britain. It was a war for which the country was totally unprepared.[14]

Unlike previous wars, at the outbreak of the War of 1812 Pennsylvania still had in place a valid militia act. It imposed the obligation for all free white males between the ages of 18 and 45 to be enrolled in a militia company.[15] Most of the militia's strength remained in the enrolled militia, even though increasing numbers of volunteer militias were being organized in many communities. However, the Pennsylvania militia only mustered and trained a few days each year and was thus hardly prepared to go to war.[16]

As was the tradition in the Commonwealth, not all members of any given unit would be required to serve the nation, because militia were called into

[13] Clarke, *Official History of the Pennsylvania Militia*, pp. 175-176.
[14] While initially the British had shown an unwillingness to repeal the Orders-in-Council, it is ironic that only five days after Congress declared war against them the contentious orders were repealed. With communications the way they were in those days, news did not reach the United States until the end of July. By that time the "die had been cast," and the government was determined to pursue the war to settle once and for all numerous differences with the British Empire. See Victor A. Sapio, *Pennsylvania and the War of 1812* (Lexington, Ky.: University of Kentucky Press, 1970), pp. 167-168.
[15] While the act imposed a universal obligation, it could be and sometimes was avoided. If a citizen had enough money, he could hire a replacement to fulfill his obligation.
[16] The 1807 act actually provided for training on multiple levels – companies, troops, battalions and regiments. It also specified the days of the month that training was to be held for the various levels. Attached to the bound copies of this act are the prescribed drill regulations: "Regulations for Order and Discipline of the Troops of the United States" – the Federal standard rather than the Commonwealth's. See *An Act for the Regulation of the Militia*, pp. 31-32.

federal service by class rather than unit. Only portions of units were activated; a part of the militia always remained in their home communities, available as a home guard to defend the Commonwealth in an emergency. This policy had a major disadvantage, however, in that it broke down the continuity of local units that had at least some practice in working together.

Problems for the militia went beyond the fragmentation of units caused by calling up soldiers by class. The lack of good, solid leadership also plagued the militia. Professionalism had not yet touched the officer ranks. In the lower grades, officers were still elected by popular vote, not chosen for military prowess. Higher ranking officers were appointed by the governor. Governor Simon Snyder acknowledged this overall unpreparedness in his annual address to the Assembly on December 5, 1811:

> *It is generally acknowledged that the present [militia] system is materially defective, and the repeated essays of the legislature, on that important subject, prove the difficulty of forming a system, that will be effective in its operation, without being oppressive to its citizens.*[17]

In further assessing the state of the militia, Snyder acknowledged the existence of a public store of arms but noted that they were deteriorating because there was no legal provision for their maintenance. For that matter, there was no provision in the various regiments for maintaining the weapons that had already been distributed. In his report to the legislature on December 3, 1812, Snyder noted:

> *The scattered, and in many cases unknown places where public arms, and the wretched rusteaten condition in which they are too often found, make it a work of time, labor and expense to collect them together, and have them put in such repair as they ought to be previous to their being put into the hands of our militia. The want of cartouch boxes, and flints and many other indispensable military equipment and stores has been sensibly felt.*[18]

In all fairness, though lack of equipment and proper training meant that these militia soldiers were not well prepared to fight, neither were the regulars of the U.S. Army. The Army's strength and readiness had hit the predictable post-war low, as had funds for military forces.[19] The unpreparedness of both

[17] Reed, *Papers of the Governors, 1785-1817*, p. 748.
[18] Ibid., pp. 781-782.

the Army and the militia hardly mattered in 1812, since the nation was rapidly moving toward war with the British.

With war on the horizon, the nation needed troops. As early as November 5, 1811, President James Madison had recommended preparations for war. Congress was called into early session the same month to address the crisis. Sharing the President's concern about British transgressions, Congress subsequently issued a call for 100,000 militiamen. Pennsylvania, which until the 1740s had distinguished itself through its inability to support any type of military force, now promptly and strongly supported military action against the British by the federal government. From the outset, the governor was firm in his support of the war. When transmitting the President's requirement through his General Order of August 12, 1812, Governor Snyder stated:

> *To obey this call in defense of rights sacred to freemen — to avenge the injuries of the nation and defend the cause of suffering humanity — the Volunteers of Pennsylvania will not hesitate a moment to meet the avowed enemy of those rights, not only within the bounds of the United States; but will, without those limits, with ardor seek, and with the determination characteristic of Freemen, punish the unprovoked invaders of our rights and property.*[20]

Snyder issued a General Order on May 12, 1812, drafting 14,000 men to fill Pennsylvania's quota. According to his order, coordinated through Adjutant General William Reed, Pennsylvania troops were to be organized as follows:

> *1st. There shall forthwith be drafted, in the manner prescribed by law, 14,000 militia, officers and privates, to be formed into two divisions, four brigades and twenty two regiments. The offer of service to the governor of any flank company, or companies, attached to any regiment of a number equal to the number of militia required to be drafted from such regiment,*

---

[19] For example, in June 1802 the Army consisted of 3,040 soldiers and 172 officers. Though the crisis with Britain continued throughout the first decade of the 19th century, by 1812 the Army still had only 6,744 men. Russell F. Weigley, *History of the United States Army*, The Macmillan Wars of the United States, Louis Morton, ed. (New York: Macmillan Company, 1967), pp. 110-112.

[20] Thomas Lynch Montgomery, ed., *Pennsylvania Archives: War of 1812-1814*, sixth series, vol. VII (Harrisburg: State Printer, 1907), pp. 901-903. Cited hereafter as Montgomery, *War of 1812-1814*.

*may be accepted in substitution of such draft from the regiment. The Corps
of artillery, cavalry, riflemen and infantry shall be in the following proportions as*

Artillery, 700   Riflemen, 1,400
Cavalry, 700   Infantry, 11,200

*2d. The whole quota required shall be apportioned among the several divi-
sions of the state, agreeably to a detail furnished by the Adjutant General.
The quotas of the several divisions of the state shall be formed into two
divisions for the present service.*[21]

The First Division (not to be confused with the modern-day term) was
commanded by Major General Issac Worrell and headquartered in Philadelphia.
It was composed of units from the eastern part of the Commonwealth. The
Second Division, commanded by Major General Adamson Tannehill, drew its
strength from the northern and western parts of the state. Close to the immediate theater of war, Tannehill's division was the one first called on to deploy in
the field of battle.

Pennsylvania had been a battleground for both the French and Indian
War and the Revolutionary War. But even though Pennsylvania's units rapidly
and in many cases enthusiastically prepared to participate in this war, no major
land campaigns were to take place on Pennsylvania soil. The only direct threat
to the Commonwealth emerged on the Great Lakes. The potential for incursions by sea into the Chesapeake and the Delaware by British ships clearly existed and ultimately occurred; but other than the British activity on the Great
Lakes, the British did not directly menace either the Commonwealth's territory
or its waterways.

When the war broke out, the closest British forces were located in
Canada, and the first clashes occurred near the Canadian border. The first
major action in this region was no compliment to American military prowess.
General William Hull, with a force consisting largely of Ohio militia, cut a road
from Urbana, Ohio to Detroit in the summer of 1812. Detroit was important
as a center of trade and diplomacy and lay close to the U.S.-Canadian border.
Hull – who was also governor of the Michigan Territory, where he had organ-

---

[21] The General Order was issued at Harrisburg by Governor Simon Snyder, with additional
detail by William Reed, the adjutant general. John B. Linn and William H. Egle, eds., *Pennsylvania
Archives: Papers and Documents Relating to the War of 1812-1814.* (Harrisburg: Clarence M. Busch,
State Printer, 1896), pp. 555-561. Cited hereafter as Linn and Egle, *Papers and Documents Relating
to the War of 1812.*

ized a territorial militia – failed miserably in defending Detroit, resulting in the city's surrender to the British. His shameful performance resulted in court-martial proceedings in which he was found guilty of neglect of duty and bad conduct.[22]   The small U.S. garrison abandoned another western outpost, Fort Dearborn (present-day Chicago). Once the garrison moved out of its prepared defenses, many were slaughtered by the Indians. Fortunately, no Pennsylvania militia troops were involved in either of these disastrous episodes.

Pennsylvania militia would be employed in a contentious area stretching from Fort Niagara on the approaches to Lake Ontario through Lake Erie and into the Ohio region. The western division under the command of General Tannehill ultimately split, with roughly half of his troops remaining in the Pittsburgh area and the rest in Meadville. Its quotas were met by using not only enrolled militia units but volunteers, volunteer companies and flank companies.[23] Some Pennsylvania volunteers eagerly sought military service. For example, on May 14, 1812, Captain Samuel Agnew, commander of the Harrisburg volunteers, wrote the governor:

> *Sir: I have the honor of informing your Excellency that the Harrisburg volunteers, who have honored me with their command, have unanimously resolved to tender their services to the Governor of Pennsylvania as part of the quota of the Pennsylvania militia.*[24]

Captain Agnew's request for inclusion in the state's quota was one of many from volunteer units received by the governor's office. The commanders of the Lancaster Phalanx, the Philadelphia Benevolent Blues, the Pittsburgh Republican Volunteers and the Nazareth Township Troop of Cavalry, as well as many others, offered their services. Pennsylvania's Militia Law contributed to the lack of an organized call-up of existing units by retaining the same system employed during the Revolutionary War: activating militiamen by class rather

---

[22] Hull's performance as a commander was considered so bad that he was originally charged with treason and cowardice as well. He was cleared of these charges but convicted on the remainder and condemned to be shot. The court, however, recommended mercy, and President Madison remitted his sentence because of his age and previous military record.

[23] The term "flank companies" is unfamiliar to most soldiers and even students of the military today. Older records refer to enrolled militia companies and flank companies. Shortly before the beginning of the war, the standard fighting unit, the regiment, had two battalions of four companies each, with each battalion having the authority to have a volunteer flank company. While this was the supposed general structure, volunteer companies were not always affiliated with a battalion, and communities often had volunteer units that were totally unaffiliated.

[24] Linn and Egle, *Papers and Documents Relating to the War of 1812*, p. 563.

than unit. Far too many of the units which mustered in the wake of Pennsylvania's mobilization were units in name only, made up of soldiers who had never worked or trained together.

According to the governor's papers, 2,516 volunteers were to rendezvous in Meadville on September 25, and on October 2 volunteers numbering 2,214 were to rendezvous at Pittsburgh. It was suggested that any surplus from these two groups be retained in Pennsylvania for the defense of the state's borders.[25] When the various detachments met in Pittsburgh, they were organized into a brigade, and Tannehill was elected as its commander, though he had to serve in the reduced rank of brigadier general. The governor, a strong supporter of the war, highlighted with pride in his annual address to the Assembly on December 3, 1812, that 4,000 Pennsylvania militiamen had been ordered into active duty in defense of the republic.[26]

While the assembly of troops at Pittsburgh and Meadville is noted with pride in several contemporary accounts, the first actual use of Pennsylvania troops in combat actually came earlier, during the summer of 1812. They were not directly employed against the British, but rather against a formidable Indian confederacy that had formed in the area between Ohio and Illinois. The tribes of the region bitterly resented the relentless pressure of American settlers after the Revolutionary War. This originated in the years following 1795 when a Pennsylvanian in the U.S. Army, General Anthony Wayne, forced a settlement from the tribes in what is now Ohio, requiring their evacuation from this lush area to lands further west. Beginning in 1809 these resentments flared up anew when several chiefs purporting to represent Delaware, Kickapoo, Eel River and Wea Indian tribes ceded even more land, including lands occupied by tribes loyal to a half Creek-half Shawnee named Tecumseh. Unique among the chiefs in the area, Tecumseh thoroughly understood the ways of the settlers and, in addition, had a natural leadership ability and a clear vision of what he wanted for the future.[27] His aim was to unite all the tribes of the Mississippi Valley and

---

[25] The General Order, dated September 5, is in Montgomery, *War of 1812-1814*, p. 905. See also Gertrude MacKinney, ed., *Pennsylvania Archives: Executive Minutes of Governor Simon Snyder, 1812-1814*, ninth Series, vol. V (Harrisburg: Commonwealth of Pennsylvania, 1931), p. 3257. Cited hereafter as MacKinney, *Executive Minutes of Governor Snyder.*

[26] Ibid., p. 781.

[27] Tecumseh spoke English well, was familiar with the works of Shakespeare and knew the Bible. He had fallen in love with a white woman, Rebecca Galloway, whom he wanted to marry. She was willing to marry him but only if he give up his Indian customs. He refused to do this, and from that point on Tecumseh began distancing himself from the white man's world. Still, he never lost his understanding of it – and through this became a formidable enemy.

stop the relentless advance of land cessions by forming a strong tribal confederacy. When a collision between Tecumseh's growing confederacy and William
Henry Harrison, governor of the Indiana Territory, seemed imminent, a meeting was held in 1810 to try to defuse the crisis and avoid war.

Tecumseh began working in earnest to put his confederacy together in
1811. Harrison became convinced that Tecumseh posed a major threat to
peace on the frontier. Thus, by mid-1811, Harrison had both regular Army
troops and militia (from Indiana and Kentucky) in the field to attempt to stop
Tecumseh and his brother, known as the Prophet. In the Battle of Tippecanoe,
Harrison succeeded in scattering most of Tecumseh's followers, but he and
some of his band managed to escape. Harrison's victory likely pushed
Tecumseh into an alliance with the British. Thus, when the War of 1812 broke
out, the British had a number of allied tribes in present-day Ohio, Indiana and
Illinois. Harrison's Tippecanoe campaign can be viewed as the precursor, if not
the opening battle, of the War of 1812.

It should come as no surprise then, that as the War of 1812 began, one
of the first contingencies that Pennsylvania troops had to face was the British-
Indian problem in Ohio. Concern existed about the Ohio region and the need
for troops to repel any incursion into this area by the British or their Indian
allies. Harrison delegated his political role as governor to a subordinate and
began planning to defend the contested region. He wanted an army of 10,000
men to protect the region against Tecumseh and the British. To build a force
of that size, he needed militia. Secretary of War William Eustis requested militia from Virginia and Pennsylvania to fill out Harrison's force. As noted previously, part of Pennsylvania's militia – more than 2,000 men – were scheduled to
report to Pittsburgh on October 2, 1812. Available records suggest that, upon
arrival, the troops were not all that well equipped. A Mr. Linnard, deputy quarter [master] general, had to supply cartouch boxes from stores in Pittsburgh,
and the governor had a contract for some 2,000 cartouch boxes. It was also
indicated that a supply of arms might be needed for issue at Pittsburgh.[28]

The crisis in the west resulted in some of these Pennsylvania troops
serving with Harrison's Army of the Northwest in a number of capacities. For
example, they helped build Fort Meigs and supply military forces in the area.
Some Pennsylvanians took part in an operation designed by Harrison to ensure
the safety of his supply lines. His force was composed of Kentucky Dragoons,
a squadron of the Second United States Dragoons, a company from the
Nineteenth Infantry, the Pittsburgh Blues and Alexander's Pennsylvania Rifle-

---

[28] MacKinney, *Executive Minutes of Governor Simon Synder,* p. 3256.

men. The expedition left on December 14, 1812. Despite severe cold the following week, they were successful in destroying three Indian villages. All the
soldiers on the expedition suffered terribly from the weather, with frostbite
causing far more damage than Indian missiles.[29] Harrison's forces, including the
Pennsylvania contingent, continued their service under him throughout the
winter of 1812-1813, when there were more casualties from cold and disease
than from actions against the enemy.

Spring, however, not only brought relief from the miserable weather
but from military service. The Virginia and Pennsylvania troops were six-
month volunteers, and their time on active duty expired as spring arrived.
Recognizing this, in early March 1813 both houses of the Pennsylvania legislature passed a bill that all militiamen from Pennsylvania serving under General
Harrison would receive a bounty of $12, paid by the state treasurer – that is, if
they agreed to continue on federal duty for an additional two months.[30] This
enticement was not enough to keep all the Pennsylvanians on duty, and a number elected to go home. That some remained on duty is affirmed by a news
report from early April 1813. It stated that troops at Fort Meigs (in present-day
Ohio) consisted of Pennsylvania and Virginia brigades. Among the units were
Colonel Campbell's Regulars, Captain Cushing's Artillery, and Petersburg,
Pittsburgh and Greensburg Volunteers. Another news item from the same period stated that the Pennsylvania legislature had granted a bounty of $20 to each
Pennsylvania militiaman and volunteer soldier serving with the U.S. Army.[31]

While this was transpiring in the Ohio region, other Pennsylvania militia were being employed in another contiguous state. On August 13, 1812,
President Thomas Jefferson sent a message requiring 2,000 Pennsylvania troops
to proceed as soon as possible to Buffalo, New York. The presidential order
was followed by Governor Snyder's General Order, issued on August 25, 1812,
requiring the 2,000 Pennsylvania militiamen to march, with the least possible
delay, from the northwestern part of Pennsylvania to Buffalo. The soldiers
were supposed to march to Meadville, their place of rendezvous, and form into
a brigade consisting of four regiments of two battalions each.[32] The troops

---

[29] A good account of this expedition and Harrison's strategy can be found in John K. Mahon,
The War of 1812 (New York: Da Capo Press, 1972), pp. 63-74. Cited hereafter as Mahon, *The
War of 1812*. Mahon reports that of the 600-man expedition, 40 soldiers were crippled by the
cold, and 303 were severely frostbitten to the point of being invalids.
[30] H. Niles, ed., "Weekly Register: Documents, Essays and Facts Together with Notices of the
Arts and Manufactures and a Record of Events of the Time: Events of the War: Military," vol.
II (Baltimore: Franklin Press, 1812), p. 32.
[31] Ibid., p. 81.

were to serve under the command of William Reed until they elected officers, to include a brigadier to command them. Once organized they were to proceed to Niagara and place themselves under the commanding general of troops there.

Preparations to use Meadville as a major mustering area had taken place in the preceding month when, in keeping with the governor's request, a build-up of arms and equipment was initiated. As a result, on July 23, 1812, three wagons of munitions, including 32 boxes of muskets, 200 pounds of lead, 1,000 flints and three kegs of powder, were sent from Harrisburg to Meadville.[33]

The military build-up in New York, in preparation for operations against the British, caused considerable anxiety for citizens on the frontier. It seemed there was little regard for their own defense. Thus, a petition was addressed to the governor in September 1812, on behalf of the people of Tioga, Potter and McKean counties. They asked the governor:

> *[about] taking some effective measures to guard against and repel the inroads and depredations of our common enemy on the unprotected inhab-itants of the counties of Tioga, Potter and McKean. We have no longer any confidence in such a part of our red brethren as have lately left their homes to join the enemy (as we suppose) and fear many acts of cruelty and barbarity may be perpetuated by those described above.*[34]

This petition asked the governor to station two regiments of militia in the northwestern counties to protect against potential raids by the Indians or their British allies. While no attacks from either source ever came, the request clearly illustrates the frontier nature of northwestern Pennsylvania and the uneasiness that its inhabitants had about the remaining native population.

A Pennsylvania brigade commanded by General Adam Tannehill marched north to the Niagara area, where they reported to Brigadier General Alexander Smyth, a "regular." In this campaign neither regulars nor militia cov-ered themselves with glory. Since Pennsylvania troops were positioned on the U.S.-Canadian border, Smyth asked Tannehill if his soldiers would cross into Canada with the regulars. Tannehill responded in the affirmative – that is, if the

---

[32] Linn and Egle, *Papers and Documents Relating to the War of 1812*, pp. 585-588.
[33] Message from N. B. Boileau to Brigade Inspector William Clark, July 23, 1812. Ibid., pp. 583-584.
[34] Representation of the frontier settlers of the northern counties, September, 1812. Ibid., pp. 598-599.

Pennsylvania troops were part of an adequate force. When it came to deploy-ing these soldiers, only 413 out of 1,500 in the brigade were actually willing to cross into Canada. The Pennsylvania brigade ultimately decided it was time to go home, and 1,150 soldiers departed, leaving 300 behind to be organized into a battalion. On December 9, 1812, the battalion was also discharged and pro-ceeded home.[35]

The query as to whether Pennsylvania militia would cross into Canada raises a significant issue which troubled military leaders and some of their troops in the War of 1812. The basis of the objection was the wording of the Constitution's militia clause, which stated that the role of the militia was to repel invasions, defend the nation and suppress insurrections. Yet some of the mili-tary operations proposed against the British in 1812 required militiamen to invade Canada.[36] Legal limitations perceived by some citizen-soldiers, as well as their political leaders, restricted employment of militia troops. New York's governor, like Pennsylvania's, was a strong supporter of the war, but when Major General Stephen van Rensselaer tried to get New York militia to cross the Niagara River and invade Canada, they refused.[37] They felt an obligation to defend the United States but not to invade foreign territory. Ohio militia, com-manded by Brigadier General William Hull, refused to cross the Canadian bor-

[35] The bitterness between the militia and the regulars reached new heights – or rather depths – in this ill-fated campaign. The worst relations were between Smyth and the commander of the New York Militia, General Peter B. Porter, who was stationed in the same area as the Pennsylvanians. Porter provoked his regular rival, Smyth, to a duel. Fortunately the officers, who both fired, were not good shots. Smyth took leave, and as he proceeded home, a New York militiaman took a shot at him – luckily, missing. Mahon, *The War of 1812*, pp. 82-85.

[36] For the militia, the most serious part of this debate was the governor's insistence that they had the ability to consider the merit of the President's call-up. For example, the governor of Connecticut found the request for militia unconstitutional, because it did not specify any of the three contingencies mentioned in the Constitution. Furthermore, the federal plan called for placing Connecticut militia under federal officers which, in the governor's eyes, was inappro-priate, since Connecticut officers were already designated for the units. When the Secretary of War entered the controversy and asserted that a British invasion was imminent, the governor stated that a British fleet cruising off the coast did not constitute a threat. Thus, Connecticut declined to send its quota of militia troops. Massachusetts also failed to do so. This legal issue was not decided until 1827, when in the case of *Martin v. Mott* the Supreme Court ruled that the President's decision to call forth the militia was binding and could not be overridden by the gov-ernors.

[37] In van Rensselaer's command a Pennsylvania brigade caused a similar problem. Crossing the border into Canada – invading a neighboring country rather than defending their own – con-cerned some of the 2,000 Pennsylvania militia troops who gathered at Pittsburgh and were sub-sequently sent into Ohio in late 1812. They were willing to assist with the defense of the Ohio, but when asked if they would cross into Canada, neither the men nor their officers showed any great enthusiasm. Thus, out of 1,500 in the Pennsylvania Brigade, only 413 were willing to

der near Detroit for the same reason as their New York peers. In Connecticut, Massachusetts and Rhode Island the situation was even worse, because the governors refused to supply the required number of troops due to anti-war, pro-British sentiments in the region. Some Pennsylvania troops refused to cross the border, but most served where they were needed.

Many problems were emerging in the first exercise of power by the American republic. Pennsylvania's Governor Snyder summed up some of them relating to the militia when he noted on December 10, 1813:

> *Organizing and officering these detachments, agreeably to the direction of the secretary of war, was attended with considerable difficulty, arising out of the inefficiency of our militia law and the discordance between our military system and that of the United States. For that matter, neither were the militia troops from the other states who were generally poorly trained and who failed to perform well in these military operations.*[38]

In many respects the military situation for American forces seemed to deteriorate in 1813, through no fault of regular Army units or the more numerous militia units. The real cause for the crisis lay with events on the European mainland. In 1813 the military fortunes of France and its emperor Napoleon began to rapidly decline. As Napoleon's army reeled from the victories of the coalition arrayed against it, the British Empire could invest more of its land and naval forces to defeat the United States. In 1813 Britain began to exercise both economic and military pressure against the United States and, in addition, took steps to bring the war to the American people, particularly around the Chesapeake Bay.[39] Beginning in the spring of 1813, British forces under Admiral Sir George Cockburn plundered the Chesapeake area. Cockburn sought to destroy American naval vessels and military supplies and disrupt American coastal trade. Above all, he wanted to bring war to the American

---

cross with a force of militia and regular Army units led by Brigadier General Alexander Smyth, a regular Army officer. Some of the problems here were command-related, because Symth was serving under van Rensselaer, a New York officer. Smyth did not like the militia, and they neither liked nor trusted him.

[38] Reed, *Papers of the Governors, 1785-1817*, p. 821.

[39] The economic pressure was in the form of a naval blockade, designed to shut down coastal trade. Initially the blockade stretched from Charleston, South Carolina to Florida. By November 1813 it had been extended to reach from just south of New England to Florida. In a sense, New England was rewarded for its reticence in supporting the federal government by being exempt from the blockade.

populace and clearly show them the consequences of opposing the British Empire. In keeping with this strategy, in April his forces burned Frenchtown, Maryland, and the following month, Havre de Grace, Georgetown and Fredericktown. When summer arrived, the British carried their attacks further south, spreading destruction around Hampton, Virginia.

Though not specifically aimed at Pennsylvania, these incursions did affect the Commonwealth. The degenerating military situation in 1813 caused the federal government to requisition additional troops from Pennsylvania. In a message to the legislature on March 29, 1813, Governor Snyder reported the federal request of two detachments of militia, "the one for the defense of the city of Philadelphia and the shores of the Delaware, the other for the protection of the Navy Yard."[40]

Throughout 1813-1814 there were repeated scares prompted by the presence of British naval forces off the coast. The two most likely objectives for the British were either Philadelphia or Baltimore, if not the country's capital. After all, British forces had targeted Philadelphia during the Revolution and had occupied the city early in the war. Hearing of the presence of a British warship in the waterways approaching Philadelphia, the governor ordered the First Division of the Pennsylvania Militia to be placed in readiness to respond to an invasion. Fortifications for the city were refurbished and new ones built, in a flurry of activity reminiscent of 1747 and 1775. On April 5, 1813, the governor ordered a detachment of 1,000 drafted militiamen to protect Philadelphia and defend the shores of Delaware from British incursions.[41] Delaware was a lucrative target, due not only to its vulnerability on the coast but also to the presence of the Du Pont facilities where explosives were being manufactured.

Even though the British actions in Maryland and Delaware held considerable significance for the nation, the military activity on Lake Erie in the fall of 1813 had equal if not greater importance. This stemmed from the fact that a battle here provided the nation with one of its most celebrated victories of the war: the Battle of Lake Erie. Even though this was a naval engagement, it involved Pennsylvania troops. As noted earlier, the British had seized the initiative in the Great Lakes early in the war, taking control of this vital waterway and the key communities of Detroit and Chicago. A plan was developed to reassert American control of the Great Lakes region. The architects of the plan were Secretary of the Navy Paul Hamilton and Daniel Dobbins, a Pennsyl-

---

[40] Reed, *Papers of the Governors, 1785-1817*, pp. 812, 813.
[41] General Order of the Governor, dated April 5, 1813, in Linn and Egle, *Papers and Documents Relating to the War of 1812*, pp. 646-647.

vanian.[42]

Dobbins was born near the present site of Lewistown in Mifflin County. He left the mid-state in 1795 and settled in Presque Isle (Erie), Pennsylvania, where he became a trader on the Great Lakes. He was rated as a master mariner on both Lake Erie and Lake Ontario. When Mackinac Island was seized by the British in July 1812, Dobbins was captured, but as was the custom of the period, he was paroled by the British and returned to territory under American control. He was captured again the following August with the surrender of Detroit. He escaped and returned to Erie and discussed his observations with Major General David Meade, who commanded the 16th Division of the Pennsylvania Militia, made up of units in northwestern Pennsylvania.[43] Meade asked Dobbins to go to the nation's capital and report his perceptions on the fall of Detroit and the danger facing the country along the lake frontier. Dobbins travelled to Washington and apprised several government officials of his observations recommending that a lake fleet be built to counter the British threat. Apparently he was convincing, because on September 15 he received instructions from Secretary of the Navy Hamilton to return to Erie and contract for materials and supplies to build four gunboats. He was appointed sailing master (a senior warrant officer) in the U.S. Navy. He was subordinate to Commodore Isaac Chauncey, commander of naval forces on Lakes Ontario and Erie, but since Chauncey was at the Brooklyn Navy Yard, the task of constructing the four ships fell initially to Dobbins.

Through the latter part of 1812 Dobbins worked to find the necessary men and supplies to build the lake fleet. It was a daunting task, due to the shortage of key materials such as sail cloth, iron and rigging and the lack of craftsmen this far inland who could build ships. The fact that Erie was a remote site, with virtually no industry and no reliable road network to bring in supplies, also worked against Dobbins' efforts. Still, the construction program was well underway when Commodore Chauncey, a bona fide naval officer, arrived to assist with preparations. The work of these two men set the stage for Oliver Hazzard Perry to complete and lead the fleet, once he arrived in March 1813.

When Perry arrived in Erie, he found the port facility, located on a body

---

[42] Fortunately Daniel Dobbins' papers have been preserved and are available on microfilm at the Buffalo and Erie County Historical Society in New York. In addition, there are a number of biographical sketches of Dobbins, including a recent publication, Robert D. Ilisevich, *Daniel Dobbins, Frontier Mariner* (Erie, Pa.: Erie County Historical Society, 1993).

[43] Details on the life and career of David Mead can be found in manuscripts in the Crawford County Historical Society in Meadville, Pennsylvania.

of water dominated by the British, to be virtually defenseless. Once again, Pennsylvania provided the needed assistance in the defense of the area. On March 31, 1813, the governor ordered 1,000 men drafted into federal service from Pennsylvania's 11th, 12th and 13th Divisions for the protection of naval armaments at Erie.[44] These militiamen were scheduled to rendezvous in Erie on April 20. After reporting, they assisted in the defense of the harbor and its incomplete warships.[45] In early August 1813 the small fleet moved out of the harbor into Lake Erie proper, where they joined a few existing U.S. vessels.[46] This in itself was a difficult task, because the new ships were built in a harbor protected by a sand bar. The sand bar stretched across the harbor mouth, shielding the brigs[47] under construction from the dominant British fleet on the lake. There were only about six feet of water over the sand bar; when the brigs were completed, floats had to be used to move them across. When Perry began to move his ships out of Erie harbor – without rigging or cannon – the British failed to take advantage of their vulnerability and stage a serious attack on the new American vessels. By August 10 Perry had his small fleet together and was prepared to engage Captain Robert Barclay's fleet.[48]

For the coming Battle of Lake Erie, Perry had a total of nine vessels available. Included in this number were his two largest, classified as brigs, the *Lawrence* and the *Niagara*. His adversary, Captain Barclay, had under his command a squadron of six vessels. Both commanders were short on qualified

---

[44] Linn and Egle, *Papers and Documents Relating to the War of 1812*, pp. 638-639.

[45] The guard duty to which they were assigned did not seem to sit well with some of the militiamen. One author reports that "when ordered to stand night guard aboard the ships, the 'boys' refused to go." When ordered out to do guard duty, only seven privates out of two companies responded. John R. Elting, *Amateurs to Arms: A Military History of the War of 1812* (Chapel Hill, N.C.: Algonquin Books, 1991), p. 91.

[46] Dobbins had initiated the construction of four ships, though on his arrival Chauncey had altered the design of two of the vessels. Five additional vessels, stationed on the Niagara River, were added to Perry's fleet, giving him a total of nine ships.

[47] For the non-nautical reader, a brig is a two-masted ship with square rigged sails, considerably smaller than a three-masted man-of-war but nonetheless lethal for lake warfare. A ship of this size could hold anywhere from ten to 32 guns. The *Niagara*, a vessel particularly linked to Pennsylvania's military history, held 20 guns.

[48] The history of the 109th Field Artillery records that, as Perry worked to effect the union of his fleet, the British squadron made an appearance. When this threat appeared, a Pennsylvania battery (known as the Kingston Matross), commanded by Captain Samuel Thomas, met them with a cannonade. Exactly when this occurred is not recorded, but the British fleet was in the vicinity of Presque Isle on several occasions between June and August, 1813. See William H. Zierdt, *Narrative History of the 109th Field Artillery, Pennsylvania National Guard, 1775-1930* (Wilkes-Barre, Pa.: Wyoming Historical and Geological Society, 1932), p. 46. Cited hereafter as Zierdt, *Narrative History of the 109th Field Artillery*.

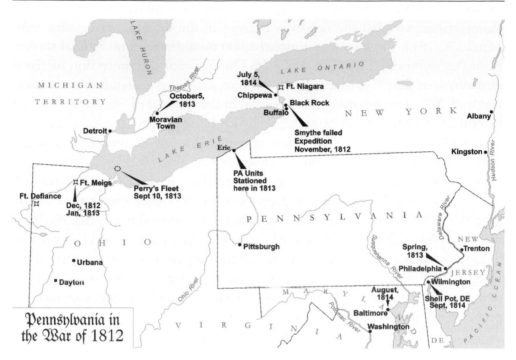

Deployment of Pennsylvania troops in the Eastern Theater (map by Jim Kistler).

sailors to man their ships. Perry, who had only 490 men but needed 740, took soldiers to fill out some of his crew. Among them were four artillerymen from a Pennsylvania militia battery, commanded by Captain Samuel Thomas. They would be put to good use manning guns on Perry's ships.[49] A total of 41 Pennsylvanians from volunteer elements became crew members on Perry's fleet, serving as fillers on various vessels.[50] Thomas' artillerymen had also emplaced guns in the harbor area to serve as shore batteries, covering the final construction and movement of the ships.

Thus, by the time Perry's small fleet engaged Barclay's smaller though

[49] Use of the Pennsylvania militia battery is well documented in archival materials. After the war Captain Thomas helped former members of his battery document their service in the Battle of Lake Erie. This recognition was significant because it meant a silver medal for each of them. Thomas supplied affidavits, as did other former soldiers documenting service in the fleet. See Thomas Lynch Montgomery, ed., *Pennsylvania Archives: Miscellaneous Papers and Drafted Troops, 1812-1814*, sixth series, vol. IX (Harrisburg: State Printer, 1907), pp. 247-290. Cited hereafter as Montgomery, *Miscellaneous Papers and Drafted Troops.*
[50] Documents in the Pennsylvania Archives validate a significant presence of Pennsylvania volunteers on Perry's ships. Forty-one silver medals were struck and engraved with their names.

capable force on September 10, 1813, Pennsylvania had an interest beyond the mere fact that Lake Erie lay on its border. A mid-stater had initiated the construction of Perry's fleet; Pennsylvania troops, both infantry and artillery, had been in place to defend Erie, if the harbor had been attacked by either Barclay's naval forces or the British army troops commanded by General Henry Proctor; and four cannoneers volunteered from Thomas' Pennsylvania militia battery for service on Perry's ships.

The Battle of Lake Erie commenced with the movement of both fleets at dawn on September 10. Perry, though having numerical superiority, was rightfully concerned about the superior range of some of the British guns and, as a result, adopted a strategy whereby his ships fought close, each with a specific British vessel to engage. Perry was on the *Lawrence*, his flagship. Within two hours, out of his crew of 100, 21 were dead and 63 wounded. Perry and four or five sailors subsequently transferred to the *Niagara* and, with the assistance of the smaller sloops in his fleet, soundly defeated the British. As he stated in his message to General Harrison, "We have met the enemy and they are ours – two ships, two brigs, one schooner and a sloop."[51]

It would be hard to overestimate the impact of Perry's victory. By the fall of 1813 the nation was desperate for a decisive victory. It had endured the loss of Detroit and Chicago, had witnessed the British offensive to close the Chesapeake and, all in all, had endured repeated disappointments. Perry gave the nation a clear-cut victory by taking Barclay's fleet and, in the process, clearing Lake Erie of British naval presence. The news was met with celebrations throughout the country, and Perry and his small fleet became national heroes overnight. The Commonwealth was rightfully proud of Perry's accomplishments, in which Pennsylvanians had a role, and the Assembly awarded a silver medal to every man in the fleet and a gold medal for Commodore Perry.[52]

Most important, however, Perry's victory proved to be the beginning of an American initiative to reestablish control over the Great Lakes. Secretary of War John Armstrong, upon hearing of Perry's victory, authorized General

---

[51] Mahon, *The War of 1812,* p. 175.
[52] The Senate and House passed resolutions on January 6-7, 1814, praising Perry for his "brilliant action" and pledged to grant him "a gold medal of fine workmanship" as well as gold medals for Commandant Jesse Duncan Elliot and Lieutenant John J. Yarnell. The Pennsylvanians who served on the fleet were to be given a silver medal of the weight of $2, with each man's name engraved on it, "in complement for their patriotism and bravery." Montgomery, *Miscellaneous Papers and Drafted Troops*, pp. 247-248. By 1817, however, numerous questions were being raised about why the medals had not been awarded. They were finally presented in 1819. Ibid., pp. 258-265.

John Armstrong, son of French and Indian War hero Colonel John
Armstrong, was Secretary of War during the War of 1812. He also
served as a Pennsylvania officer during the Revolutionary War
(reproduced by permission of the Pennsylvania Historical and
Museum Commission).

Harrison to resume operations to regain control of the lakes. Units from
Harrison's command advanced from Erie to Cleveland and, at the end of the
month, in cooperation with Commodore Perry's naval units, crossed into
Canada. Included in Harrison's force were a number of Pennsylvania troops.
One Pennsylvania militia regiment, like some of its peers from New York earlier in the war, objected to serving outside the borders of the country. Thus,
when the invasion occurred, only 150 Pennsylvanians were willing to cross the
border. The invasion force ultimately consisted of two brigades of regular
Army troops, about 3,000 volunteers from Kentucky and the 150 militiamen
from Pennsylvania. Captain Thomas' battery, which had supported Perry at
Erie, was also involved.[53]

    Harrison's troops, more than half of them volunteers, crossed the

[53] Zierdt, *Narrative History of the 109th Field Artillery*, pp. 46-47. See also Mahon, *The War of 1812*, pp. 82-83.

Detroit River and advanced on General Henry Proctor's defending forces. Initially, Proctor had given ground while searching for suitable terrain to defend. On October 5, 1813, in the vicinity of Moraviantown, Proctor, together with Tecumseh and his Indian forces, assumed battle positions and awaited Harrison's attack. For the second time in 30 days, American troops gave the nation victory. Harrison defeated Proctor (who was later court-martialed). Tecumseh was killed, depriving the Indians of a natural leader who had worked hard to cut across tribal divisions and unite them against the relentless expansion of American settlement.

The pace of military operations continued brisk throughout 1813 and well into 1814. Pennsylvania troops were part of a force sent to attack a British strongpoint at Niagara. Some had to be pressured to take part, but a brigade with 300 Pennsylvanians and 400 Indian allies, commanded by a New Yorker, Brigadier General Peter B. Porter, became heavily involved in what became known as the Battle of Chippewa. This engagement occurred near the confluence of the Chippewa and Niagara Rivers on July 5, 1814. Brigadier General Winfield Scott, who held a command on the field and would later become well known in American military history, was one of the brigade commanders. Scott's and Porter's brigades inflicted significant casualties on the British – 148 killed, 321 wounded – a solid defeat in a traditional stand-up battle.

The British offensive along the east coast continued through 1813 and 1814. In the spring the British continued to press the coastal area around Baltimore, in hopes of enticing an American flotilla of armed barges to fight, but they found the American commander only willing to fight on his terms. In the summer the British decided to carry their final land campaign on the east coast to the capital of the American republic. On August 21, 1814, British troops brushed aside American defenders and attacked Washington, D.C., burning and looting most of the public buildings, including the White House.

No Pennsylvania militia troops were involved in the half-hearted defense of the capital, but the attack shook the country. Together with the incursions of 1813 mentioned above, it caused considerable concern in both Pennsylvania and its neighboring state Maryland.[54]

---

[54] The attack on Washington and the general unpreparedness of the capital's defenses destroyed the career of a famous former Pennsylvanian, John Armstrong. Armstrong, son of the famous General John Armstrong of Carlisle, had left the Commonwealth after the Revolution and became a resident of New York. Ever active in military matters, Armstrong had been appointed Secretary of War. Abrasive, with a deserved reputation as an intriguer, he insisted that Baltimore was a far more lucrative target for the British due to its importance as a port. Thus, he focused his attention on fortifying Baltimore rather than the nation's capital. When

A message from Washington on August 18, 1814, alerted Pennsylvania's Governor Snyder that a large British force was at the mouth of the Potomac and the President required 5,000 men to help defend the country. On behalf of the President, Brigadier General William Winder, commander of the Tenth Military District, requested volunteers from the counties nearest his district to assist in the capital's defense.[55] Since Baltimore seemed the next likely target, Snyder ordered selected militia units to defend Baltimore and protect the port of Philadelphia. Five thousand men, drawn from the Second Brigade, Third Division and the Fourth, Fifth and Sixth Divisions were mobilized and rendezvoused in York. Because the soldiers were drawn from different locations, as was the practice of the time, the various companies had to pause in York to be regimented. The companies from York and Hanover, however, had not waited for arrivals from other communities and marched on, reporting for duty on August 28-29. Arriving at Baltimore, the Pennsylvania elements joined a brigade of Virginia militia and the Maryland Militia. The term of service for Pennsylvania troops was to be six months, unless released sooner by the federal government.[56] The militia assembled at York were placed under the command of Major General Nathaniel Watson of Lancaster County and Brigadier Generals John Forester, Harrisburg, and John Adams, Lancaster.

These militia troops would be desperately needed because on September 12, 1814, General Robert Ross landed a British army of 4,500 men at North Point. Ross almost immediately set his troops marching toward Baltimore, a mere 14 miles away. The defending troops marching out to meet Ross were largely militia and were placed under the command of Brigadier General John Stricker, a prominent Baltimore figure in both the militia and the banking community. The Pennsylvania units from York and Hanover which had arrived early were attached to the defending forces and participated in the engagement. The British, who hoped for support from Admiral Alexander Cochrane's ships in taking Baltimore, were ultimately disappointed, because Cochrane could not take Fort Henry, and thus the harbor was still controlled by the Americans. To further complicate their situation, when Ross rode forward to reconnoiter American lines, he was killed by sharpshooters, forcing a change in command during the battle. Militia resistance was stiff and organized, caus-

Washington fell, many citizens blamed him, and local militia even refused to obey his orders. In the wake of Washington's burning and the subsequent looting of Alexandria, Armstrong left for Baltimore and resigned from his cabinet position.

[55] Letter from Brigadier William H. Winder to Governor Simon Snyder, August 18, 1814, in Linn and Egle, *Papers and Documents Relating to the War of 1812*, pp. 734-735.

[56] Ibid., pp. 736-737.

ing the British to erroneously think they were outnumbered. As a consequence, after the day's fighting, they withdrew in the middle of the night, leaving the field to the militia.

Because Philadelphia was also a potential target for a British attack from the beginning of Admiral Sir George Cockburn's advance into Maryland waters, Pennsylvanians were repeatedly alerted or positioned to defend the city.[57] For example, 1,000 militiamen were sent to Shell Pot, north of Wilmington, Delaware. Troops under the command of General Thomas Cadwalader were ordered to set up at Camp Dupont, near Wilmington, to protect the Delaware and Elk Rivers. In Pennsylvania, Camp Gainer was established near Marcus Hook, where Pennsylvania units were posted to protect the Philadelphia area.

As the year 1814 drew to a close, the War of 1812 was also in the process of concluding. On December 24, 1814, the Treaty of Ghent was signed, ending the war. With communications as they were in 1814, official notification did not reach New York until February 11, and the President did not announce it to the nation until February 18.[58] Consequently, the war continued into 1815, with the Battle of New Orleans concluding on January 8, 1815. Several significant engagements occurred at sea in early 1815, in addition to some small land battles. Major General Jacob Brown, commanding units on the Niagara front in 1814, had already planned for a new campaign to invade Canada in 1815. To do so he needed 40,000 men – not only regulars, but 25,000 militia from New York, Vermont, Ohio, Pennsylvania and western Virginia. With the war's end, Pennsylvania would never have to address this call for volunteers.

Reviewing the Pennsylvania militia and its performance in the War of 1812 produces a mixed assessment. The militia's pre-war commander, Governor Simon Snyder, could not have been more supportive of the national government. He not only supplied the troops requested by the President, he consistently supported the war and castigated the British government for its abuses of the United States and its citizens. Snyder was also a realist when it came to the status and capabilities of the militia. From the outset of the war he high-

---

[57] Thus, on August 28, 1814, with Washington burned and Baltimore thought to be the next target, the governor ordered the assembly of a military force at Philadelphia to protect the city. Ibid., p. 742.

[58] According to the governor's records, on February 17, 1815, a message was presented to both houses of the legislature announcing that an honorable peace treaty had been negotiated and the war had been over since December 24. Gertrude MacKinney, ed., *Pennsylvania Archives: Executive Minutes of the Commonwealth of Pennsylvania, Executive Journal*, ninth series, vol. VI (Harrisburg: Commonwealth of Pennsylvania, 1931), p. 4243.

lighted its poor training and criticized the number and condition of its weapons. Nonetheless he strongly supported the Commonwealth's involvement in the war.

As for the militia itself, it exhibited weaknesses symptomatic of those noted by the governor. Because of shortcomings in both the national Militia Act and the state statutes that implemented it, funds for equipment, weapons and training were in short supply. Ill-trained and ill-equipped, the militia possessed only one key advantage: the dedication of those who served. Records show that this dedication may have been lacking in some units, and desertion was a problem. In repeated instances soldiers failed to obey orders – not as often as those of sister states, but still far more often than they should have.

One weakness that was becoming evident in Pennsylvania's system was its traditional – since the Revolutionary War – method of calling up soldiers for duty. Because Pennsylvania militiamen were called up by class, rather than by unit, they often lacked the cohesion that comes with long-term association. This problem, together with the difficulty of ordering state soldiers to serve outside the United States, meant that the militia needed prompt legislative attention to make it what one of its former officers, General George Washington, sought: an instrument of national defense. Considering the circumstances – a militia and a nation ill prepared for war – Pennsylvania forces probably acquitted themselves as well as could be expected. Governor Snyder perhaps summed up their performance best when he stated:

> During the late war the soil of this commonwealth was never trodden by an hostile foot, yet it had at one time a greater number of militia and volunteers in the service of the United States than were at any time greater in the field from any other state in the union. Our militia volunteers were actually engaged with the enemy in Canada, on lake Erie, at Baltimore and elsewhere, and stood ready to repel him from the states of New York and New Jersey. These are proud facts for Pennsylvania.[59]

---

[59] Reed, *Papers of the Governors, 1785-1817*, p. 883.

CHAPTER 9

The Era of Volunteer Militias

An efficient defense must, in my judgement, be sought in a select militia. Such a body, always organized, disciplined and well appointed, can on any emergency be promptly brought into the field; and, so long as freedom is appreciated and patriotism inherited from a brave ancestry, we shall never want abundant materials to form such a force.

— Governor Simon Snyder, 1815

With the end of the War of 1812, belatedly announced on February 11, 1815, the United States entered what would become a traditional cycle for post-war America. With the threat of British invasion gone, the nation and the Commonwealth began to hastily and, at times, haphazardly demobilize their military forces, many of them volunteers or militia. With the return of peace, several problems began to emerge for Pennsylvania's militia. For the individual militiaman who had fought in the war, the most serious issue was financial. Pay to militiamen for their federal service was not always prompt in the 18th or 19th centuries. In a speech to the legislature on February 17, 1815, immediately following the war's end, Governor Simon Snyder noted that neither the Commonwealth nor Congress had the funds to pay all the Pennsylvania troops that fought in the War of 1812.[1] It was not until February 1816 that the governor announced provision by the "general government" of funds to complete the payment of militia troops for their service in the war. Once the federal funds had been received, the governor directed prompt payment of the Commonwealth's soldiers.[2]

---

[1] George E. Reed, ed., *Pennsylvania Archives: Papers of the Governors, 1785-1817*, fourth series, vol. IV (Harrisburg: State of Pennsylvania, 1900), p. 885. Cited hereafter as Reed, *Papers of the Governors, 1785-1817*.

[2] Letter from General George Cadwalader, dated February 16, 1816, in Gertrude MacKinney, ed., *Pennsylvania Archives: Executive Minutes of the Commonwealth of Pennsylvania, Executive Journal,*

Funding payment for militia units was only one of the issues that troubled post-war Pennsylvania. Equally important was how to equip militia troops in the post-war era. Adjutant General Robert Carr's report for 1821 noted that the entire state had only 40 pieces of artillery, and these were unfit for service. The two 12-pound brass pieces in the state's inventory were so badly worn that a 16-pound ball could be put into them. The 27 brass 4-pounders were also worn and "honeycombed" and considered dangerous to use. When this report was filed, the state did not own even a single caisson. The state was supposed to have 44,831 muskets and rifles, but the Adjutant General's Office could only find 28,465. Between 1819 and 1821 alone, 2,481 weapons disappeared from the state's inventory.[3] The Adjutant General's Report of 1820 highlighted the shortage. According to Adjutant General W. N. Irvine, until these weapons could be collected, after having been "scattered over the face of the state for more than 20 years," Pennsylvania had little knowledge of the actual number of small arms in its inventory.[4]

The major problem for the post-war militia was more than financing and accountability; it was a basic structural flaw. As noted previously, according to the federal act of 1792, the militia was a military organization that imposed universal service on all free white males between the ages of 18 and 45. Pennsylvania passed additional militia acts in 1814, 1816, 1818 and 1821, but the militia remained essentially the same.[5] Universal enrollment for all free white males was retained, as was the practice of dividing the manpower pool

1814-1818, ninth series, vol. VI (Harrisburg: Commonwealth of Pennsylvania, 1931), p. 4432. It should also be noted that on June 26, 1816, the governor recognized a group of Pennsylvania volunteers with a cash award. Governor Snyder authorized $10 bounties for 54 men from John McMillan's company, 61 from Lieutenant John Gardner's company of Adams County militia, 48 from Captain George Hendel's company, 64 from Captain David Moreland's company, and 39 from Captain John Roberts' Company of Cumberland County militia. This bonus was for service in Upper Canada in 1814 while these troops were under the command of Major General Brown. Ibid., p. 4515.

[3] "Report of the Adjutant General Robert Carr for the Year 1821," dated February 8, 1822, in George E. Reed, *Pennsylvania Archives: Papers of the Governors, 1817-1832*, fourth series, vol. V (Harrisburg: State Printer, 1900), pp. 346-348. Cited hereafter as Reed, *Papers of the Governors, 1817-1832*.

[4] Ibid., pp. 215-216.

[5] These are only a few of the militia acts passed during this period. There was very little substantive change in any of them. Thus, for example, the Militia Act of 1828 provided for the same essential membership, i.e., "every free able bodied white male person ... between the ages of eighteen and forty five"; gave the same exemptions; specified how officers were to be elected; allowed volunteer units; and so on. See *An Act for the Regulation of the Militia of the Commonwealth of Pennsylvania* (Harrisburg: Office of the Reporter, 1828), p. 72.

into classes.[6] The structure of divisions and brigades was occasionally altered, as was the structure of the smaller units. A basic weakness, however, continued: the imposition of military duties on all, making it difficult if not impossible to ensure that proper training and equipment were provided.[7] Even though Governor William Findlay claimed on December 3, 1818, "The last enrollment of our militia exhibits the number of 118,016, ready to be called into public service," the report filed by Adjutant General W. N. Irvine, on March 15, 1820, was more realistic. It openly questioned the ability of the militia system to properly function:

> *It is much to be lamented that the present militia system does not give even to the most vigilant and zealous officers all the power necessary to call forth and report the full strength of their brigades, either as soldiers in the field for training or on an exempt list. I allude now more particularly to the report of Major Stanley, Inspector of the 2d Brigade, 3d division of the Militia not only because the report of this officer affords the most flagrant instance of the insufficiency of the system, exhibiting to you and to the legislature a regiment consisting of only forty officers, non-commissioned officers and privates, districted in a thickly settled part of the country but because of my knowledge of that gentleman, I am fully convinced that he has used every exertion that the law has afforded him, to compel the inhabitants within the bounds of his brigade to a performance of their duties.*[8]

Due to the difficulty of enforcing what was essentially universal military service, in the 1820s enrolled militias suffered a decline in reputation and ultimately in numbers. Untrained and undisciplined, the enrolled militia was recognized as a largely ineffective force not only by the society supporting it but by many militiamen as well. As an example, members of the 84th Regiment in Philadelphia openly ridiculed the institution in 1824. They elected John Pluck,

---

[6] Another problem was the practice, dating from the Militia Act of 1777, of levying fines on those citizens who failed to report for militia musters. This meant that some citizens would find it more convenient to pay a fine – which virtually became a tax – rather than fulfill their military obligation. Obviously this did not support the defense needs of the Commonwealth or the nation. As a further drawback, as time passed these fines came to be relied on as a source of revenue for the government.

[7] The lack of training was a source of amusement among the enrolled militiamen, whose only real military requirement was "toeing the curb," i.e., falling in along the curbstone for the obligatory annual formation.

[8] Report of Adjutant General W. N. Irvine, March 15, 1820, in Reed, *Papers of the Governors, 1817-1832*, pp. 215-216.

an ignorant stableman, as their colonel. A board of officers declared the election illegal, but when a second election was held, the regiment again chose Pluck. In the spirit of buffoonery, Pluck ordered that a parade be held on May 19, 1824. His own battalion marched in this charade, with a number of soldiers wearing outlandish costumes and carrying imitation weapons.[9] The *U.S. Gazette* commented, "The military system is a farce. Demagogues have been using commissions in the militia as stepping-stones to offices of profit and honor. A cure must be found for the evil, which is to make fun of it."[10]

The problems with the militia system had been recognized earlier by Governor Snyder, a prime backer of the War of 1812, who had carefully monitored the Commonwealth's troops in the war. In his speech to the legislature on February 17, 1815, the governor, while praising the service of the volunteers and militia in the war, clearly stated that "experience has shown the futility of the idea of converting every man to a soldier."[11] Instead, Snyder proposed the reorganization of the militia, creating a different state defense force than existed in either the enrolled militia or the volunteer militia. He stated:

> *An efficient defense must in my judgement be sought in a select militia. Such a body, always organized, disciplined and well appointed, can on any emergency be promptly brought into the field; and so long as freedom is appreciated and patriotism inherited from a brave ancestry, we shall never want abundant materials to form such a force.*[12]

What Governor Snyder proposed was a select militia, whose members would be given adequate training and a "liberal" remuneration for uniform and accoutrements. This force would be exempted from participation in the activities of the enrolled militia; the latter, in accordance with the Militia Act, could be held as a reserve. Under Snyder's plan, the resources of the Commonwealth would be expended on bringing the select militia to a higher standard of readiness, rather than trying to teach the masses the military art.[13] In 1816 Snyder

---

[9] J. Thomas Scharf and Thompson Wescott, *History of Philadelphia, 1609-1884*, vol. I (Philadelphia: L. H. Everts & Co., 1884), p. 615. Cited hereafter as Scharf, *History of Philadelphia*.
[10] William Clarke, *Official History of the Militia and National Guard of Pennsylvania from the Earliest Period of Record to the Present Time*, vol. II (Philadelphia: Charles J. Hendler, 1909), p. 32. Cited hereafter as Clarke, *Official History of the Pennsylvania Militia*, vol. II.
[11] Reed, *Papers of the Governors, 1785-1817*, p. 883.
[12] Ibid., pp. 882-883.
[13] Governor Snyder's concept of a select militia was very close to Washington's plan for a national militia, as proposed in the original Militia Bill of 1791, submitted by then-Secretary of

again proposed that the legislature establish a select militia, stating:

> *The attempt to convert every man, under a certain age into a soldier, is demonstrably futile. The ambition and the military pride essential to a soldier is only to be found among the young and vigorous; and such material formed in select corps, well appointed and equipped, would constitute pride and strength, the safety and glory of our country.*[14]

The following year, when he addressed the legislature for the last time, Snyder reminded them that he had proposed a new concept for the militia but that he had nothing more to add, indicating that his recommendations stood. Snyder's administration ended the same year, and later governors failed to pursue his initiative. Instead, many Pennsylvanians elected to continue the trend that had begun at the first part of the century, placing more faith in volunteer militias. Pennsylvania had utilized a combination of enrolled militia and volunteer militia in the War of 1812, but within the enrolled militia, the lack of training and the calling up of individuals by class meant that such units lacked cohesion and training. Even though no documented studies seem to exist which validate a higher level of performance for volunteer militia units, evidence does indicate that they possessed a higher level of *esprit de corps* than their enrolled militia peers. Still, in Pennsylvania enrolled militia continued to exist concurrently with volunteer militia from the 1820s through the end of the 1840s.[15] The Adjutant General's Report of 1825, dated February 9, 1826, provided the following assessment of the Commonwealth's strength:

Governor and Commander-in-Chief	*1*
Major Generals	*16*
Brigadier Generals	*32*
Adjutant General	*1*

War Henry Knox. In fact, in the governor's address in 1816 he stated, "I am of the opinion, to make it [the militia] an efficient national force, it ought to be organized, armed and disciplined under the authority of Congress." He, like Washington, would find the nation and its individual states wary of any national military force that could be used as an instrument of tyranny.

[14] Reed, *Papers of the Governors, 1785-1817*, p. 921.

[15] The most complete listing of Pennsylvania units in this period can be found in the State Archives in a series of microfilmed records in the Bureau of Elections, Pennsylvania Department of State. These records, consisting of 11 volumes, show the names and locations of Pennsylvania units from 1800 to 1861.

Staff of General Officers   *162*
Infantry (Militia) including Officers   *134,337*
Volunteer Cavalry (36 Troops)   *1,905*
Volunteer Artillery (39 companies)   *1,820*
Volunteer Infantry (226 companies)   *15,340*
Volunteer Riflemen (159 companies)   *9,374*[16]

These statistics listed the enrolled militia strength as 134,337 and the four components of the volunteer force at 28,239, for a combined strength of 162,576. Thus, even though the volunteer militia was building a reputation for better training and more spirit, it was still overshadowed in numbers by the enrolled militia. Of interest is the listing of enrolled militia as infantry, whereas the more specialized and expensive units, artillery and cavalry, were volunteer units. This trend continued, as evidenced by the Adjutant General's Report of 1830. It noted, "In many parts of the state there exists a great aversion to military training." In 1829 the adjutant general noted there were 33,048 soldiers in the volunteer militia. By 1830, the number had increased to 34,377. Most of the increase in volunteer militia enrollment was in artillery and cavalry units.[17]

The problem of how to develop a stronger, better trained militia, and thus a better system of defense for both the Commonwealth and the United States, would elude resolution in the years between the War of 1812 and the Mexican War. The basis of the problem, which faced all the states, was the weak and ineffective federal law of 1792, which each state implemented through its own statutes.[18] Since congressional action did not occur, Governor George Wolf, in his annual address to the Assembly on December 2, 1835, offered a solution:

---

[16] Report of Adjutant General G. B. Porter, dated February 8, 1825, in Reed, *Papers of the Governors, 1817-1832*, pp. 574-575.

[17] Report of Adjutant General Samuel Power, dated February 16, 1831. Ibid., pp. 930-932. Readers should also consider the impact of militia affairs on politics of the period. In his 1830 report, the adjutant general reported the total strength of the militia in both categories as 182,285. In 1830 the population of Pennsylvania was 1,348,233, which meant that 13.5 percent of the citizenry had some militia affiliation.

[18] Pennsylvania was not the only state trying to resolve the inherent weakness of the enrolled militia. In 1832 Pennsylvania Governor George Wolf received a joint resolution passed by both houses of the Indiana legislature urging Congress to pass a law to provide "for a more perfect and uniform organization of the militia of the several States of the Union, in pursuance of the Constitution of the United States." This Indiana Resolution was to be transmitted to all the governors in the Union. George E. Reed, *Pennsylvania Archives: Papers of the Governors, 1832-1845*, fourth series, vol. VI (Harrisburg: Commonwealth of Pennsylvania, 1901), p. 13.

The Militia system is deplorably defective, and requires prompt attention to its reorganization and thorough amendment. It ought if possible be raised above the reproach and ridicule which its inefficiency and general defectiveness have brought upon it. It is true that, to make it what it should be, the action of Congress must be brought to bear upon it — but by encouraging voluntary Associations, you may provoke a military ardor, which will add much to the efficiency of the system, and infuse a spirit of subordination and discipline into the whole body of the militia which will inspire confidence, and make it in a measure what it ought to be, the bulwark of the nation.[19]

In Pennsylvania, Wolf's idea of encouraging volunteers, in lieu of action by Congress, was a workable solution for developing a more acceptable military force – a force of volunteers within the militia system rather than an organization to supplant the enrolled militia. This would be Pennsylvania's method of developing an improved militia for the next 25 years.

In the two decades following the War of 1812, Pennsylvania was fortunate because it was not plagued by any serious internal or external threats. Since the nation was not involved in any wars, there were no federal calls to active duty during the 1820s and 1830s. Indian campaigns were not needed in Pennsylvania either, since the Commonwealth had essentially passed its frontier stage. During this period, several Indian campaigns were conducted in the eastern half of the United States, but not on Pennsylvania soil. Consequently, they did not include Pennsylvania militia units, but rather units from the states where the Indian tribes were located. Any serious threat of Indian insurrection for Pennsylvania ceased with the 1790 campaign waged by General Josiah Harmar, commander in chief of the United States Army (who in 1793 became Pennsylvania's first adjutant general).

The only contingencies requiring military force after the War of 1812 would come from civil disorder. In the decade following the war, one event occurred which was significant for the militia in general and the Pennsylvania militia in particular. In September 1824, the Marquis de Lafayette, a famous Revolutionary War figure, paid an official visit to the United States and was given a military escort for a visit to Philadelphia. The First City Troop – by this time well experienced in escorting dignitaries – and the First County Troop escorted the marquis.[20] After leaving Pennsylvania he travelled to New York,

[19] Ibid., p. 238.
[20] For example, the First City Troop escorted General George Washington at the outset of the

where he reviewed the 7th New York. Lafayette referred to the regiment as the "Garde Nationale" – the National Guard. This term, though not immediately adopted as a new name for the volunteer militia, would slowly grow in popularity, increasingly so after the Civil War. Some states, including Pennsylvania, would begin using this name for state troops in the 1870s. Through federal legislation passed in 1916, the term National Guard would be adopted as the official name for all state defense forces.

Beginning in the 1830s, a number of minor military operations were conducted within the Commonwealth, all of them related to civil disorder. On August 12, 1834, race riots broke out in southern Philadelphia. The initial cause appears to have been a perceived affront to some of Philadelphia's white citizens by members of the city's growing black community. The real cause, however, was likely the tension brought about by the activities of abolitionists in the city. The riots, which resulted in destruction of property and numerous assaults on black citizens, could not be contained by civil authorities. Both the First City Troop and the Washington Grays were called out on three successive nights to restore order.[21]

In 1838 a contested election in Pennsylvania caused considerable turmoil in Harrisburg. Governor Joseph Ritner, a leader in the Anti-Masonic Party, was defeated in his re-election bid. Ritner had won the governor's race in 1835 backed by a conglomeration of factions composed of Anti-Masons, Whigs and Abolitionists. David Rittenhouse Porter, a Democrat, defeated Ritner in 1838. The election was almost immediately contested, with the Anti-Masons conspiring to hold on to some of their seats in hopes of controlling the legislature. Because the vote was split by the emergence of a third-party candidate, Ritner became governor without a clear majority of the votes. (He received 94,023 votes out of 200,413 cast.) The close election and such campaign issues as abolition and Masonry resulted in a contentious squabble over seats in the legislature – particularly from the Philadelphia area, where fraudu-

Revolutionary War and again during the Whiskey Rebellion. They escorted Andrew Jackson in 1833 and Martin Van Buren in 1839. Due to the prestige of the members and the significance of Philadelphia in early American history, they had many such ceremonial duties during the late 18th century and throughout the 19th. See First Troop, Philadelphia City Cavalry, *History of the First Troop, Philadelphia City Cavalry, together with an Introductory Chapter Summarizing the Early History and the Rolls Complete from 1774* (Philadelphia: Winchell Company, 1991), pp. 4-5, 281. Cited hereafter as *History of the First City Troop.*
[21] Scharf, *History of Philadelphia,* pp. 637-638. Scharf and Westcott mention additional riots related to the growing number of blacks in Philadelphia and the activities of abolitionist groups that openly fraternized with black citizens. (See pp. 641, 652-53.) In these instances, however, police were able to contain the situation.

lent returns were also a factor. Two different parties claimed identical seats. The bitter dispute and the ensuing riotous behavior in the House, complicated by mobs of outsiders who supported the two parties, resulted in Governor Ritner ordering Major General Robert Patterson to call out militia troops.

Patterson marched the First Division to Harrisburg to put down what the governor viewed as an insurrection. Both brigades of the division were based in Phildadelphia. In ordering out the militia, the governor had the troops draw "buck and ball" loads, paper cartridges consisting of a .69 caliber ball and three buckshot.[22] Due to this choice of munitions, the civil disturbances of this period resulting in the use of militia troops became known as "Buckshot Wars." In the end, the adjutant general determined that the governor was not using the militia to suppress insurrection as much as to further his own political agenda. Patterson refused to become involved in the squabble and, in the end, only pledged to protect public property and the lives of his soldiers. The governor briefly attempted to obtain federal troops from Carlisle Barracks, as well as support from President Martin Van Buren. The governor finally sent the 1,000 militiamen home and called up militia troops from the 1st Brigade, 11th Division (from Cumberland County), but ultimately he had to be content with the legislature settling its own problems through the civil rather than the military process.

The pace of militia responses to civil disorder became brisk in the first half of the 1840s. Beginning in August 1842, the First Division was called out to deal with further race riots in the Southwark section of Philadelphia. The First City Troop was on state duty in Philadelphia August 1-3, 1842, to assist in restoring order.[23] During the first few days of August, militia troops established their headquarters on Washington Square, using it as a cantonment in order to protect their members and equipment from the rioters.

In 1843 Philadelphia was again plagued by a series of riots requiring militia action. Immigration in the first four decades of the 19th century had brought a wave of new population into Pennsylvania, bringing both social and

[22] This load, extremely effective at ranges of 75 to 100 yards, had its origins in the previous century, when it proved popular due to the infantryman's ability to hit something with it, despite the inherent inaccuracy of smoothbore weapons at longer ranges. It remained as the favorite load for some infantry units, such as the famed 69th Irish Brigade, until the end of the Civil War. This was despite the fact that in the Civil War the smoothbore musket was being rapidly phased out in favor of the rifled musket, with greater accuracy and range. See Joseph G. Bilby, "A Better Chance to Hit: The Story of the Buck and Ball," *The American Rifleman* (May 1993), pp. 48-49, 78-80.
[23] *History of the First City Troop*, p. 5-6.

One of the earliest known images of a Pennsylvania volunteer depicts William H. Yeaton, of the Washington Grays of Philadelphia, circa 1840s.

economic pressures on the Commonwealth. In the mid-1830s, some native-born citizens, concerned about the growth of foreign influence in the country and opposed to "foreigners" voting in American elections, formed the Native American party. A major issue for this party's members was the growth of Roman Catholic influence, prompted by the increasing number of Irish Catholics arriving in the Philadelphia area. In largely Protestant America, some regarded Catholics with considerable suspicion because of their ties to a foreign leader: the Pope, who resided in Rome. The crisis began on May 3, 1844, when the Native American party met to organize a new local chapter in Kensington, a district with a sizable Irish Catholic population. The Irish Catholics, offended by a meeting of Native Americans in their presence, attacked the group, and a riot ensued. Not to be deterred, the Native Americans staged a second rally on May 6, and the area's Irish attacked again, this time with bricks and guns. A Native American was killed, and several others were wounded. On May 7 the

Native Americans rallied again on Independence Square. Despite pleas for calm, the crowd moved out of the square and proceeded to Kensington, where they fought with the Catholic residents, causing additional casualties and considerable destruction of both private and church property.

When it was determined that the sheriff could not control the situation, the First Brigade, First Division from Philadelphia County was called out. By May 8 most of the militia were withdrawn, but when rioters learned the military presence had been reduced, they again began to torch buildings, including the Roman Catholic Church of St. Michael. On the afternoon of May 9, Brigadier General George Cadwalader, in command of the First Brigade, arrived. Dividing his brigade into two columns, he drove the rioters from the streets. Despite progress in the Kensington district, rioting broke out within the city limits of Philadelphia, with rioters burning St. Augustine Catholic Church. Militia troops were subsequently moved into Philadelphia proper to establish control. Governor Porter made a personal visit to the scene of the riots on the same day. With his presence, the militia troops and some assistance from a detachment from the *USS Princeton*, the rioting subsided.

The causes of the sectarian strife, however, remained. In July riots again erupted, initially focused on the Church of St. Phillip de Neri in Philadelphia. Local volunteers designated to protect the church were beleaguered by disgruntled crowds and had to be reinforced on the evening of July 6 by volunteer militia from the Washington Blues, Cadwalader Grays, Montgomery Hibernia Greens and the Markle Rifles. When the situation seemed to calm, the military force was reduced to three companies, including the Hibernia Greens (whose ethnic composition should be obvious from their name). On July 7 a virtual battle broke out in and around the church, as rioters, in possession of an old field piece, fired a load of slugs and nails on the church and its militia protectors. Negotiations began, the volunteers agreed to withdraw, and the mob leaders agreed to protect the church. As the volunteers withdrew, the wrath of the mob was turned on the Hibernia Greens, who were stoned, resulting in the death of one man.[24] Militia troops were subsequently called into the Southwark area, and another battle erupted, as militiamen with fixed bayonets attempted to drive back the rioters and the rioters responded with cannon and small arms fire. Fighting continued throughout the evening and into the next day, when the militia, exhausted and without food or ammunition, had to be withdrawn. Five thousand fresh militia troops were brought

[24] Clarke, *Official History of the Pennsylvania Militia*, vol. II, pp. 38-40.

in from the Philadelphia area. Their presence over the next three weeks resulted in peace and order returning.[25]

The Native American riots proved to be the most serious civil disorders
that confronted the Pennsylvania militia in the pre-Civil War era – and the last
of the Buckshot Wars before the beginning of the Mexican War in 1846. If the
names of units involved in the Buckshot Wars are reviewed, it becomes clear
that the authorities used volunteer units to restore order rather than the enrolled
militia. Volunteer militia were much better organized and more easily deployed
than enrolled militia. This should come as no surprise, because from the beginning of the 19th century volunteer militia had become increasingly popular in
many communities and had been recognized as a legal alternative to militia service. As the crisis with Mexico developed, volunteers would again represent the
military force of choice.

The origins of the war with Mexico can be traced back to the
Declaration of Independence by Texas on December 20, 1835. Although
Mexico had grudgingly agreed to Texas' independence, following a successful
revolution led by American settlers, Mexico still claimed part of Texas as its territory. The leadership of the Texas government wanted the newly independent
"country" to become a part of the United States, but at first the U.S. government was hesitant to take this step. By the mid-1840s, however, the federal government was decidedly expansionistic in philosophy and, in cooperation with
the Texas government, began to move toward the annexation of the "Lone
Star" state. Newly elected President James K. Polk wanted to establish the Rio
Grande River as the southern border of Texas and sought to stand firm in the
face of Mexican pressure and, through diplomacy, resolve the crisis.

Tensions along the border rose throughout 1845, culminating with the
December 22, 1845, approval by Congress of annexation. In July 1845 troops
under Brigadier General Zachary Taylor, commander of U.S. troops in the
Southwest, had been ordered to Texas to defend the border of the newly
acquired state. Mexico did not accept the Rio Grande as the southern border.
Thus, on March 8, 1846, when Taylor moved troops into the area between the
Nueces River and the Rio Grande, the stage for conflict was set. Taylor took
up a position along the Rio Grande directly across from the Mexican town of
Matamoros. From Mexico's perspective, U.S. troops were in Mexican territory

---

[25] Among the troops brought into the riot area were the Reading Artillerists, who were in gar-
rison at the Pennsylvania State Arsenal and later at the Girard Bank. See W. J. Creed, *Historical
Sketch and Souvenir, Reading Artillerists, Company A, Fourth Regiment Infantry, Third Brigade, NGP*
(Reading, Pa.: B. F. Owen Publishers, 1894), p. 24.

and certainly too close to the border as claimed by the United States. Clashes began with the ambush of U.S. dragoons on April 25 and continued with the Battles of Palo Alto and Ressaca de la Palma during the second week in May. The deepening border crisis caused President Polk to send a message to Congress on May 11, 1846, declaring that a state of war existed between Mexico and the United States. On May 13, 1846, the President issued a proclamation affirming the state of war.

The President had no choice but to call for volunteers, much as was done in 1812, because the U.S. Army was minuscule. It totaled just 8,509 officers and enlisted men.[26] Volunteers drawn from militia and volunteer regiments, augmented by additional patriotic citizens, would have to assist in defending American interests. Congress responded to the President's proclamation by providing funds and authorizing a call for 50,000 volunteers.

With war declared and the call for volunteers issued, the Commonwealth's governor, Francis R. Shunk, alerted the Pennsylvania militia through the adjutant general and told the troops to hold themselves in readiness. On May 19 an official notification from the Secretary of War indicated that Pennsylvania's quota would be six regiments. The governor's call for six regiments of ten companies each was issued on May 26, and recruiting was to be completed by July 11. The response to the call was overwhelming. On July 15, only a few days past the deadline, enough soldiers had volunteered to man between 90 and 100 companies, rather than the 60 that were required. The governor wrote to the President of the United States with considerable satisfaction:

> It is earnestly hoped that in case these troops are required to be mustered into the service, a reasonable time will be allowed for the organization of the regiments, and for their discipline, before they shall be ordered to march. In concluding this report I cannot refrain from expressing the gratification I derive from the patriotism and ardor of the citizen soldiers of my native state, who remote from the scene of action, have responded to the country's call with so much promptitude.[27]

American soil had been violated and American soldiers had been

---

[26] Russell F. Weigley, *History of the United States Army*, The Macmillan Wars of the United States, Louis Morton, ed. (New York: Macmillan Company, 1967), pp. 566-567.
[27] George E. Reed, ed., *Pennsylvania Archives: Papers of the Governors, 1845-1858*, fourth series, vol. VII (Harrisburg: State Printer, 1902), p. 107. Cited hereafter Reed, *Papers of the Governors, 1845-1858*.

attacked — a sure formula to evoke a solid response from American citizens, then or now. Governor Shunk, on receiving the declaration of war, issued a proclamation in which he clearly demonstrated solid support for the war. He called on the Commonwealth's forces to "hold themselves in readiness prompt-ly to meet and repel the enemies of the republic and to preserve the rights and honor and secure the perpetuity of the Union."[28] A rapid and sincere out-pouring of patriotic fervor accompanied the prospect of Pennsylvania troops defending American honor on the border. Militia companies throughout the state scrambled to be properly uniformed, armed and prepared in the hope that they would be among those accepted for service. The 90 companies who vol-unteered represented a broad geographical distribution from all over the Commonwealth. Among them were the Steuben Fusiliers from Philadelphia, the Gettysburg Guards, the Berks County Washington Grays, Luzerne County's Wyoming Artillerists, the Irish Greens from Pittsburgh and the St. Thomas Artillery from Franklin County.

Despite this flurry of activity and the fact that Governor Shunk sent a message to the President on July 15, enumerating the companies that were avail-able for federal service, a lull developed.[29] For the next four months, it seemed that neither six regiments nor 90 companies would be called to serve. Pennsylvania militiamen waited impatiently but ultimately settled back to a peacetime existence, since the federal notice failed to arrive. On November 16, 1846, however, Pennsylvania was informed that one regiment of volunteers was required from the state.[30] Only ten companies were accepted, in keeping with the standard force structure of the period.[31] The First Pennsylvania Regiment was under the command of Francis M. Wynkoop. Most of its units came from either Philadelphia or Pittsburgh. Philadelphia contributed six companies:

> The Monroe Guards, Company C
> The City Guards, Company D
> The Washington Light Infantry, Company E
> The Philadelphia Light Guards, Company F
> The Jefferson Guards, Company G

[28] Ibid., p. 105.
[29] A list providing the names of 90 companies, together with their commanding officers, can be found in Reed, *Papers of the Governors, 1845-1858*, pp. 108-111.
[30] Ibid., p. 118.
[31] From the start of the 19th century through the Civil War, the regiment consisted of ten com-panies, usually with 35-40 soldiers each. A regiment could conceivably have up to 1,000 sol-diers, with the companies being larger than described, but its strength would normally fall between 350 and 400 soldiers.

The Caldwalader Grays, Company H

Pittsburgh contributed two companies:

The Jackson Independent Blues, Company A
The Duquesne Grays, Company K

The only other areas of the state represented were Pottsville and Wilkes-Barre:

The Washington Artillery, Company B
The Wyoming Artillerists, Company I

A short time later, on December 14, 1846, the President requested a second regiment from the Commonwealth. It was mustered at Pittsburgh on January 5, 1847.[32] The Second Pennsylvania was under the command of Colonel William B. Roberts.[33] More geographically diverse than the First Regiment, the Second was composed of the following elements:

The Reading Artillery, Company A (Berks County)
The American Highlanders, Company B (Summit, Cambria County)
The Columbia Guards, Company C (Columbia County)
The Cambria Guards, Company D (Ebensburgh, Cambria County)
The Westmoreland Guards, Company E (Westmoreland County)
The Philadelphia Rangers, Company F
The Cameron Guards, Company G (Dauphin County)
The Fayette County Volunteers, Company H
The Independent Irish Greens, Company I (Pittsburgh)
The Stockton Artillerists, Company K (Carbon County)[34]

These two regiments of Pennsylvania volunteers were not mobilized merely for

---

[32] Reed, *Papers of the Governors*, 1845-1858, p. 119.
[33] Allan Peskin, ed., *Volunteers: The Mexican War Journals of Private Richard Coulter and Sergeant Thomas Barclay, Company E, Second Pennsylvania Infantry* (Kent, Ohio: Kent State University Press, 1991), pp. 14-15. Cited hereafter as Peskin, *Journals of Richard Coulter and Thomas Barclay*.
[34] Regrettably, the lineages of today's Pennsylvania National Guard do not include a historical trace for all this these units. Official Center for Military History lineages show the 109th Field Artillery, the Wyoming Guards, still have Mexican war credits; the 337th Engineer Battalion has the Mexican War credits for the Reading Artillerists; Detachment 1, Battery A, 213th Air Defense Artillery has the credits for the Washington Artillerists; the 128th Forward Support Battalion has the Duquesne Greys' lineage; C Company, 728th Main Support Battalion has the Franklin Guards' lineage; and the 213th Artillery Regiment (deactivated in 1968), originally entitled The First Defenders, had Mexican War credits.

General Winfield Scott reviews the Pennsylvania militia at Reading, May 19, 1842 (courtesy Historical Society of Berks County, Reading, Pa.).

domestic garrison duty; they were destined to take an active role in the campaign against Mexico.

For both regiments, the official muster and entry into federal service came at Pittsburgh. By December 15, all ten companies of the First Pennsylvania had arrived in Pittsburgh, by various means of transport.[35] As was the established practice with militia units, the First Pennsylvania elected officers on December 18. The First was to remain in Pittsburgh until December 21-22, 1846. The Second Pennsylvania, which completed the arrival of its companies by January 5, elected officers on the next day.[36] They departed Pittsburgh on

[35] According to Randy Hackenburg, U.S. Army Military History Institute, the troops from Philadelphia came first by rail and then by the Pennsylvania Canal or the Philadelphia-Pittsburgh Turnpike (as did the Pottsville unit). The Wyoming Artillerists moved toward Pittsburgh on the Susquehanna Canal. Randy W. Hackenburg, *Pennsylvania in the War with Mexico* (Shippensburg, Pa.: White Main Publishing Co., 1992), p. 4. Cited hereafter as Hackenburg, *Pennsylvania in the War with Mexico*.

[36] Sergeant Thomas Barclay noted that each soldier was paid bounty money of $21, in lieu of six months' clothing, and stated, "We have today ceased to be 'free and independent citizens' and are become the property of Uncle Sam, who has the sole and exclusive right to our labor, lives and all our energies." Peskin, *Journals of Richard Coulter and Thomas Barclay,* p. 13.

January 8-9, 1847.

The first stop on the way to war was New Orleans. Both regiments trained briefly at Camp Jackson, prepared for embarkation and sailed for Mexico by the end of the month. Other than some disturbances caused by rowdies in the First Regiment at both Pittsburgh and New Orleans, the entry of the Pennsylvania volunteers into federal service had gone well. The journey into the Gulf, however, proved to be a major challenge for the Second Regiment. On February 2 a fierce tropical storm struck the convoy of ships carrying Pennsylvania troops to Mexico. It buffeted the convoy for 40 hours. Though none of the vessels sank, the misery inflicted on the Pennsylvania volunteers by high seas was substantial.[37] The skies cleared on February 3, buoying the morale of the troops, but on February 10 another storm hit. For the next 56 hours the Second Regiment endured an even more violent storm. No ships were lost, but the troops were not in very good shape.[38]

Rather than immediately invade Mexico, both regiments landed on Lobos, a Caribbean isle. Elements of the First Regiment arrived on February 11-12, the Second Regiment on the 14th. The only major hitch in the deployment of Pennsylvania troops occurred when smallpox was discovered on a transport carrying companies B, D and G of the Second Regiment. With Lobos an unhealthy place anyway, these companies had to be quarantined on board the ship until March 3, by which time the other companies had departed for Mexico.

The Pennsylvania forces were not the only troops on Lobos. There were other state regiments from New York, both Carolinas, Mississippi and Louisiana. General Winfield Scott – who had worked with Pennsylvania militia during the War of 1812 and had even reviewed Pennsylvania volunteers at Reading and Danville in 1842 – was the commander. Arriving on February 21, 1847, Scott organized his troops into three divisions. Two were composed of regulars, and the third, commanded by Major General Robert Patterson, was made up of volunteers, including both the First and Second Pennsylvania.

---

[37] According to Barclay's diary entry, "The traveler overwhelmed with terror and admiration of the grandeur of the works of nature ... The sublime above the deck is in strange contrast with the ludicrous below. The oaths, laughter and songs of the hearty are mingled with the groans of the sick ... The boxes and barrels loosed from their fastenings are merrily dancing and at every lurch, pitch and roll the length of the vessel." Ibid., p. 24.

[38] Private Richard Coulter reported that soldiers were roused at 5 a.m. by the ferocity of the storm. Since they could not cook meals, "our fare, raw flitch [bacon] principally fat, the rank taste killed with vinegar and crackers with scarcely sufficient water to wash it down." Ibid., p. 28.

Major General Robert Patterson, originally a Pennsylvania volunteer and, in the war with Mexico, the commander of one of General Winfield Scott's three divisions (reproduced by permission, U.S. Army Military History Institute).

Patterson was originally a Pennsylvania volunteer officer who, as noted above, had commanded troops in Philadelphia during the Buckshot Wars. The two Pennsylvania regiments (minus the three companies in quarantine) embarked from Lobos on March 2, 1847.[39] The short voyage to Vera Cruz was uneventful but at the same time significant, because U.S. troops, using specially constructed boats, made one of the earliest amphibious landings in U.S. military history. Conducted about two miles south of Vera Cruz on March 9, the landings were successfully executed with no loss of life.

Initially, enemy opposition was conspicuously absent. However, once Pennsylvania and Tennessee troops began advancing on Vera Cruz, in preparation for besieging the city, Mexican lancers and infantry resisted, resulting in a small engagement on March 10.[40] After routing the Mexicans, U.S. forces con-

[39] A total of 16 men came down with smallpox, and the extended quarantine on the ship meant that many other soldiers were not in the best of health. As a consequence, these soldiers stayed on the island until the health of the companies had been restored. After the rest of the Pennsylvania troops left Lobos on March 2, the quarantined troops were moved to the island on the 3rd. They finally left Lobos on April 8 to join up with the rest of the Army.

[40] See Thomas Barclay's diary entry for March 10, in Peskin, *Journals of Richard Coulter and Thomas Barclay*, p. 43.

tinued their progress toward the city.

On March 22, having properly emplaced guns and occupied suitable terrain, General Scott offered the Mexican commander the opportunity to surrender. This offer, intended to spare the inhabitants the misery of war, was refused. On the same day U.S. batteries opened up on the city. On March 26 the city's garrison commander sent out a flag of truce, and the formal surrender of the city occurred on March 29. Even though troops had not been required to storm the city, small engagements and skirmishes necessary to occupy the favorable ground cost the Pennsylvania regiments 15 casualties – 12 from the First Regiment and three from the Second. Three of these were killed in action, and one died of wounds.[41] Once the city was secured, there was a brief pause for the volunteers, and then they pressed on with the intent of taking Mexico City. While moving toward their goal, the U.S. troops became involved in another battle. The engagement was fought at Cerro Gordo, a naturally defensible position where the National Road ran through a narrow pass between the heights, called Cerro Gordo, and the Rio del Plan. The commander of Mexican forces, General Antonio Lopez de Santa Anna, was determined to stop American forces here, but General Scott was equally determined to press on to Mexico City.

On April 18 approximately 8,550 U.S. troops attacked the 11,000 Mexicans under Santa Anna's command. The battle was a hard fought engagement against superior numbers in prepared defensive positions. Both Pennsylvania regiments were involved, and both took casualties – 10 from the First and 13 from the Second.[42] U.S. forces won the battle, capturing 3,000 Mexican soldiers and a substantial amount of military equipment.[43] Afterward, between April 19 and 21, the Americans advanced to Jalapa. The Second Pennsylvania, later joined by elements of the First, took up residence in Mexican barracks, where they served to garrison the town and protect the Army's lines of communication.

Following the battle at Cerro Gordo and the establishment of a substantial garrison at Jalapa, several months elapsed when there were no signifi-

---

[41] Hackenburg, *Pennsylvania in the War with Mexico*, p. 29-30.

[42] The best source for rosters of members from Pennsylvania, casualties and dates of service is Randy Hackenburg's *Pennsylvania in the War with Mexico*.

[43] While noting that the battle did not go exactly as planned, Sergeant Barclay of the Second Pennsylvania stated proudly, "Had we been defeated or repulsed at Cerro Gordo, the Army would have been forced back to Vera Cruz in the sick season. Nothing could have been accomplished until the arrival of reinforcements from the United States." Peskin, *Journals of Richard Coulter and Thomas Barclay*, pp. 78-80.

cant engagements between Santa Anna's forces and U.S. troops. Mexican troops and guerrillas remained nearby to harass Americans in the field and pick off unsuspecting stragglers, but they did not risk a general engagement. In early June, General Scott abandoned Jalapa and elected to garrison only Vera Cruz, Perote and Puebla. While U.S. troops were being consolidated in the three locations, there was a small engagement at La Hoya and Las Vegas, but there were no Pennsylvania casualties, and the consolidation was completed.

Scott's pause in moving on Mexico City was caused by the need for additional troops. A call for more volunteers had been issued on April 19, and Pennsylvania was quick to respond. The adjutant general identified two additional Pennsylvania companies, the Independent Grays from Bedford and the Wayne Guards from Mifflin County. Like their predecessors, the two companies proceeded to Pittsburgh, where they were mustered into federal service. They went on to New Orleans, shipped out to Vera Cruz and landed in the vicinity of the city on June 27.[44]

Throughout the first half of July, Scott made preparations to leave the coastal region and march on Mexico City, in hopes of bringing the war to an end. Preliminary moves started on July 16, with two Pennsylvania volunteer companies taking part in a brief fight on July 21. The First Pennsylvania, however, was soon disappointed. They were informed that they would be left behind to assist in garrisoning the cities of Perote and Puebla, with four companies in the first location and six in the latter, along with a company of dragoons and a detachment from the First U.S. Artillery.[45] Their commander in Puebla, Lieutenant Colonel Samuel W. Black, attempted to resign in protest but was persuaded to stay. For soldiers who had left their homes and loved ones behind in Pennsylvania to fight, this news was nonetheless unwelcome. They would soon discover that this garrison duty would not be an easy task and that the war would indeed come to them.

Even though the populace seemed ambivalent about the presence of U.S. troops, once Scott's main body left, Mexican General Joaquin Rea sent agents into Puebla to turn the citizens against the occupiers and undermine U.S. morale. Trouble for the garrison began on July 26, when the Mexicans staged a raid on Puebla. When American forces responded, the Mexicans launched a

---

[44] Hackenburg, *Pennsylvania in the War with Mexico*, p. 49.
[45] The six companies were the Jackson Independent Blues from Pittsburgh (A Company), the Monroe Guards from Philadelphia (C Company), the City Guards from Philadelphia (D Company), the Jefferson Guards from Philadelphia (G Company), the Wyoming Artillerists from Wilkes-Barre, and the Duquesne Grays from Pittsburgh (K Company).

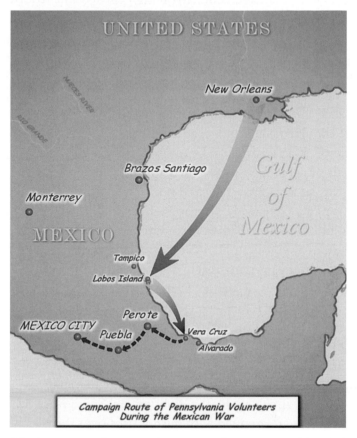

Campaign Route of Pennsylvania Volunteers
During the Mexican War

Mexican campaign route for troops of the First and Second
Pennsylvania in the Mexican War.

flank attack that resulted in 20 American casualties out of a force of 30. On
September 13 General Rea had several thousand of his troops move into
Puebla. For most of the month, the garrison was pressed hard by the Mexicans,
who held part of the town and blocked access to their food supply. The garrison, commanded by Colonel Thomas W. Childs, was offered two chances to
surrender but elected to hold out until they could be relieved by American reinforcements.[46] General Joseph Lane proceeded from Vera Cruz on September 19
and, after numerous delays, reached Perote on October 5.[47]

[46] While Pennsylvania troops fought well against Mexican incursions into the areas they controlled, a major factor in their successful defense was that the U.S. garrison included the First
U.S Artillery, which provided needed firepower.
[47] A good primary source for the actions occurring at Puebla can be found in Jacob Oswandel's

Several notable engagements involving Pennsylvania troops followed, as Santa Anna unsuccessfully tried to ambush this sizable force of more than 3,000 men. On October 12 Lane's troops, including elements of the First Pennsylvania, engaged Mexican troops in Puebla who were attempting to evacuate the town. In the process of clearing the city, Company K of the First Pennsylvania took 13 casualties. During the siege, 21 Pennsylvania volunteers were either killed in action or died of their wounds.[48]

While the skirmishes and siege at Puebla had been occurring, action by the main body of Scott's army had been proceeding well. Scott had led his column out of the Puebla area to proceed toward Mexico City in early August. Mexico City was an attractive objective not only because it was the capital, but also because it had a large body of troops defending it, which gave Mexico the ability to continue the fight. Scott's force was organized into four divisions; the Second Brigade of the Fourth Division was an expanded Second Pennsylvania Regiment. The American Army reached the vicinity of Mexico City on August 15 and engaged in a series of battles four days later. The Second Pennsylvania was not involved in the initial engagements at San Antonio, Contreras and Churubusco because it had the task of protecting the supplies and trains at San Augustin. On September 12, when the Army began its move against Mexico City in earnest, the Second became a part of the force designated to storm the Mexican fortifications, including the citadel of Chapultepec. Pennsylvania troops were heavily involved in the fighting on September 12-13, and two Pennsylvania officers are credited with raising flags over the castle, signifying an American victory.[49] Regrettably, Santa Anna's troops had eluded the attackers; as noted above, it was they who gave the First Pennsylvania such difficulty at Puebla. Storming the citadel and subsequent fighting by the Second Pennsylvania and other U.S. units gave the Army possession of the city and a clear-cut victory. The cost, however, was high. Eight Pennsylvania soldiers were killed and 89 wounded, 11 of whom later died of their wounds.[50]

The victory at Mexico City did not, however, bring about a prompt end to the war or an immediate return of the Keystone soldiers to their home state. Instead, there would be a period of occupation duty, marked by guerrilla activ-

Notes of the Mexican War, 1846-47-48 (Philadelphia: 1885).

[48] Hackenburg, *Pennsylvania in the War with Mexico*, p. 73.

[49] Both Hackenburg and Clarke's *Official History of the Pennsylvania Militia* credit Captain Edward C. Williams, Company C, with raising the first American flag over the citadel. Hackenburg credits Captain Samuel H. Montgomery, formerly a private in Company E, later a Quartermaster Department captain, with raising a Pennsylvania flag over the castle.

[50] Hackenburg, *Pennsylvania in the War with Mexico*, p. 60.

ity interspersed with periods of boredom and homesickness.[51] By December 8 both Pennsylvania regiments were together in Mexico City, but training, parades and garrison duties were the order of the day until the peace treaty was finally signed on May 30, 1848. The Pennsylvania regiments began moving toward Vera Cruz at the first of June, and at the end of the month, both regiments were loaded onto steamers for the return trip home. During the second week of July the troops finally reached home – veterans not only of the Mexican War but of the first war fought on foreign soil by volunteer militia troops. While Pennsylvania's regiments could deservedly claim a solid role in the victories won in Mexico, those victories had come at a price. A total of 2,415 men served in the two regiments; of them, 477 died – 52 from battle-related injuries – and hundreds more fell sick. Through battle casualties or disease, half of those who originally volunteered failed to come home.[52]

Both the War of 1812 and the Mexican War made it increasingly obvious that the enrolled militia was not a suitable military force to defend either the Commonwealth or the nation. Volunteer militia, allowable in Pennsylvania from the beginning of the 19th century, had more and more carried the burden of defense for the Commonwealth as the century proceeded. Recognizing the increasing dependence of the Commonwealth on the volunteers, a new militia act was passed in April 1849. While still obligating all able-bodied free white males from 18 to 45 for military service, it gave every eligible citizen one month to provide himself with a proper uniform for a volunteer company.[53] Citizens

---

[51] The mood of the men went beyond homesickness for both Pennsylvania volunteers and those from other states. For example, on November 30 Richard Coulter reported that New York and South Carolina regiments had prepared petitions requesting that their regiments be disbanded so they could return home. A similar attempt was conducted in Coulter's regiment, but, as he noted, "Many officers, the colonel at their head, opposed it as derogatory to the character of the Regiment." A petition, however, was drafted and signed by 300 men on December 9, highlighting the dissatisfaction of these soldiers who were clearly ready to go home. Peskin, *Journals of Richard Coulter and Thomas Barclay*, p. 217.

[52] Once troops shipped out to Mexico, there were several successful attempts to recruit additional troops as replacements. As late as mid-April, recruits were drawn from Pennsylvania. Thus, the formation of the two original regiments was not the only effort by Pennsylvania to supply troops for the Mexican War. In addition, the 11th U.S. Infantry was composed of primarily Pennsylvania militia companies which were converted into "regulars." See Hackenburg, *Pennsylvania in the War with Mexico*, p. 88.

[53] Governor William F. Johnson noted in his annual address to the legislature on January 1, 1850, that while the new militia law required additional revision, it was still a welcome change. He noted, "The abolition of the mockery of parades incident to the old system and the establishment of an effectual uniformed militia, well disciplined and drilled, has been productive of general utility." Reed, *Papers of the Governors, 1845-1857*, p. 389.

so equipped were then to form themselves into companies of no less than 30 soldiers, elect their officers, draw up their own by-laws and levy and collect fines from any members failing to make training sessions. These volunteer companies were required to meet at least twice a year for training, and each battalion and regiment composed of these companies was to meet at least once a year for training and inspection. These changes effectively spelled the end for the enrolled militia in Pennsylvania, since most citizens either adopted a volunteer affiliation or paid the required tax.[54]

Volunteers were exempted from paying fines for non-attendance at enrolled militia musters – an exemption dating from 1803. Others, however, faced financial consequences for failing to attend. Under the provisions of the new law, county commissioners, once they received a list of delinquent militiamen from the company captains, were required to add a fine for non-attendance to the state tax of the delinquent soldier. The tax collected did not all go into the state's coffers; instead, $50 annually was appropriated out of a military account established for each company, to be used for armory maintenance and music expenses.[55]

Additional acts were passed in 1851, 1852 and 1853, but the major change in militia legislation came in 1858. The Militia Act passed on April 21, 1858, clearly placed the organized or volunteer militia in the forefront as the Commonwealth's established military force. Under this act, assessors were required to make a list of all citizens between the ages of 21 and 45 who were eligible for military duty in the service of the United States. As with the law of 1849, a copy of this list was to be filed with the county commissioners and posted in public places throughout the Commonwealth. Commanders of uniformed or organized militia companies were also to forward copies of their rosters to county commissioners. Citizens who were eligible for military service – other than the normal exceptions – but had not elected to join an organized company were required to pay a tax for non-participation.

With the excellent record of Pennsylvania volunteers in the Mexican War – and the legislation passed in the decade immediately following the war – the stage was set for the next and most significant military operation of the 19th century, the American Civil War.

---

[54] Nevertheless, the militia law remained on the books. Thus, during the Civil War, militia would be called out and used when Pennsylvania was threatened by Confederate incursions.
[55] Exceptions were ministers of the gospel, school teachers, directors of educational institutions, judges and individuals who had been honorably discharged from military service according to the laws of the Commonwealth.

CHAPTER 10

Pennsylvania Volunteers Come of Age: Pennsylvania in the Civil War

When the history of the volunteers and militia of Pennsylvania ... shall have been completed, the great sacrifice made by Pennsylvania in support of constitutional law and the integrity of the Union may be properly comprehended and appreciated.

– Brigadier General A. L. Russell
The Adjutant General, 1866

As the decade of the 1850s came to a close, the nation and the Commonwealth witnessed a developing crisis that would affect, directly or indirectly, the lives of millions of Pennsylvanians. This crisis was the polarization of the nation over states' rights and slavery, which ultimately resulted in the American Civil War. Pennsylvania, like most of the original colonies, had at one time permitted citizens to own slaves. As early as 1688, however, the same groups that had opposed military appropriations for the defense of the Commonwealth also opposed the institution of slavery. Thus, by the mid-18th century the Quakers, supported by the Mennonites, were aggressively and by and large successfully promoting an anti-slavery agenda.[1] As early as 1808, the laws of the Commonwealth made it extremely difficult to own slaves, and by 1831 it was virtually impossible to hold a slave in Pennsylvania under 50 years of age.[2] In short, despite the fact that Pennsylvania

---

[1] Pennsylvania was the home of several notable anti-slavery organizations. The Society for Promoting the Abolition of Slavery was organized in Philadelphia in 1774, and in 1833 the National Anti-Slavery Society was founded there.

[2] Pennsylvanians, however, were divided on the issues of slavery and the rights of freed blacks. For example, the Commonwealth's Constitution of 1838 excluded blacks from voting. Race riots broke out in Philadelphia when a rumor circulated that blacks and whites were walking arm in arm following a lecture on May 14, 1838. While white society tended to oppose slavery, it was not generally in favor of full social or political equality for black citizens.

shared a common border with two slave states, Maryland and Virginia, by the time of the Civil War its opposition to slavery was well established.

The proximity of Pennsylvania to the slave states caused it to be involved, although indirectly, in one of the major crises leading up to the war. In 1859, as the nation moved toward the secession of the southern states, John Brown, assisted by thirteen whites and five free blacks, seized the federal arsenal at Harpers Ferry, West Virginia. Brown had once lived in northern Pennsylvania and used Pennsylvania as a staging area for his raid. From Harpers Ferry he attempted to spark a slave revolt, but a military relief force under then-Lieutenant Colonel Robert E. Lee captured Brown and his followers.[3] Brown's raid, while it failed to spark a revolt, was a key event that galvanized the emotions of North and South.

In this emotionally charged environment over slavery, two Republicans were elected to their respective offices, Abraham Lincoln as President of the United States and Andrew G. Curtin as governor of Pennsylvania. While the election of Lincoln, an anti-slavery candidate, and its implications on the American political scene are well known, Curtin is sometimes overlooked. He became the first Republican to lead his party to a statewide victory. Even though he was an elected official of the nation's anti-slavery party, Curtin, like Lincoln, hoped to avert the secession of the southern states and the breakup of the Union. In his inaugural address on January 15, 1861, the new governor stressed that the election result was not a reason to dissolve the Union and the Commonwealth should repeal any laws that were offensive to the South or in contradiction to national laws. Nonetheless, Curtin also emphasized that the Union's integrity was paramount and Pennsylvanians would stand behind their government to preserve that integrity.[4] Despite his desire for a peaceful resolution of the issues, a few months later Pennsylvanians would be required to sup-

---

[3] John Brown had connections with Pennsylvania. Though he was originally from Connecticut and became infamous for his activities in Kansas, he had lived in Richmond, Pennsylvania, where he operated a tannery. Just before his now-famous raid, Brown, under the alias of Doctor Smith, had a residence in Chambersburg.

[4] Governor Curtin stated in his address, "If we have any laws upon our statute books which infringe upon the rights of the people of the states or contravene any law of the Federal government, they ought to be repealed." He also said, "The supremacy of the National government has been so fully admitted and so long cherished by the people of Pennsylvania and so completely has the conviction of its nationality and sovereignty directed their political action, that they are surprised at the pertinacity with which a portion of the people elsewhere maintain the opposite view." George E. Reed, ed., *Pennsylvania Archives: Papers of the Governors, 1858-1871*, fourth series, vol. VIII (Harrisburg: State Printer, 1902), pp. 332-333. Cited hereafter as Reed, *Papers of the Governors, 1858-1871*.

Pennsylvania's Civil War governor Andrew G. Curtin. Strong supporter of the Union and consistent recruiter of regiments, Curtin was one of the strongest wartime governors.

port their national government. On April 12, 1861, southern troops opened fire on Fort Sumter, South Carolina, initiating America's Civil War.

Similar to the situation in 1812 and 1846, the federal government was faced with a quandary. Troops had to be fielded to quell a rebellion, but because federal forces were minuscule the government lacked the ability to do so quickly. In many respects, the situation was even worse in 1861 than in 1812 or 1846 because the small federal Army's loyalties were divided. Some regulars from the southern states were more attached to their states than the national government. As a consequence, proven military leaders like Richard Ewell, James Longstreet, Lewis Armistead, Robert E. Lee and J. E. B. Stuart, among others, tendered their federal commissions rather than take up arms against their home states. With such defections, the federal force with which Lincoln had to work was even smaller. The only choice for fielding a sizable body of troops was to appeal to the states for volunteers. On April 15, 1861, the President issued a call for 75,000 volunteers.

With the President's call, Pennsylvania was given a quota of fourteen regiments for three months of federal service. These regiments were to be consistent in structure with the regulars, which meant that each was to have ten companies and the necessary regimental staff. In its pre-war volunteer force Pennsylvania had 19,000 officers and men in 339 infantry, 84 artillery and 53 cavalry units – more men than the regular Army.[5] Pennsylvania's forces would become even larger, for when the call for volunteers came, the Common-wealth's citizens flocked to the colors, enthusiastically volunteering to help put down the rebellion. This patriotic outpouring resulted in Pennsylvania furnish-ing 25 regiments for three months' service, exceeding the federal quota by 11 regiments.[6] Altogether, 20,175 men served in the three-month regiments.[7] Despite Pennsylvania's success in filling and exceeding its quota, volunteers continued to step forward.

A geographic breakdown of the units that volunteered early in the war proves interesting. For example, the First and Second Pennsylvania were pure volunteer regiments, composed of citizens who had answered the call to defend the Union. The Third Regiment, however, consisted of companies that exist-ed prior to the war, with units from the following locations:

Hollidaysburg Fencibles, Company A
Altoona Guards, Company B
Williamsburg, Company C
Tyrone, Company D
Altoona (Logan Rangers), Company E
Johnstown, Companies F and G
Hollidaysburg, Company H
East Liberty, Company I
Johnstown, Company K

The Fourth Pennsylvania Volunteer Regiment drew most of its strength

[5] At the beginning of the war the U.S. Army consisted of a little over 15,000 enlisted men and 1,108 officers. As a further complication, of the Army's 198 companies, 183 were scattered over the western frontier at some 79 posts and thus were not immediately deployable for the crisis along the Eastern seaboard. The only way to mobilize quickly was to call up militia. Use of enrolled militia, which in reality existed only on paper, was not an option. The best avail-able manpower could be secured through the use of organized or volunteer militia. See Russell F. Weigley, *History of the United States Army*, The Macmillan Wars of the United States, Louis Morton, ed. (New York: Macmillan Company, 1967), pp. 198-199.
[6] According to Governor Curtin's comments to the General Assembly on April 30, 1861, the governor felt Pennsylvania would need more than its original quota, so he continued to take vol-unteers until reaching the equivalent of 23 regiments. By the end of the month, circumstances proved Curtin correct, because Pennsylvania had furnished 25 regiments of three-month vol-unteers instead of the 14 that had originally been requested. Reed, *Papers of the Governors, 1858-1871*, pp. 375-376.
[7] Annual message of the governor to the General Assembly, January 8, 1862. Ibid., p. 421.

from the Norristown area, although companies from Pottstown, Media, Lewisburg and the Eagle Guards from Bellefonte were added to bring the regiment to full strength. Colonel John F. Hartranft, who would later become famous in the history of the Commonwealth and the National Guard of Pennsylvania, commanded the Fourth Regiment. The Fifth and Sixth Pennsylvania Volunteer Regiments were also composed of companies formed specifically to fill federal requisitions, but the Eighth Regiment included companies with volunteer militia backgrounds. For example, Company C had been a cavalry company in Wilkes-Barre known as the Wyoming Light Dragoons. Companies F and G had been the Wyoming Artillerists and the Wyoming Yaegers from Wilkes-Barre. From existing records it would be a simple task to enumerate the origins of the first 25 regiments organized to meet Pennsylvania's quotas, but that would take this book beyond the intent of providing a basic overview of Pennsylvania militia history to 1870. The reader who seeks additional details about these regiments and their companies should consult Samuel P. Bates' five-volume set entitled *History of Pennsylvania Volunteers, 1861-1865*.[8]

Pennsylvania had enough manpower to form a total of 39 regiments, but federal authorization to muster these troops did not exist. The War Department was unwilling to take additional troops because, as Lincoln told the Congress in July 1861, "One of the greatest perplexities of the government is to avoid raising troops faster than we can provide for them."

The Commonwealth had been faced with the problem of excess volunteers some 15 years before, at the outset of the Mexican War, and had not been able to obtain federal permission to accept them at that time either. While in the Mexican War many would-be Pennsylvania patriots never had the opportunity to serve, in the Civil War the governor developed a strategy that would permit additional volunteers to serve and, at the same time, provide a larger manpower pool for the nation. Governor Curtin, who would ultimately control all recruiting in Pennsylvania, recommended that the General Assembly pass an Act of May 15, 1861, which would create a Pennsylvania Reserve Corps consisting of 13 regiments of infantry, one of cavalry and one of artillery.[9] This

[8] Samuel P. Bates, *History of Pennsylvania Volunteers, 1861-1865; Prepared in Compliance with the Acts of the Legislature* (Harrisburg: State Printer, 1870). Cited hereafter as Bates, *History of Pensylvania Volunteers.*
[9] The order placing the governor in charge of recruiting was issued by Simon Cameron, Secretary of War, who stated, "All men now enrolled or mustered into the service of the United States for brigades, regiments, or companies in the state of Pennsylvania under the direct authority of the Secretary of War are placed under the command of the Governor of

corps would be enlisted for a period of three years and would be paid, armed and equipped by the Commonwealth. A loan of $3 million was authorized to defray the cost of implementing this act. Major General George A. McCall was commissioned to command the troops raised under its provisions.[10] In essence, Pennsylvania would accept these volunteers and "bank" them, keeping them in reserve for future calls for volunteers which, in Curtin's opinion, would in all likelihood occur. Such calls would come if the war was anything more than a short one, because Lincoln's original call was only for three-month regiments. Of equal importance, Pennsylvania, bordering slave states, had reason to be concerned about the safety of its citizens. The Reserve Corps could function as a force to protect the southern border of Pennsylvania.

In April 1861, however, the key issues were mustering into federal service the necessary units to meet the immediate quota; arming and equipping them; and moving them into position to defend the nation. For the authorized regiments, two mustering points were established, Philadelphia and Harrisburg. Some regular Army officers were sent to Pennsylvania to assist in mustering the troops. Fitz-John Porter, who would later become a general officer, was sent to Harrisburg to supervise the induction and equipping of the troops. Porter commented on the confusion in the mustering center, noting, "The absence of arms, ammunition and equipment of all kind could not have been worse had it been premeditated ... The state had no arms whatever or equipments for cooking purposes ... and I had to resort to extraordinary expedients of hotels and restaurants to feed the men until the commissary department could be organized."[11]

Some of these troops, however, did mobilize rapidly, for they were desperately needed to defend the nation's capital. Washington, D.C. sat directly on the Virginia border, and an incursion by Confederate troops or the outright seizure of the capital was a definite threat. Maryland, immediately north of the

Pennsylvania who shall organize them as may be deemed most advantageous to the interests of the General Government." Reed, *Papers of the Governors, 1857-1871*, p. 409.
[10] General George A. McCall was an excellent choice for this position. He was a native Pennsylvanian, born in Philadelphia, and an 1822 graduate of the U.S. Military Academy. He served with distinction in the Seminole Wars and the Mexican War. At the time of his appointment he had retired to Chester County due to health problems. J. R. Sypher, *History of the Pennsylvania Reserve Corps: A Complete Record of the Organization of the Different Companies, Regiments and Brigades, Containing Descriptions of Expeditions, Marches, Skirmishes and Battles, together with Biographical Sketches of Officers and Personal Records of Each Man during His Term of Service* (Lancaster, Pa.: Elias Barr & Co., 1865), pp. 60-61.
[11] Fitz-John Porter, as quoted in Philip S. Klein and Ari Hoogenboom, *A History of Pennsylvania* (New York: McGraw Hill Co., 1973), p. 249.

An element of the Pennsylvania Reserve Corps – Company B, 33rd Regiment, Pennsylvania Volunteer Infantry, 4th Pennsylvania Reserves (photo reproduced by permission of the Massachusetts Commandery, Military Order of the Loyal Legion, and the U.S. Army Military History Institute).

capital, was a slave state, and pro-southern sentiment in that state's capital was clear. The most obvious method to quickly bolster the capital's defense was by using Pennsylvania troops. On April 18, 1861, only three days after Lincoln's call for volunteers, five companies of volunteers from the 25th Pennsylvania Infantry boarded a train in Harrisburg and proceeded to Baltimore.[12] The companies that entrained were the Ringgold Light Artillery of Reading, the Allen Rifles from Allentown, Logan Guards from Lewistown, National Light Infantry and the Washington Artillerists from Pottsville. Their rapid response to the threat to the nation's capital earned them distinction as "The First Defenders."[13]

The movement of Pennsylvania troops to defend Washington resulted in the first action of the Civil War involving Commonwealth troops. Rail trans-

[12] On the same date Camp Curtin was established in Harrisburg for mustering and training troops from south central Pennsylvania.
[13] A remembrance of this event is evident today in the distinctive unit insignia worn by the 213th Air Defense Artillery. The red crest shows the dome of the nation's capital, and the motto

port through Baltimore required units, including Pennsylvania's five companies and some U.S. regulars, to detrain and march to another rail station where they could re-embark for the final leg of their journey to Washington. When the troop train arrived, a crowd gathered that jostled the soldiers, spat at them and hurled insults. When the regular Army unit left the column of marching troops, protected by Baltimore police, and proceeded toward Fort Henry, the fury of the mob was directed squarely against the five Pennsylvania companies. Pennsylvania troops had to endure the howling mob and the stones they hurled. Fortunately the rioters did not have ammunition, thus avoiding a full shooting war on the streets of Baltimore. With no serious casualties, the companies successfully entrained and reached the capital that evening.[14] They were the first Union troops to arrive in Washington, which was literally surrounded by either Confederate or pro-Confederate territory.[15] Their role was appropriately recognized in July 1861 when Congress passed a resolution praising the 530 soldiers who pressed forward through the Baltimore mob and began the defense of the capital.[16]

proudly proclaims, "The First Defenders." The author acknowledges that there were other "first defenders." On the day following the mustering of these first five companies, additional companies were mustered: the Worth Infantry (York County), Company A, 16th Infantry and Company K from the York Rifles, 2nd Infantry.

[14] The popular enthusiasm for forming volunteer regiments and the pro-Southern sentiments in Baltimore were illustrated through Governor Curtin's address to the General Assembly. He reported that a large body of men, not organized as a part of the militia and under the command of officers without any official commissions, attempted to proceed from Pennsylvania through Baltimore and assist with the defense of the capital. They were attacked by the Baltimore mob; four were killed, and a number of these would-be volunteers were wounded. Most returned to Philadelphia, and at the time of the governor's speech they were being organized into a regiment with appropriately commissioned officers. Reed, *Papers of the Governors, 1858-1871*, p. 376. Frederic Godcharles noted that these volunteers were ten unarmed and un-uniformed companies under the command of William F. Small. He also noted that they were in the company of the 6th Massachusetts, who also suffered casualties (four killed in action) from the Baltimore mob. See Frederic A. Godcharles, *Pennsylvania: Political, Governmental, Military and Civil*, military volume (New York: American Historical Society, 1933), p. 364.

[15] According to William Clarke's history, the impact of the First Defenders' arrival was considerable. The companies were supposed to have a strength of 530, but in reality they had 476. The Washington papers, however, reported the Pennsylvania strength as 5,300, thus creating the impression of considerable reinforcements to deter any Confederate incursions. See Major William P. Clarke, *Official History of the Militia and National Guard of Pennsylvania from the Earliest Period of Record to the Present Time*, vol. II (Philadelphia: Charles J. Hendler, 1909), pp. 72-74.

[16] The resolution by the 32nd Congress on July 22, 1861, stated, "Resolved that the thanks of this House are due and are already tendered to the five hundred and thirty soldiers from Pennsylvania who passed through the mob at Baltimore and reached Washington on the 18th day of April last for the defense of the National Capitol."

In the capital region, where Pennsylvania troops were concentrated, an uneasy and unofficial truce took hold. Neither army seemed anxious to engage in battle and spill American blood. By mid-summer, however, the situation had changed. The Union Army, commanded by General Irwin McDowell, had taken a defensive position near Centreville, about 20 miles southwest of Washington. A Confederate force under General Pierre G. T. Beauregard was positioned to the west of Washington, at Manassas, where it was defending the vital Orange and Alexandria Railroad. McDowell was under pressure through the political leadership to break the military stalemate. After some preliminary maneuvering, on July 21, 1861, the two armies engaged at Manassas (or Bull Run) in the first major battle of the war. Bull Run is rightfully regarded as a federal rout and had little result other than to prove that it was going to be a long and arduous task to bring the nation back together. It also proved that, at least for the Union, the initial method used to raise manpower would have to be reevaluated. The President had initially called for 75,000 troops for three months' duties. By the time the Battle of Bull Run occurred, the initial enlistment of Pennsylvania troops, as well as many of those from other states, had already expired.[17] Volunteers, little more than raw recruits, had served their time.[18] As a result, in late July Congress authorized the president to accept up to 500,000 volunteers with terms of service from six months to three years. Fortunately, in Pennsylvania, where the governor had provided outstanding leadership, the volunteers needed to meet additional manpower requirements were available, uniformed and trained.

The forethought of Governor Curtin is evident. With more troops needed to protect the capital, the Reserve Corps – recruited, equipped and trained by the Commonwealth at four separate camps – was a logical source of manpower. Elements of the Reserve Corps had already been employed in the

[17] The government quickly learned its lesson about calling up short-term volunteers. On April 28 Major General Patterson informed Governor Curtin that word had been received stating no additional three-month regiments would be needed. Any further requisitions from Pennsylvania would be for longer periods of service. See message by Major General R. Patterson, H.Q. Military Department of Pennsylvania, to the governor on April 30, 1861, and Governor Andrew G. Curtin to the Assembly on May 2, 1861, in Reed, *Papers of the Governors, 1858-1871*, pp. 380-382.

[18] This release of troops was almost as disorganized as their original mustering. Governor Curtin reported to the legislature that in July the discharge of the three-month regiments "dumped" 8,000 to 10,000 veterans into Harrisburg, where some waited as much as ten days for their pay. Their tents and cooking equipment had been taken from them in Maryland, and they had no way to fix meals, even though the federal commissary had rations. The Commonwealth stepped in to provide food and shelter for the men. Ibid., p. 421.

defense of the Union. Beginning on June 22, 1861, two regiments under the command of Charles J. Biddle and Seneca G. Simmons and two companies of artillery under the command of Colonel Charles T. Campbell were sent to assist Union troops at Cumberland, Maryland. They spent about six weeks there and in western Virginia engaged in military operations. When the First Battle of Bull Run occurred, the federal government requisitioned the Pennsylvania Reserve Corps. Within four days after the battle, eleven regiments of the corps – trained, clothed and armed by Pennsylvania – were in Washington and ready to defend the capital against any Confederate incursions. The two regiments and companies mentioned previously, which had been stationed in western Virginia, were pulled back and restationed in Washington, bringing the total Reserve Corps strength in the capital to 15 regiments. Similar to the record of "The First Defenders," who rushed from southern Pennsylvania in April 1861, Pennsylvania volunteers in July 1861 again rapidly moved to defend the capital. The corps was still commanded by George McCall, now a federally recognized brigadier general.

The commitment of the Commonwealth and its governor to the defense of the Union is well illustrated by the Reserve Corps. The corps was an expensive endeavor for Pennsylvania, in both human and financial terms. Fielding this corps, consisting of 15,856 men, cost the Commonwealth a total of $855,444.87. This figure does not include the cost of transporting the regiments or other corps elements to training camps. Nevertheless, when a crisis emerged, the Reserve Corps, a state effort, provided the nation with the necessary soldiers.

Building a federal Army, largely composed of volunteers, continued through the rest of the year. In his annual speech to the Assembly, Governor Curtin stated that by the end of the year, the state had regiments numbered to 115.[19] Included in this were two of the three-month regiments that went into service in later requisitions. By the end of the year a total of 92 regiments were either in U.S. service or preparing for it, with 109,615 soldiers among them. When the three-month volunteers are included, a total of 129,790 soldiers from the Commonwealth were either serving or had served in the defense of the nation.[20] During the first year of the war, Pennsylvania's volunteers were sta-

---

[19] The student of Civil War history will find the numbering system for Pennsylvania's volunteer and militia units baffling. In some instances, the same number was given to more than one regiment, while in other cases the same unit was known by several designations. Sanford W. Higginbotham, et. al., *Pennsylvania and the Civil War: A Handbook* (Harrisburg: Pennsylvania Historical and Museum Commission, 1961), p. 10.

[20] There is some acknowledged duplication in this figure. Some of the three-month volunteers

tioned in a number of locations besides Washington.   The report to the
Assembly shows:

> *The 11th and 15th Regiments of Infantry, Pennsylvania Volunteers at*
> *Annapolis, Md.;*
> *The 21st, 28th, 29th, 66th, 71st, 72nd, and 106th Infantry,*
> *Pennsylvania Volunteers, under the command of Major General*
> *Nathaniel P. Banks in Virginia;*
> *The 45th, 50th, 76th, 100th Regiments of Infantry, Pennsylvania*
> *Volunteers were stationed in South Carolina;*
> *The 48th Infantry, Pennsylvania Volunteers was stationed at Hatteras*
> *Inlet;*
> *The 108th Infantry and the 11th Cavalry were at Fortress Monroe in*
> *Virginia;*
> *The 77th, 78th, and 79th Infantry Regiments, 7th and 9th Cavalry, one*
> *Troop of Horse, one Squadron of Cavalry and two Battalions of*
> *Artillery were in Kentucky;*
> *The 84th and 11th Infantry were stationed in Western Virginia;*
> *The 87th Infantry, Pennsylvania Volunteers, three companies of Infantry,*
> *four companies of cavalry, five companies of light artillery were located at*
> *Cockeysville, Maryland;*
> *A company of Artillery was located at Ft. Delaware;*
> *All remaining Pennsylvania troops were located in the Washington D.C.*
> *vicinity.*[21]

Pennsylvania's contribution to the defense of the Union, beginning with
the spring of 1862, was so significant that it would be difficult to detail the
organization and disposition of every regiment, their leaders or their battle honors. For the purposes of this work, a survey of militia and volunteer history in
the Commonwealth, the key period to be covered, best illustrating Pennsylvania's contributions to the Union victory, runs from the late summer of 1862
to the end of the 1863 Gettysburg Campaign. This period was selected because
it was then that the greatest military threat to the Union and to Pennsylvania

---

re-enlisted in the new three-year regiments. The figure given includes these re-enlistments, in
essence providing an inflated figure. Determining the exact duplicate count would be difficult
if not impossible.
[21] Report of the Governor to the Assembly on January 8, 1862, in Reed, *Papers of the Governors,*
1858-1871, pp. 413-435.

Officers of the 3rd Pennsylvania Heavy Artillery (reproduced by permission of the Massachusetts Commandery, Military Order of the Loyal Legion, and the U.S. Army Military History Institute).

itself existed. Contiguous to slave states and blessed with mineral and agricultural resources, Pennsylvania was a natural target for the Confederates. Direct threats to the Commonwealth were to come in both 1862 and 1863.

The focal point for the fighting in the late spring of 1862 was General George B. McClellan's so-called Peninsula Campaign. A Pennsylvanian by birth, McClellan launched his campaign and moved on Richmond, Virginia with the intention of taking the Confederate capital.[22] Initially it seemed that "Little Mac" was going to achieve his aim, but just as success drew near, on June 1, 1862, General Robert E. Lee was appointed commander of the now-famous force that he re-named the Army of Northern Virginia. In a series of bloody engagements, known as the Seven Days Battles, Lee forced McClellan to raise

---

[22] Pennsylvania troops took part in this campaign as well – among them, the 83rd Pennsylvania, which would be on Little Round Top on July 2, 1863; the 72nd Pennsylvania; and the well-known First Troop, Philadelphia City Cavalry.

his siege of Richmond and retreat. These events prompted the first direct threat to the citizens of Pennsylvania.

That threat came in the fall of 1862. After a string of victories in Virginia, Lee wrote to the Confederate president, Jefferson Davis, that now was the most propitious time to invade the Union. His intention was to invade central Maryland and proceed into south central Pennsylvania, ultimately reaching Harrisburg. His goals were threefold. First, he intended to offer the citizens of Maryland, a southern state, an opportunity to rise up against their northern oppressors; second, he hoped his action would help the South in its efforts to gain diplomatic recognition in Europe; and finally, he intended to wreck the transportation network across the Susquehanna River which led westward into the Ohio River Valley. Lee's army began crossing the Potomac on September 5, 1862, proceeding into northern territory. Within a few days they were headquartered in Frederick, Maryland. Lee's orders of September 9 detailed General Thomas "Stonewall" Jackson's reinforced wing of the army to move into position to take Harpers Ferry. Lee was virtually on the Pennsylvania border.

This direct threat to the Commonwealth seemed to leave Governor Curtin in a quandary. Since the beginning of the rebellion, Curtin had been a strong supporter of the national government and a dedicated recruiter of troops for the Union Army. But these troops were under federal command and control. In fact, many were a part of the federal response force being thrown together under McClellan.[23] Thus, although there were 55 Pennsylvania regiments in the Army that McClellan would use to pursue Lee, these troops were not being used specifically for the defense of the Commonwealth. The Pennsylvania Reserve Corps, Curtin's innovation, was also in service of the national government. On September 7 the corps was a division under the command of General "Fighting Joe" Hooker, commander of the Union Army's First Corps, who had recently arrived in Washington, D.C. It would move out of Washington, under the command of General John Reynolds (a native of Lancaster, Pennsylvania), and join the Union forces moving into Maryland to block the Confederate advance northward.

Governor Curtin, however, was not without resources. On April 9, 1861, as Pennsylvania and the nation were rapidly preparing for a response to the southern states' secession, the governor had directed the attention of the legislature to the lack of preparedness on the part of the Pennsylvania militia.

---

[23] At the time of the Confederate incursion, McClellan, who had failed with his Peninsular Campaign in the summer of 1862, was in charge of all troops for the defense of Washington. When Lee's Army moved north, McClellan was hastily designated to organize a response force.

On April 12 the legislature had passed "An Act for the better organization of the Militia of this Commonwealth" and appropriated $500,000 for arming and equipping the militia.[24] It is obvious that the intent was to bolster the strength of volunteer regiments, which soon after the act's passage would begin filling Pennsylvania's first quota of volunteers. The passage of such an act, however, underscores the fact that Pennsylvania had current militia legislation on the books, and – although volunteer militias were the force of choice for the Commonwealth – other militia could be organized under existing legislation.

Even though federal authorities could not immediately determine Lee's line of march, Curtin was convinced of his intent to ultimately invade Pennsylvania. On September 4 he issued a proclamation alerting the Pennsyl-

General George Gordon Meade, a Pennsylvania officer who became famous for his defense of the Union at Gettysburg, July 1-3, 1863 (photo reproduced by permission of the Massachusetts Commandery, Military Order of the Loyal Legion, and the U.S. Army Military History Institute).

[24] Governor Curtin's address to the Assembly on January 8, 1862, in Reed, *Papers of the Governors, 1858-1871*, p. 420.

vania militia to the danger and calling for them to organize into companies and prepare to defend the Commonwealth. On September 11, with Lee's forces in Maryland besieging the Harpers Ferry arsenal, Curtin issued a call for 50,000 militia to defend the Commonwealth. The militia force rapidly proceeded into the Cumberland Valley, with a vanguard of one regiment and eight companies. The militia units moved from Harrisburg on the night of September 12, with additional regiments following as they reported. According to the governor's records, 15,000 of these volunteers took up positions at Hagerstown and Boonsboro, Maryland, and 10,000 were positioned in the vicinity of Greencastle and Chambersburg, Pennsylvania. About 25,000 militiamen remained in Harrisburg awaiting orders. One regiment was sent into Delaware, at the request of General-in-Chief of the Union Army Henry Halleck, to guard the DuPont powder mills. At Curtin's request, General Reynolds, commander of the Pennsylvania Reserve Corps, was detached from his command and allowed to return to Pennsylvania to command the militia forces. Although the militia was in place to block the Confederate incursion, McClellan's Army of the Potomac stopped Lee at the battles of South Mountain and Antietam. The militia was released from duty on September 24, having served as an additional source of manpower in the event that Lee had continued to move north.

Lee's first major problem with his campaign into the north occurred when a Union soldier found Lee's Special Order 191, issued on September 9, at an abandoned campsite. The order alerted McClellan to the fact that Lee had committed the cardinal error of dividing his force in the face of a superior enemy. Although it took him some 16 hours to respond, McClellan moved against Lee with uncharacteristic energy and resolve, forcing the latter to defend the passes on South Mountain with a mere three divisions, pitted against McClellan's vastly superior Union Army. To unravel Lee's position, three federal corps attacked, using a considerable number of Pennsylvania regiments. The Union First Corps, commanded by General Joe Hooker, with three divisions, had the preponderance. Hooker's Third Division, commanded by a Pennsylvanian, Major General George Gordon Meade, was composed of units of the Pennsylvania Reserve Corps, who still considered themselves part of that organization despite their new federal designation.[25] Meade's Division included

[25] Examples of the changes in unit designations are as follows: the First Pennsylvania Reserves became the 30th Pennsylvania Volunteer Regiment; the Second Pennsylvania Reserves became the 31st Pennsylvania Volunteers; the 13th Pennsylvania Reserves became the 42nd Pennsylvania Volunteers. The fact that the soldiers valued their reserve corps affiliation is obvious, when one observes the monuments along Cornfield Avenue in the present battlefield park.

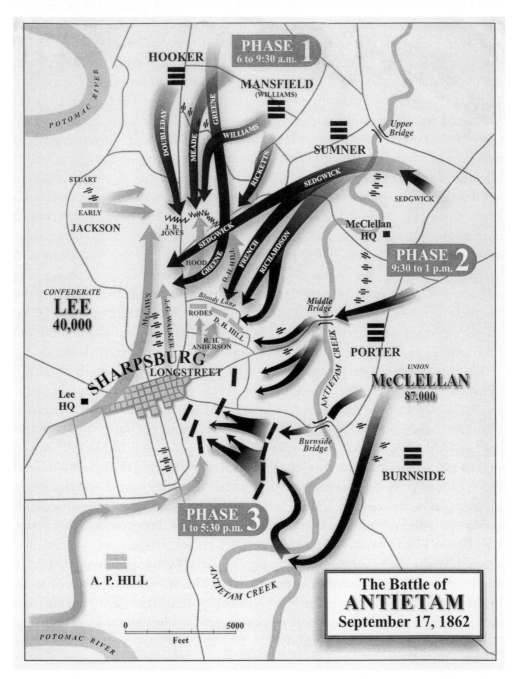

Map showing the three phases of the Battle of Antietam on September 17, 1863 (reproduced by permission of the U.S. Army War College).

14 Pennsylvania regiments and three artillery batteries. Meade and his Pennsyl-vanians were given the task of striking the left flank of Confederate General Rodes' Division which was defending Turners Gap, through which the old National Road ran. The attack was led by the Pennsylvania "Bucktail" Regi-ment. Meade's troops fought Rodes' seasoned veterans from about 2 p.m. until dusk in an action that resulted in the Confederates withdrawing, giving the Union control of both Turners and Fox's Gap.

Lee then retired with his available forces to the little Maryland town of Sharpsburg and took up a defensive position, hoping that Jackson's wing of his army would arrive in time to stage a credible defense. McClellan initially con-centrated his troops west of Sharpsburg on September 15. Characteristic of McClellan's leadership style, he failed to act on the 15th, when he had a clear advantage. Instead, on the evening of September 16 he sent his First Corps, commanded by Hooker, to the north side of the town in preparation for an assault the next day. McClellan's battle plan for September 17 is not totally clear today nor was it clear to his corps commanders at that time. But on the morn-ing of the 17th Hooker launched his attack parallel to the Hagerstown Pike, not around the Confederate flank in the vicinity of Nicodemus Hill but straight into "Stonewall" Jackson's Confederate wing. As noted above, Hooker's command, the First Corps, had most of the Pennsylvania troops on the battlefield – 17 regiments and four artillery batteries in all.

In succession during the early morning hours, the three divisions of Hooker's Corps assaulted the positions manned by the seasoned, recently arrived Confederate soldiers commanded by Jackson. Poor tactics on the bat-tlefield by McClellan and, in many respects, by Hooker himself, rather than a lack of courage by Hooker's soldiers, caused substantial casualties and failed to dislodge Jackson's troops. Despite some initial successes, the repeated assaults by the First Corps were stopped largely due to a spirited counterattack into the corps center by John Bell Hood's Texans.

As the First Corps attack stalled, the Union Twelfth Corps, command-ed by General J. K. F. Mansfield, entered the field and continued the attempt to unravel Jackson's position. The Twelfth Corps, which promptly lost its com-manding general, included 11 Pennsylvania regiments, two artillery batteries and one cavalry detachment. Mansfield's corps, despite some local successes, was also unable to break Jackson's defense force. Skillful use of interior lines in Lee's defense allowed him to rush reinforcements to areas where Union troops were in danger of breaking through. No one can question the valor of the individual regiments that tried to drive Lee from the field – only the competence of their senior commanders.[26]   Even as Mansfield's attack was winding down, a division from a third Union corps drove across the northern part of the battlefield on an east-to-west axis.

This third federal corps, commanded by Major General Edwin Sumner, advanced with precision and discipline, but two of the divisions veered to the left and became separated from the corps' Second Division, commanded by Major General John Sedgwick, and their corps commander, who was leading from the front. Sedgwick's Second Brigade, known as the Philadelphia Brigade, was composed of four Pennsylvania volunteer regiments.[27] The Pennsylvanians drove deep into the southern lines, reaching what was known as the West Woods, but despite their progress, they soon found themselves in a maelstrom. Unbeknownst to the Philadelphia Brigade, a Confederate brigade commanded by General Jubal Early and a fresh division commanded by General Lafayette McLaws, recently arrived from Harpers Ferry, worked around the vulnerable flank of Sedgewick's Division and attacked. Within minutes the division found itself under intense fire from the front and the flanks. In a documented incident of fratricide, Sedgwick's second line mistakenly opened fire on the first line.   Within minutes, 2,200 casualties were strewn over the battlefield, and Sedgwick's Division retreated from the field. Today, a striking obelisk stands in the vicinity of what were the West Woods, marking the spot where the Philadelphia Brigade suffered its heavy casualties.

The remaining two divisions from Sumner's Second Corps, which had veered south, ran into Daniel Harvey Hill's Confederate Division, which had taken up a formidable defensive position along a sunken road (since called "bloody lane").[28] The two divisions, including a total of five Pennsylvania vol-

[26] The writer refers to McClellan, Hooker and Mansfield, not Meade. McClellan had ample resources to crush Lee, but his command of troops on the ground was hesitant and indecisive. Hooker attacked straight into the face of the enemy, rather than Lee's left, with disastrous results. General Mansfield, who had never commanded a large formation of troops on the battlefield, attempted to maneuver his troops but was mortally wounded before his corps even got into action.
[27] The 69th, 71st, 72nd and 106th Pennsylvania Volunteers comprised the Philadelphia Brigade. All four regiments had been organized in Philadelphia in 1861 as three-year regiments and, with the exception of a few officers, largely retained a Pennsylvania base.
[28] Israel Richardson's First Division included the famous Irish Brigade commanded by Thomas Meagher. As originally conceived, the brigade was to have had units from New York, Boston and Philadelphia, but Pennsylvania balked over the question of whether these would have counted as Pennsylvania or New York volunteers. When the Irish Brigade suffered frightful casualties at Antietam, the 116th Pennsylvania (recruited in Philadelphia on September 1, 1862) was added to the Irish Brigade on October 10, while the Irish were still in Maryland. Though in the lower ranks it had a number of German-sounding names, the 116th was integrated into

Independent Battery E, Pennsylvania Volunteer Light Artillery, "Knapp's Battery," immediately following their participation in the Battle of Antietam (photo reproduced by permission of the Massachusetts Commandery, Military Order of the Loyal Legion, and the U.S. Army Military History Institute).

unteer regiments, engaged in the battle for the sunken road. After heavy fighting, the Confederate defense collapsed, and the remaining forces withdrew, temporarily causing a major problem in Lee's center.[29] A hastily reorganized Confederate defense, however, prevented the Union from achieving a clear breakthrough and the possibility of a victory on the field.

The fighting then shifted south to the third and final phase of the battle, the attack of Major General Ambrose Burnside's Ninth Corps, whose task was to advance on the lower bridge over Antietam Creek and then presumably

the brigade and fought with distinction at Fredericksburg and Gettysburg. Joseph G. Bilby, *The Irish Brigade in the Civil War: The 69th New York and Other Irish Regiments of the Army of the Potomac* (Conshohocken, Pa.: Combined Books, 1998), pp. 60-62.

[29] A noteworthy episode occurred in the advance of one of General William French's two Union divisions. Confederate Generals John Gordon and James Longstreet commented on the precision and discipline of the Union advance, but the 132nd Pennsylvania Volunteers, one of French's regiments, briefly lost their discipline, but not due to enemy fire. When the 132nd marched through the Roulette Farm, a Confederate shell hit a cluster of beehives, and the soldiers found themselves dodging both swarms of angry bees and Confederate bullets. The officers worked to get the regiment under control, but the skirmish with the bees while under fire from the Confederates remained indelibly impressed on the minds of the soldiers, long after the event. *Pennsylvania at Antietam, Report of the Antietam Battlefield Memorial Commission of Pennsylvania* (Harrisburg: State Printer, 1906), p. 190.

John F. Hartranft served the Commonwealth in many capacities during the mid-nine-teenth century. He was a respected Pennsylvania Volunteer officer in the Civil War, a leader with the rank of major general in the immediate post-war years, and governor during the turbulent 1870s.

cut off or roll up Lee's right flank. Burnside's attack jumped off late, because of either his own hesitancy or an ambiguous order from McClellan. When the attack was finally launched, Burnside's troops were unable to make progress because they were proceeding across a one-lane bridge, which canalized them and forced them to face an enemy with possession of a commanding height. Connecticut troops, together with troops from Maryland and New Hampshire, attempted without success to dislodge Brigadier General Robert Toomb's Georgians from the heights overlooking the bridge. The Union division com-mander, Brigadier General Samuel Sturgis, ordered the commander of his sec-ond brigade, Brigadier Edward Ferrero, to lead another attempt to take the bridge. The 51st Pennsylvania, commanded by Colonel John F. Hartranft, led the attack. Followed and closely supported by the 51st New York, they carried the bridge after heavy fighting.[30] The heights overlooking the bridge were also

[30] When General Ferrero addressed the 51st Pennsylvania and the 51st New York and asked them if they would take the bridge, Corporal Lewis Patterson from Company I of the 51st Pennsylvania called out, "Will you give us our whiskey if we make it?" The question came

taken, and the stage was set for an advance on Lee's right which, if successful, could have cut off his lines of communication or at least his escape route south. Despite the achievement of the Pennsylvania and New York troops, this opportunity escaped the Union, and the fighting at Sharpsburg at day's end resulted in a bloody draw, with neither Lee nor McClellan achieving their stated goals.

Although McClellan still outnumbered Lee after the conclusion of the battle and had a significant number of regiments that had not even fired a shot, he failed to renew the battle or pursue his adversary.[31] Instead, he remained on the ground over which his troops had so bravely, although futilely, fought. Rather than pursue and engage Lee's weakened army, McClellan requested reinforcements and began organizing and training his troops. As a result, this would be his last command.

McClellan's indecision prompted yet another crisis for his home state. With the Union force in a static position, Lee ordered a second incursion into the Keystone State. This time his goal was the Cumberland Valley Railroad bridge just a short distance above Chambersburg. On October 9, 1862, Major General J. E. B. Stuart left Darkesville in western Virginia with 1,800 men and, after passing through Maryland, arrived in Chambersburg on October 10 shortly after dark. Stuart did not encounter any resistance since most of the Union Army in the area was still positioned at Sharpsburg, Maryland. The Pennsylvania militia, which had been called to duty in early September, had been sent home on September 24. Governor Curtin did move two companies of regulars and the Anderson Cavalry from Carlisle Barracks toward Chambersburg and South Mountain and alerted troops at Camp Curtin, but Stuart was moving too fast.[32] Thus, with minimum inconvenience, Stuart was able to destroy railroad shops and rolling stock and seize Union arms and ammunition. He could not accomplish his mission, however, because the bridge he was supposed to destroy was built of iron and he had failed to bring explosives. As a result, he proceeded east toward Gettysburg, but at Cashtown he turned south and by October 14 returned to Virginia. The Union Army, still at Sharpsburg

---

because the 51st had a reputation for its drinking, and the brigade commander had stopped their whiskey rations. Ferrero responded, "Yes by God, you shall have as much of it as you want if you take the bridge ... [if] I have to send to New York and pay for it out of my own private purse." Thomas A. Parker, *History of the 51st Regiment of Pennsylvania Volunteers* (Philadelphia: Kind and Baird Publishers, 1869), pp. 232-239.

[31] For example, the Sixth Army Corps, commanded by one of McClellan's favorites, General William Franklin, was not used in the bitter one-day engagement. The corps included four Pennsylvania regiments.

[32] Reed, *Papers of the Governors, 1858-1871*, p. 458.

(with elements in Harpers Ferry), had failed to respond, and Stuart returned home with considerable booty and not a single casualty. To the Union's embarrassment, Stuart had ridden completely around the Union Army and this time had actually succeeded in invading Pennsylvania. Naturally, the citizens of south central Pennsylvania were quite upset.

The immediate threat to Pennsylvania seemed to fade with the advent of fall. McClellan's army remained in position at Sharpsburg until October 26, when it began slowly moving units into Virginia. Totally out of patience with the snail's pace by which McClellan waged war, on November 7, 1862, Lincoln relieved him and entrusted command of the Army of the Potomac to Ambrose Burnside, who had commanded the left wing of the Union Army at Antietam. Burnside took the initiative, moving the war in the critical Eastern seaboard from the embattled area of central Maryland and Pennsylvania to Virginia. Burnside planned to take Fredericksburg, Virginia and then, following a successful battle there, move on to Richmond and take the Confederate capital. By November 20 he had 110,000 soldiers concentrated at Falmouth, Virginia, in

The 110th Pennsylvania Volunteer Infantry in winter camp, probably in the vicinity of Fredericksburg in the winter of 1862-1863 (photo reproduced by permission of the U.S. Army Military History Institute).

preparation for the attack on Fredericksburg.

Despite the size of Burnside's force and the level of preparation he and his staff made, the assault on Fredericksburg proved to be a disaster for him and far too many of his soldiers. Many of the problems in this campaign can be attributed to Burnside himself. A commander must have confidence in both his soldiers and himself, but even prior to his appointment Burnside did not feel he was competent to command an army of this size. Despite this accurate assessment, he was unwilling or unable to refuse command. To complicate the situation, when Burnside moved his army to Fredericksburg, Lee's Army of Northern Virginia had possession of Fredericksburg and the heights overlooking the town. Thus, Union troops would have to cross the Rappahannock and the river below, in order to engage Lee's army under fire. As the Union Army began arriving at Falmouth in preparation for the attack, the Rappahannock was rising, making it extremely difficult to move a large army across a single ford. To make matters worse, the pontoon bridges that General-in-Chief Henry Halleck had promised to supply did not arrive when they were supposed to. The resulting delay in the Union Army's river crossing allowed Lee to assemble his army to meet an attack that was obviously going to occur. On December 11, 1862, when the bridge was finally completed, Union troops began crossing but paused to sack the town. Burnside finally launched his attack on Confederate positions on December 13. In a mere several days, Union troops had to cross a river under fire, fight in a town and attack Lee's army, which held terrain above it. Burnside's assault – in particular, the attack against Marye's Heights – was a disaster. The Union Army suffered 12,653 casualties, almost 8,000 of them along a stone wall at the base of Marye's Heights. Despite this heavy expenditure of manpower, Burnside's attack failed to put him on the road to Richmond. The slaughter of Union troops at Fredericksburg caused Lee, surveying the action, to say, "It is well that war is so terrible – we should grow too fond of it."[33]

A review of the regiments under Burnside's command during this ill-fated campaign shows the substantial contribution made by Pennsylvania. Of his army, 70 infantry regiments were Pennsylvania volunteers, as were nine artillery batteries and three cavalry regiments.[34] Pennsylvania's contribution to

[33] Burnside would make one final attempt on January 20 to successfully engage Confederate troops at Fredericksburg. He attempted to move some of his units westward up the Rappahannock, cross the fords and drive behind the Army of Northern Virginia. This turned into a disaster when torrential rains hit and the attacking force became mired in a sea of mud. A number of Pennsylvania units were also involved in the infamous "Mud March."

[34] These figures are taken from M. Jay Luvaas and Harold W. Nelson, eds., *The U.S. Army War*

the war was in part due to the leadership provided by Governor Curtin. The governor best summed up the Commonwealth's role when he addressed the Assembly on January 7, 1863. He noted that President Lincoln had called for 300,000 volunteers on July 7, 1862. During 1862, 38 new regiments were raised in Pennsylvania, along with three unattached companies of infantry. Four additional regiments authorized before this call had also been recruited and were in the process of being organized. The governor also reminded listeners that 50,000 militia had been called up for the Antietam campaign. In short, since the beginning of the war, Pennsylvania had supplied 200,000 men for the war effort (plus the 50,000 militia noted).[35]

These troops and many more would be sorely needed, because poor leadership in the person of Ambrose Burnside cost the Union many good soldiers. General Hooker replaced Burnside as commander of the Army of the Potomac on January 26, 1863. Because Hooker was appointed commander in mid-winter, he had the opportunity to reorganize his army and integrate new units into his weakened force. During the Civil War, commanders normally avoided major campaigns during the dead of winter, preferring to wait for more favorable weather in the spring and summer. Hooker, however, had the same vision as his two predecessors: to move on Richmond and take the capital of the Confederacy. Thus, when spring came, he would launch a campaign.

Hooker put his Army in motion on April 27 and prepared to attack Lee. To defeat Lee and take Richmond, Hooker assembled a force of seven Army corps and one cavalry corps, for a total strength of 134,000 men (and 413 artillery pieces). In this sizable army, Hooker had a total of 76 volunteer infantry regiments, eight artillery batteries and nine cavalry units from Pennsylvania. His plan to defeat Lee and open the road to Richmond was audacious and complex. Hooker intended to detach three infantry corps from the main body of his army and send them on a wide flanking movement, requiring them to move 20 miles up the Rappahannock, cross the river and then proceed back toward Fredericksburg. There they would join up with another federal corps and poise 70,000 Union soldiers to strike the left flank of Lee's outnumbered army. The three Union corps which would be the striking force of Hooker's flanking movement – the 11th, commanded by Major General Oliver O. Howard; the 12th, commanded by Major General Henry W. Slocum; and the 5th, commanded by Pennsylvanian George Gordon Meade – included 26

Pennsylvania volunteer infantry regiments and two artillery batteries.

Initially, Hooker's plan seemed to work perfectly. The three Union corps moved into position on Lee's flank, and Lee was simply unaware of their position. A Union officer, Lieutenant Clay McCauley from the 126th Pennsylvania, an element in Meade's Corps, reflected in his journal the optimism of the day. He noted that Hooker's General Order No. 47 stated they had "completely surrounded the rebel … [and that they would] either have to fly ingloriously or come out from their breastworks, where destruction was certain."[36] Despite the Union's success in maneuvering a force into a position of advantage, Hooker and at least one of his subordinates stalled, giving Lee the opportunity to determine that a Union force was on his flank and adjust his own force accordingly. Lee threw together about 40,000 men to face Hooker's flank threat, and belatedly, on May 1, Hooker put his troops in motion to attack Lee's flank. At the same time, Confederate troops from General Thomas Jackson's command, under the newly arrived General Lafayette McLaws, advanced to attack Union troops. Initially the Union troops made progress, but then Hooker seemed to lose his nerve and ordered his corps commanders to break off the advance. Meade, advancing virtually unopposed, was amazed. Even more astonishing, Hooker prepared to go over to the defense. While Hooker's units were taking up positions, some of Confederate General Jeb Stuart's scouts reported that General Oliver Howard's Corps had an open flank. Not lacking nerve – like the Union commander – on the late afternoon of May 2, 1863, Jackson, with Lee's permission, threw his corps against the exposed Union right flank. The surprised soldiers from Howard's Corps began an embarrassing retreat, which degenerated into a rout. The chaos resulting from this flank attack was described by Lieutenant Colonel Adolph von Hartung, 74th Pennsylvania Infantry, part of Howard's Eleventh Corps. He reported:

> At about 5:30 p.m. were suddenly attacked in very great force by the enemy, and his attack was directed on our right flank and back. The regiment on our right broke through the ranks of the Seventy-Fourth Regiment in such a manner that the regiment got at once thrown in such disorder that a restoring of order was an utter impossibility. The first we ever knew of the enemy was that our men, sitting on knapsacks and ready to spring to their arms, were shot from the rear and flank. [The surprise] was so complete that the men had not even time to take their arms before

[36] Lieutenant Clay McCauley, as quoted in James McPherson, *1863: Turning Point of the Civil War* (New York: Time-Life Books, 1998), p. 35.

they were thrown in the wildest confusion.[37]

Only the coming of darkness and the wounding of General Jackson averted a total Union disaster. When the next day dawned, more federal units had crossed the river, bringing the Union strength to 76,000 men, almost twice the number in the Army of Northern Virginia. Despite the Union's numerical superiority, it was the Confederates who aggressively attacked, pressing the Union Army until its commander, rather than the Army itself, broke. The Union Army began a withdrawal to more defensible positions. In this engagement known as Chancellorsville, the Union suffered 17,287 casualties in three days of fighting.[38]

With the guns of Chancellorsville barely cooled, Lee began preparing to wage his most significant campaign into the North. This, the Gettysburg Campaign, would greatly affect south central Pennsylvania and a large number of Pennsylvania volunteers. The campaign was the brainchild of Lee, with the concurrence of Jefferson Davis and the Confederate strategy board. Disengaging from Hooker's Army of the Potomac, still positioned in Virginia, on June 13, 1863, Lee began moving the Army of Northern Virginia into south central Pennsylvania. Despite his losses at Chancellorsville, he was able to field an army of three corps, a total of about 76,000 men. His goal was Harrisburg, with its transportation network which led west and linked the industrial East to the Ohio River Valley and the supply center of Chicago.

As Lee crossed into Pennsylvania, the losses suffered by the citizens of the state were considerable. Living off the lush farms of Pennsylvania, Confederate troops demanded supplies, and sometimes money, from virtually defenseless communities.[39] By June 26, General "Dick" Ewell, in command of Lee's

---

[37] *The War of the Rebellion: Compellation of the Official Records of the Union and the Confederate Armies*, vol. XIX, part I (Washington, D.C.: Government Printing Office, 1887), p. 665. Cited hereafter as *Official Records of the Union and Confederate Armies*.

[38] As noted by one writer, however, "Chancellorsville was a bittersweet success. Lee lost nearly 13,000 men killed wounded and missing – 22 percent of his entire army. In contrast ... [the Union's loss] was relatively much lower, slightly more than 17,000." Given the demographics of the North and South, the Confederacy could not long endure these sorts of "victories." Gary W. Gallagher, *The Battle of Chancellorsville* (NP: Eastern National Park and Monument Association, 1995), p. 53.

[39] As Lee began his invasion, President Lincoln called for the states to raise militia, even though in most states the militia system had fallen into disuse. Governor Curtin, responding to the President's call and recognizing that Confederate troops were only 26 miles from Harrisburg, issued a call on June 26, 1863, for 60,000 volunteer militia to assist in repelling the invasion of the state. They were to be mustered for a period of 90 days and were to serve only "so much

Second Army Corps, a large corps which was the vanguard of Lee's advance, had troops in Carlisle, Camp Hill-Mechanicsburg and Hanover.[40] The two remaining Confederate corps, commanded by General A. P. Hill and General James Longstreet, were in Chambersburg, together with Lee and his headquarters. Lee hoped he could move most of his troops into Pennsylvania before Union authorities knew his army was in motion, but Hooker, despite his failure at Chancellorsville, sensed that Lee was up to something. Union troops were alerted, and Lee was detected early on, as he began moving his corps up the Shenandoah Valley. Once it was evident that a raid toward Washington was not part of the Confederate strategy, federal troops began moving north out of the nation's capital.

As the Union response was forming, Hooker was relieved on June 28, due to a disagreement with the President on troop dispositions. One of his subordinate corps commanders, the Pennsylvanian Meade, was designated commander of the Army of the Potomac. Whether Meade would have engaged Lee, had he the choice to do so, is uncertain, because he took command as the Army of Northern Virginia had the initiative and was already in motion. Meade's task was to locate Lee, fix the Confederate force and engage him. With this goal in mind, Union cavalry moved north from Frederick, Maryland, to locate Lee's exact position. Two brigades of a cavalry division commanded by General John Buford arrived at Gettysburg on the last day of the month. Buford, with an excellent eye for terrain, quickly determined that Gettysburg, with its crucial road network, was important to hold and very defensible. Buford sent word to the commander of the Union First Corps, Pennsylvanian General John Reynolds, to bring his troops forward as soon as possible, because he could only delay the superior Confederate force for a couple of hours if attacked. Buford's cavalry, which included the 17th Pennsylvania, would in fact be attacked because, on the 30th, the Confederates had conducted a reconnaissance of Gettysburg and determined it was only occupied by militia troops. Since they regarded the town as poorly defended, Confederate General Henry Heth requested permission from his corps commander, General A. P. Hill, to advance into Gettysburg to procure supplies. Although Lee had given orders that a general engagement was to be avoided, a clash with local militia, in order to obtain needed supplies, did not seem to violate the order.

What resulted, however, was a three-day general engagement that we

of the period of muster as the safety of our people and the honor of our state may require." See the "Proclamation for Sixty Thousand Men to Repel Invasion of the State," in Reed, *Papers of the Governors, 1856-1871*, pp. 502-504.

Undated photo of a monument west of Gettysburg on Chamberburg Pike, commemo-
rating the bravery of Sgt. Ben Crippen on the afternoon of July 1, 1863 (photo reproduced by permission of the U.S. Army Military History Institute).

now know as the Battle of Gettysburg. It began on the morning of July 1,
1863, when Heth's Division moved up Chambersburg Pike and attacked the
westernmost brigade of Buford's Cavalry Division. Buford delayed the
Confederate advance with his veteran troopers, well-armed with breech-loading
carbines, and shortly after 9 a.m. elements of John Reynolds' First Corps began
arriving and deploying on the field. Bitter fighting raged over the field for the
next two hours as Reynolds' troops skilfully stopped the Confederate advance.[41]
In the process, a soldier from Pennsylvania achieved notoriety on the battlefield.
As the Union First Corps took its position on McPherson's Ridge, an old gray-

[40] As General John B. Gordon, in command of the Georgia Brigade, approached Wrightsville,
he encountered Pennsylvania troops that had erected earthworks and were prepared to delay the
Confederate advance. In one of the famous episodes in this part of the campaign, the Union
troops, under pressure from the superior Confederate force, retreated across the long covered
bridge and set fire to it midway so Gordon's troops could not follow them. Unfortunately, this
successful firing caused the town to catch fire as well.
[41] Reynolds, a respected general from Lancaster, became the first general officer casualty on the
battlefield. With his death, the First Corps command passed to General Abner Doubleday, bet-

haired gentleman, John Burns, trudged across the battlefield, musket in hand, and was approached by Major Thomas Chamberlain of the 150th Regiment, Pennsylvania Volunteers. Burns' request was simple: he merely wanted a chance to fight. Despite his 69 years, Burns was placed along the edge of Herbst Woods, where the Iron Brigade was located, and fought well. During the first day's engagement, Burns was wounded three times but survived, undoubtedly making him the oldest soldier on the field.[42]

Around 11 a.m., a lull developed on the west side of the battlefield, and the action shifted to the north. In mid-day General Oliver Howard arrived in Gettysburg and positioned two divisions of his Union Eleventh Corps on the north side of town. At about the same time, elements of Richard Ewell's Second Confederate Corps began arriving and took up positions north of town. After consolidating their positions, the Southern troops resumed the attack from the north and west of Gettysburg and began pushing the Union troops back. On the west side of town, where the Union First Corps had so bravely defended that morning, the determination of A. P. Hill's troops and the sheer weight of their numbers caused the Union line to waver and fall back. The 143rd Pennsylvania, one of those units that gave ground, did provide one memorable moment for the state's military history. As the regiment withdrew, albeit in a disciplined fashion, the color sergeant, Ben Crippen, firmly held the regiment's colors. Then, as he shook his fist in defiance at the advancing Confederates, he was killed. Lieutenant Colonel Arthur J. Freemantle, a British observer with Lee's army, reported his bravery with admiration, stating:

> *A Yankee colorbearer floated his standard in the field, and the regiment fought around it, and when at last it was compelled to retreat, the color-bearer retreated last of all, turning around now and then to shake his fist in the face of the advancing Confederates. He was shot. General Hill was sorry when he met his fate.*[43]

ter known for his title as the father of baseball than for his military laurels.

[42] Soldiering was nothing new to John Burns. As a young man he had fought in the War of 1812 at Lundy's Lane, served in the post-war militia and volunteered to fight in the Mexican War, but his volunteer regiment was not taken. Before volunteering to fight with the 150th Pennsylvania, he had also been arrested and briefly held as a prisoner when General Jubal Early's Division passed through Gettysburg on June 26. Lincoln rewarded him for his service through special recognition at Gettysburg in November 1863, when the President was there for the dedication of the National Cemetery. Samuel P. Bates, *Martial Deeds of Pennsylvania* (Philadelphia: T. H. Davis and Co., 1875), pp. 988-999.

[43] William H. Zierdt, *Narrative History of the 109th Field Artillery, Pennsylvania National Guard, 1175-1930* (Wilkes-Barre, Pa.: Wyoming Historical and Geological Society, 1932), p. 79.

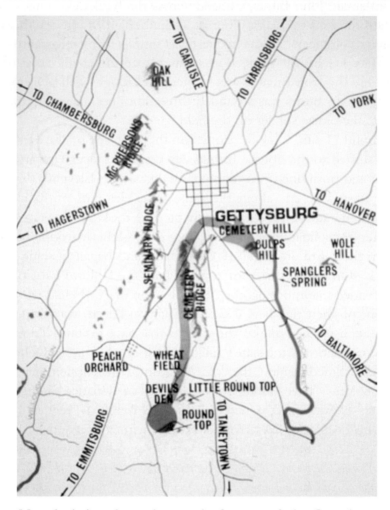

Map depicting the major terrain features of the Gettysburg vicinity, highlighting the famous fishhook defensive position (reproduced by permission of the U.S. Army War College).

Under pressure from the divisions of Confederate Generals Rodes and Early, General Howard was pushed back through Gettysburg. His troops and those of Doubleday's First Corps fell in on the heights south of town known as Cemetery Hill (and Ridge). The first day of Gettysburg, best described as a meeting engagement, was over. Although Union troops had fought well, the two Union corps had barely survived destruction. Eleven Pennsylvania Volunteer Infantry regiments and a cavalry and artillery unit fought with the Union First Corps west of town. Altogether, 17 Pennsylvania Volunteer Infantry reg-

iments took part in the first day's engagement at Gettysburg, as well as two cavalry units and one battery of light artillery.[44] Units like the 56th and 121st Infantry took significant losses (51 and 68 percent respectively). The 149th Pennsylvania Volunteer Infantry, positioned along Chambersburg Pike, suffered 75
percent casualties. Five members of these regiments – three enlisted men and
two officers – were awarded Medals of Honor for actions on July 1.[45]

Neither Lee nor the new Union commander, George Meade, had directed the first day's battle. As a meeting engagement, the battle occurred as troops
arrived at Gettysburg, and neither commander came on the scene until the battle was in progress. On the second day, however, Lee was determined to pun-
ish the Union Army. The strength of both armies was still building. On the
evening of July 1, two fresh divisions of General Longstreet's Corps had arrived
and would be the key elements for Lee's concept of operations on July 2.
Fortunately for Meade, whose two corps had narrowly escaped destruction,
four more federal corps arrived during the night, giving him the fresh Second,
Third, Fifth and Twelfth Union Corps. At this point in the battle, the Union
defense took on the familiar "fishhook" position that followed the natural terrain. According to Lee's plan, the main effort on the second day was a flanking movement, designed to strike the left of Meade's position, in the vicinity of
Devil's Den and the Peach Orchard, and roll up the federal line. Federal attention was to be diverted from Longstreet's maneuver by attacks on the Union
center by A. P. Hill's Corps and Dick Ewell's Corps on the Union right.

Lee's plan almost worked. Hill's and Ewell's attacks accomplished little,
but despite the lack of enthusiasm by their commander, Longstreet's soldiers
fought like Longstreet's always fought. Attacking *en echelon*, complete with classic "rebel yells," they hammered away at the Union left. Under such heavy pressure, the far left Union corps, General Dan Sickles' Third Corps, began to give
way. As Colonel Henry J. Madill, 141st Pennsylvania Volunteers, reported, they
had little choice. Madill stated in his after action report:

> *My regiment suffered so severely; 25 of my men were killed here and 5 of*
> *my officers were severely wounded ... I took 200 men into the fight, with*

[44] The number of Pennsylvania units cited comes from the force structure information provided in M. Jay Luvaas and Harold W. Nelson, *The U.S. Army War College Guide to the Battle of
Gettysburg* (Carlisle, Pa.: South Mountain Press, 1986), pp. 216-233.

[45] For details on these units and the exact location of their monuments, see Richard Rollins and
Dave Shultz, *Guide to Pennsylvania Troops at Gettysburg* (Redondo Beach, Calif.: Rank and File
Publications, 1998), pp. 2-20. Cited hereafter as Rollins and Shultz, *Pennsylvania Troops at
Gettysburg*. Note that one of these regiments was a militia unit, the 26th Militia or the 26th

9 officers. Out of that number, I lost 145 men and 6 commissioned officers, the largest proportional loss in the corps in that fight.[46]

Even as disaster seemed imminent, the Union anchored its line on Little Round Top, and the federal left held — but just barely. As the forces employed to block Lee's advance on July 2 are reviewed, the contribution of Pennsylvania volunteers is again impressive. Sixty-three Pennsylvania Volunteer Infantry regiments, eight artillery batteries and seven cavalry units were on the field for the second day's fighting. Thirty-eight of the infantry regiments were on the south end of the battlefield, where Lee placed his main effort.[47] Eleven Pennsylvania volunteers were awarded Medals of Honor for their actions of the second day at Gettysburg. Pennsylvania units were heavily concentrated in the vicinity of the Wheat Field, where some of the bloodiest fighting occurred.[48]

Despite his inability to defeat the Union forces on two days in succession, Lee was determined to resume the battle a third day, in order to win a major engagement on Northern soil. With Longstreet's last fresh division, commanded by General George Pickett, and with Jeb Stuart finally rejoined with the Army of Northern Virginia, Lee planned a final assault to win his victory.[49] General Ewell's Corps would again attack the Union right and attempt to seize Culp's Hill. Longstreet, joined by his fresh division, would attack the Union center, and Stuart's cavalry would ride around the Union right and hit the rear of the Union center. The plan seemed sound, but it required solid coordination to successfully unhinge the Union defense.

From the outset things went awry. In the early morning, the Union Twelfth Corps launched an attack to clear the slopes of Culp's Hill of Confederates. Thus, the action on Culp's Hill began prematurely and died out before noon, totally uncoordinated with the rest of Lee's actions. Stuart's ride was also

Emergency Infantry Regiment, "Home Guard," organized at Camp Curtin on June 21-24, 1863, on the eve of the battle.

[46] *Official Records of the Union and Confederate Armies*, vol. XXVII, part I, pp. 504-505.

[47] One of the most distinctive units was the 114th Pennsylvania Volunteer Infantry, also known as Collis' Zouaves. Colorfully uniformed in the traditional manner of Civil War Zouaves, this unit, positioned in the vicinity of the Peach Orchard, was hit by General William Barksdale's Mississippi Brigade. The Zouaves were forced to give ground under the fury of the Mississippi attack, suffering almost 60 percent casualties.

[48] Rollins and Shultz, *Pennsylvania Troops at Gettysburg*, p. 21.

[49] For the reader unfamiliar with the battle, Stuart was essentially detached from the main body of Lee's army for most of the battle. He was supposed to keep in touch with General Ewell's right as the Army of Northern Virginia moved north but failed to do so. Thus, on the day the battle began, Stuart was waging his own battle in the little town of Carlisle rather than serving as the eyes and ears of Lee's army.

unsuccessful. Stuart was observed as he made his advance, and Union cavalry were sent to stop him. This resulted in a spirited engagement, but Stuart's troops ran low on ammunition and had to leave the battlefield, neither defeating the Yankee cavalry nor accomplishing their assigned task. This left the third advance, the main effort for Lee's third day, without a supporting or diversionary attack.

Lee began his artillery preparation at about 1 p.m. Artillery blazed for several hours, as Confederate gunners pounded Cemetery Ridge and Union gunners replied with counter-battery fire. At about 3 p.m., roughly 12,000 Confederate soldiers left their staging areas and, with a nod of Longstreet's head, began one of the most famous infantry charges of all time: "Pickett's Charge." Union artillery cut swaths of destruction through the almost parade-ground Confederate formations, but the troops in butternut brown pressed on with discipline and courage. The Confederate line paused briefly before Emittsburg Road, reorganized and then surged forward toward Cemetery

Band of the 114th Infantry Regiment, Pennsylvania Volunteers (also known as "Collis' Zouaves"), a regiment raised in Philadelphia in 1862 (photo reproduced by permission of the Massachusetts Commandery, Military Order of the Loyal Legion and the U.S. Army Military History Institute).

Ridge. Aiming toward the now famous copse of trees, the Confederates pene-
trated the line and pressed forward. Directly in front of the trees, the
Philadelphia Brigade wavered and began to break, but in the end the Union line
was simply too strong. The efforts of the brave Southerners were in vain. By
the time Lee's soldiers had reached and briefly breached the Union lines, they
no longer had the strength to exploit their breakthrough. The remnants retreated under Union fire and, under Lee's orders, prepared for the Union counterattack that never came. The Battle of Gettysburg was over.

The contribution of Pennsylvania volunteers to this battle was substantial. Seventy-nine Pennsylvania units, most of them volunteer infantry, were on
the Gettysburg battlefield. The majority were in combatant roles. This
amounted to 24,412 men, drawn from a broad geographical spectrum of the
state. The total casualties for Pennsylvania were 5,887, with 741 killed in action.
Seventeen Pennsylvanians, all of them from volunteer or Pennsylvania Reserve
elements, won Medals of Honor.[50] At Gettysburg, a crucial battle for the
Keystone State as well as the nation, Pennsylvania was well represented.

Although the Battle of Gettysburg and the simultaneous fall of Vicksburg marked the beginning of the end for the Confederacy, many hard battles
remained before Lee's surrender at Appomattox. President Lincoln was well
aware of this and on October 17, 1863, called for another 300,000 volunteers
from the states. Pennsylvania's share of this quota was 38,268. The governor
responded by issuing a proclamation on October 28 that called on the citizens
to heed the call by January 5, 1864. When he addressed the Assembly on
January 7, 1864, Governor Curtin was deservedly proud of his citizens, noting
that since the war began, 277,409 men from the Commonwealth had left for
"general or special support" of the war effort and the "storehouses and depots
literally overflowed" with supplies.[51]

During 1863 Pennsylvania also began to utilize another source of manpower, black soldiers. Records indicate that in the early part of the war, a few

---

[50] Even as Pennsylvania was supplying a significant number of troops for the defense of the
Commonwealth, it is important to remember that Pennsylvania volunteers were serving in the
defense of the nation, not just the Commonwealth. Thus, in spite of the obvious danger posed
to Pennsylvania by the Confederate invasion, Pennsylvania volunteers were in the Western theater as well. In Grant's Army of Tennessee, there were four Pennsylvania Volunteer Infantry
regiments and one artillery battery. In the siege that climaxed on July 4, 1863, and resulted in
the surrender of the Confederate stronghold on the Mississippi, Vicksburg, the Union force
included the 51st Pennsylvania.

[51] Annual message of Governor Andrew Gregg Curtin to the Assembly, in Reed, *Papers of the
Governors, 1858-1871*, pp. 508-510, 529-530.

The 32nd U.S. Colored Troops in formation at Camp William Penn, Chelten Hills, Pennsylvania (photo reproduced by permission of the National Archives).

blacks were able to join volunteer militia units, despite the segregated society of the period. For example, when the "First Defenders" marched through Baltimore, Nicholas Biddle, a black man from Pottsville, was a member of an artillery element and was bloodied by stones thrown by the pro-Southern mob. George Stephens, a Philadelphia cabinetmaker, joined the 26th Pennsylvania Volunteers as a cook for the regiment.[52] These enlistments, however, were exceptions. It was obvious that if blacks were going to fight for the Union, they would have to have their own units.

Almost from the inception of the war, proposals were made by various Union officers to recruit, train and employ black soldiers. Early initiatives to create black regiments were made in South Carolina, Louisiana and Kansas, but federal authorities were initially dubious if not outright opposed to the effort.

[52] Noah Andre Trudeau, *Like Men of War: Black Troops in the Civil War, 1862-1865* (New York: Little Brown and Co., 1998), pp. 7, 11.

Systematic recruitment of black units began with General Order 143, which authorized the formation of the United States Colored Troops (U.S.C.T.). At first, free Pennsylvania blacks found it convenient to travel to Massachusetts, long a hotbed of Abolitionist sentiment, to join units forming there. However, beginning in March 1863, efforts were made in Philadelphia to recruit and enlist black units. With Lee's Army of Northern Virginia in motion toward Pennsylvania, on June 17, 1863, Secretary of War Edwin Stanton gave permission to Philadelphian Thomas Webster to raise three regiments of black soldiers. Within a week, a camp was established at Chelten Hills, near Philadelphia, to muster and train black regiments.[53] The first 80 recruits reported to Chelten Hills, now called Camp William Penn, on June 26, 1863. The first recruits were organized into the 3rd Infantry Regiment, U.S.C.T., and before the end of the war another ten regiments were organized at Camp William Penn.[54]

As 1864 began, the war was approaching its fourth year. Along the East Coast, where most Pennsylvania troops were located, the pattern had been established that once spring arrived, a new campaign year would begin in earnest. In 1864, however, a new factor was present. As of March 9, 1864, the Union Army in the east was under new leadership. General U. S. Grant had taken command. In his characteristic style, on May 5, 1864, he took the initiative and began the Battle of the Wilderness, in which a considerable number of Pennsylvania volunteers were involved. The Wilderness was promptly followed by the Battle of Spotsylvania. These two battles resulted in the Union Army suffering some 33,000 casualties, including a good number of Pennsylvanians. Units like the 48th Pennsylvania, from the Pottsville area, and the 119th Pennsylvania took significant losses. Both the Union Army and General Lee were experiencing Grant's leadership style: the bulldog-like determination with which, despite a heavy casualty rate, he refused to leave the Army of Northern Virginia in peace. His determination would eventually defeat them.

While the eastern Union Army and most Pennsylvania volunteers were focused on the campaigns planned in Virginia, Pennsylvania received another unwelcome guest. General Jubal Early dispatched a raiding force for the final Confederate incursion into the Keystone State. Similar to the fall of 1862, the goal of the Confederates was Chambersburg. The raid had no real strategic goal but was rather an act of revenge against the Union for the excesses of

---

[53] The history of these black regiments, mustered and trained at Camp William Penn, can be found in Bates, *History of Pennsylvania Volunteers*, vol. X, pp. 925-1140. This citation is taken from the 1993 reprint by Broadfoot Publishing Co., Wilmington, N.C.
[54] William A. Gladstone, *Men of Color* (Gettysburg, Pa.: Thomas Publications, 1993), p. 64.

Union troops in Virginia's Shenandoah Valley. Approximately 2,600 Confederate soldiers under the command of General John McCausland proceeded into Pennsylvania and on July 30 reached Chambersburg. As in 1862, the town was largely undefended. Union General Darius Couch had his headquarters there, but his command consisted of little more than 100 men scattered around the countryside as scouts. McCausland entered the town and demanded $100,000 in gold or $500,000 in greenbacks. When the citizens refused to comply, Confederate troops systematically burned the town, plundering and looting as they went. After virtually destroying the town, the raiders withdrew.[55]

While the 1864 campaign was underway, the legislature passed an act that deserves mention. On several occasions since the beginning of the war, the governor had informed the Assembly that the militia law was inadequate. In April 1861, a new militia act had been passed, but it offered no real changes in the organization of the militia. In 1864, however, the militia law was entirely revised. According to the act passed on May 4, 1863, the concept of enrolling all able-bodied white male citizens of the state in the militia was retained. Although the old enrolled militia had been largely discredited in the first half of the 19th century, in both 1862 and 1863 militia had been called for and performed a useful function during the direct Confederate threats to Pennsylvania. The militia essentially served as a home guard, for limited periods of service. Under the new act, the enrolled militia would be limited to a similar function – not subject to any active duty unless there was war, rioting or invasion or threat of invasion. The volunteer militia, the second component of the militia force, was to be the first ordered into active service. When the enrolled militia was ordered out, the governor was to organize it into the necessary companies, battalions and regiments. Much of the act was then devoted to the structure of the volunteer militia, which would be the trained, organized and equipped force.

One episode from 1864 deserves particular attention, due to the significant participation of Pennsylvania troops. After the costly battle at Cold Harbor, on June 1-3, the Union Army attacked Confederate forces at Petersburg, Virginia. From 1861 to 1863, neither army placed much emphasis on building trenches or sandbagged and fortified positions. Beginning with Cold Harbor, however, Union troops had to contend with well-prepared

---

[55] The destruction was considerable. Two hundred sixty-six private homes or businesses, 98 barns or stables and 173 miscellaneous structures were destroyed. B. S. Schneck, *The Burning of Chambersburg, Pennsylvania* (Philadelphia: Lindsay and Blakiston, 1865), pp. 67-74. This small book gives a detailed list of all of the structures burned and a map of their locations.

The crater at Petersburg as seen from Union lines, a product of the mining skills of the 48th Pennsylvania Volunteer Infantry (photo reproduced by permission of the U.S. Army War College).

Confederate defenses. Such defenses had caused Grant frightful casualties at Cold Harbor, and when his army moved to Petersburg, it was again faced by trenches and well-prepared strongpoints that threatened heavy Union losses. Men from the 48th Pennsylvania, who had considerable experience in mining, suggested another idea. Instead of direct assaults, they proposed to tunnel under the Confederate entrenchments, plant a mine and literally blow a hole through the Confederate lines. The plan was approved by General Ambrose Burnside, and for three weeks the Pennsylvania miners worked away. They dug 20 feet underground for a length of 510 feet, then planted four tons of explosives. On June 29 the charge was blown, throwing men, timbers and gun carriages into the air and creating a crater 30 feet deep and 170 feet long.

Unfortunately, such a crater became an obstacle in itself, and there developed a "Battle of the Crater." Although troops had been trained to move forward quickly and exploit the break in Confederate lines, last-minute changes caused the troops to be shifted, and in the end the desired breakthrough was not achieved. The overall operation cost the Union about 4,000 casualties and was deemed a failure by General Grant. Although no great advantage was gained by the Union Army, the miners of the 48th Pennsylvania accomplished their task well and left a unique episode of the war as their legacy.

By the last half of 1864, it became increasingly clear that no amount of trenches or strongpoints could save the Confederacy. At the same time Grant was hammering Lee in Virginia, General William Tecumseh Sherman moved his army south, and on September 2 he captured Atlanta. He then proceeded east, and on December 22 Sherman's army captured Savannah, Georgia, cutting the Confederacy in two. It had previously been cut in two in the west with the fall of Vicksburg on July 4, 1863. For the Confederacy, the end was near.

A review of the Commonwealth's accomplishments in 1864 confirms Pennsylvania's significant role in supplying troops for the suppression of the rebellion. The figures supplied to the Assembly by the governor in his January 4, 1865, address show the following:

Troops sent into service during 1864

Organizations for three year terms	*9,867*
Organizations for one hundred days terms	*7,675*
Organizations for one year term	*16,096*
Volunteer recruits	*26,567*
Drafted men and substitutes	*10,651*
Recruits for Regular Army	*2,974*

Re-enlistments of Pennsylvania Volunteers

Infantry	*13,862*
Cavalry	*2,834*
Artillery	*799*
Accredited to other states	*389*
Total	*91,704*[56]

Curtin also provided the legislators with a recapitulation of Pennsylvania's contributions since the beginning of the conflict:

[56] Curtin later stated in his annual address to the Assembly on January 30, 1866, that in 1864, under various calls by the federal government, 32 regiments, two battalions and eight attached companies were organized and sent into the field. With reenlistments amounting to 17,876, a total of 91,704 men were furnished. Reed, *Papers of the Governors, 1857-1871,* p. 719.

During the year 1861   *130,594*
During the year 1862   *71,100*
During the year 1863   *43,046*
During the year 1864   *73,824*
Re-enlistment of Pennsylvania Volunteers *17,876*
         Total *336,444*[57]

   Although in 1865 the war only lasted for a little more than three months, Pennsylvania continued to recruit and field troops. Before 1865, Governor Curtin had suggested that rather than continue the policy of creating new regiments, the emphasis should be on organizing new companies to fill out veteran regiments whose strength had been reduced by casualties. This concept was adopted, and in 1865, 75 companies were organized and assigned to veteran regiments. Three completely new regiments were recruited, however, and by the end of the war the total number of soldiers recruited by Pennsylvania for the year 1865 was 25,790.[58] In reality, additional recruitment was not needed because the war was rapidly coming to an end. On April 4, 1865, the governor announced that Richmond, "the center of treason," had fallen. Five days later, on April 9, 1865, General Lee and his Army of Northern Virginia surrendered at Appomattox Court House. The war was over.

   Pennsylvania's role in the Civil War and the contribution of its volunteer units were considerable. The Adjutant General's Report for 1865 shows that Pennsylvania supplied 248 regiments to the Union Army – 128 of which were enlisted for three years, 18 for one year, 33 for nine months, three for six months, and 59 for three months, 100 days or 90 days. (In addition, seven regiments were formed in response to the 1863 Confederate invasion, and emergency militia regiments and smaller units also served in the 1862-63 campaigns.) Of these 248 regiments, 218 were infantry, 25 were cavalry and five were artillery.[59] This number of volunteers and the leadership provided by Governor Curtin truly made Pennsylvania a "Keystone" in the defense of the Union.

---

[57] Ibid., p. 662.
[58] Ibid., p. 719.
[59] The five artillery regiments were heavy artillery. Pennsylvania also contributed light artillery.

Epilogue

If we are to have a militia system at all, it should be an uniform one, and well sustained by liberal provisions and appropriations for its organization and support.

— Brigadier General Lemuel Todd, 1866

With the surrender of Robert E. Lee and the remnants of his Army of Northern Virginia on April 9, 1865, the long and hard-fought war had finally come to an end. And so began the traditional demobilization whereby the members of the largely volunteer Army (with some draftees) returned home and resumed their peacetime pursuits. In Pennsylvania the process began in the late spring of 1865 and continued through the remainder of the year. It was not possible to immediately demobilize all the units, because the victorious Union Army garrisoned parts of the South in order to reestablish the authority of the federal government and ensure that rebel troops were fully demobilized. Thus, at the end of 1865, while the vast majority of Pennsylvania volunteers had returned home, Adjutant General A. L. Russell reported that six regiments of infantry were still in federal service. They were listed as follows: the 47th, at Charleston, South Carolina; the 58th, at various locations in Virginia; the 77th, in Victoria, Texas; the 188th, 195th and the 214th near Washington, D.C.; a regiment of artillery in Virginia; and one battalion of the 19th Pennsylvania Cavalry at Baton Rouge, Louisiana.[1]

As the Commonwealth returned to a peacetime existence, however, its government began to exercise the provisions of the 1864 Militia Act and organize volunteer militia forces in order to be prepared for any future emergencies for either the Commonwealth or the nation. In Philadelphia, York, Luzerne County and many other locations, volunteer militia companies were organized. Even so, the pace was slow. This was likely attributable to a post-war lethargy regarding military matters and to the fact that in order to organize a company

---

[1] Brigadier General A. L. Russell, *Annual Report of the Adjutant General of Pennsylvania, Transmitted to the Governor in Pursuance of the Law, for the Year 1866* (Harrisburg, The State Printers, 1867), p. 6. Cited hereafter as Russell, *Report of the Adjutant General for 1866.*

(under the 1864 act), there had to be a total of 80 enlisted men and three officers to gain recognition. By 1867, there were only 31 volunteer militia companies organized in the state.

The most troublesome part of the 1864 act was its establishment of a system composed of volunteer militia and an enrolled militia. Even though volunteer companies were being established, many around Civil War cadres, the system for an enrolled militia was again not functioning. The state Inspector General, Lemuel Todd, reported to the governor:

> *From the fact of the utter prostration of the militia system throughout the Commonwealth, it will be a most arduous, tedious and expensive undertaking to effect any organization under that act [of May 4, 1864] ... If we are to have a militia system at all, it should be an uniform one, and well sustained by liberal provisions and appropriations for its organization and support.*[2]

It was a familiar problem facing the state's military officials. The 1864 act had repeated the errors of both state and federal legislation from the beginning of the Republic. The act had provided for volunteer militias, but it required an enrolled militia, a provision that imposed a universal obligation on all white male citizens. By imposing an obligation on all, in the end it required service, even "toeing the curb," by none. As General Todd noted in his report, the enrolled militia required effective county organizations to enforce it. The cost to do this, in his opinion, would be excessive. Calling forth the militia during the Civil War had proven to be feasible because the danger posed by Confederate incursions was obvious and the citizenry were willing to defend their homes. In time of peace, for many citizens a militia obligation was too much of a bother. Thus, Pennsylvania was again faced by a militia law which was simply not enforceable.

Militia acts were passed in 1865, 1866, 1867 and 1869, but none of them altered the basic structure established in the 1864 act. It was not until April 7, 1870 that an act was passed which substantially altered the structure of the Commonwealth's military force. In that year Pennsylvania's lawmakers began the process of creating a new organization that would become today's National Guard. Under the provisions of this act, the active militia of the state was called the National Guard of Pennsylvania. The commander in chief of the

---

[2] Russell, *Report of the Adjutant General for 1866,* pp. 11, 12.

Guard was given the authority to organize this force into companies, battalions, regiments, brigades and divisions. If an able-bodied male did not belong to a Guard company, he was fined unless exempted from military service. The term of enlistment, five years, was specified, as was the term of officers' commissions. Pay, although the paltry sum of $12 annually, was established, and this pay was in proportion to the number of drills or parades that the Guardsman attended.[3]

Through this 1870 act, the Pennsylvania militia began the slow but steady process of becoming a modern and dependable force for the defense of the nation and the Commonwealth. Many more legal and structural changes, on both the state and national level, would be necessary before this transition was complete. The process, however, had begun.

---

[3] Major William P. Clarke, *Official History of the Militia and the National Guard of the State of Pennsylvania* (Philadelphia: Charles P. Hendler, 1909), pp. 47-50.

254

Bibliography

Government Documents

An Act for the Regulation of the Militia of the Commonwealth of Pennsylvania. Harrisburg: Office of the Reporter, 1828.

An Act for the Regulation of the Militia of the Commonwealth of Pennsylvania. Lancaster, Pa.: John R. Matthews, 1807.

The Annals of Congress, 1789-1790, First Congress, Second Session, vol. II. Washington: Seaton and Gales, 1849.

Beckman, Gail M., *The Statutes at Large of Pennsylvania at the Time of William Penn, 1680-1700*, vol. I. New York: Vantage Press, 1976.

Egle, William H., ed., *Pennsylvania Archives: Pennsylvania in the War of the Revolution, Associated Battalions and Militia, 1775-1783*, second series, vols. I and II. Clarence M. Busch: State Printer, 1896.

Hazard, Samuel, ed., *Pennsylvania Archives: Selected and Arranged from Original Documents in the Office of the Secretary of the Commonwealth Conformably to the Acts of the General Assembly, Commencing 1760*, vol. IV. Philadelphia: Joseph Severns and Co., 1853.

_____, *Pennsylvania Archives: Selected and Arranged from Original Documents in the Office of the Secretary of the Commonwealth Conformably to the Acts of the General Assembly, Commencing 1783*, vol. X. Philadelphia: Joseph Severns and Co., 1854.

_____, *Pennsylvania Archives: Selected and Arranged From Original Documents in the Office of the Secretary of the Commonwealth Conformably to the Acts of the General Assembly, Commencing 1776*, vol.V. Philadelphia: Joseph Severns and Co., 1853.

Hoban, Charles F., ed., *Pennsylvania Archives: Votes of the Assembly, January 7, 1771-September 26, 1776*, eighth series, vol. VIII. Harrisburg: Department of Property and Supplies, 1935.

Linn, John B. and William H. Egle, eds., *Pennsylvania Archives: Pennsylvania in the War of the Revolution, Battalions and Line, 1775-1783*, second series, vol. II. Harrisburg, Lane S. Hart, State Printer, 1880.

_____, *Pennsylvania Archives: Roll of Pennsylvania Volunteers in the War of 1812-1814*, second series, vol. XII. Harrisburg: State Printer, 1890.

_____, *Pennsylvania Archives: Papers and Documents Relating to the War of 1812-1814*, second series, vol. XII. Harrisburg: Clarence M. Busch, State Printer, 1896.

_____, *Pennsylvania Archives: Papers Relating to the French Occupation in Western Pennsylvania, 1631-1764*, second series, vol. VI. Harrisburg: State Printer, 1891.

_____, *Pennsylvania Archives: Provincial Affairs in Pennsylvania: Papers Relating to the Dutch and Swedish Settlements on the Delaware, 1682-1750* and *Papers Relating to the Boundary Dispute between Pennsylvania and Maryland, 1734-1760*, second series, vol. VII. Harrisburg: E. K. Meyers, State Printer, 1890.

MacKinney, Gertrude, ed., *Pennsylvania Archives: Votes of the Assembly, October 14, 1741-September 11, 1753*, eighth series, vol. IV. Harrisburg: State Printer, 1931.

_____, *Pennsylvania Archives: Votes of the Assembly, October 15, 1753-September 24, 1756*, eighth series, vol. V. Harrisburg: State Printer, 1931.

_____, *Pennsylvania Archives: Executive Minutes of Governor Simon Snyder, 1812-1814*, ninth series, vol. V. Harrisburg: Commonwealth of Pennsylvania, 1931.

_____, *Pennsylvania Archives: Executive Minutes of the Commonwealth of Pennsylvania, Executive Journal, 1814-1818*, ninth series, vol. VI. Harrisburg: Commonwealth of Pennsylvania, 1931.

Minutes of the Common Council of Philadelphia, 1704-1776. Philadelphia: N.P., 1847)

Montgomery, Thomas Lynch, ed., *Pennsylvania Archives: Officers and Soldiers in the Service of the Province of Pennsylvania, 1744-1765*, fifth series, vol. I. Harrisburg: Harrisburg Publishing Co., 1906.

_____, *Pennsylvania Archives: War of 1812-1814,* sixth series, vol. VII. Harrisburg: State Printer, 1907.

_____, *Pennsylvania Archives: Miscellaneous Papers and Drafted Troops, 1812-1814*, sixth series, vol. IX. Harrisburg: State Printer, 1907.

Pennsylvania Archives: Colonial Records of Pennsylvania, Minutes of the Provincial Council of Pennsylvania from Organization to the Termination of the Proprietary Government, vol. I. Philadelphia: Joseph Severns and Co., 1852.

Pennsylvania Archives: Colonial Records of Pennsylvania, Minutes of the Provincial Council of Pennsylvania from Organization to the Termination of the Proprietary Government, vol. II. Philadelphia: Joseph Severns and Co., 1857.

Pennsylvania Archives: Colonial Records of Pennsylvania, Minutes of the Provincial Council of Pennsylvania from Organization to the Termination of the Proprietary Government, vol.V. Harrisburg: Theo. Fenn & Co., 1851.

Pennsylvania Archives: Colonial Records of Pennsylvania, Minutes of the Provincial Council from Organization to the Termination of the Proprietary Government, vol. VIII. Harrisburg: Theo. Fenn & Co., 1852.

Pennsylvania Archives: Colonial Records of Pennsylvania, Minutes of the Provincial Council from Organization to the Termination of the Proprietary Government, vol. IX. Harrisburg: Theo. Fenn & Co., 1852.

Pennsylvania Archives: Colonial Records of Pennsylvania, eighth series, vol.VII. Philadelphia: Joseph Severns and Co., 1852.

Pennsylvania Archives: Minutes of the Provincial Council, vol. V. Philadelphia: Joseph Severns and Co., 1840.

Pennsylvania Archives: Votes of the Assembly, January 7, 1771-September 26, 1776, eighth series, vol. VIII. Harrisburg: State Library, 1935.

Pennsylvania at Antietam: Report of the Antietam Battlefield Memorial Commission of Pennsylvania. Harrisburg: State Printer, 1906.

Pennsylvania Military Regulation No. 80, March 1, 1937.   Harrisburg: Adjutant General's Office, 1937.

Reed, George E., ed., *Pennsylvania Archives: Papers of the Governors, 1681-1747*, fourth series, vol. I. Harrisburg: State of Pennsylvania, 1900.

_____, *Pennsylvania Archives: Papers of the Governors, 1747-1759*, fourth series, vol. II. Harrisburg: State of Pennsylvania, 1900.

_____, *Pennsylvania Archives: Papers of the Governors, 1759-1785*, fourth series, vol. III. Harrisburg: State of Pennsylvania, 1900.

_____, *Pennsylvania Archives: Papers of the Governors, 1785-1817*, fourth series, vol. IV. Harrisburg: State of Pennsylvania, 1900.

_____, *Pennsylvania Archives: Papers of the Governors, 1817-1832*, fourth series, vol. V. Harrisburg: State Printer, 1900.

_____, *Pennsylvania Archives: Papers of the Governors, 1832-1845*, fourth series, vol. VI. Harrisburg: Commonwealth of Pennsylvania, 1901.

_____, *Pennsylvania Archives: Papers of the Governors, 1845-1858*, fourth series, vol. VII. Harrisburg: State Printer, 1902.

_____, *Pennsylvania Archives: Papers of the Governors, 1858-1871*, fourth series, vol. VIII. Harrisburg: State Printer, 1902.

_____, *Pennsylvania Archives: Papers Relating to What Is Known as the Whiskey Rebellion in Western Pennsylvania, 1794*, second series, vol. IV. Harrisburg: E.K. Meyers, State Printer, 1890.

Russell, A. L., *Annual Report of the Adjutant General of Pennsylvania, Transmitted to the Governor in Pursuance of the Law for the Year 1866*. Harrisburg: State Printer, 1867.

Scott, Major James B. ed., *The Militia, Senate Document 695, January 12, 1917*. Washington, D.C.: Government Printing Office, 1917.

Statutes at Large of Pennsylvania, 1682-1801, vol. V, 1744-1759. Harrisburg: State Printer, 1898.

The War of the Rebellion: Compellation of the Official Records of the Union and the Confederate Armies, vols. XIX and XXVII. Washington, D.C.: Government Printing Office, 1887.

Published Books - Primary Sources

Fleming, Thomas, ed. *Benjamin Franklin: A Biography in His Own Words.* New York: Harper and Row, 1943.

Larabee, Leonard W., ed, *The Papers of Benjamin Franklin, January 1, 1735-December 31, 1744*, vol. 2. New Haven, Conn.: Yale University Press, 1960.

_____, *The Papers of Benjamin Franklin, January 1, 1745-June 30, 1750*, vol. 3. New Haven: Yale University Press, 1961.

_____, *The Papers of Benjamin Franklin, July 1, 1750-June 30, 1753*, vol. 4. New Haven: Yale University Press, 1961.

_____, *The Papers of Benjamin Franklin, July 1, 1753-March 31, 1755*, vol. 5. New Haven: Yale University Press, 1962.

_____, *The Papers of Benjamin Franklin, April 1, 1755-September 30, 1756*, vol. 6. New Haven: Yale University Press, 1963.

Oswandel, Jacob, *Notes of the Mexican War, 1846-47-48.* Philadelphia, 1885.

Parker, Thomas A., *History of the 51st Regiment of Pennsylvania Volunteers.* Philadelphia: Kind and Baird Publishers, 1869.

Peskin, Allen, ed., *Volunteers: The Mexican War Journals of Private Richard Coulter and Sergeant Thomas Barclay, Company E, Second Pennsylvania Infantry.* Kent, Ohio: Kent State University Press, 1991.

Schneck, B. S., *The Burning of Chambersburg, Pennsylvania.* Philadelphia: Lindsay and Blakiston, 1865.

Smith, William, *A Brief State of the Province of Pennsylvania.* London: NP, 1755.

Van Doren, Carl, ed., *Benjamin Franklin's Autobiographical Writings.* New York: Viking Press, 1945.

Waddell, Louis, John L. Tottenham and Donald H. Kent, eds., *The Papers of Henry Bouquet*, vol. II. Harrisburg: Pennsylvania Historical and Museum Commission, 1978.

Washington, George, *The Journal of Major George Washington; An Account of His First Official Mission, October 1753-January 1754*. New York: Dominion Books, 1963.

Washington, George, "Sentiments on the Peace Establishment," appendix I in John McCauley Palmer, *Washington, Lincoln and Wilson*. New York: Doubleday, 1930.

Williamson, Hugh, *The Plain Dealer or Remarks on Quaker Politicks in Pennsylvania*. Philadelphia: 1764.

Published Books - Secondary Sources

Bates, Samuel P., *History of Pennsylvania Volunteers, 1861-1865, Prepared in Compliance with the Acts of the Legislature*. Harrisburg: State Printer, 1870.

_____, *Martial Deeds of Pennsylvania*. Philadelphia: T. H. Davis and Company, 1875.

Bilby, Joseph G., *The Irish Brigade in the Civil War: The 69th New York and Other Irish Regiments of the Army of the Potomac*. Conshohocken, Pa.: Combined Books, 1998.

Boyd, Stephen R., *The Whiskey Rebellion: Past and Present Perspectives*. Westport, Conn.: The Greenwood Press, 1985.

Brunhouse, Robert L., *The Counter-Revolution in Pennsylvania, 1776-1790*. Harrisburg: Pennsylvania Historical and Museum Commission, 1971.

Buranelli, Vincent, *The King and the Quaker: A Study of William Penn and James I*. Philadelphia: University of Pennsylvania Press, 1962.

Clarke, Major William P., *Official History of the Militia and National Guard of Pennsylvania from the Earliest Period of Record to the Present Time*, 2 vols. Philadelphia: Captain Charles J. Hendler, 1909.

Clouse, Jerry A., *The Whiskey Rebellion: Southwestern Pennsylvania's Frontier Population Test the American Constitution*. Harrisburg: Pennsylvania Historical and Museum Commission, 1994.

Donehoo, George P., *Pennsylvania: A History*, vol. II. New York: Lewis Historical Publications, 1926.

Eddy, Melvin V. Jr., *William Penn and Early Quakerism*. Princeton, N.J.: University Press, 1973.

Ellis, Franklin and Samuel Evans, *History of Lancaster County Pennsylvania with Biographical Sketches of Many Pioneers and Prominent Men*. Philadelphia: Everts and Peck, 1883.

Elting, John R., *Amateurs to Arms: A Military History of the War of 1812*. Chapel Hill, N.C.: Algonquin Books, 1991.

Egnal, Marc, *A Mighty Empire: The Origins of the American Revolution*. Ithaca, N.Y.: Cornell University Press, 1988.

First Troop, Philadelphia City Cavalry, *History of the First Troop, Philadelphia City Cavalry, together with an Introductory Chapter Summarizing the Early History and the Rolls Complete from 1774*. Philadelphia: Winchell Co., 1991.

Gallagher, Gary W., *The Battle of Chancellorsville*. NP: Eastern National Park and Monument Association, 1995.

Gladstone, William A., *Men of Color*. Gettysburg, Pa.: Thomas Publications, 1993.

Godcharles, Frederic A., *Pennsylvania: Political, Governmental, Military and Civil*, Governmental Volume. New York: American Historical Society, 1933.

_____, *Pennsylvania: Political, Governmental, Military and Civil*, Military Volume. New York: American Historical Society Inc., 1933.

Hackenburg, Randy W., *Pennsylvania in the War with Mexico*. Shippensburg, Pa.: White Main Publishing Co., 1992.

Hanna, William, *Benjamin Franklin and Pennsylvania Politics*. Stanford, Calif.: Stanford University Press, 1965.

Hassler, Edgar W., *Old Westmoreland: A History of Western Pennsylvania during the Revolution*. Pittsburgh: J. R. Weldin and Co., 1900.

Hickey, Donald R., *The War of 1812: A Forgotten Conflict*. Chicago: University of Illinois Press, 1989.

Historical Society of Pennsylvania, *Collections of the Historical Society of Pemnsylvania*, vol. 1. Philadelphia: N.P., 1853.

Honeywell, Roy J., *Chaplains of the United States Army*. Washington, D.C.: Department of the Army, 1958.

Hunter, William A., *Forts on the Pennsylvania Frontier, 1753-1758*. Harrisburg: Pennsylvania Historical and Museum Commission, 1960.

Ilisevich, Robert D., *Daniel Dobbins, Frontier Mariner*. Erie, Pa.: Erie County Historical Society, 1993.

Jackson, John J., *The Pennsylvania Navy, 1775-1781*. New Brunswick, N.J.: Rutgers University Press, 1974.

Jennings, Francis, *Empire of Fortune*. New York: W .W. Norton and Co., 1988.

Jones, Rufus M., *The Quakers in the American Colonies*. London: Macmillan and Co., 1911.

Kennedy, William V., *Thompson's Pennsylvania Rifle Battalion: Keystone of the Army*. Lemoyne, Pa.: Thompson Battalion Memorial Project, 1985.

Klein, Philip S. and Ari Hoogenboom, *A History of Pennsylvania*. New York: McGraw-Hill Co., 1973.

Leach, Douglas E., *Arms for the Empire: A Military History of the British Colonies in North America, 1607-1763*. New York: Macmillan Co., 1972.

_____, *Roots of Conflict*. Chapel Hill, N.C.: University of North Carolina Press, 1986.

Luvaas, M. Jay and Harold W. Nelson, eds., *The U.S. Army War College Guide to the Battles of Chancellorsville and Fredericksburg*. Carlisle, Pa.: South Mountain Press, 1988.

_____, *The U.S. Army War College Guide to the Battle of Gettysburg*. Carlisle, Pa.: South Mountain Press, 1986.

Mahon, John K., *The War of 1812*. New York: Da Capo Press, 1972.

Manders, Eric I., *The Battle of Long Island*. Monmouth Beach, N. J.: Phillip Freneau Press, 1978.

McPherson, James, *1863: Turning Point of the Civil War*. New York: Time-Life Books, 1998.

Millet, Allan R. and Peter Maslowski, *For the Common Defense: A Military History of the United States of America*. New York: Free Press, 1984.

Millet, Allan R., *"Semper Fidelis": The History of the United States Marine Corps*. New York: Free Press, 1986.

Minor, Charles, *History of Wyoming*. Philadelphia: J. Drissy, 1845.

Montgomery, Morton L., *History of Berks County in Pennsylvania*. Philadelphia: Everts, Peck & Richards, 1889.

Norton, Herman A., *Struggling for Recognition: The United States Army Chaplaincy, 1791-1865*. Washington, D.C.: Office of the Chief of Chaplains, 1977.

Oberholtzer, Ellis P., *Philadelphia: A History of the City and Its People*. Philadelphia: S. J. Clark Publishing Company, n.d.

Palmer, David R. *1794: America, Its Army and the Birth of the Nation*. Novato, Calif.: Presidio Press, 1994.

Richards, Henry M. M., *The Pennsylvania-German in the Revolutionary War, 1775-1783*. Lancaster, Pa.: Pennsylvania German Society, 1908.

Richardson, Edward W., *Standards and Colors of the American Revolution*. Philadelphia: University of Pennsylvania Press, 1982.

Rollins, Richard and Dave Shultz, *Guide to Pennsylvania Troops at Gettysburg*. Redondo Beach, Calif.: Rank and File Publications, 1998.

Rossman, Kenneth R., *Thomas Mifflin and the Politics of the American Revolution*. Chapel Hill, N.C.: University of North Carolina Press, 1952.

Rosswurm, Steven, *Arms, Country and Class: The Philadelphia Militia and the "Lower Sort" during the American Revolution.* New Brunswick, N.J.: Rutgers University Press, 1987.

Sapio, Victor A., *Pennsylvania in the War of 1812.* Lexington, Ky.: University of Kentucky Press, 1970.

Scharf, J. Thomas and Thompson Westcott, *History of Philadelphia, 1609-1884*, vol. I. Philadelphia, L. H. Everts & Co., 1884.

Schwartz, Sally, *A Mixed Multitude: The Struggle for Toleration in Colonial Pennsylvania.* New York: University Press, 1987.

Sharpless, Isaac, *A Quaker Experiment in Government: A History of Quaker Government in Pennsylvania, 1682-1783.* Philadelphia: Ferris and Leach, 1920.

_____, *A History of Quaker Government in Pennsylvania: The Quakers in the Revolution*, vol. II. Philadelphia: T. S. Leach and Co., 1899.

Sipe, C. Hale, *The Indian Wars of Pennsylvania: An Account of Indian Events in Pennsylvania, of the French and Indian War, Pontiac's War, Lord Dunmore's War, the Revolutionary War, and the Indian Uprising from 1789 to 1795.* Harrisburg: Telegraph Press, 1931.

Smyth, Henry Albert, *The Writings of Benjamin Franklin: The Autobiography of Benjamin Franklin.* New York: Macmillan Co., 1905.

Stille, Charles J., *Major General Anthony Wayne and the Pennsylvania Line in the Continental Army.* Philadelphia: J. B. Lippincott, 1893.

Stroh, Oscar H., *Thompson's Battalion.* Harrisburg: Graphic Services, 1976.

Sypher, J. R., *History of the Pennsylvania Reserve Corps: A Complete Record of the Organization of the Different Companies, Regiments and Brigades, Containing Descriptions of Expeditions, Marches, Skirmishes and Battles, Together with Biographical Sketches of Officers and Personal Records of Each Man during His Term of Service.* Lancaster, Pa.: Elias Barr and Co., 1865.

Trudeau, Noah Andre, *Like Men of War: Black Troops in the Civil War, 1862-1865.* New York: Little Brown and Co., 1998.

Trussell, John B. B., *The Pennsylvania Line: Regimental Organization and Operations, 1776-1783*. Harrisburg: Pennsylvania Historical and Museum Commission, 1977.

_____, "From Revolution to Whiskey Rebellion," in *The First Century: A History of the 28th Infantry Division*, Col. Uzal Ent, ed. Harrisburg: Stackpole Books, 1979.

_____, *William Penn: Architect of a Nation*. Harrisburg: Pennsylvania Historical and Museum Commission, 1994.

Tucker, Glenn, *Mad Anthony Wayne and the New Nation*. Harrisburg: Stackpole Books, 1973.

Van Doren, Carl, *Mutiny in January: The Story of a Crisis in the Continental Army Now for the First Time Fully Told from Many Hitherto Unknown or Neglected Sources*. New York: Viking Press, 1943.

Volweiler, Albert T., *George Croghan and the Westward Movement, 1741-1782*. Cleveland: Arthur H. Clark Co., 1926.

Wainright, Nicholas B., *The Schuylkill Fishing Company of the State in Schuylkill, 1732-1982*. Philadelphia: Sutter House, Lititz, Pa., 1982.

Wallace, Paul A. W., *Conrad Weiser, Friend of Colonist and Mohawk*. Philadelphia: University of Pennsylvania Press, 1945.

West, J. Martin, ed., *War for Empire in Western Pennsylvania*. Fort Ligonier, Pa.: Fort Ligonier Association, 1993.

Wildes, Harry E., *William Penn*. New York: Macmillan Co., 1974.

Weigley, Russell F., *History of the United States Army*, The Macmillan Wars of the United States, Louis Morton, ed. New York: Macmillan Co., 1967.

_____, *The American Way of War: A History of United States Military Strategy and Policy*. New York: Macmillan Co., 1973.

_____, "The Colonial Militia," in *The First Century: A History of the 28th Infantry Division*, Col. Uzal W. Ent, ed. Harrisburg: Stackpole Books, 1979.

Wright, Robert K. Jr., *The Continental Army*, The Army Lineage Series. Washington, D.C.: Center of Military History, 1983.

Zierdt, William H., *Narrative History of the 109th Field Artillery, Pennsylvania National Guard, 1775-1930*. Wilkes-Barre, Pa.: Wyoming Historical and Geological Society, 1932.

Articles, Pamphlets and Periodicals

Anderson, Niles, "Bushy Run: Decisive Battle in the Wilderness," *Western Pennsylvania Historical Magazine* (vol. 46, 1963), pp. 211-245.

Bilby, Joseph G., "A Better Chance to Hit: The Story of the Buck and Ball," *The American Rifleman* (May 1993), pp. 48-49, 78-80.

Branch, Douglas E., "Henry Bouquet: Professional Soldier," *Pennsylvania Magazine of History and Biography* (vol. 62, 1939), pp. 41-50.

Creed, W. J., *Historical Sketch and Souvenir, Reading Artillerists, Company A, Fourth Regiment Infantry, Third Brigade, NGP*. Reading, Pa.: B. F. Owen Publishers, 1894.

Crist, Robert Grant, *Captain William Hendricks and the March to Quebec, 1775*. Carlisle, Pa.: Hamilton Library and Cumberland County Historical Society, 1960.

Devine, Francis E., "The Pennsylvania Flying Camp, July-November 1776," *Pennsylvania History* (vol. 46, 1979), pp. 59-78.

Griffith, Sally F., "'Order, Discipline, and a Few Cannon': Benjamin Franklin, the Association, and the Rhetoric and Practice of Boosterism," *Pennsylvania Magazine of History and Biography* (vol. CXVI, April 1992), p. 134.

Harp, Chadwick Allen, "Remember the Ladies: Women in the American Revolution," *Pennsylvania Heritage: Quarterly of the Pennsylvania Historical and Museum Commission* (vol. XX, spring 1994), pp. 33-37.

Higginbotham, Sanford W., et. al., *Pennsylvania and the Civil War: A Handbook*. Harrisburg: Pennsylvania Historical and Museum Commission, 1961.

Hindman, William B., "The Great Meadows and the Climaxing Battle at Fort Necessity," *West Virginia Historical Review* (vol. 16, 1954-55), pp. 65-89.

Hindle, Brook, "The March of the Paxton Boys," *William and Mary Quarterly* (vol. 3, 1946), pp.463-464.

Hunter, William A., "First Line of Defense, 1755-1756," *Pennsylvania History: Quarterly Journal of the Pennsylvania Historical Association* (vol. XXII, no. 3, 1955), pp. 229-255.

_____, "Victory at Kittanning," *Pennsylvania History: Quarterly Journal of the Pennsylvania Historical Association* (vol. 23, 1956), pp. 376-407.

Jordan, John W., "Biographical Sketch of Reverend Bernhard Adam Grube," *Pennsylvania Magazine of History and Biography* (vol. XXV, 1901), p. 17.

Kent, Donald H., "Henry Bouquet," *American Heritage* (vol. 4, no. 3, 1952-53), p. 43.

Ketcham, Ralph, "Conscience, War and Politics in Pennsylvania, 1755-1757," *William and Mary Quarterly* (vol. XX, 1963), pp. 418-419.

Keyser, Paul D., "Memoirs of Colonel Jehu Eyre," *Pennsylvania Magazine of History and Biography* (vol. III, 1879), pp. 296-307, 412-425.

Kings, J. W., "Colonel John Armstrong: His Place in the History of Southwestern Pennsylvania," *Western Pennsylvania Historical Magazine* (vol. 10, 1927), pp. 129-145.

Kirby, James, "The Return of the Paxton Boys and the Historical State of Pennsylvania, 1764-1774," *Pennsylvania History: Quarterly Journal of the Pennsylvania Historical Association* (vol. 38, 1971), pp. 117-133.

Kyte, George W., "General Wayne Marches South, 1781," *Pennsylvania History: Quarterly Journal of the Pennsylvania Historical Association* (vol. 30, 1963), pp. 301-315.

Lacey, John, "Memoirs of Brigadier-General John Lacey of Pennsylvania," *Pennsylvania Magazine of History and Biography* (vol. XXV, 1902), pp. 101-111, 265-270.

Landis, Captain John B., "Investigation into the American Tradition of Woman Known as Molly Pitcher," *Journal of American History* (vol. V, 1911), pp. 83-95.

Nead, Benjamin N., "A Sketch of General Thomas Proctor, with Some Account of the First Pennsylvania Artillery in the Revolution," *Pennsylvania Magazine of History and Biography* (vol. IV, 1880), pp. 474-470.

Newman Dorland, W. A., "The Second Troop, Philadelphia City Cavalry," *Pennsylvania Magazine of History and Biography* (vol. XLVI, 1922), pp. 55-57, 154-172, 346-365.

Nichols, Franklin Thayer, "The Organization of Braddock's Army," *William and Mary Quarterly* (vol. IV, 1947), pp. 125-147.

Niles, H., "Weekly Register: Documents, Essays and Facts Together with Notices of the Arts and Manufactures and a Record of Events of the Time" (vols. I and II). Baltimore: Franklin Press, 1812-1813.

No author, "The Restoration of the Schuylkill Gun to the State in Schuylkill," *Pennsylvania Magazine of History and Biography* (vol. VIII, 1884), pp. 198-215.

Montgomery, Thomas H., "Diary of Lieutenant Francis Nichols of Colonel William Thompson's Battalion of Pennsylvania Riflemen, January to September 1776," *Pennsylvania Magazine of History and Biography* (vol. XX, 1896), pp. 504-515.

Pennsylvania Gazette, The, September 3, 1740; September 8, 1740; May 14, 1741; April 8, 1742; July 31, 1746; July 2, 1747; December 3, 1747; January 9, 1748; March 8, 1748; September 1, 1748; June 27, 1754; October 15, 1754; August 21, 1755; February 17, 1757; February 9, 1764.

Pennypacker, Samuel W., "Samuel John Atlee," *Pennsylvania Magazine of History and Biography* (vol. II, 1878), pp. 74-84.

Rice, William H. "The Gnadenhutten Massacres: A Brief History of Two Historic Tragedies," *The Pennsylvania German: A Popular Magazine of Biography, History, Genealogy, Folklore, Literature, etc.* (vol. 7, no. 1, January 1906), pp. 26-31.

Schaeffer, Paul N. "Pennsylvania's Draft Laws during the Revolution," *Historical Review of Berks County* (October 1940), pp. 2, 3.

Stein, Clyde S., "A Former Berks Militia Unit, Company C, 103rd Quartermaster Regiment," *Historical Review of Berks County* (October 1940), pp. 18-20.

Stephenson, R.S., "Pennsylvania Provincial Soldiers in the Seven Years War," *Pennsylvania Magazine of History and Biography* (vol. LXII, no. 2, 1938), pp. 199-200.

Ward, Matthew C., "An Army of Servants: The Pennsylvania Regiment during the Seven Years War," *Pennsylvania Magazine of History and Biography* (vol. CXIX, no. 1/2, 1995), pp. 79-93.

Weiner, Frederick B., "The Militia Clause of the Constitution," *Harvard Law Review* (December 1940).

Wellenreuther, Hermann, "The Political Dilemma of the Quakers in Pennsylvania," *Pennsylvania Magazine of History and Biography* (April 1970), p. 154.

Williams, Edward G., "The Orderly Book of Colonel Henry Bouquet's Expedition against the Ohio Indians," *Western Pennsylvania Historical Magazine* (vol. 43, 1959), pp. 179-206, 283-302.

Letters, Manuscripts and Tracts

Benson, Michael R., "The Early History of the Artillery Battalion of Philadelphia, 1760-1777," March 19, 1976.

Franklin, Benjamin, A Tradesman of Philadelphia, *Plain Truth: or, Serious Considerations on the Present State of the City of Philadelphia, and Province of Pennsylvania* (Philadelphia: 1747).

Loxley, Benjamin, "Benjamin Loxley's Daybook, 1771-1785," Historical Society of Pennsylvania, Philadelphia.

Maule, Thomas, *Tribute to Caesar, now paid by the best Christians, and to what purpose. With some remarks on the late vigorous expedition against Canada. Of civil Government, how inconsistent it is with the Government of Christ in his Church, compared with the ancient just and righteous principles of the Quakers, and their modern practice and doctrine. With some notes upon the discipline of their Church in this province, especially at Philadelphia.*

Palmer, Brig. Gen. John MacAuley, "The Military Policy of the United States," lecture delivered at the U.S. Army War College, September 21, 1928 (p. 13 of the manuscript).

Penn, John, letter to George Thomas, dated August 2, 1739, in "The Pennsylvania Manuscripts: Thomas Penn Letterbook," microfilm roll 1, Letterbooks, January 19,1729-August 1742 (Philadelphia: Historical Society of Pennsylvania), pp. 306-307.

Penn, Thomas, letter to Richard Peters, dated June 9, 1748, in "The Pennsylvania Manuscripts: Thomas Penn Letterbook II" (Philadelphia: Historical Society of Pennsylvania), p. 232.

Seymour, Joseph, "Four Independent Companies of Foot, May 1746-November 1747," December 22, 1998.

_____, "Soldiers of the Quaker City: The Story of the Philadelphia Artillery, 1747-1783," July 1997.

Index